The Mosques
of the Indian Subcontinent

The Mosques
of the Indian Subcontinent

Their Development and Iconography

Fredrick W. Bunce, PhD.
Professor Emeritus of Art
Indiana State University

D.K. Printworld (P) Ltd.
New Delhi

Cataloging in Publication Data — DK
[Courtesy: D.K. Agencies (P) Ltd. <docinfo@dkagencies.com>]

Bunce, Fredrick W. (Fredrick William), 1935-
The mosques of the Indian subcontinent, their development and iconography / Fredrick W. Bunce.
p. cm.
Includes bibliographical references (p.)
ISBN 13: 9788124604588
ISBN 10: 8124604584

1. Mosques–India–Designs and plans. 2. Architecture, Islamic–India–History. I. Title.

DDC 726.209 54 22

ISBN 13: 978-81-246-0458-8
ISBN 10: 81-246-0458-4
First Published in India in 2008

Published and printed by:
D.K. Printworld (P) Ltd.
Regd. office : *'Sri Kunj,'* F-52, Bali Nagar
Ramesh Nagar Metro Station
New Delhi - 110 015
Phones : (011) 2545 3975, 2546 6019; *Fax* : (011) 2546 5926
E-mail : dkprintworld@vsnl.net
Web : www.dkprintworld.com

Contents

Contents (Continued)

List of Plates

List of Plates (Continued)

Miscellaneous Plans

List of Plates (Continued)

Miscellaneous Elevations

List of Figures

List of Figures (Concluded)

Abbreviations

A H	A.B.M. Husain, *Fatehpur-Sikri and Its Architecture.*
A M	Anisha Shekhar Mukherji, *The Red Fort of Shahjahanabad.*
C A	Catherine B. Asher, *Architecture of Mughal India.*
C S	C.M. Villiers Stuart, *Gardens of the Great Mughals.*
C T	Christopher Tadgell, *The History of Architecture in India.*
E G	Ernst Grube, et al., George Mitchell (ed.) *Architecture of the Islamic World: Its History and Social Meaning.*
EH	E.B. Havell, *Encyclopaedia of Architecture in the Indian Subcontinent.*
FWB	Fredrick W. Bunce, *The Iconography of Plans: A Study of the Influence of Buddhism and Hinduism on Architectural Plans of South and South-East Asia.*
FWB 2	———, *Numbers, Their Iconographic Consideration in Buddhist and Hindu Practices.*
FWB 3	———, *Islamic Tombs in India: The Iconography and Genesis of Their Design.*
GM	George Michell, ed., *Architcture of the Islamic World.*
GM II	George Michell, *The Royal Palaces of India.*
GT	G.H.R. Tillotson, *Mughal India.*
H C	Henry Cousens, *Bījāpur and Its Architectural Remains: With a Historical Outline of the Adil Shahi Dynasty.*
HS	Henri Stierlin (ed.), *Architecture of the World: Islamic India.*
HS 2	Henri Stierlin, *Islam from Baghdad to Cordoba: Early Architecture from the 7th to the 13th Century.*
IS	Issam El-Said and Ayse Parman, *Geometric Concepts in Islamic Art.*
JP	Jose Pereira, *Islamic Sacred Architecture: A Stylistic History.*
KR	K.V. Soundara Rajan, *Islam Builds in India.*
MF	Martin J. Frishman and Hasan-Uddin Khan, eds., *The Mosque: History, Architectural Development & Regional Diversity.*
MS	Mehrdad Shokoohy, *Muslim Architecture of South India.*
MW	Mohammad Waliullah Khan, *Lahore and its Important Monuments.*
PB	Percy Brown, *Indian Architecture* (*Islamic Period*).
RH	Robert Hillenbrand, *Islamic Art and Architecture.*
RH 2	———, *Islamic Architecture: Form, Function & Meaning.*
RM	Rustam Mehta, *Masterpieces of Indo-Islamic Architecture.*
RN	R. Nath, *Fathepur Sikri and its Monuments.*

Abbreviations (Continued)

R N 2	———, *History of Mughal Architecture.*
R N 3	———, *History of Sultanate Architecture.*
R N 4	———, *Indigenous Characteristics of Mughal Architecture.*
S G	Satish Grover, *Islamic Architecture in India.*
S S	Shehbaz H. Safrani, *Golconda and Hyderabad.*
V S	Vibhuti Sachdev and Giles Tillotson, *Building Jaipur: The Making of an Indian City.*

Preface

I came to Islamic iconography late in my various considerations, particularly, via Buddhist and Hindu iconography. This produced, first: *Islamic Tombs of India: The Iconography and Genesis of Their Design* and then *Royal Palaces, Residences and Pavilions of India: An Iconographic Consideration,* which in part dealt with Islamic palaces. Partially, this interest arose because I also chose to retire in a predominantly Islamic country — Malaysia.

In preparing these two manuscripts, noted above, for publication I visited the American Institute of Indian Studies, Gurgaon, and the Department of Archaeology, Archaeological Survey of India, New Delhi, in order to obtain photographs that might be applicable to these two studies. Alas, in both institutions, there was a dearth of photographic material in relation to Islamic monuments in which I was interested. It wasn't because the monuments in which I was concerned with were little known or of little importance. Buddhist and Hindu photographic documentation was thoroughly represented, but Islamic monuments were not. I was, to put it mildly, taken a back!

India and the Indian subcontinent possess a myriad of important Buddhist, Hindu and Islamic architectural monuments. Can anyone, who has been introduced to Buddhism, not be aware of the Stūpa I at Sāñcī? Who, Similarly, can one, is moderately familiar with Hindu monuments, not be conversant with the Shore Temple at Mahabalipuram? Of course, the Taj Mahal is one of the monuments that stands among the most important and well-known architectural monuments in the world, rightly or wrongly.

Yet, the obvious is ignored! Islamic structures appear to be given second class status in India. Great, important and impressive *masjid*s — e.g. the Adina Masjid, Pandua; Masjid-i Jami, Jaunpur; Masjid-i Jami, Bījāpur; and Masjid Badshahi, Lahore — are seemingly ignored by these important research repositories! This fact is not only regrettable, but absolutely ludicrous considering the elevated status of scholarship within India. Happily, the printed word, scholarly research in India and publication are not so disinclined!

I have learned that India and the Indian subcontinent possess one of the richest, if not the richest assemblage of architectural monuments in the world going back several millennia. It would appear to be short-sighted that one of the more important aspects of this culture is apparently ignored, or at best under-represented by these repositories.

Fredrick W. Bunce

Introduction

Indian Subcontinent after CE 1950

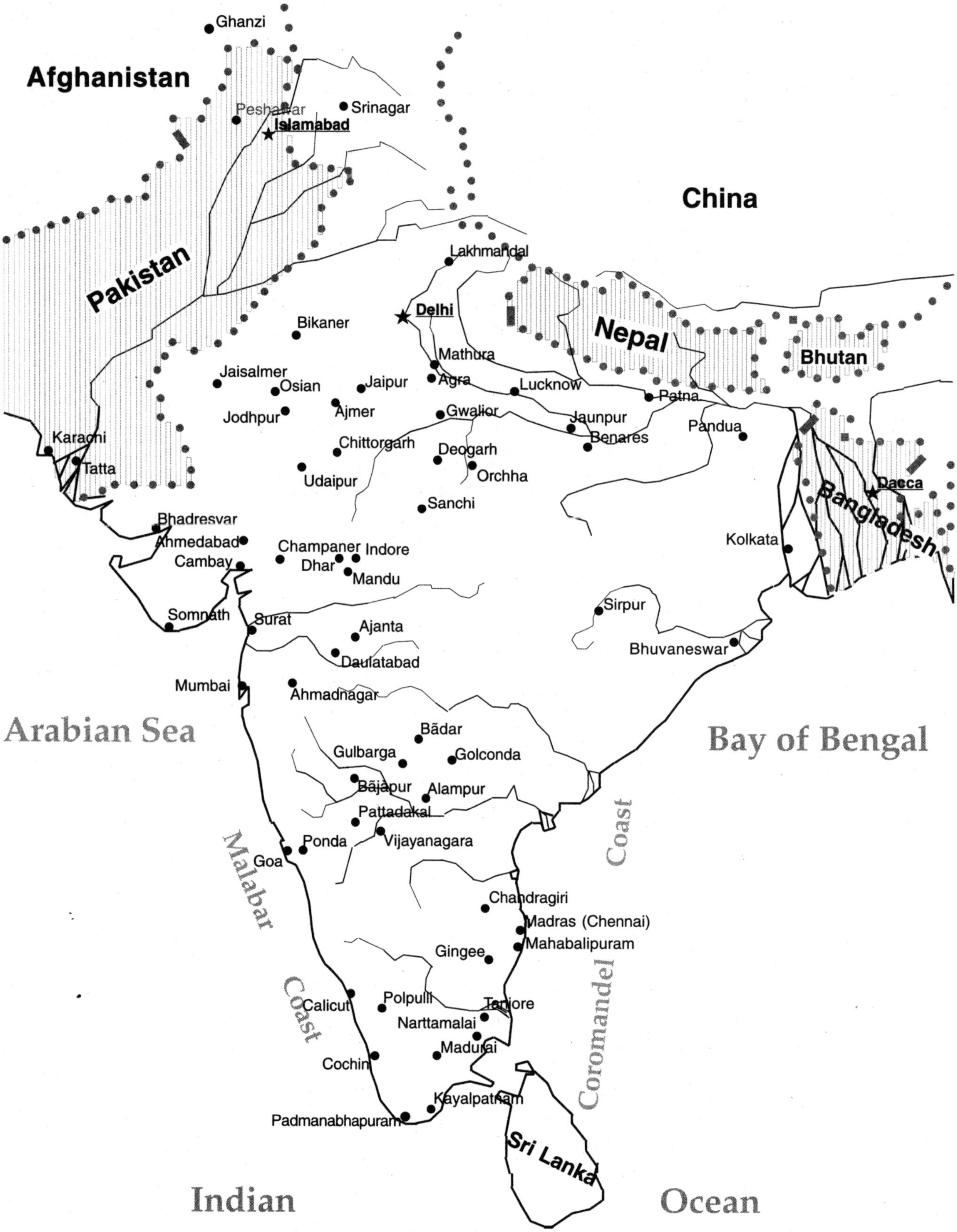

Introduction

> Among the many gifts which God has bestowed upon me, His humble servant, was a desire to erect public buildings. So I built many mosques and colleges and monasteries that the learned and the elders, the devout and the holy, might worship God in these edifices, and aid the kind builder with their prayers.[1]
>
> — Firuz Shah Tughluq (r. CE 1351–88)

SOON after the death of Abu'l Qassim Muhammad ibn 'Abdallah al-Hashimi (The Prophet or Nabi Muhammad) in CE 632, Islam began to spread. A religion born of a son of the desert, its appeal was enormous to those of the Arab world and by the tenth century it had reached eastward as far as present-day Afghanistan before flowing southward into north-west India.

Within Islam there is the concept of intercession (Arabic: *shafá'a*). Normally Islamic pilgrims would visit the tombs of great saints and holy men seeking their intercession, their *shafá'a*. *Shafá'a* may be seen to operate in the reverse as well. It is believed by some that if one builds a *masjid*, particularly if it is attached to a mausoleum (Arabic: *madfam* or *lhad*) and numerous pilgrims or devotees come there to pray, this will somehow benefit the one(s) interred in that place. This concept is similar to the Roman idea of immortality as embodied in the "State Portrait." In the Roman belief it is supposed that one's immortality is assured if people in viewing the portrait, recognize the greatness and worth of the individual.

The great and powerful of Islamic India built elaborate mausolea to remind subsequent viewers of their position, thereby affecting their position in the Hereafter through *shafá'a* or intercession. There were certain passive restrictions within Islam against the construction of elaborate tombs as voiced by The Prophet, Nabi Muhammad. Rulers, as well as the rich and famous of the Islamic world in general, and India in particular, somehow circumvented or ignored these caveats and raised some of the most elaborate burial monuments in the world. Yet, there was, generally, always a mosque, or a *qiblā* with *mehrāb*, incorporated into the tomb or *rauza*, however insignificant in size or decor. Perhaps these inclusions — i.e. a *masjid*, or a *qiblā* with *mehrāb* — were seen as a way of skirting or neutralizing the restrictions against ostentatious tombs.

The construction of a *masjid* was normally undertaken by a man of wealth or a titled individual or a polity. To construct a mosque is also seen as a spiritual deed that may bring certain spiritual benefits not only to the builder but also to those who come to offer their obligatory prayers. This concept — spiritual benefit — is similar to the Theravāda Buddhist concept of "merit." Furthermore, the construction of a *masjid* is not dissimilar to the European monarchs' construction of elaborate chapels or great churches for the "Glory of God" and their own position in the Hereafter.

At first, the basically pacific character of the Hindu faith was no match against the aggressive nature of Islam as it entered the vast subcontinent. Not only was north-west India relatively easily invaded and conquered, converts to Islam were numerous. This was particularly true of the two lower castes — i.e. vaiśya and śūdra. Islam did not hold the restricting caste (Ind.: *varṇa*) levels that the Hindu

---

[1] R.C. Majumdar, *An Advanced History of India*, London: 1960, p. 332, quoting, in translation, Firuz Shah.

Introduction (Continued)

faith espoused. However, centuries or millennia of culture and tradition would not be easily or totally overthrown. A basic flaw in the intended or unintended Islamization of India was the importation of foreign rulers — i.e. Afghani, Turkic and Persian. These rulers were significantly harsher than the indigenous Hindu rulers. That is not to say that Hindu monarchs of the period were kind, benevolent or magnanimous; but there was a sharp, swift, deadly edge to the Islamic rulers' governance that made the rājās, the *rāo*s, etc. seem preferable. This was particularly true among the independent and fractious Rājpūts as well as the fiercely independent, Draviḍian south. The coexistence between the two religious groups was often tempestuous. Numerous Afghani, Turkic and Persian rulers were aware that they were in the distinct minority. Some trod with a light foot. Others were not as tolerant. Two Islamic Emperors indicate this polarity — i.e. Akbar the Great and his great-grandson Aurangzeb — one tolerate to a fault, the other a narrow-minded, conservative bigot.

Ghazni in present-day Afghanistan was ruled by the newly created Sultan Sabuktigin (r. CE 977–97) (see **Appendix D**), a Yamanid. He was the son of Aptigin (r. CE 962–63), a Turkish slave commander in the Ghazni sultanate. Sabuktigin invaded southward and claimed the area north of the Indus as part of his domain. The Yamanids of Ghazni, after their initial advance, pursued a policy of peace and appeasement. It was during the reign of the Zahir-ud-Dawlah Ibrahim (r. CE 1059–99) that the Ibrahim Shrine/Masjid (see **Plate 1**) at Bhadresvar and the large Masjid-i Jami (see **Plate 5**) of Ajmer were built. In both instances both Turkic and Persian influences can be seen.

Prince Ghiyath-ud-Din Mohammed II (r. CE 1163–1203) of the Ghauri Dynasty, defeated the weak Yamanid Sultan, Taj-ud-Dawlah Khusraw Malik, and claimed that part of India conquered by the Yamanids as his own as well as the title of Sultan. Towards the end of his reign Mohammed II had advanced as far as Delhi. His armies pressed even farther eastward. One general subdued Nālandā and another Benares. It was during the reign of the last Ghauri Sultan, Shihab-ud-Din Mohammed III (r. CE 1173–1206), that the famed Quwwat-ul-Islam Masjid (see **Plate 4**) of Delhi was begun. After nearly eighty years in construction, it was to become the largest and most important mosque in northern India for quite some time.

Qutb-ud-din Aibak, the occupier of Benares, after the assassination of Mohammed III, was nominated as the supreme commander. He assumed the title of *sultan* and made Delhi his capital. He, therefore, became the first independent Islamic ruler of India and the first Sultan of Delhi (r. CE 1206–10). In northern India, until CE 1266 the Slave or Mamluk Sultans reigned. Some time at the end of Sultan Qutb-ud-din Aibak's life, or the beginning of the reign of Sultan Aram Shah (r. CE 1210-11), the second stage of the Quwwat-ul-Islam Masjid (see **Plate 6**) of Delhi was raised.

After the supplanting of the original Mamluk Dynasty; a little over fifty years saw two additional dynasties rise and fall — i.e. the House of Balban (CE 1266–90) and the Khalji (CE 1290–1320). These were turbulent years as one after the other jockeyed for power and the throne of the Sultanate. Assassinations were the coin of the day. Significantly, it was during the reigns of the first three Khaljis — i.e. Jalal-ud-din Firuz Khalji (r. CE 1290–96), Rukn-ud-din Ibrahim (II) (r. CE 1296) and 'Ala-ud-din Muhammad Khalji (r. CE 1296–1316) (see **Appendix D**) — that the Quwwat-ul-Islam Masjid (see **Plate 8**) was finished, reaching the size that is seen today.

Introduction (Continued)

Turkic and Afghani related Sultans again reigned in Delhi for a little over two centuries. First the Turkic Tughluq Dynasty. In CE 1320 Ghiyas-ud-din Tughluq Shah I (r. CE 1320–25) took command of the government from the incompetent Khalji. His reign was short and relatively peaceful. However, Shah I and a young son were killed in an "accident" near Delhi when a pavilion mysteriously collapsed upon them cutting short the reign of the sultan. There followed his son, Muhammad Shah Tughluq, Shah II (r. CE 1325–51), a ruler of great villainy and ferocity. By the mid-fourteenth century, Firuz Shah Tughluq (r. CE 1351–88) ascended the throne and a series of building projects were begun, many of which were most important, historically. The Tughluqs reigned in Delhi until CE 1414. At the end of the fourteenth century, the Mongols under Qutb ad-Din Timur ibn Taragai (Timur the Lame aka Tamerlane) (r. CE 1380–1405) invaded northern India and broke the yoke of the Turkic Sultans. In their place the Afghani Sayyid Dynasty's (CE 1414–50) Khizir Khan Sayyid (r. CE 1414–21) was placed upon the throne. Soon the Afghani Lodi Dynasty (CE 1451–1526) replaced them and they reigned until the Timurud Dynasty asserted their power in CE 1526 (see **Appendix D**).

As the Tughluq reigned in Delhi, the fourteenth century saw numerous and significant mosques constructed throughout India. Among the most notable were the Masjid-i Jami (see **Plate 10**) at Cambay (CE 1325), the Masjid Begampuri (see **Plate 15**) of Delhi (*c.* CE 1325), the Jami' al-Kabir (see **Plate 11**) in Kayalpatnam (*c.* CE 1333), the Masjid Kalan (see **Plate 17**) of Delhi (*c.* CE 1351), the impressive Adina Masjid (see **Plate 13**) in Pandua (CE 1364), the majestic Masjid-i Jami (see **Plate 14**) at Gulbarga (*c.* CE 1367), the Khiṛkī Masjid (see **Plate 18**) of Delhi (*c.* CE 1375), and the important Masjid-i Jami (See **Plate 19**) of Srinagar (*c.* CE 1385). Similarly, the fifteenth century with the Sayyids and Lodis in Delhi produced in India an equally impressive array of mosques — the Atala Masjid (see **Plate 20**) of Jaunpur (*c.* CE 1408), the interesting Solah Khambā Masjid (see **Plate 24**) at Bīdar (*c.* CE 1424), the Rānī Rūpmatī Masjid (See **Plate 25**) in Ahmedabad (*c.* CE 1430), the impressive Masjid-i Jami (see **Plate 27**) of Jaunpur (*c.* CE 1438), the Masjid-i Jami (see **Plate 28**) at Mandu (CE 1440), the dramatic Masjid-i Jami Sarkhej (see **Plate 30**) in Ahmedabad (CE 1451), and the large Masjid-i Jami (see **Plate 32**) of Campāner (*c.* CE 1485).

The brilliant Afghani-Mughal (Mongol) Zahir-ud-din Muhammad Babur, King of Ferghana, also known as "the Great Mughal" (r. CE 1526–30) pushed south from his small kingdom and defeated the Delhi Sultan Ibrahim Shah Lodi (II) (r. CE 1517–26), thus establishing one of the most spectacular and long lasting dynasties in Asia — the Timurid or Mughal Dynasty (CE 1526–1876) (see **Appendix D**). A brief interruption — the Suri Period (CE 1540–55) — did little to tarnish this dynasty's lustre. His son Nasir-ud-din Humayun (r. CE 1530–40 and 1555–56) was the least successful of the early Mughals, however; in the end he prevailed. But, it was Jalal-ud-din Akbar the Great (r. CE 1556–05), Nur-ud-din Jahangir (r. CE 1606–27) and Shihab-ud-din Shah Jahan (r. CE 1628–66) that stand out as great rulers and builders during this period.

Architecturally, the sixteenth and seventeenth centuries each saw a dominant figure — Akbar the Great and Shah Jahan, respectively. That is not to say that Akbar's son and Shah Jahan's father, Jahangir

Introduction (Continued)

was without merit, but he paled in comparison to his father and son. Jahangir's greatest monuments were the Tomb of Akbar at Sikandra and his own tomb in Lahore. Doubtless, Akbar had overseen the original plans for his tomb, but it was left to Jahangir to attend to the major share of the construction.

The sixteenth and seventeenth centuries saw a plethora of great monuments. For example, there is the elaborate Safa Masjid (see **Plate 37**) at Ponda (*c.* CE 1550), Bījāpur's Masjid-i Jami (see **Plate 38**) (*c.* CE 1560), the monumental Badshahi Masjid (see **Plate 39**) of Fatehpur Sikri, the elegant Ali Shahid Pir Masjid (See **Plate 41**) (*c.* CE 1600) and the strange Aṇḍā Masjid (see **Plate 42**) (CE 1608) both in Bījāpur, the Masjid Wazir Khan (see **Plate 46**) of Lahore (CE 1634), Shahjahanabad's sublime Pearl Mosque (see **Plate 47**) (*c.* CE 1639), the Masjid-i Nagina (see **Plate 45**) of Lal Qila, Agra (*c.* CE 1628), the truly monumental Masjid-i Jami (see **Plate 48**) of Delhi (*c.* CE 1644) the largest in India, and the grand Masjid Badshahi (see **Plate 54**) in Lahore (CE 1673).

Along with the impressive and great monuments noted above, there are myriad examples of *masjid* constructed by men of far less financial resources and/or power than the rulers. Many of these may be found along the Malabar and Coromandel coasts in port cities inhabited by merchants and traders. Many of these businessmen had immigrated to these rich ports from the Islamic centres to the west and north while others were indigenous, sons of the soil — i.e. *bhūmiputras*. They constructed modest structures for the local faithful as well as for their own *shafá'a*.

The Solahkhambī Masjid (see **Plate 2**) at Bhadresvar (*c.* CE 1166), the Ahmad Nainar Masjid (see **Plate 12**) of Kayalpatnam (*c.* CE 1350), Qadiriya Masjid (see **Plate 29**) also at Kayalpatnam (*c.* CE 1450), and the elaborate Safa Masjid (see **Plate 37**) of Ponda (*c.* CE 1550) are but a few examples of *masjid* raised by local entrepreneurs. They may be far less ostentatious, but, nonetheless, important as they offer the other side of the coin.

Islam may have been a religion that was imposed or insinuated itself into or upon the Hindu/Jain/Buddhist fabric of India. Without exception, the Sultans of Delhi, Ahmednagar, Baroda, Berar, Bīdar, Bījāpur, Golconda, Jaunpur, Kashmir, Malwar, and of course the Mughals were first Islamic, but secondly sons of another soil, another land. Initially they were either Turkic, Persian or Afghani. The last Mughal, Siraz-ud-din Bahadur Shah II (r. CE 1857-76), could trace his ancestry back to Babur and even claim descendence from Genghis Khan and Tamerlane, but one-hundred-fifty years since the Great Mughals had diluted the energy and through intermarriage had made this last Emperor of India, less Mughal than Indian. However, whether imposed or insinuated, the Islamic faith provides some of the most spectacular architectural monuments of that vast subcontinent, Mother India.

The Mosque (Masjid)

Islam is a congregational religion, not unlike Christianity and Judaism. In order for the faithful to gather, particularly for Friday prayers or *solat jumaat*, a structure, a physical form was needed, hence, the *masjid*. As with most ecclesiastical structures, there were certain requirements to which a *masjid* must conform. Frishman lists nine components.[1] These elements are: (1) a space which is partially open

[1] MF, pp. 32-41.

to the sky and partially covered, (2) the *qiblā* and *mehrāb* perpendicular to and oriented towards Mecca, (3) a pulpit (*minbar*), (4) the *dikka* for the *qadi* of the *masjid*, (5) the *kursi* or lectern, (6) the *maqsura* or protective area for the Caliph or a prince which was later abandoned, (7) the *fisqiya* or *haud*, a ritual ablution pool, (8) the *minaret* for the calling of the faithful, and (9) the portal. Of these nine "components," nowadays, the required elements are: the space, *qiblā* and *mehrāb*, the *minbār*, the *kursi*, the *fisqiya*, the *minaret*, and quite naturally the portal. The *dikka* may appear, but only in large *masjids*, and the *maqsura* is only seen in the older *masjids*.[1]

Frishman views the *masjid*, especially the major monuments before the twentieth century, as falling into five categories.[2] These categories apply mainly to the plans or general layout of the *masjid*, but also consider certain elevation features as well (see **Figure 1**). The first is a structure in which there is a covered area and an open court (see **Figure 1-A**) which he views as being favoured in Arabia, Spain

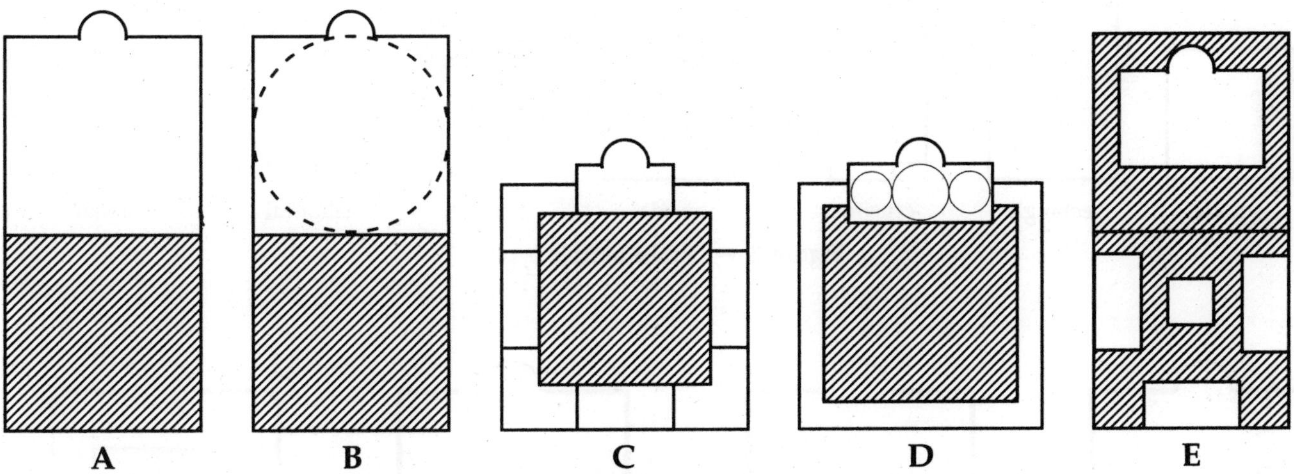

Figure 1 — Mosque catagories according to MF

and North Africa. The second category is an edifice in which the covered area is surmounted by a large dome (see **Figure 1-B**) employed frequently by the Ottomans. Third is a form in which the central court is flanked, biaxially, with large, vaulted structures or *iwans* (see **Figure 1-C**) and is encountered most often in Iran. The fourth example is a form he views as being found essentially in India and is composed of a large open court with a triple domed *haram* (see **Figure 1-D**). Finally, there is a *masjid* that is composed of a number of detached structures within a common enclosure and may be seen in China (see **Figure 1-E**). *En plan*, there is virtually little difference between example **A & B**. Also, **C & D** are similar inasmuch as they generally fall within a square shape. However, these general categories are interesting inasmuch as they offer a general outline, and one which was used to develop the various categories that appear within India.

---

1 Islamic doctrine saw all equal under Allah. The disappearance of the *maqsura* and the egalitarian aspect may be attested to the fact that in Morocco, when the King attends prayers, he is segregated from the other worshippers by a ring of pillows, but is not elevated or behind a protective screen.

2 MF, pp. 12-13.

Introduction (Continued)

The Mosque (Masjid) in India

Ecclesiastical structures in India may take many forms, *en plan*. Hindu temples offer the most variety of form. From the earliest extant structures or ruins, those forms are: square, rectangular, cruciform, apsidal, circular, elliptical and stellar (see **Figure 2**). There are regional preferences, to be sure — one encounters a large number of circular temples in Kerala — but the overwhelming majority throughout India fall within these seven basic plans/forms.

On the other hand, the *masjid* of India, particularly the free standing structures, may be encountered in either a square or a rectangle, *en plan*. Within the Islamic world there are examples of octagonal *masjid*-chapels which are incorporated within a larger structure, particularly a palace — the famed

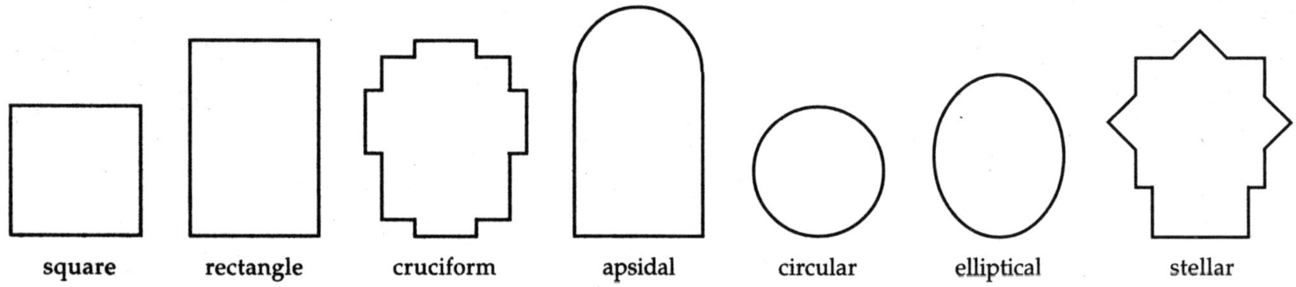

Figure 2 — Hindu temple types

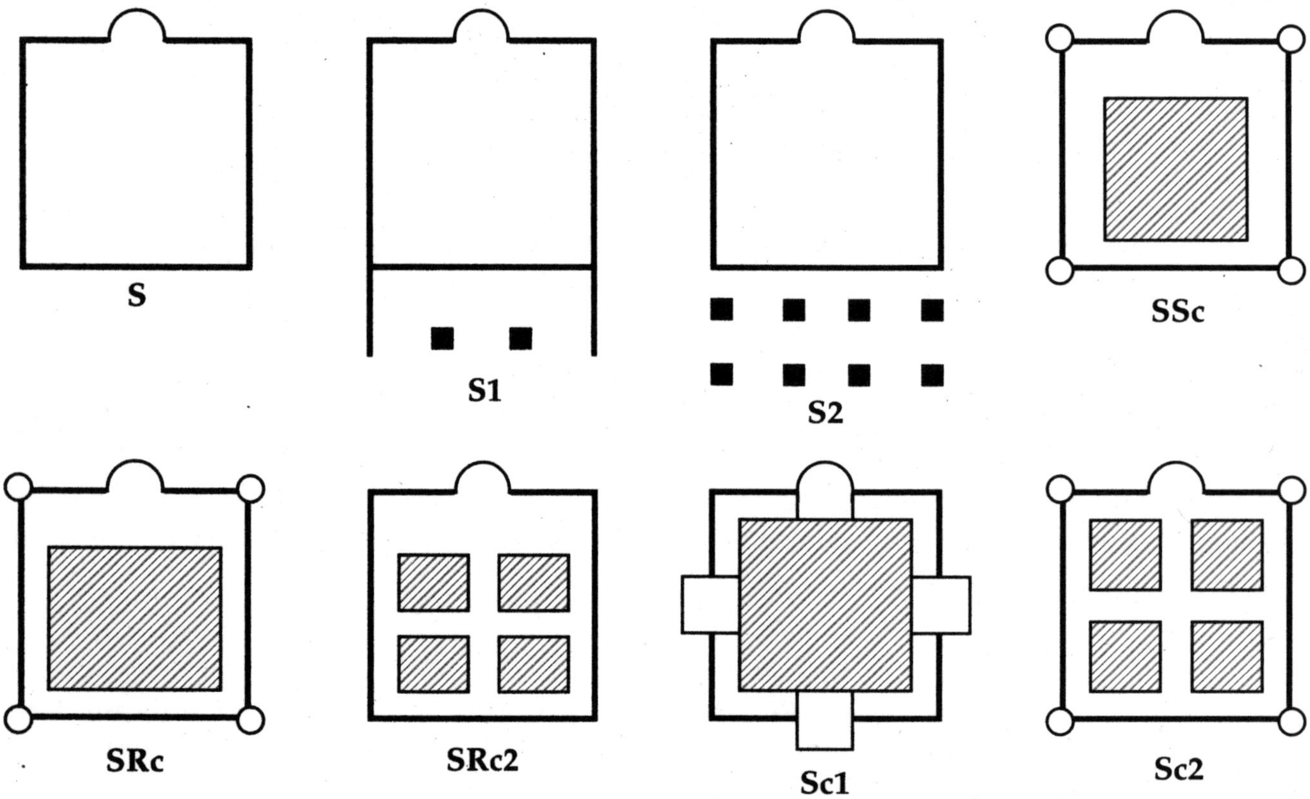

Figure 3 — Square *masjid* types

Introduction (Continued)

chapel of the Aljaferiya Palace at Zaragoza, Spain — and the isolated circular plan of the Mahlara Mosque at Kayalpatnam. The latter is a relatively modern design — i.e. CE 1871. However, both the square and the rectangular forms appear in numerous variations within India as free standing structures.

The square masjid occurs in large numbers throughout India. Outside of India, it occurs less often. There are, however, notable examples — the Bab Mardum Mosque of Toledo, Spain (*c.* CE 1000); the Masjid-i-Jami in Tinmal, Morocco (*c.* CE 1153); and the Masjid al-Hakim in Cairo, Egypt (CE 990–1013) to name but three. The frequency of the square *masjid* encountered in India may be, in part, due to the preference of the square in the plans of Hindu temples (see **Figure 3**). The simple square plan is perceived to exhibit seven variations. The *Masjid* which consists of a simple square is noted as **S** (see **Figure 3 - S**), e.g. the Qadiriya masjid of Kayalpatnam (see **Plate 29**). This elemental square type, the simplest of all plans, is rarely found except when a *qiblā* and *mehrāb* are found within a tomb — Tomb of Sultan Iltutmish (see **Plate 8** [to the left]) — thereby promoting the resting place to a place of prayer as well. The first variation of the **S** form resembles the Greek *in antis* temple, *en plan*, and is noted as **S1** (see **Figure 3 - S1**). Here the cella wall extends enfolding two or more columns across the front. This form may be seen in the Ibrahim Shrine/Masjid at Bhadresvar (see **Plate 1**). A second variation on the simple **S** form, is a square plan with two or more rows of columns in front and without surrounding or enclosing walls. This form is noted as **S2** (see **Figure 3 - S2**) and may be seen to be related to the Etruscan or podium style Roman temple. The Solahkhambī Masjid at Bhadresvar is an example of this type (see **Plate 2**). A square *masjid* with a square court, generally offset away from the *qiblā* is noted as **SSc** (see **Figure 3 – SSc**) and is the third variant. An example of this plan may be seen in the Masjid-i Jami of Mandu (see **Plate 28**). The fourth variation on the square is a square *masjid* with a rectangular, open court. This variation is noted as **SRc** (see **Figure 3 - SRc**). Frequently this variation will be seen with either round or octagonal towers (*minarets*) at the four corners and is represented by the Masjid Aṛhāī-din-kā-Jhoṅpṛā of Ajmer (see **Plate 5**) as well as in the Tomb of Sultan Ghari in Delhi.[1] A fifth variation on the square masjid is one in which there is four, open rectangular courts. This is noted as **SRc2** (see **Figure 3 - SRc2**). An example of this variation is seen in the Masjid Kalan of Delhi (see **Plate 17**). A sixth variation on the square is similar to **Sc**, but with prominent entrances opposite the *qiblā/mehrāb* and perpendicular to it. This variance from the simple square is noted as **Sc1** (see **Figure 3 - Sc1**) and may be seen in the Masjid Begampuri in Delhi (see **Plate 15**) and equates with Frishman's category **C** (see **Figure 1 - C**). A seventh and last variation on the square which is also similar to **Sc** and related to **SRc2** is a square with four, square, open courts. This form is noted as **Sc2** (see **Figure 3 - Sc2**). This type may be encountered in the Khiṛkī Masjid of Delhi (see **Plate 18**).

The second major form of *masjid* found in India is the rectangular plan (see **Figure 4**). The rectangular plan may be seen in a majority of *masjid*s throughout greater India. Outside of India, the rectangular plan predominates in overwhelming numbers. This form within India is seen to possess six variations.

1 The burial component of this tomb is visually secondary to the whole, consisting of an octagonal, raised form in the centre of the court with a stairway leading down to the crypt. In truth, the *qiblā* and *mehrāb* are far more prominent and architecturally dominate the whole.

Introduction (Continued)

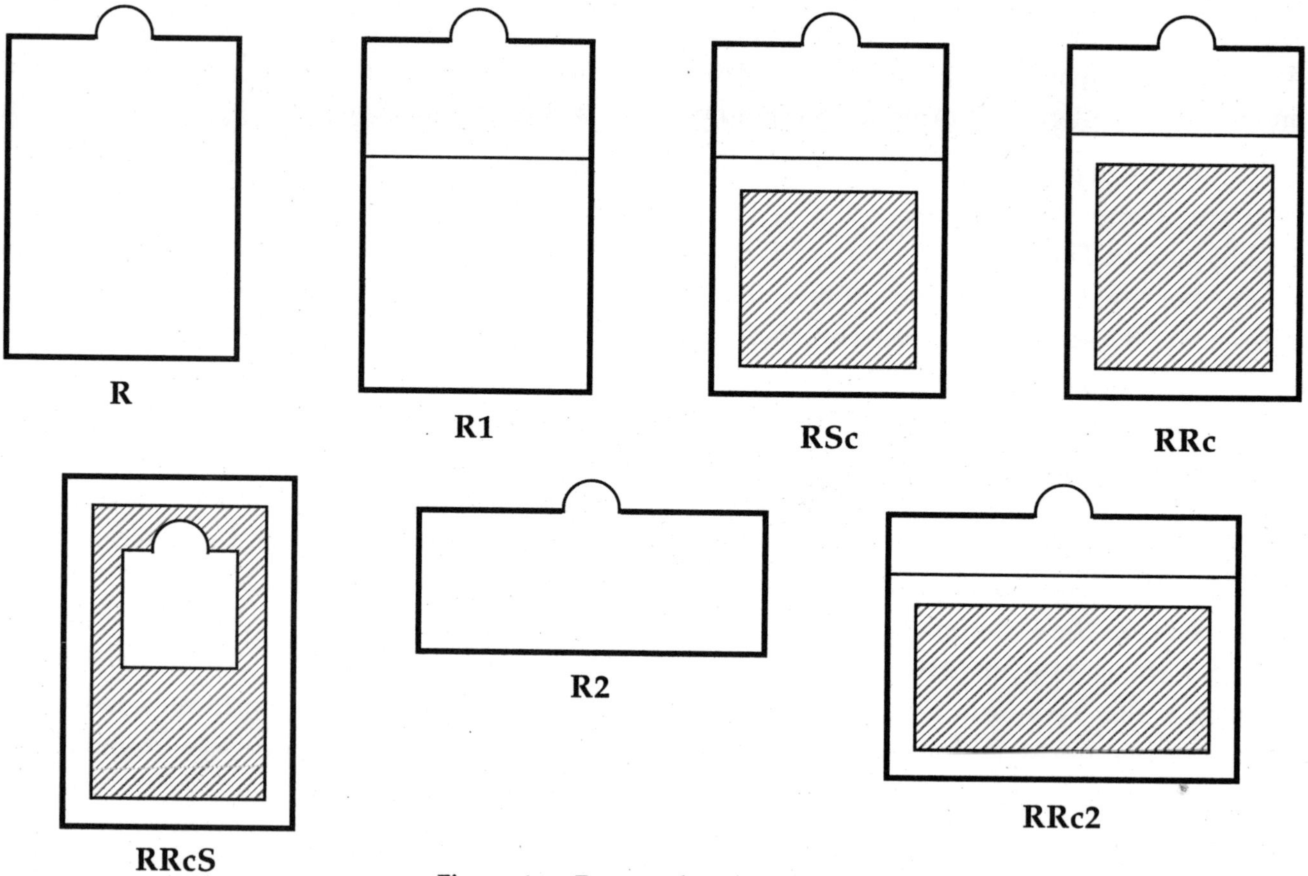

Figure 4 — Rectangular *masjid* types

The simplest type of this plan is that in which a rectangular, walled structure exists without internal divisions and lacking an open court. This basic type is noted as **R** (see **Figure 4 - R**) and may be seen in the immense Masjid-i Jami of Gulbarga (see **Plate 14**). A variation on **R**, the first, is seen in that *masjid* in which the basic design is rectangular and possesses one or more covered interior spaces parallel with the *qiblā/mehrāb*. This variation is noted as **R1** (see **Figure 4 - R1**). Numerous early examples may be found; the Ahmad Nainar Masjid at Kayalpatnam (see **Plate 12**) is but one of them. The second variation on the simple rectangle is the rectangular *haram* with a square open court. This type is indicated as **RSc** (see **Figure 4 - RSc**) and is exemplified in the Chhoti Masjid in Bhadresvar (see **Plate 3**). A further mutation, the third variant, is found in a rectangular *haram* with a rectangular court and noted as **RRc** (see **Figure 4 - RRc**). The venerated Quwwat-ul-Islam Masjid, first stage, in Delhi (see **Plate 4**) as well as the Masjid-i Jami of Tatta (see **Plate 49**) are examples of this type. The fourth rectangular variation is unique. It consists of a rectangular court with a square *haram* set within the court, and is noted as **RRcS** (see **Figure 4 - RRcS**). The single example is encountered in the unusual Mecca Masjid of Bījāpur (see **Plate 52**). A fifth variation is that rectangular *masjid* which is a lateral design — the length of the rectangle is parallel with the *qiblā/mehrāb*. This form is noted as **R2** (see **Figure 4 - R2**). There are numerous examples of this variation. This form seems to be particularly popular in the west, especially Gujarat as well as in the Sultanate of Bījāpur — Gunmani Masjid from Gaur (see **Plate 31**), the Safa

Masjid of Ponda (see **Plate 37**) and the Gol Gumbaz Masjid at Bījāpur (see **Plate 44**). Finally, the sixth and last variant is a lateral plan with a lateral, rectangular court. This plan is noted as **RRc2** (see **Figure 4 - RRc2**), and may be seen in the Adina Masjid in Pandua (see **Plate 13**).

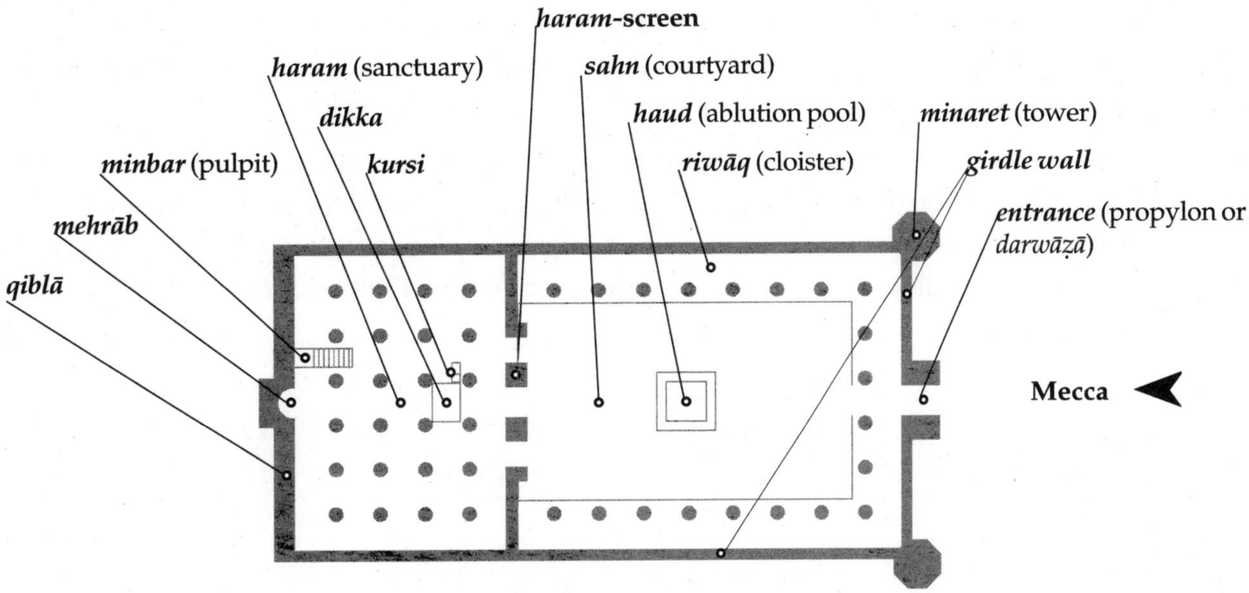

Figure 5 — Major elements of a *masjid*

The *masjid*, traditionally, consists of a *qiblā, mehrāb, haram, sahn, haud* and *minaret* (see **Figure 5**). As time progresses certain requirements change — in the *masjid* associated with a *rauza*, often times, a *sahn* is not included (see **Plate 25**) and the Bengali mosque frequently is without a *sahn* as well (see **Plate 31**).

There are three terms used herein that need additional explication — *haram, haram*-screen and *darwāẓā*. To many contemporary devotees of Islam, *haram* refers to those things which are forbidden, proscribed or condemned — the consumption of alcohol and/or pork. This is an interpretation that takes the term to its narrowest meaning, and one often used by the *shari'a.* A broader interpretation of the term refers to an area where one comes for prayers, and, in attending, must be "clean" both physically and spiritually — the Masjid-al Haram at Mecca where the *Ka'ba* is found, or the Haram al-Sharif in Jerusalem consisting of the Dome of the Rock and the Masjid al-Akasa. In both the Masjid-al Haram and the Haram al-Sharif, the interpretation of the term *haram* implies that when one comes there, he must throw off all impurities, both physical and spiritual. Within this study, the term *haram* is used to denote the sanctuary of a mosque. It is a definition utilized by many scholars today.[1] Second, the term *haram*-screen has been employed to define that architectural feature which acts as a transition between the *sahn* and the *haram* and refers to the "screen" or that architectural feature which separates and protects. It may refer to a series of similar arcuated or trabeated openings. It may also refer to a combination of arcuated or trabeated openings combined with a larger, monumental element, sometimes referred to as an *iwan* or *liwan*, terms which are imprecise and/or inadequate. Herein, the term will be

1 HS 2, p. 235; MF, p. 282; and GM, p. 281.

Introduction (Concluded)

employed as it applies to that element(s) which separate(s) the *sahn* from the *haram*. Finally, the term *darwāẓā* which is a term generally applied to a monumental entrance or gate as in the Delhi Darwāẓā of Shahjahanabad or the Buland Darwāẓā of the Badshahi Masjid of Fatehpur-Sikri. Many Indian *masjids* exhibit a large, prominent, sometimes monumental east entrance. The term "propylon" is applied at times, especially to the *masjid* of Jaunpur which has a pylon-like shape. Within this study the term *darwāẓā* will be applied to any monumental or large entrance block of a *masjid*, especially found in the eastern entrance, but may occur in the north or south entrances as well.

The choice of the *masjid* included in this study was made for two salient reasons — their adherence to the twelve variations noted and the manner in which they vary from the norm. Further, the examples selected were those which are most often seen as being exemplars within a region or of a type that is noteworthy. The distribution of the various types identified in **Figures 3 & 4** within this study are illustrated in **Figure 6**.

	1				5					10					15					20					25					30					35					40					45					50				
S																													X													X												
S1	X																																																				
S2		X																																																			
SSc																												X																										X
SRc					X					X									X																																				
SRc2																	X																																				
Sc1															X					X																												X						
Sc2																		X																																			
R														X																																							
R1							X									X																				X				X															
RSc											X										X						X												X							X										
RRc			X						X			X										X			X				X	X								X								X	X		X					
RRcS																																																			X			
R2																						X		X	X						X		X	X	X		X				X		X	X						X		X	X	
RRc2				X		X		X					X																																									

Figure 6 — Appearance of *masjid* types within this study

Finally, **Appendix C** is devoted, primarily, to "proportional elevations." These elevations are not purported to be precise in their many architectural details, but indicate major proportions and divisions. These elevations were composed using Adobe PageMaker 6.0.

The Mosques of the 12th Century

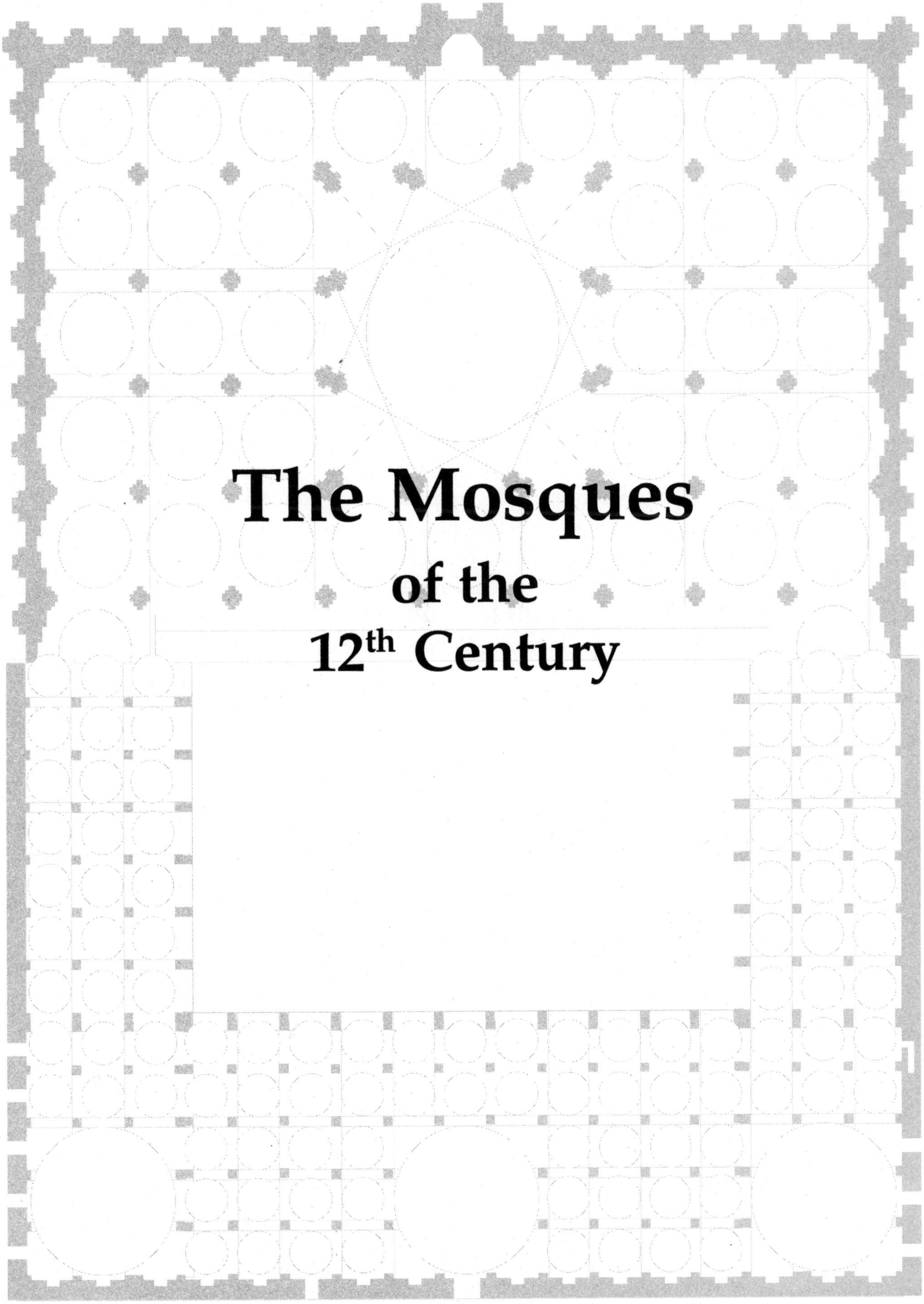

Ibrahim Shrine/Masjid, Bhadresvar (CE 1159)

One of the earliest Islamic *masjids* in India is the Ibrahim Shrine/Masjid located in Bhadresvar, in the state of Gujarat and known locally as Dargah La'l Shahbaz.[1] Just who, or which Ibrahim, the shrine/*masjid* is dedicated to is unknown.

Bhadresvar was known in ancient times as Bardaxima and later as Barda and was on a major trade route (see map: "Indian Subcontinent after CE 1950," indicating major sites, p. 2.). Islam came early to this area of India, partially because of Bhadresvar's proximity to Iran and the Arabic Peninsula and, also because it was a noted port of the day. Apparently the first Muslims came as traders rather than invaders and they quickly spread down the Malabar Coast, the western coast of India.

A relatively small structure, the Ibrahim Shrine/Masjid is essentially square with a portico to the east. As would be expected, this structure is aligned towards Mecca. It consists of a square cella with a deep *mehrāb* in the *qiblā* wall. This type of *mehrāb* was widely employed during the earliest periods of the Islamic influence within India. Later, the *mehrāb* was little more than a semicircular indention within the *qiblā*. Four windows, two to the south and two to the north, punctuate the walls and provide adequate light for the interior. An entrance towards the east opens onto a vestibule with four pillars across the front, two being engaged to the wall's extension. This provides a more imposing entrance than a simple wall with a door as seen in the **S** type plan (see **Figure 3**). At the roof-line the square cella is transformed to an octagon which is supported by eight piers, two on each wall of the interior. The octagon transmutes to a circle. The plan appears Islamic, however, a typical Indian "dome" — circular and corbelled — rises upwards (see **Appendix B — Plate 82**). Doubtless, the plan was initially drawn by the resident Muslims and left to the local Hindu *sthapati* to execute, not an unheard of practice.

The Ibrahim Shrine/Masjid appears to be an example of an **S1** type plan (see **Figure 3 — S1)** — a square cella with extended walls enfolding pillars. It is related to the Greek *in antis* temple type common to smaller temples of the Hellas.

1 MS, p. 12.

Plate 1 — Ibrahim Shrine/Masjid, plan

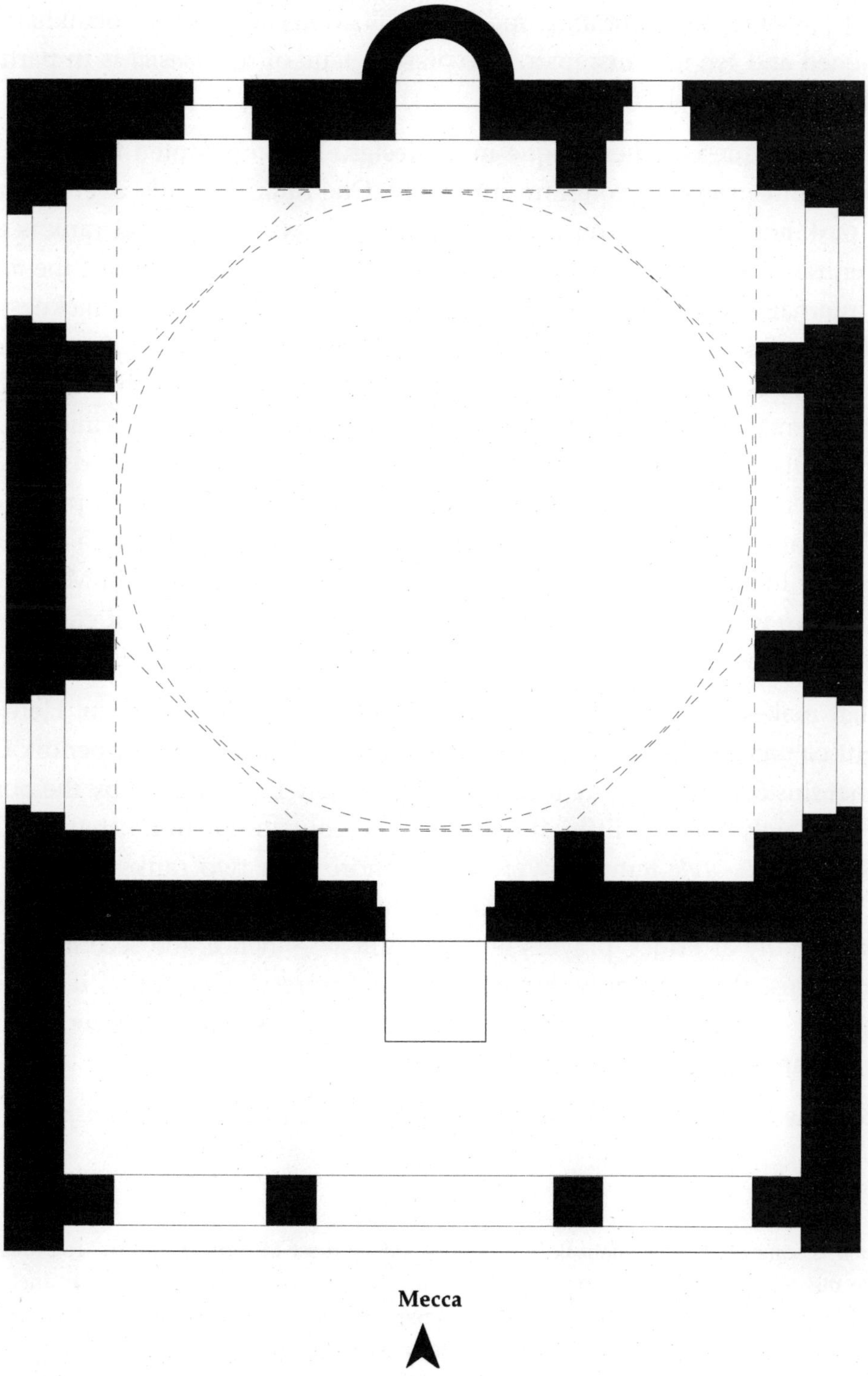

Solahkhambī Masjid, Bhadresvar (CE 1166)

One of the first *masjids* of some importance and size in Bhadresvar was the Solahkhambī Masjid. Long ago it was abandoned and fell into disrepair. The present state of this *masjid* is in partial ruin and it is constantly inundated with the shifting sands.

Nonetheless, this mosque is rather unique in its design. It is constituted by a *haram*[1] that is nearly square, *en plan*, with three ranks of columns, internally. One rank is a little over two metres from the *qiblā*, the second rank nearly five metres from the same wall, while the third rank is a little over two metres from the entrance wall, the east wall. As with many of the early *masjids*, the *mehrāb*, *en plan*, is prominent both internally and externally. Here the *mehrāb* is as deep as the thickness of the western wall and extends beyond in a half circle of the same width. Numerous later *masjids*, even within monumental mosques, possess a *mehrāb* which is only a half circle set in the thickness of the *qiblā* and of minor importance, *en scale*. It is to be noted that there is a second *mehrāb* — a semicircle, *en plan*, and set within the eastern wall south of the entrance. This may well have been added later. There are four windows piercing the thick walls, two to the north and two to the south which provide adequate light to the interior. The walls are fairly thick which appear a necessity to maintain a cooler interior in this hot and arid region of India. Unlike mosques of the near east, the Solahkhambī Masjid does not exhibit a dome, although there is a square element between the two eastern ranks of columns that may have supported a wooden dome.

However, what makes the Solahkhambī Masjid truly unique is the portico. Here one encounters four ranks of eight columns each, forming seven bays across the front (see **Appendix C — Plate 86**). It has been noted that this feature is highly unusual and probably is influenced by the porticoes of Indian Hindu temples.[2] Certainly there is little, if any, evidence outside of India that would relate to this feature. Greco-Roman *octa-style* temples were rarely more than two ranks deep as in an *octa-style, dipteral* temple.[3] This colonnaded, roofed portico may have served as an overflow space for the rather small interior, particularly at Friday prayers — Solat Jum'at — hence, the second *mehrāb*. In addition, the eight columns across the front provided not only an impressive entrance, it refers to the number eight which is also a sacred number in Islam. Islamic belief acknowledges eight paradises — *hasht bishisht* — and eight angels who uphold the Divine Throne.

The open, columned portico clearly places the Solahkhambī Masjid as a *masjid* of the **S2** type (see **Figure 3 — S2**).

---

1 The term *haram* is somewhat problematical. It is understood by most Muslims to mean "forbidden" or "prohibited." However, the meaning of the term more specifically means "set aside." As such it may include the meaning of "forbidden." However, the Great Mosque of Mecca is referred to as The Mosque of the Haram (Masjid al-Haram). It also refers to an area set aside in a home and later refers to a *harem* or *zenana*. In this study it is employed, referring to the enclosed prayer hall of a *masjid* where a *mehrāb* is found. Occasionally, the term *liwan* is used for the same area.

2 The Kālasaṁhāramūrti Temple at Triprangod, or the Śiva Temple of Kaviyur both possess a *namaskāra-maṇḍapa*. Although a separate structure from the sanctum, this feature, common to a number of earlier Hindu temples, may have been an influence.

3 An *octa-style, dipteral* temple would have eight columns across the front and back, two rows or ranks deep. The number of columns along the length may vary.

Plate 2 — Solahkhambi Masjid, plan

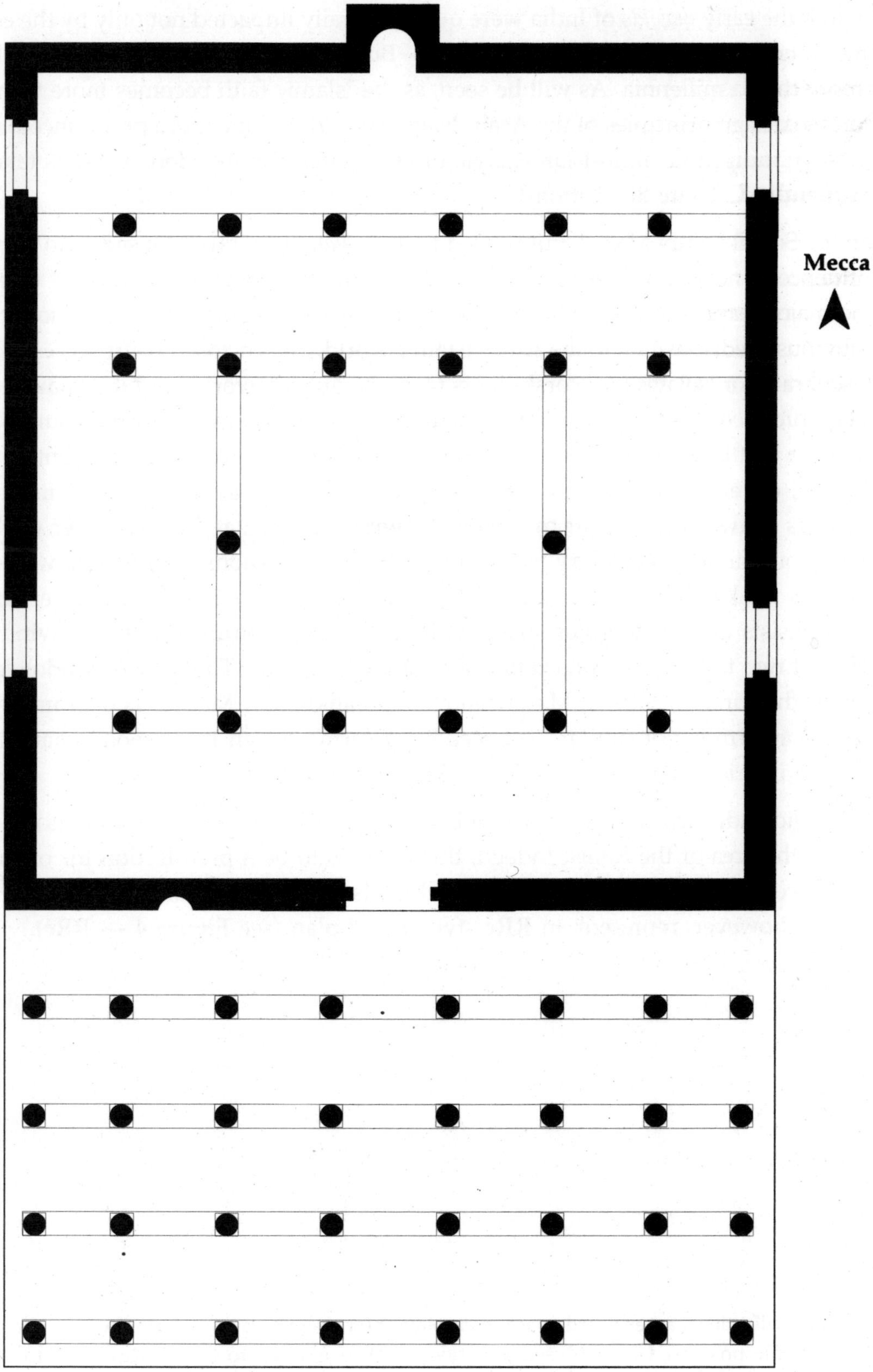

Chhoti Masjid, Bhadreśvar (CE 1166)

It is noteworthy that the early *masjids* of India were quite naturally impacted not only by the construction techniques of India, but also by the design principles — Buddhist, Hindu and Jaina — which had been in practice for more than a millennia. As will be seen, as the Islamic faith becomes more firmly planted, the reliance upon the design principles of the Arab/Islamic world become more pronounced. Eventually, India evolves its own indigenous Indo-Islamic style of *masjid* architecture. Here a step is taken towards that end (see **Appendix C, Plate 86** [bottom]).

Smaller than the Solahkhambī Masjid, but related to it, *en plan*, the Chhoti Masjid, also of Bhadresvar, indicates the influence of near-eastern *masjid* design in the employment of an open court (see **Appendix B, Plate 55**). The major feature of the Chhoti Masjid is the enclosed courtyard, nearly square in shape. It indicated an obvious predisposition to the Arab/Islamic world. The enclosed court serves two purposes — it physically separates or isolates the worshippers from the outside world, and it contains or coalesces these worshippers into a communal whole. The separation or isolation aspect of the court is an ancient iconographic concept that is applicable to many faiths.[1] Within this court one is confronted with a two ranked, colonnaded, covered entrance area, but not as grand or as deep as is seen in the previous *masjid*. Twelve pillars in two ranks, eight free-standing with four engaged to the outer wall create the portico space. Here one finds a secondary *mehrāb* of minimal dimensions, and in line with that of the *masjid* proper. This is flanked by two entrances into the *haram*. The sanctum is of a lesser size than the portico area and consists of a rectangular space with one rank of columns and four windows — i.e. two to the north and two to the south bracketing the rank of columns. The *qiblā* is windowless and the *mehrāb*, like that of the Ibrahim Shrine/Masjid and the Solahkhambī Masjid, is a prominent feature. However, the exterior form is not similar — a rectilinear form as seen in the Solahkhambī Masjid — rather, it mimics the interior configuration and is semicircular, *en plan*.

The Chhoti Masjid indicates what appears to become the rule in the *masjids* of India — an open court which dwarfs the area of the *haram*. Indeed, this appears to be a predilection for other *masjids* in the Islamic world except Turkey where the prayer hall tends to be larger than the court (see **Appendix B, Plate 58**). It does, however, represent an **RRc** style *masjid* plan (see **Figure 4 — RRc**).

---

1 In the earliest of civilizations, an enclosed space is employed for protection of outside invaders, hence influence. The Egyptian temple possessed an enclosed *peristyle* which was open to those who came to worship. The enclosed garden in Judaeo-Christian iconography is seen as symbolic of purity and/or virginity. Within the later Islamic world it becomes the feature of the *zenana*. The Forbidden City of Beijing is walled to ensure that the only functioning male within at nightfall is the person of the Emperor.

Plate 3 — Chhoti Masjid, plan

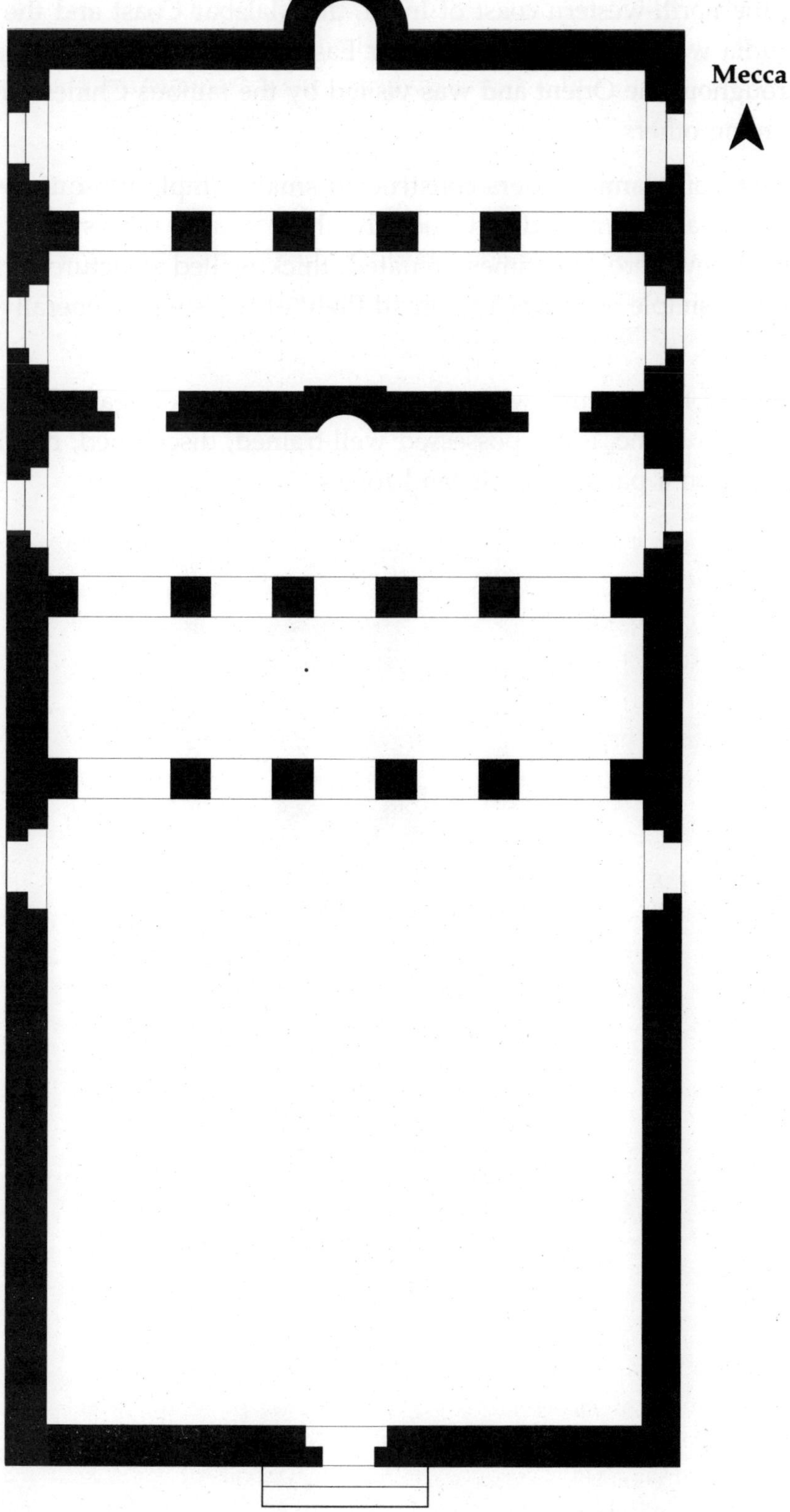

Twelfth Century

The earliest *masjid*s found in India were raised not by generals of armies but generals of commerce. For centuries traders from north-eastern Africa, the Arabian peninsula and Persia had availed themselves of the ports along the north-western coast of India, the Malabar Coast and the Coromandal Coast. As a trading centre, India was also known in the Far East as well. On the Malabar Coast, Calicut was a renowned port throughout the Orient and was visited by the famous Chinese trader-adventurer Zheng He (Cheng Ho), among others.

The small enclaves of Islamic traders constructed small, simple mosques which, due to their size would be characterized as a *surau* today. Generally, these *masjid*s consisted of a *haram* and a covered portico or vestibule. They were sometimes arcuated, thick walled structures with the requisite *mehrāb* in the *qiblā*. Doors were simple openings and broad flight of stairs were generally not seen in these plain, modest structures.

Towards the end of the century when the Islamic invasions began in earnest, the armies came overland rather than sea borne. Islam possessed well-trained, disciplined, nearly invincible armies. Its navy, frankly, was not on a par with their land forces.

The Mosques
of the
13th Century

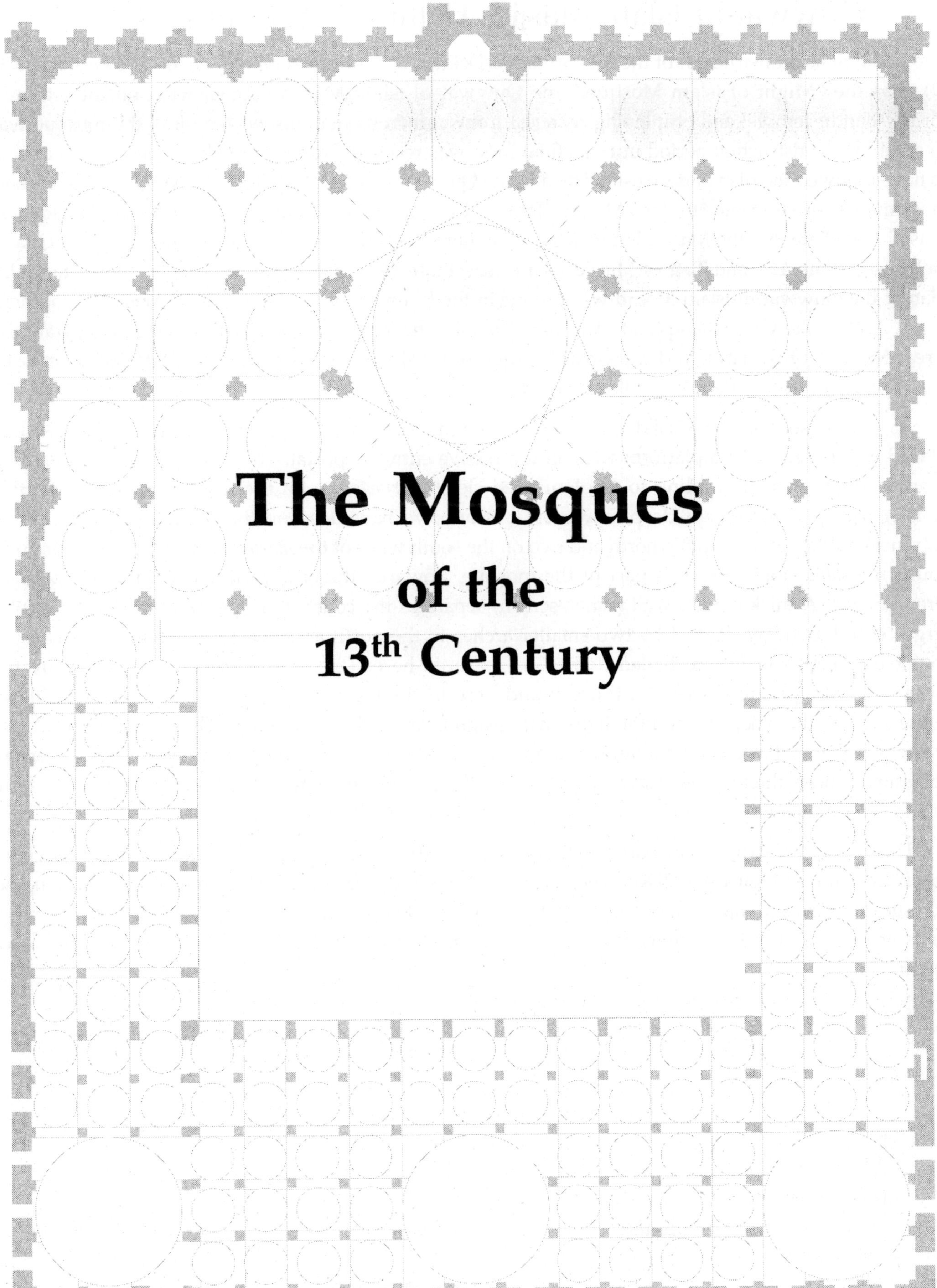

Quwwat-ul-Islam Masjid, Delhi, 1st Stage (*c.* CE 1199)

The initial major construction of the first Sultan of Delhi, Qutb-ud-din Aibak (CE 1206–10) (see **Appendix D**), was the "Might of Islam Mosque," the Quwwat-ul-Islam Masjid. Constructed on the site of a former Hindu temple[1] and employing material from numerous demolished temples,[2] the mosque was to see a long construction period until its final form was reached. Numerous subsequent *masjids* appear to have followed the plan pattern established in the Quwwat-ul-Islam Masjid — the Masjid-i Jami Sarkhej of Ahmedabad (see **Plate 30**), the Masjid-i Jami at Campāner (see **Plate 32**), Fatehpur Sikri's Badshahi Masjid (see **Plate 39**), the Masjid Wazir Khan of Lahore (see **Plate 46**), Pearl Mosque at the Lal Qila in Delhi (see **Plate 47**), and Tatta's Masjid-i Jami (see **Plate 49**). That is not to say that the rectangular plan of the Quwwat-ul-Islam Masjid was unique in the Islamic world — the Shibam Masjid of southern Saudi Arabia, the Great Mosque at Qairouan, Tunisia; the Tarik Khana Masjid at Damghan, Iran; the Great Mosque of Samarra; and the Great Mosque of Cordoba (see **Appendix B, Plate 56**) all may be seen to be reflected in the plan of the Delhi *masjid*.

As will be seen in the Masjid Aṛhāī-din-kā-Jhoṅpṛā at Ajmer (see **Plate 5**), the Quwwat-ul-Islam Masjid was raised upon a platform with an impressive entrance portal. This entrance was achieved by a broad flight of stairs leading to a colonnaded cloister (*riwāq*) — on the front or eastern side, this cloister (*riwāq*) is three bays deep; however, it is but two bays deep on the north and south. Lesser entrances are found: two on the north and two on the south walls of the *masjid*. A large, open, rectangular court, the *sahn*, dominates this part of the mosque. Towards the *qiblā* in this court there is a small circular *haud*. A thick curtain wall (*haram*-screen) separates the court from the *haram* and consists of a large central archway flanked by two smaller arches to the north and two to the south. The *haram* is four bays deep, and five corbelled domes are featured here. The focus of these five domes are the *mehrāb*. Unlike previous *mehrābs*, those found here in the Quwwat-ul-Islam Masjid are singularly subservient to the whole, being little more than insignificant niches in the *qiblā*. The central, semicircular *mehrābs* is somewhat more pronounced than the four flanking *mehrābs*, but still little more than an accessory. Unlike the previous *masjid*, there is no indication on the outer surface of the *qiblā* of the form or placement of the *mehrāb*(s).

This *masjid* constructed, in part, for the glory of Sultan Qutb-ud-din Aibak is of the **RRc** style of *masjid* design (see **Figure 4 — RRc**). The additions that were to be imposed — Iltutmish's addition and Jalal-ud-din Firuz Khalji's grand enlargement — shifted this **RRc** style *masjid* to an **RRc2** style. Either in its original form or in its enlarged state the Quwwat-ul-Islam Masjid was a *masjid* fit for the Sultan of Delhi.

---

1 Lāl Koṭ Temple, CT, p. 156.

2 Ibid. It is said that twenty-seven Hindu and Jaina temples were torn down in and around Delhi for this *masjid*'s construction.

Plate 4 — Quwwat-ul-Islam Masjid, 1st stage plan

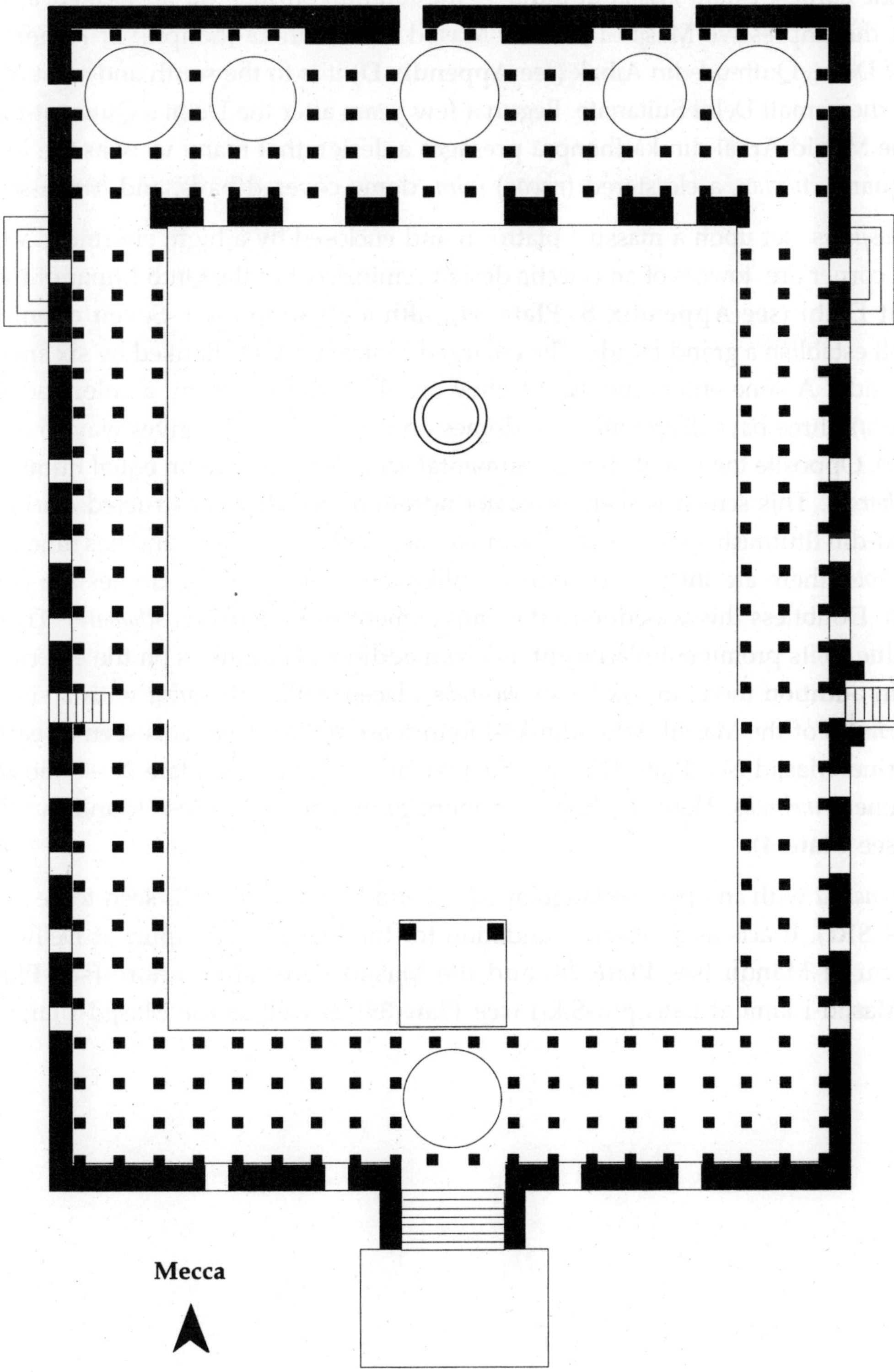

Masjid Aṛhāī-din-kā-Jhoṅpṛā, Ajmer (*c.* CE 1211)

Nearly six-hundred years from the death of the Prophet Mohammad and one-hundred years from the appearance of the earliest extant *masjid* in India — the Ibrahim Shrine/Masjid located in Bhadreśvar — one encounters the impressive Masjid-i Jami or Masjid Aṛhāī-din-kā-Jhoṅpṛā[1] at Ajmer. Initially built by the Sultan of Delhi, Qutb-ud-din Aibak (see **Appendix D**) it is to the south and west of Delhi, on the outskirts of the then small Delhi Sultanate. Begun a few years after the Delhi's Quwwat-ul-Islam Masjid (see **Plate 4**), the Masjid Aṛhāī-din-kā-Jhoṅpṛā presages a design that many view as the Indian standard — generally square, *en plan*, a cloistered (*riwāq*) *sahn*, dome covered bays, and *haram*-screen.

Here, the *masjid* is set upon a massive platform and enclosed by a high, enormous wall over 250 ft square. At each corner are towers of an eclectic design reminiscent of the Qutb Minar of the Quwwat-ul-Islam Masjid at Delhi (see **Appendix B, Plate 59**), although simplified. Seven openings along the easternmost wall establish a grand façade. The enlarged central portal is flanked by six smaller openings, three on either side. As one enters the *masjid*, they are first confronted by a colonnaded cloister-like ambulatory (*riwāq*), three bays deep with nine domes on three sides. This gives way to a massive, open court yard (*sahn*). Opposite the portals is a monumental *haram*-screen with an equal number of entrances leading to the *haram*. This screen is seen as a later addition, possibly constructed during the reign of Sultan Shams-ud-din Iltutmish (CE 1211–36). The prayer area is five bays deep and has nine domes adjacent to the *qiblā*. *En toto*, there are thirty-two domes. Unlike later *masjids*, these domes are corbelled in the Hindu tradition. Doubtless this was due to the employment of indigenous *sthapatis*. There is a central *mehrāb* which, due to its prominent placement, is given additional emphasis on the exterior in a stepped conformation. In addition there are six lesser *mehrābs* placed within the *qiblā* with a simple rectilinear exterior. The *mehrābs* of the Masjid Aṛhāī-din-kā-Jhoṅpṛā are not as deep as is seen in earlier *masjids* — the Ibrahim Shrine/Masjid (see **Plate 1**) or the Solahkhambī Masjid (see **Plate 2**) — and tend to mirror later, less prominent *mehrābs*. They are, however, more prominent than those found in the Quwwat-ul-Islam Masjid (see **Plate 4**).

This square *masjid* with an open, rectangular court and a roofed *haram* is seen to be of the **SRc** style (see **Figure 3 — SRc**). It acts as a design foundation for the Masjid Begampuri at Delhi (see **Plate 15**), the Masjid-i Jami of Māṇḍu (see **Plate 28**) and the Masjid Badshahi, Lahore (see **Plate 54**) and is related to the Masjid-i Jami at Fatehpur-Sikri (see **Plate 39**) as well as the Masjid-i Jami of Delhi (see **Plate 48**).

[1] The name translates: "two-and-a-half-day cottage," referring to the time of construction. EH, vol. II, p. 43, states that "if the walls of the quadrangle and the arches in front of the *liwan* (*haram*) are left out of account, such a performance . . . would not be altogether incredible." However, the size of this *masjid* makes such a feat "incredible," indeed.

Plate 5 — Masjid Aḁhāī-din-kā-Jhoṅpḁā, plan

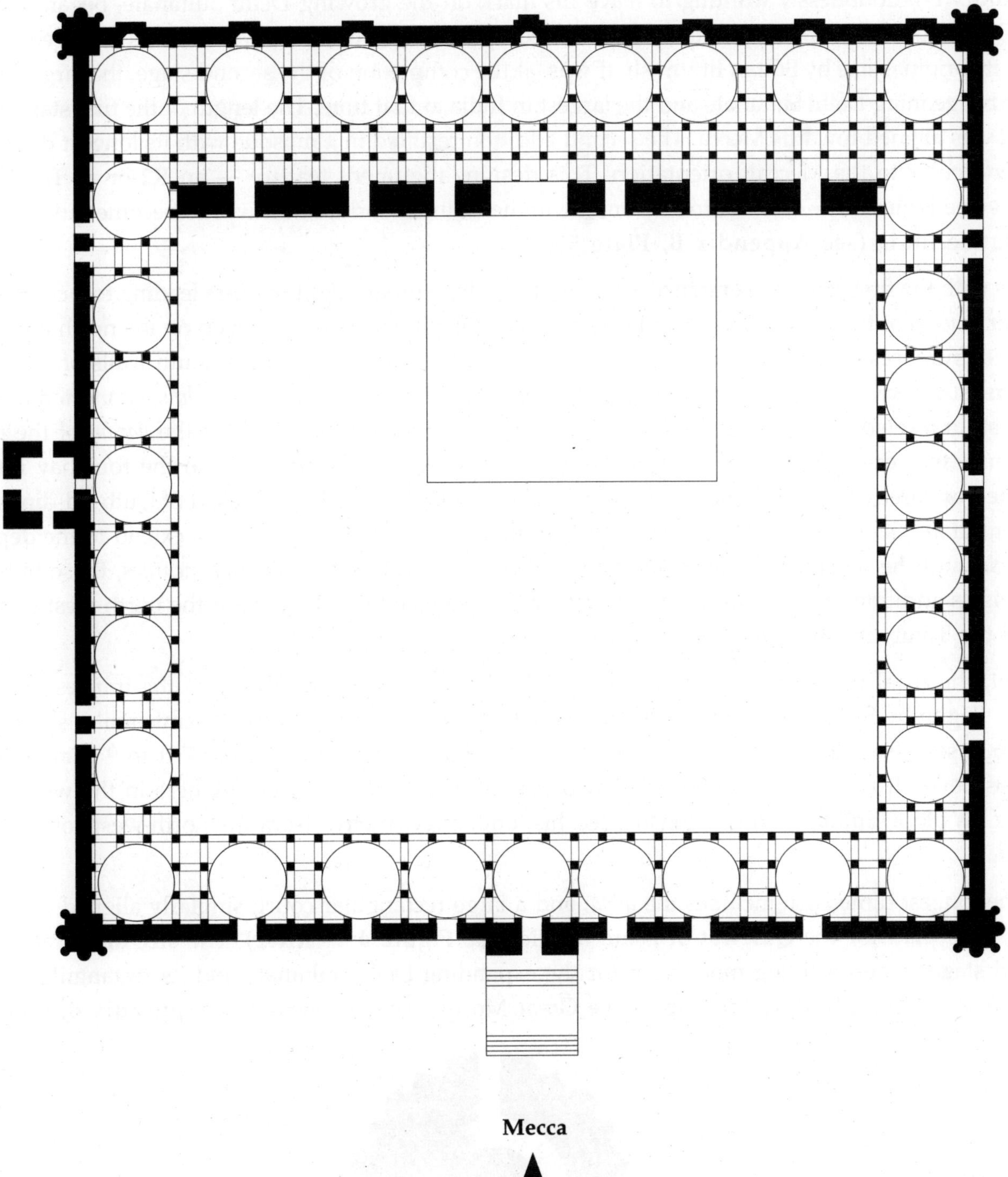

Quwwat-ul-Islam Masjid, Delhi, 2nd Stage (*c.* CE 1229)

The third ruler of the Mamluk Dynasty, the powerful Sultan Shams-ud-din Iltutmish (CE 1211–36) (see **Appendix D**), doubtlessly wanting to leave his mark on the growing Delhi Sultanate, began to build. The Quwwat-ul-Islam Masjid, initially constructed by Sultan Qutb-ud-din Aibak, was enlarged to over twice its original size by Sultan Iltutmish. It was, at the completion of the second stage, the largest *masjid* in the burgeoning Delhi Sultanate and the largest in India at that time. The length of the first stage of this *masjid* was aligned towards Mecca. The second addition resulted in a mosque with its longest dimension perpendicular to the Meccan orientation. This design/alignment feature — an **R2** or an **RRc2** style design (see **Figure 4**) — was not totally unique in the Islamic world, but it was to become quite popular in Islamic India (see **Appendix B, Plate 55**).

As with the first stage, the entrance was dominated by a broad flight of stairs leading to a colonnaded cloister (*riwāq*) of three bays deep. Similar to the first stage it was two bays deep on the north and south aspects. Entrances of similar scale and import are found on the north and the south walls of the *masjid*. The first stage was totally contained within Iltutmish's second stage. Two large *sahns*, connected towards the east, bracketed the original *masjid*. The *haram*-screen between the *sahn* and the *haram* of the initial structure, was duplicated in the double court. Here three portals give way to the four-bay interior crowned by three corbelled domes. However, unlike the Quwwat-ul-Islam Masjid of Qutb-ud-din Aibak, the central *mehrāb* is treated in a manner more attuned with earlier *masjids*. They extend to the depth of the *qiblā*, and the rectilinear forms extend beyond the *qiblā* wall. Unlike earlier *mehrābs*, those of Sultan Iltutmish's addition are rectilinear, *en plan*, rather than semicircular. Finally, in the north-west corner is found the Tomb of Iltutmish.

Yet, the focal point of the second stage of the Quwwat-ul-Islam Masjid is the impressive Qutb Minar. Begun by Sultan Qutb-ud-din Aibak, its plan consists of rectilinear and semicircular shapes (see **Figure 7;** see also: **Appendix B, Plate 59**). The tower tapers from its base of 47 ft to 9 ft at its 238 ft topmost level. It is seen as a monument "without parallel in Islamic art anywhere in the world."[1] To ensure his place, Sultan Iltutmish constructed his tomb a few metres from the north-west corner of the *masjid*.

The longest dimension includes the *qiblā*, and a large rectangular court, similarly aligned creates an **RRc2** style plan for the Quwwat-ul-Islam Masjid (see **Figure 4 — RRc2**). The size and scale of the second stage creates a fitting monument for the expanding Delhi Sultanate and its rectangularity may be seen to be influenced by the impressive Great Mosque of Damascus (see **Appendix B, Plate 55**).

Figure 7 — Qutb Minar, ground plan

1 SG, p. 8.

Plate 6 — Quwwat-ul-Islam Masjid, 2nd stage plan

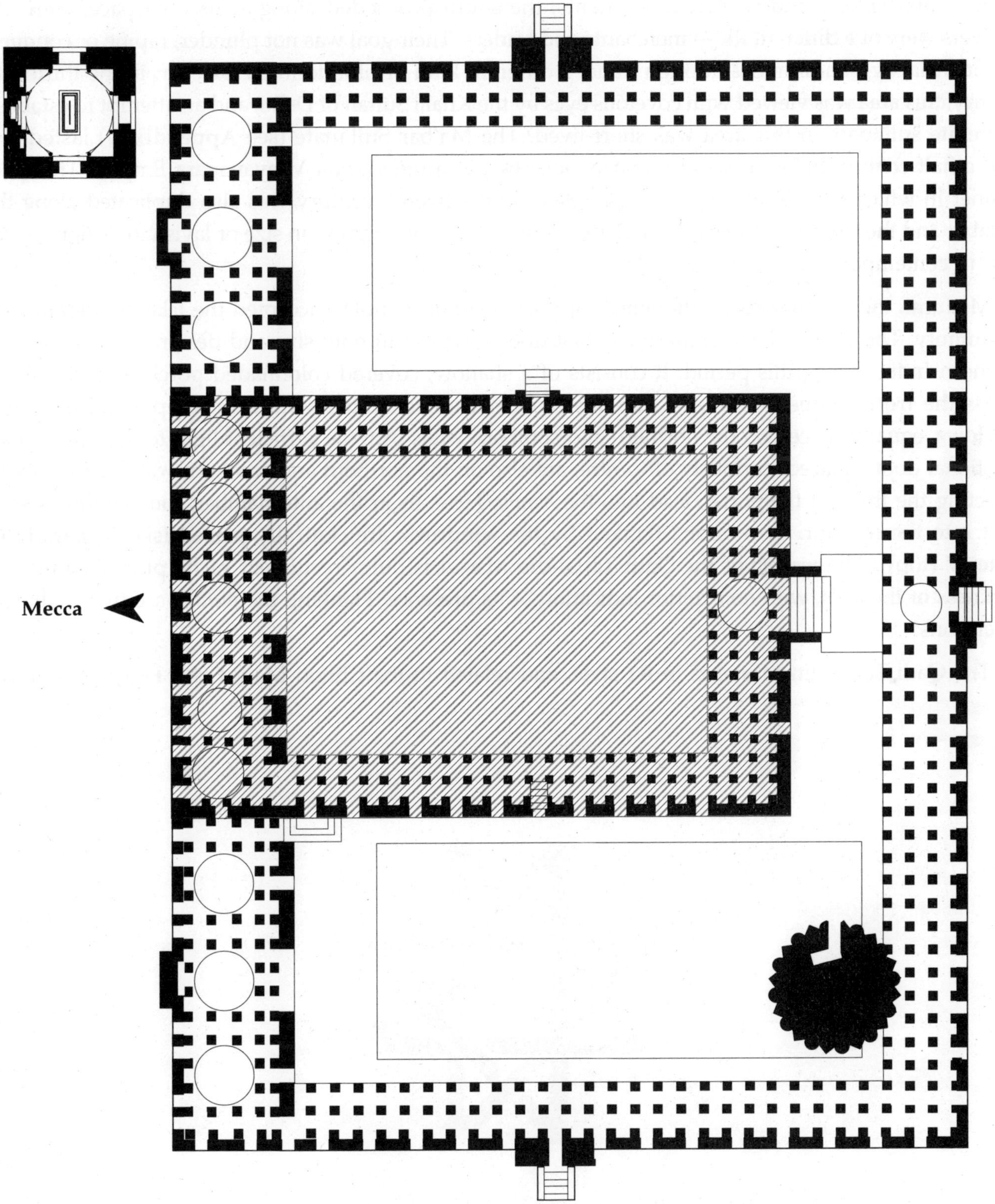

Qadi Taj al-din Masjidi, Madurai (*c.* CE 1292)

While the Turkic-Afghani invaders were expanding, conquering and building in the north, creating monumental *masjid*s and secular monuments, the south proceeded along at its own pace. Here the invaders were of a different ilk — merchants and traders. Their goal was not plunder, rapine or conquest but financial aggrandizement through trade, a different kind of plundering. However, in the thirteenth century, this area was viewed with covetous eyes by the Khalji Sultan of Delhi, and an attempt to establish a satellite sultanate in this area was short-lived. The Ma'bar Sultanate (see **Appendix D**) lasted less than a half century before it was ultimately absorbed into the vibrant Vijayanagara Empire. The quiet manner in which *masjid*s appeared in Bhadreśvar in the twelfth century was also duplicated along the Malabar and the Coromandel coasts. Here the *masjid*s were not as grand in size or lavish in design as was seen in contemporaneous imperial Delhi.

Madurai, the site of some of the most impressive Hindu temples, accepted the Islamic traders with equanimity. The Qadi Taj al-din Masjid at Madurai, is typical in both size and design of the *masjid*s of southern India during this period. It consists of a shallow, covered colonnaded porch with six pillars across the front. Three doors lead into a rectangular antechamber with four support pillars. Four windows, equally spaced on the northern and southern walls provide sufficient light to this space. Two additional doors, placed, curiously off centre, are also on the northern and southern walls. Three doors, reflecting the three of the portal, lead into the *haram*. Here, as in the antechamber, four windows shed light into the interior. Two doors, flanked by the windows, are centrally placed (see **Appendix C, Plate 87** [top]). The *mehrāb* of the Qadi Taj al-din Masjid is but a rectilinear niche placed within the thickness of the *qiblā*, with no exterior indication of its presence. Flanking the *mehrāb* are two shallower indentions.

The Qadi Taj al-din Masjid is in **R1** style, and related to the Chhoti Masjid (see **Figure 4 — R1**).

Plate 7 — Qadi Taj al-din Masjid, plan

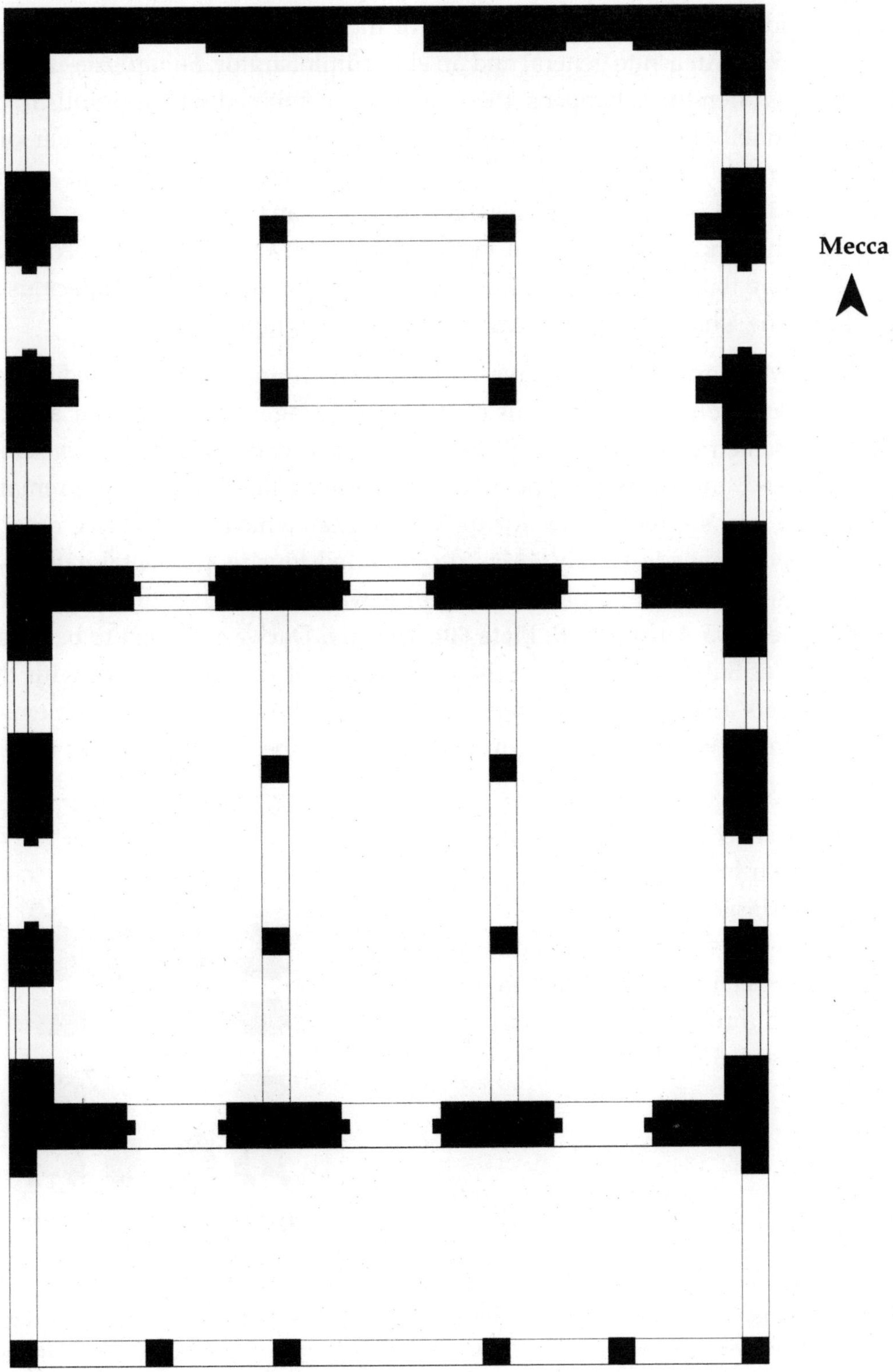

Quwwat-ul-Islam Masjid, Delhi (*c.* CE 1295) last stage

Dwarfing the first and second stage of the Quwwat-ul-Islam Masjid, Sultan 'Ala-ud-din Muhammad Khalji (r. CE 1296–1316) (see **Appendix D**), known as the Great Khalji, built big! His addition to the Quwwat-ul-Islam Masjid was over ten times the area of the original *masjid*, creating a monument that measured some 750 × 450 ft. An astute general and an able administrator, Sultan 'Ala-ud-din was also an extremely pious man. As often times happens, these qualities, combined with absolutism, created a man of extreme cruelty.[1] Nonetheless, he caused to be constructed, or began a number of noteworthy monuments during his reign besides the final stage of the Quwwat-ul-Islam Masjid — the Alai Minar (unfinished), the royal city of Siri, the Haus Khas, the Jam'at Khana Masjid and the Alai Darwāẓā. His last years were to see this once great Sultan, a victim of his own megalomania, become a compulsive paranoiac, and little more than a puppet. Within four years of his death, three rapacious sultans ruled and were dispatched. The Khalji Dynasty succumbed to the Tughluq Dynasty.

Sultan 'Ala-ud-din Muhammad Khalji increased the northern limits of the *masjid* by forty-five bays and twenty bays eastward from the dimensions of the second stage. He added four additional *mehrābs* to his extension in the same mode as Sultan Iltutmish had done extending the *haram*-screen the whole 750 ft length of the *masjid*, and continued the arcuated cloister (*riwāq*) around the remainder. In true megalomaniac style, he laid the foundation for the Alai Minar which would have dwarfed the Qutb Minar had it ever been completed.[2] Finally, 'Ala-ud-din added four monumental gateways: one to the north, two to the east and one to the south — the Alai Darwāẓā — which is the only extant example of the four (see **Figure 8;** see also **Appendix B, Plate 60**). The Alai Darwāẓā is seen to be a design solution hinted at by the Tomb of Sultan Iltutmish — the articulation of the hemisphere with the cube. This monumental gateway sets a standard that finds its ultimate solution in the monuments of the Great Mughals and is considered "the first building (in India) to reflect the . . . Indo-Islamic style."[3]

The longest dimension of the whole includes the *qiblā*, and a series of courts, similarly aligned create an **RRc2** style plan for the final stage of the Quwwat-ul-Islam Masjid (see **Figure 4 — RRc2**). As noted above, this rectangular design finds favour early in the Islamic world and is to be repeated within India throughout its history (see **Appendix B, Plate 55**).

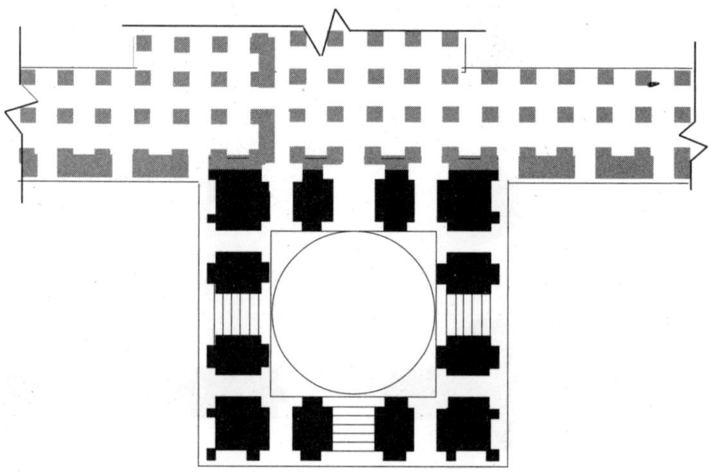

Figure 8 — *Alai Darwaza,* plan

1 It is said that "he shed more innocent blood than even (the) Pharoah was guilty of," SG, p. 20; this during a time when cruelty and vicious behaviour was the norm. Again, as might be expected 'Al-ud-din Khalji developed into a full blown meglomaniac and saw himself as the second Alexander.

2 The 238' Qutb Minar would have been dwarfed by the 392+' Alai Minar had it been completed.

3 MF, p. 163.

Plate 8 — Quwwat-ul-Islam Masjid, final plan

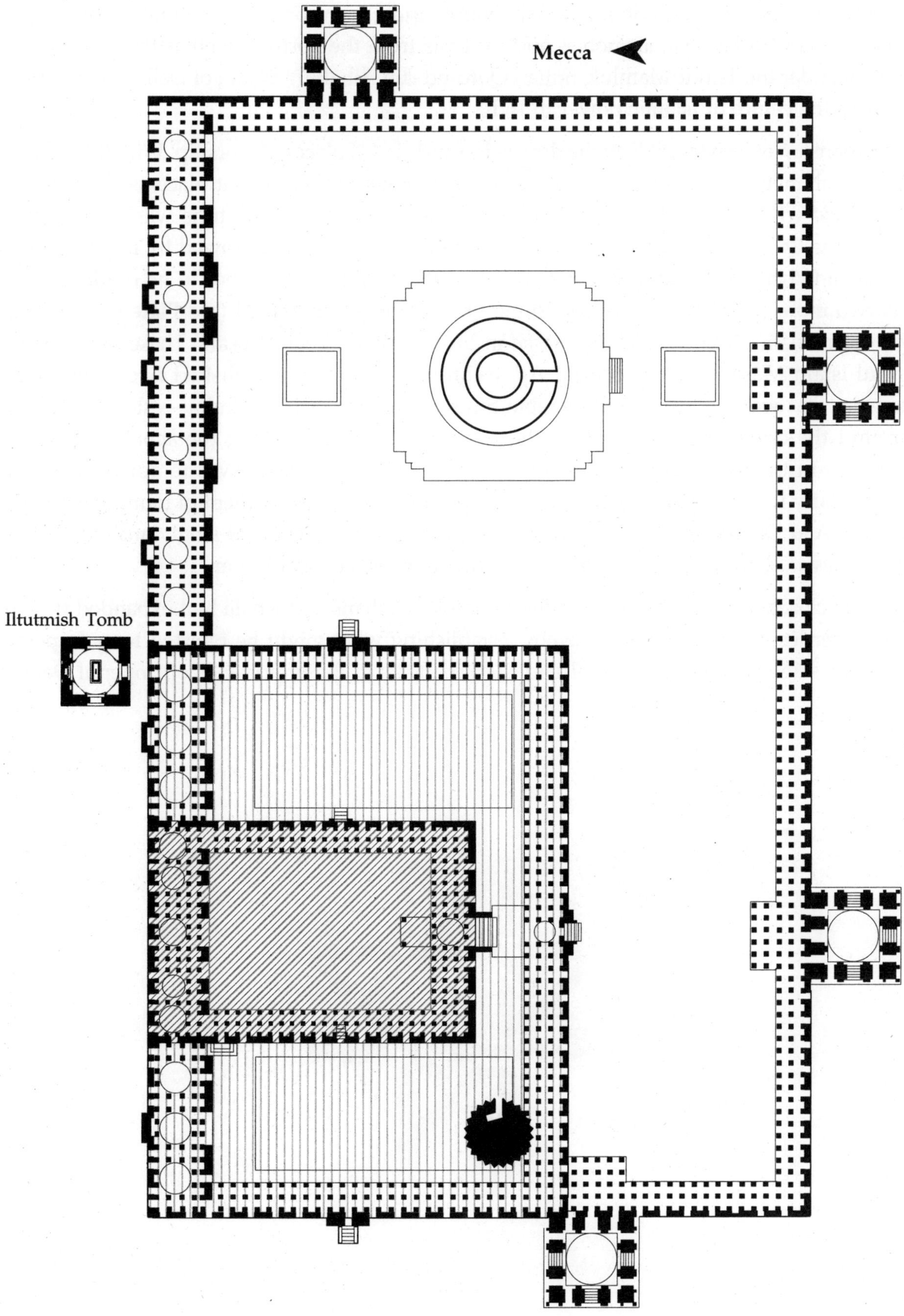

Thirteenth Century

The thirteenth century was a period of consolidation and expansion — consolidation of those regions conquered by the invading Islamic nobles and generals from the north as well as the expansion of their realm. It was under the Turkic Mamluk, Sultan Qutb-ud-din Aibak, 1st Sultan of Delhi (r. CE 1206–10), that Delhi became the centre of Islamic power in India.

Their expansion is seen tangibly in the dimension and size of places of worship. With the establishment of the Delhi Sultanate, a *masjid* was needed to reflect the importance of that place as a centre of power. At first a *masjid* which was considered large by Indian standards of that time was constructed — the first stage of the Quwwat-ul-Islam Masjid (see **Plate 4**). This was soon followed by the larger and more complex Masjid Aṛhāī-din-kā-Jhoṅpṛā at Ajmer (See **Plate 5**). Delhi was not to be outdone. In CE 1229 and 1295 two more additions were made to the Quwwat-ul-Islam Masjid (see **Plate 6** & **8**). This made the Quwwat-ul-Islam Masjid the largest *masjid* in India for a number of years. These two *masjid*s — the Quwwat-ul-Islam Masjid and the Masjid Aṛhāī-din-kā-Jhoṅpṛā — established two important design characteristics that were repeated innumerable times throughout Islamic India — the employment of a *riwāq* around the open court or *sahn* and the *maqsura* or screen fronting the *haram.* Another feature was employed in the third stage of the Quwwat-ul-Islam Masjid which was to appear time and time again, particularly in the *masjid* of northern India, and that is, the employment of monumental entrances. Although the Alai Darwāẓā was one of four, it, nonetheless, was repeated singly and on a far grander scale in the *masjid* of the Imperial Mughal Style nearly three centuries later.

The Khalji closed out the century. But, the Mamluks, Balbans and Khalji had expanded their domain to include other lesser Islamic rulers, thereby, establishing what might be referred to as Imperial Delhi rule. The third stage of the Quwwat-ul-Islam Masjid attests to the importance of Imperial Delhi.

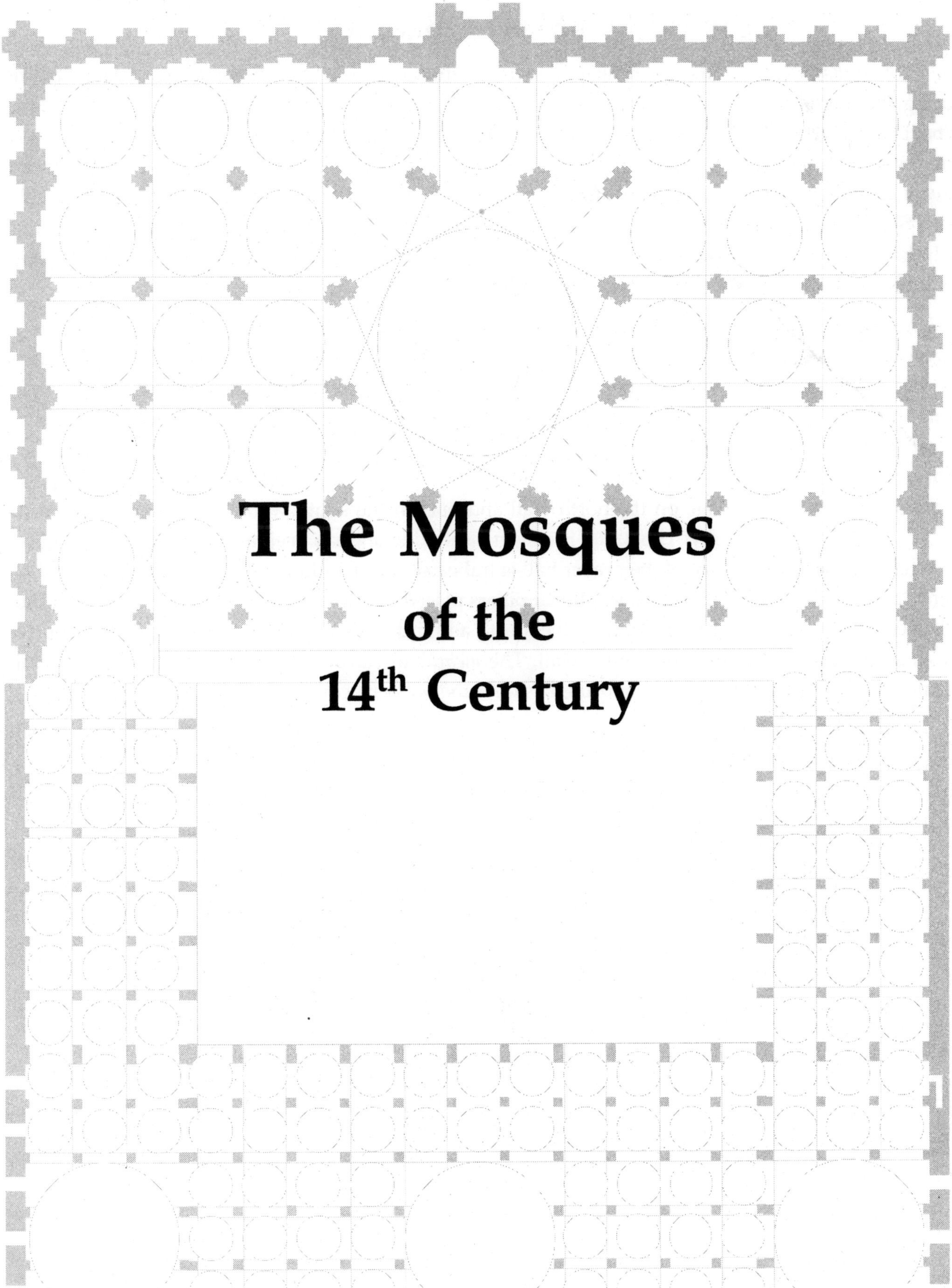

The Mosques of the 14th Century

Karim-ud-Din Masjid, Bījāpur (*c.* CE 1320)

The earliest *masjid* of any import in Bījāpur is the Karim-ud-Din Masjid. It was constructed some time during the reigns of 'Ala-ud-din Muhammad Khalji (CE 1296–1316) and Ghiyas-ud-din Tughluq Shah I (Ghazi Malik) (CE 1320-25) Sultans of Delhi (see **Appendix D**), and probably by one of their generals. This mosque reflects the style or plan that had become standard throughout Islamic India since the advent of the Delhi Sultanate. With the decline and fall of the Bahmani Sultanate, Bījāpur under the 'Adil Shahi Dynasty, of Turkic origin, rose, meteorically and produced some of the finest monuments in India. If the Karim-ud-Din Masjid appears, *en plan*, to resemble other *masjid*s in India, subsequent 'Adil Shahi *masjids* would vary dramatically from this early monument.

The plan may appear typical, but there are a number of features which vary from the norm. The Karim-ud-Din Masjid, as many mosques in areas that were conquered, pillaged surrounding Hindu and Jaina temples, particularly the pillars and stone slabs, and employed them in their *masjid*. Across the front of the mosque are a number of columns — sixteen in all and distributed in an unequal manner. The entrance pavilion to this Bījāpur *masjid* goes a step further; it is the *maṇḍapa* of a pre-existent Hindu temple with its soaring roof removed. The unremarkable courtyard or *sahn* is rectangular in shape with two additional entrances: one on the north wall and one on the south wall. These two entrances were placed, it seems, haphazardly. The *haram* is eleven bays wide and six deep and is made up of a number of different pillars. The whole of the prayer hall is trabeated and would have been oppressively dark if it weren't for the clerestory created by additional pillars placed on top of the central sixteen. Two additional entrances are found in the haram between the fourth and fifth rank of columns. Flanking these doorways are deep niches set into the thick outer wall. The *mehrāb* of Karim-ud-Din Masjid is well articulated, square, *en plan*, and extending beyond the *qiblā*. At the western corners are circular turrets.

The Karim-ud-Din Masjid exhibits a Persian trait which is to become one of the hallmarks of Indian mosque architectural design — the open court or *sahn* — which has notable predecessors: the Quwwat-ul-Islam Masjid (see **Plates 4, 6 & 8**) and the Masjid Aṛhāī-din-kā-Jhoṅpṛā (see **Plate 5**). Even the later mosques of Bījāpur rely upon the open court — an interesting fact since the 'Adil Shahi are Turks where enclosed mosques were the norm.[1]

Essentially, the mosque appears to be an **RRc** style design, with an entrance gate, *sahn*, pillared *haram* and an articulated *mehrāb* (see **Figure 4 — RRc**).

1 Inclement winter weather and snow created a need for an enclosed mosque. This was not the case in India.

Plate 9 — Karim-ud-Din Masjid, plan

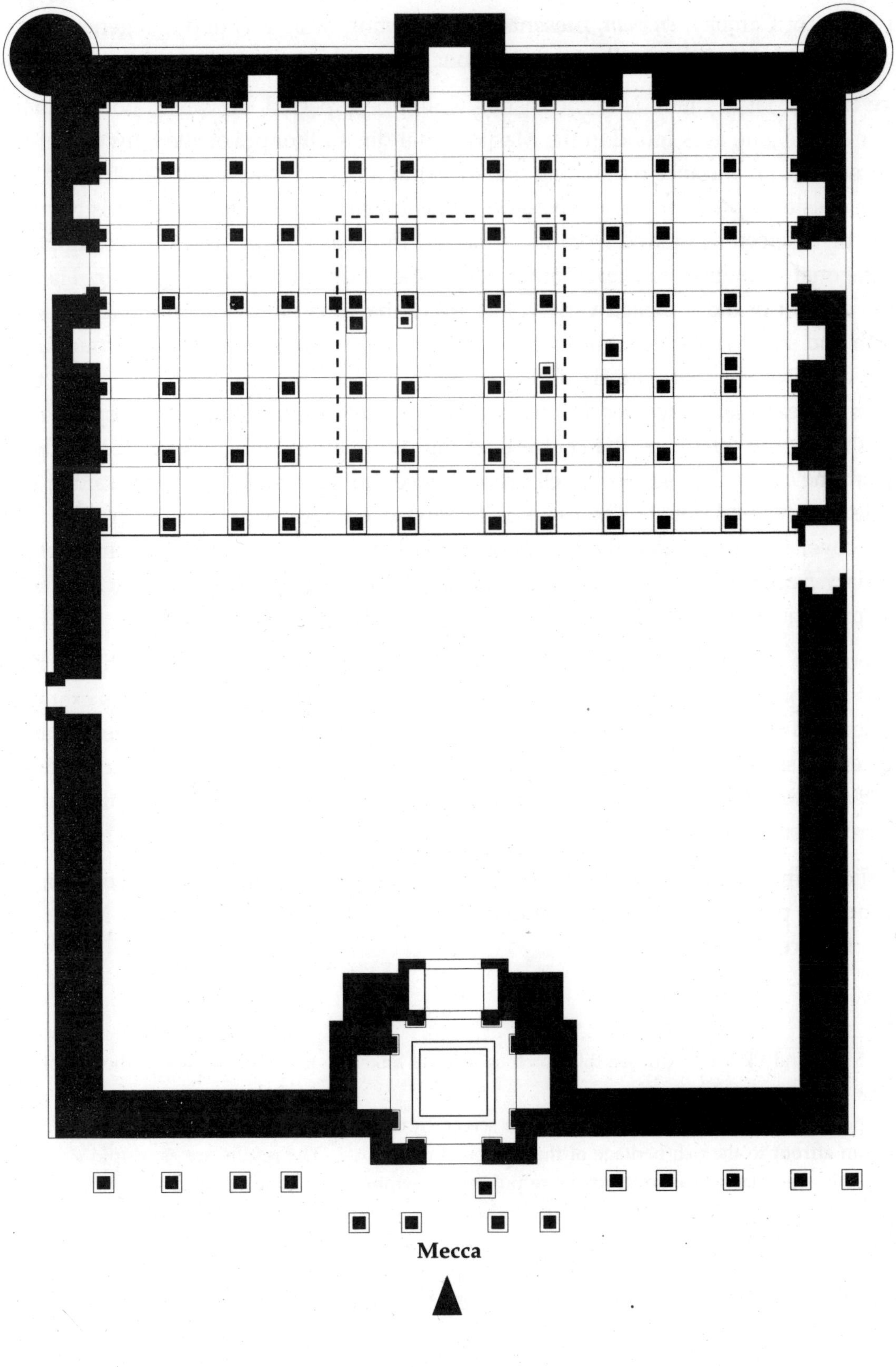

Masjid-i Jami, Cambay (CE 1325)

Constructed in viceregal Gujarat while the Sultans Ghiyas-ud-din Tughluq Shah I (Ghazi Malik) (r. CE 1320–25) and Muhammad Shah Tughluq Shah (II) (r. CE 1325–51) reigned in Delhi (see **Appendix D**), the Masjid-i Jami of Cambay, *en plan*, presents an interesting design. It finds its genesis, in part, in the design of the Masjid Aṛhāī-din-kā-Jhoṅpṛā at Ajmer (see **Plate 5**).

Entrance to the Masjid-i Jami is to the east as would be expected. However, not via that traditional, elaborate or massive gate as is found in the Masjid Aṛhāī-din-kā-Jhoṅpṛā or the Quwwat-ul-Islam Masjid. Here one encounters an entrance resembling one found in a Hindu temple but constructed with a dome.[1] Passing into a cloistered *riwāq*, an impressive *sahn* is encountered. The eastern cloister is twenty-seven bays wide, *en toto*, or nineteen as viewed from the *sahn* and four bays deep. Nine domes supported by eight pillars in octagonal formation abut each other across the width of the *masjid* proper. The domes of the Masjid-i Jami are not of the corbelled variety, but are of the voussoir-style dome (see **Appendix B, Plate 82**). The north and south *riwāq* are eighteen bays wide as viewed from the *sahn* and four bays deep. Here reflecting the depth of the court, are six domes similarly disposed to the north and six to the south. The juxtaposing of trabeated and arcuated elements creates an interesting plan and prospect. A thick *haram*-screen with three large openings, the centre opening dominating, and two small portals separate the courtyard from the *haram*. This screen is well proportioned, but that is all that can be said of this otherwise unremarkable architectural detail.[2] The *haram* is twenty-seven bays wide and seven deep. Two ranks of seven domes cover this area minus three bays on either side. The *qiblā* exhibits a central *mehrāb* and two lesser, secondary *mehrābs* — all corresponding with the three large openings in the screen. Similarly three semicircular projections from the rear wall, *en plan*, denote the internal forms.

To the south of the *masjid* proper, but connected, is the Tomb of Umer bin Ahmed Kazaruni. The connection of a tomb with a *masjid* is not unusual within Islam. There are numerous examples in which it occurs.[3] The main entry to this area is achieved via an imposing entrance in the south wall. Frequently, main entrances to Islamic tombs are to the south. Within its narrow enclosure and towards the west is a small *masjid* or *surau*, which is related in plan to its larger neighbour. This hints at the *rauza* plan that is to become prominent in Gujarat as well as Bījāpur (see **Appendix B, Plates 66, 72, 75 & 77**).

The Masjid-i Jami of Cambay reflects the **SRc** type of design. Its *haram* screen may be a point of contention, but its plan indicates an elegance that will find its ultimate fruition in the later Mughal *masjids* (see **Figure 3 - SRc**).

---

1 EH, pp. 51-53, and Pl. XII & XIII, see this porch as directly linked to the *sabhāmaṇḍapa* of the Solanki Sūrya Temple, Moḍherā.

2 The vituperative quality of the criticisms of this screen by numerous architectural historians is mirrored in SG, p. 62: ". . . an affront to the rich heritage of the Cambay builders. . . . The results are as insipid as those of the *Jamat Khana*, ... a dull blanket cast over the more pulsating rhythm of the Hindu and Jaina columns. . . ." The screen's surface is unadorned, unfortunately? Its proportions are admirable. Are we seduced by surface decoration?

3 The Mausoleum of Oljeitu Hudabanda, Sultaniya; the Tomb of Sultan Hasan, Cairo; and the Tughtabeg Khatun Tomb, Urgench, are tombs which are attached to or in close proximity to important *masjids*. Some tombs even incorporate a *mehrāb* within the *qiblā* of the tomb — the Doner Kumbet, Kayseri; the Tomb of Mehmet I, Bursa; and the Tomb of Adham Khan, Delhi.

Plate 10 — Masjid-i Jami, plan

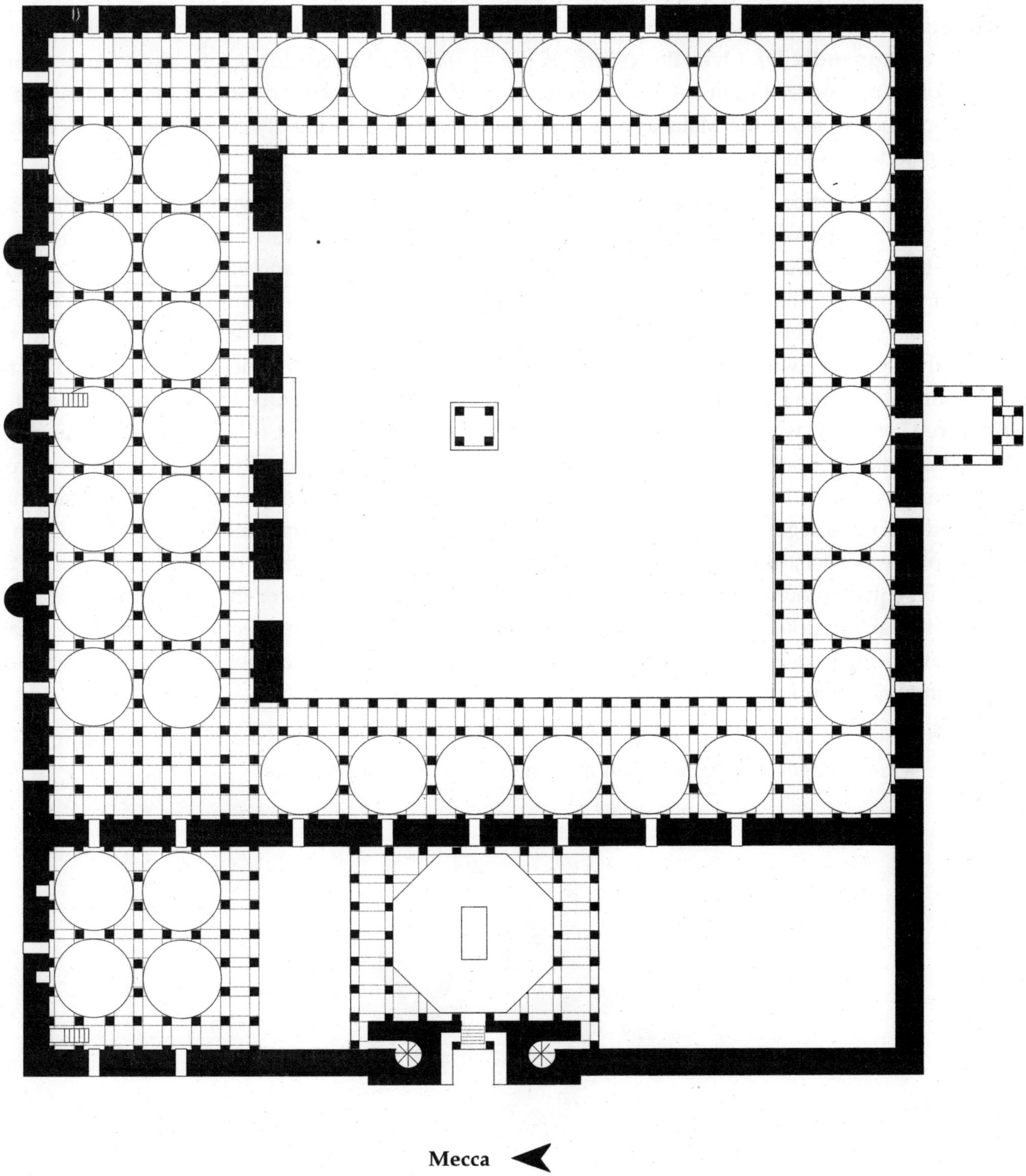

Jami' al-Kabir, Kayalpatnam (*c.* CE 1333)

The history surrounding the Jami' al-Kabir or Khutba Perriapalli at Kayalpatnam, and its construction is somewhat confusing. The mosque is generally dated between 1333 and 1338. Further, it was probably constructed by the Sultan Jalal al-din Absan, the first ruler of the short-lived Ma'bar Sultanate (CE 1333-56) (see **Appendix D**). Over the centre of the *masjid* is a raised dome, of classic proportions, obviously of more modern origins. A trabeated monument of stone, the plan hints at the frequent use of wooden construction along the Malabar and Coromandel coasts, and the effect that the monsoons had upon the regional design.

An impressive portico composed of two ranks of eight columns each, set within the extension of the cella wall, covered the whole eastern front of the *masjid*. Three doorways — at the second, fifth and eighth bay-file — and two windows between the doors allow both ingress and egress as well as light into this part of the *masjid*. The *haram* consists of nine bays with eight files of columns running east to west and eleven bays with ten ranks of columns north to south — a total of seventy-six columns. In the middle of this space, between the third and seventh ranks is an open area which now is covered by the above mentioned dome (see **Appendix C, Plate 87** [bottom]). In the centre of this area was a *haud*, now covered, which was open to the sky. The trabeated interior, a forest of columns with the single opening to the sky, not only held the devotees who came to pray, it also provided them protection from the monsoonal rains. As has been and will be seen, the open *sahn* typical of the more arid northern and western India is not a regular feature of the Malabar and Coromandel coasts and Bengal.[1] In addition to the doors of the portico, three doors are to be found on the north and three on the south sides of the *haram* and an equal amount of windows. These, along with the opening over the original *haud*, allowed for adequate light to pour into the interior. The *qiblā* with its prominent, rectilinear *mehrāb*, exhibits four windows which are evenly placed within that wall. To the south is a later addition which is now used for ritual ablution since the original *haud* has been covered.

The design of the Jami' al-Kabir is considered to be of the **RSc** type (see **Figure 4 — RSc**). This designation acknowledges its original open area over the now covered *haud*.

1 The monsoons sweep in from the south-south-west and flow up the west coast of India. A portion also flows up the east coast. Both drop copious amounts of rain and can cause considerable flooding, especially along the Ganges Delta.

Plate 11 — Jami' al-Kabir, plan

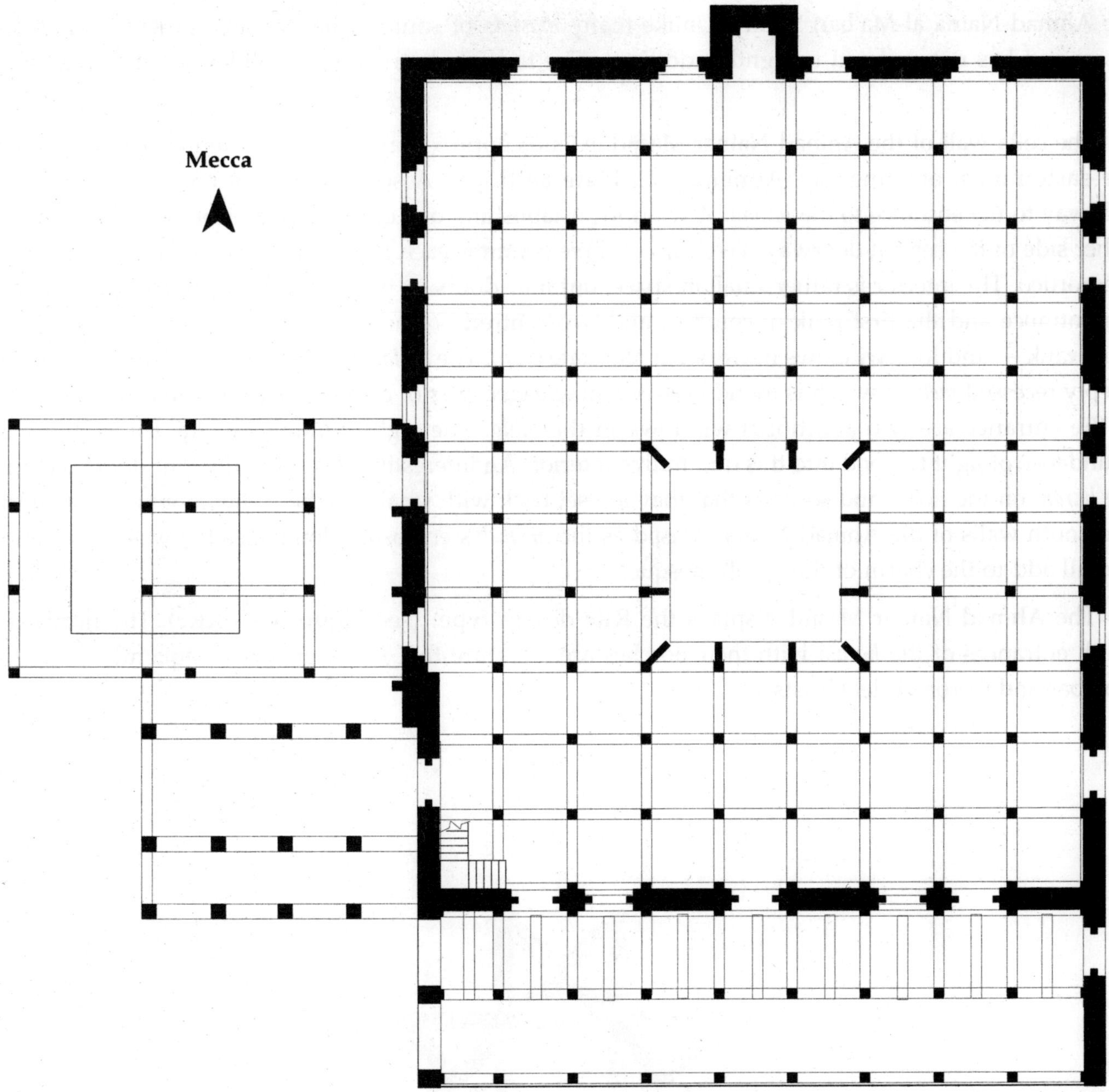

Ahmad Nainar Masjid, Kayalpatnam (*c*. CE 1350)

The Ahmad Nainar Masjid is considered by some residents of Kayalpatnam to be the oldest *masjid* of that city, possibly of the early fourteenth century. It is associated with the Qadi 'Ala al-din as well as the Ahmad Naina al-Ma'bari family. Unlike many *masjids* of south India, this monument is relatively intact and has not suffered unsightly additions. The trabeated structure is solid, even massive for its size.

The cella wall of the Ahmad Nainar Masjid extends approximately 4 m, bracketing two columns at the easternmost opening (see **Appendix C, Plate 88** [top]). A second rank of columns is set back half way to the entrance to the *haram*. A window, establishing one of the two interior aisles, is found on either side of the central doorway. Two files of three columns each mirror the spacing of the columns of the portico. The interior is rather small in space, but four doors — two centred on the first bay between the entrance and the first rank of columns and two centred on the third bay between the second and third rank — and four windows mirrored in alternate bays. The *qiblā* is dominated by a large, rectilinear, deeply recessed *mehrāb* which is found between an engaged pair of columns. Opposite the two windows of the entrance are two additional windows in the *qiblā*. The eight windows of the *haram* allow an abundance of light to flood into this diminutive interior. An interesting feature of the four doors entering the *haram* on the north and south is that they are set back with small porches. They dominate the north and south walls of the Ahmad Nainar Masjid as the *mehrāb*'s enclosure dominates the western exterior, and all add to the charm of this small mosque.

The Ahmad Nainar Masjid displays the **RRc** design type (see **Figure 4 — RRc**). The north and south entrances of the *haram* with their porches are a feature that is encountered frequently along the Malabar and Coromandel Coasts.

Plate 12 — Ahmad Nainar Masjid, plan

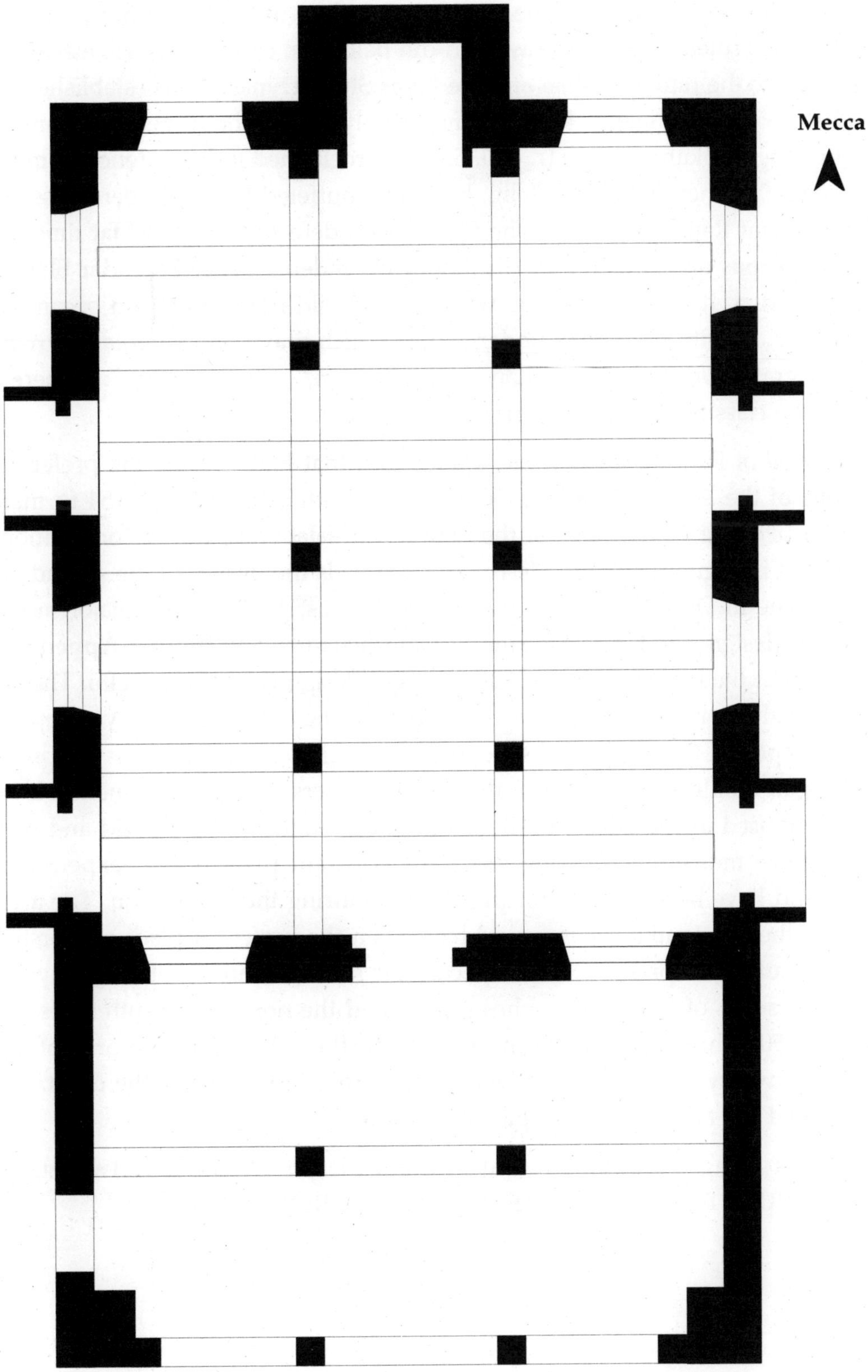

Adina Masjid, Pandua (CE 1364)

As the Delhi Sultanate expanded, it insinuated its imperial desires eastward. In CE 1266 the Bengal Sultanate was established as a satellite to the expanding and, at times, contentious empire. This was at the time when Delhi was ruled by Sultan Ghiyas-ud-din Balban (r. CE 1266–87). He elevated Nasir-ud-din Bughra (r. CE 1282–91) to the rank of Sultan and the Iliyas Shahi Dynasty was established (see **Appendix D**). From CE 1182 to 1352 the Beṅgālī rulers remained firmly within the Imperial Sultanate's fold. Then, the tenth Sultan of Bengal, Sikandar Shah (r. CE 1358–90), proclaimed independence from Imperial Delhi. The powerful Firuz Shah, then Sultan of Delhi, had been buffeted by a number of issues, the least of which were the truculent Rajasthan rulers. The Iliyas Shahi defection was, at that time, the least of his problems. In an audacious and pretentious display of his independence Sikandar Shah constructed a massive *masjid* at Pandua. It was initially known as the Masjid-i Jami but then became known as the Adina Masjid. Further, as with numerous undertakings which may seem singular in their concept, this *masjid* has been denigrated as: "little better than a gigantic barn."[1] Grover states ". . . there is little in this building that could be classified as great or original architecture."[2]

The massive *masjid* of Pandua forsook the square *sahn* that had become the preferred design. The exterior dimensions of the Adina Masjid are 507 × 285 ft, with a court 400 × 154 ft, making it at that time second only in size to the final stage of the Quwwat-ul-Islam Masjid. The orientation of the *masjid* is such that the length is aligned towards Mecca. This parallels the design of the second and third stage of the Imperial mosque in Delhi — the Quwwat-ul-Islam Masjid. One other major mosque is seen to display this unusual design, the Great Mosque of Damascus (CE 709–15) (see **Appendix B, Plate 55**), but it is more likely that the impetus for the Adina Masjid design came from Delhi. The arcuated *masjid* is three bays deep on the north, south and east aspects, and the *haram* is five bays deep. Two-hundred-sixty stone pillars supported three-hundred-seventy-eight brick domes. Brick was the preferred material utilized by the Beṅgālī builders, and, indeed, they were masters at its employment. However, the low fired bricks that were used in the domes needed constant attention in the humid and wet atmosphere, particularly during the monsoons, making upkeep a constant priority and expense. The *sahn* was impressive and would have been utilized for prayer only during the dry season. The arcuated, domed cloisters (*riwāq*) and the substantial *haram* would have been the preferred place of worship. The *mehrāb* is here given a particularly impressive, even spectacular setting. Three east-west bays are utilized to define a space, and a series of five ogive arches punctuated the north and south sides of this space. A soaring vault, some 50 ft high, springs from one side to the other. To the north of the *mehrāb* is a mezzanine involving twenty-one bays which was utilized for the women of the court. Entrance to this mezzanine was gained via a structure set against the *qiblā*.

The Adina Masjid along with the Quwwat-ul-Islam Masjid are the only two major mosques in India that utilize the **RRc2** type of design (see **Figure 4 — RRc2**).

1 SG, quoting Cunningham, p. 55.

2 Ibid.

Plate 13 — Adina Masjid, plan

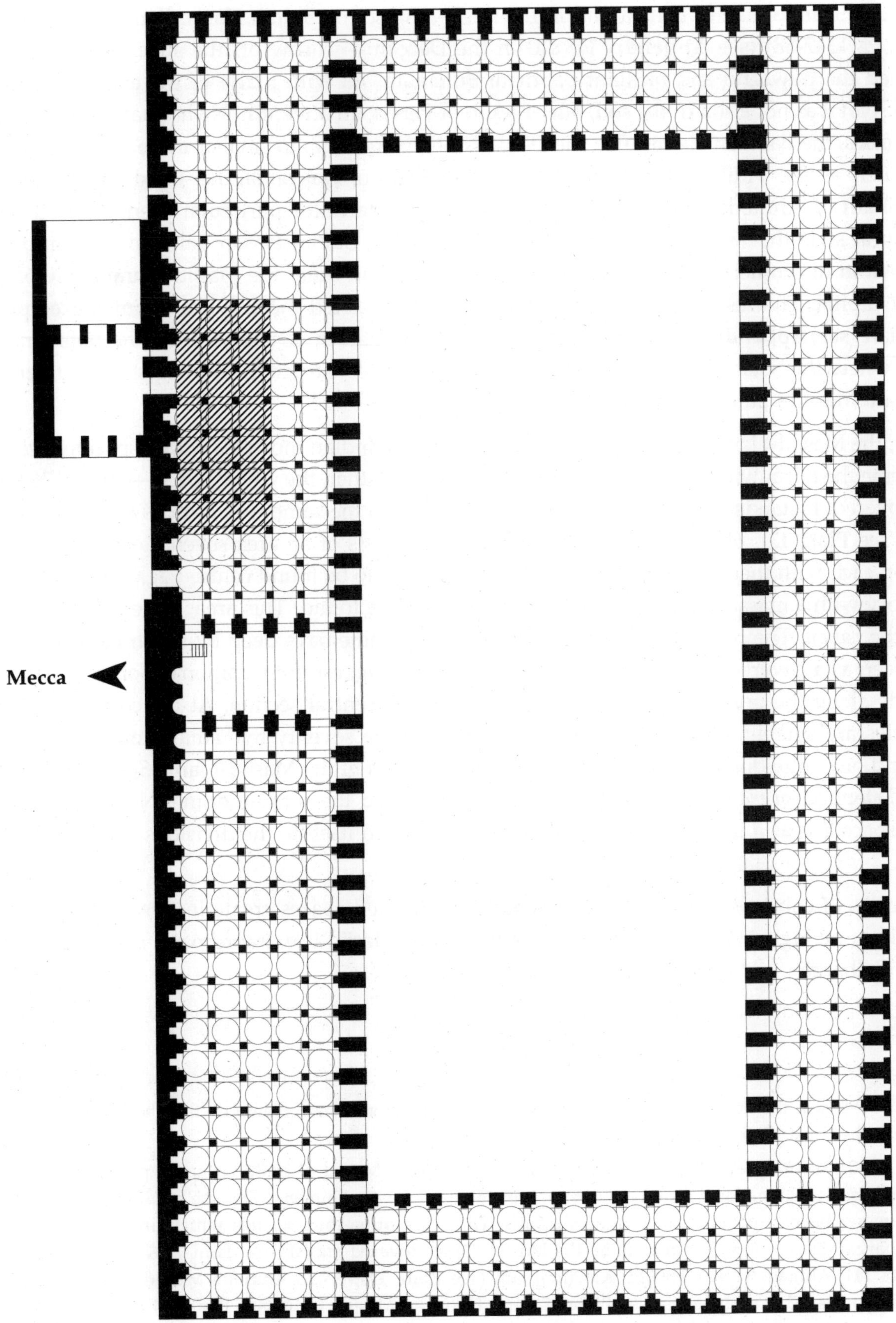

Masjid-i Jami, Gulbargā (*c.* CE 1367)

As Sikandar Shah, Sultan of Bengal, did in the north-east, so too Sultan Hasan Bahman Shah ('Ala-ud-din I) (r. CE 1347-58) (see **Appendix D**) did in the Deccan — throw off the suzerainty of Delhi and established the powerful and brilliant Bahmanī Sultanate. As with many of the early Islamic rulers, Bahman Shah was not a son of the soil, but of a son of Persia, an adventurer who made good. For nearly two centuries, the Bahman Shahi ruled the Deccan only to succumb to smaller more vibrant Persian and Turkic rulers — the 'Adil Shah of Bījāpur; the Qutab Shahi of Golconda; the 'Imad Shahi of Berar; the Nizam Shahi of Ahmednagar; and the Barid Shahi of Bidar. Not particularly enamoured with the architectural style that was prevalent within northern India, Sultan Hasan Bahman Shah imported an architect from his homeland, one Rafi of Qazvin to design and build the Masjid-i Jami at Gulbargā, the Bahmanī capital. The result was singular and spectacular, related more to the Spanish exemplar than the Persian (see **Appendix B, Plate 56**).[1] Sultan Ahmad Shah in CE 1422 shifted the Bahmanī capital to Bidar where the Solah Khambā Masjid (see **Plate 24**) was constructed, an interesting counterpoint to the brilliant Masjid-i Jami of Gulbargā.

Here, the Masjid-i Jami did not follow the contemporary Indian mosques with a spacious *sahn* which had become the norm within the Delhi sphere of influence. Rather, the whole space — 216 × 176 ft — was totally covered. It stands as an unparalleled monument much the same way as does the Adina Masjid in Pandua (see **Plate 13**). The inner portion of the *masjid* consists of an area seven bays wide and twelve bays deep each with their own small dome. The exception is to be found centred against the *qiblā.* There, a clerestory with a massive dome raised on nine bays is to be found. This area, three bays deep, may be seen as the *haram.* The remainder of this central section — nine bays deep by seven bays wide — may also be seen as a covered court area. Cross-spanned aisles suggest the traditional cloister. They are two bays wide along the north, south and east, and enfold the central section. At the corners and ends of these aisles are smaller subsidiary domes. *En toto,* there are seventy-five small domes, four medium domes and one large dome covering the vast 37,916 sq ft area of the Masjid-i Jami. Set within the *qiblā* is a *mehrāb,* stepped *en plan,* highlighted by the open space and the soaring dome. Nonetheless, the total covered space acts as a unified whole and does not easily lend itself to the divisions traditionally seen in a *masjid.*[2]

The mass of columns, the myriad domes and the arcuated spaces create in this unique *masjid* an **R** type design (see **Figure 4 — R**). As the plan of the Adina Masjid is extraordinary, so too is the Masjid-i Jami at Gulbargā.

---

1 CT, p. 198, sees the treatment of the arches as reflecting Persian influence. However, the plan is another matter and recalls the Great Mosque at Cordoba or the Masjid Qarawiyyin of Fez.

2 SG, p. 32, equates the Gulbargā Masjid-i Jami with the Khiṛkī Masjid of Delhi, as an "experiment" and sees that it violates "congregational aspect" and compartmentalizes the worshippers. The use of an area which is covered has never been antithetical to Indian Muslims. There are numerous *masjids* which are totally covered. The Gulbargā Masjid-i Jami happens to be the largest. Other covered *masjids* are: Jami 'al-Kabir, Kayalpatnam (see **Plate 11**); Ahmad Nainar Masjid, Kayalpatnam (see **Plate 12**); Solah Khambā Masjid, Bidar (see **Plate 24**); Qadiriya Masjid, Kayalpatnam (see **Plate 29**); and Gunmani Masjid, Gaur (see **Plate 31**) to name but a few.

Plate 14 — Masjid-i Jami, plan

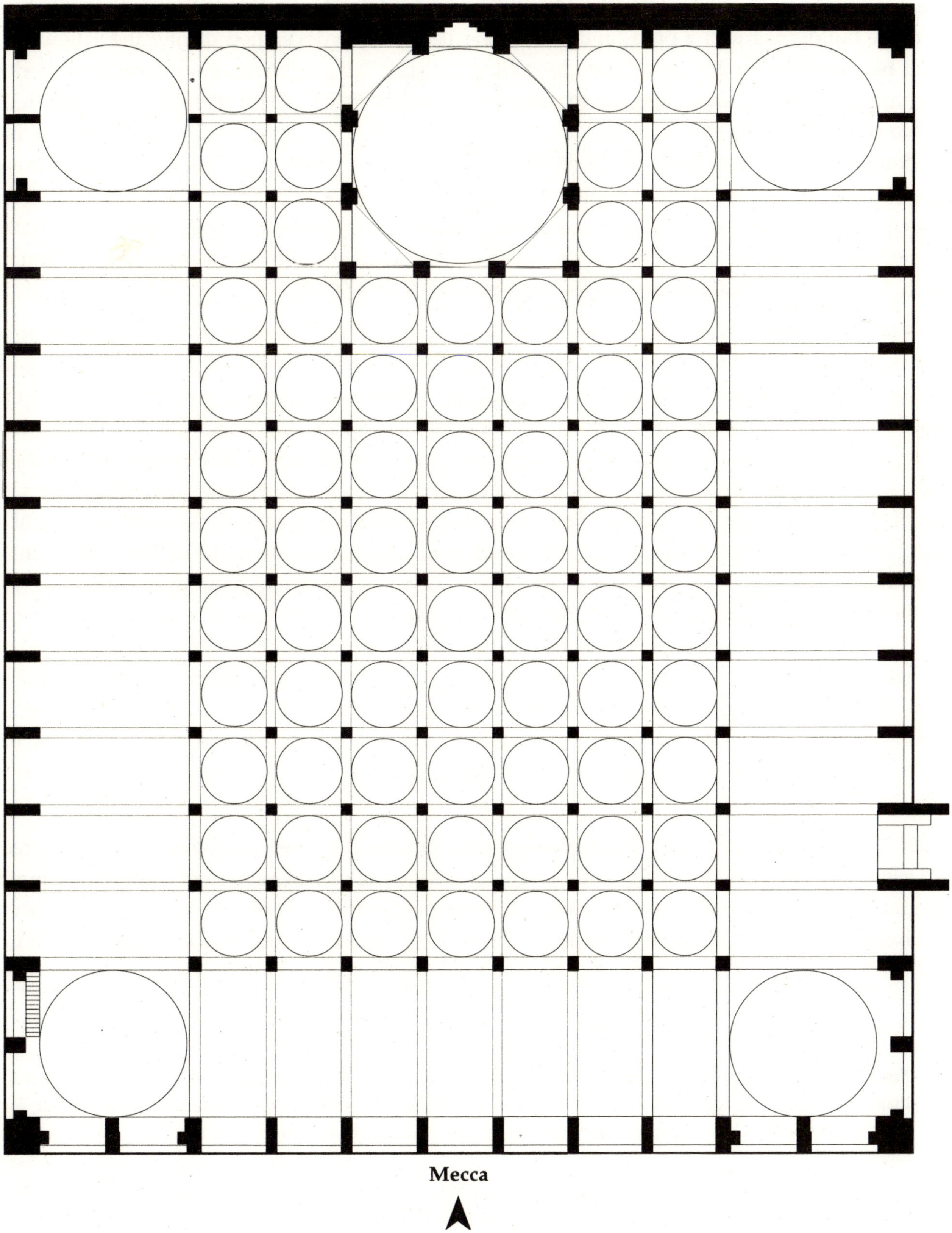

Masjid Begampuri, Delhi (*c.* CE 1370)

One of the numerous *masjid*s which were constructed under the reign of the Sultan Firuz Shah Tughluq (r. CE 1351–88) (see **Appendix D**) is the Masjid Begampuri (aka Begumpura).[1] Sultan Firuz Shah was an inveterate builder[2] as well a pious and merciless ruler. A style developed during the Tughluq's reign which has been referred to as a "pseudo-militaristic style." It might more aptly be identified as the "Tughluq Style." This "style" appears to possess six characteristics: (1) the *masjid*s are constructed upon a raised platform requiring grand stairs to gain entrance, (2) an imposing entrance, generally in the form of a domed cube, (3) a massive, tall central element as part of the *haram*-screen rather than the multi-arched screen, (4) a single arched opening into the *haram* proper, (5) engaged turrets or towers, generally battered at the corners, and (6) the cloisters surrounding the *sahn* are generally open to the outside or screened (*jālī*). In addition it indicates an interesting relationship with the Masjid Jami of Samarqand, which is roughly contemporaneous (see **Appendix B, Plate 57**).

En plan, the Masjid Begampuri resembles a prototypical Persian *masjid* — a form in which the central court is flanked, biaxially, with large, vaulted structures or *iwān*s (see **Figure 1 — C**). Broad stairs lead up to a substantial, cubic-block, entrance covered by a dome. Once inside, a *riwāq*, one bay deep with domes over each bay, fronts the north, south and east sides of the spacious *sahn*. The north and south cloister is dominated by a cubic, domed pavilion which allows ingress and egress to the *masjid*. The north, south and eastern exterior walls are punctuated by screened openings corresponding with the bays of the cloister. The *haram* is two bays deep and exhibits eight bays to the north and eight to the south. The outer fourteen bays on each side are domed similar to those of the cloister. Here, unlike the Quwwat-ul-Islam Masjid of Delhi (see **Plate 8**), the Masjid Aṛhāī-din-kā-Jhoṅpṛā at Ajmer (see **Plate 5**) and the Masjid-i Jami of Cambay (see **Plate 10**), the *haram* does not possess a screen that involves the whole of the western side of the *sahn*. Rather, a substantial central element with a single arched opening and battered towers at the corner dominate this aspect of the *masjid*. The monumental dome which covers the area behind the *maqsura* is masked by its height. The *qiblā* has five *mehrāb*. The central form is somewhat larger, *en plan*, than the other, flanking four. The five *mehrāb*s are signified on the exterior wall by rectilinear projections; however, there are no openings or *jālī*s in this wall as there are in the outer walls of the cloister.

The Masjid Begampuri (aka Begumpura) sets a standard for later *masjid*s that are associated with the Delhi Sultanate and later Mughal Empire — a mosque of considerable size commensurate with an imperial capital. There will be seen certain variations particularly with the *haram* screen or *maqsura*, but the Masjid Begampuri is a clear example of the **Sc1** type mosque design (see **Figure 3 — Sc1**).

---

1 Frequently *masjids* are named after the builder or major benefactor. In this case it is doubtlessly named after the major wife. *Begum* or *begam* is the first wife, or Sultana, or Queen — the Tomb of Jahan Begum at Bījāpur. *Pura, puri* or *pur* refers to city. Hence, Begumpurī would refer to the "Queen's city," an apt reference to a *masjid* endowed by a Queen or Sultana.

2 Among the many monuments constructed during his reign are: the Firuz Shah Kotla (*c.* CE 1354), the Khiṛkī Masjid (*c.* CE 1375); the Kalan Masjid (*c.* CE 1375), and additions to the Hauz Khas (*c.* CE 1375) including a *masjid*, *madrasa* and his tomb.

Plate 15 — Masjid Begampuri, plan

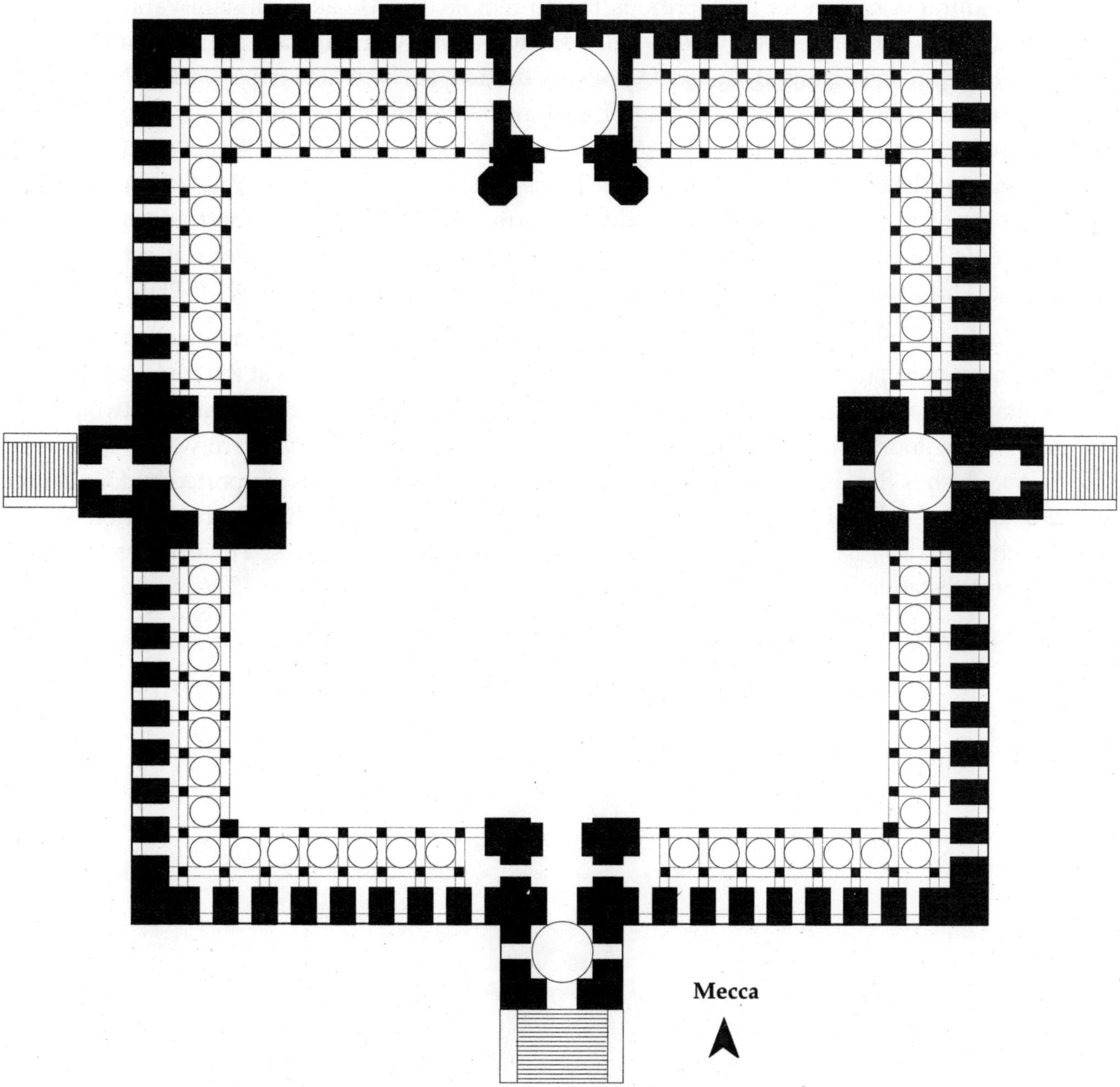

Masjid 'Ala al-din, Madurai (*c.* CE 1375)

While Muhammad Shah Tughluq Shah (II) (r. CE 1325–51) was Sultan of Delhi, the Sultan al-Sharif Jalal al-din Ahsan Shah (r. CE 1333–38) (see **Appendix D**) of Madurai rebelled and formed the Ma'bar Sultanate. Madurai is known for its enormous Hindu temple, the Minākṣī Sundareśvara Temple. The diminutive *Masjid 'Ala al-din* (r. CE 1338-39) also known as the Goripalayam Masjid stands near the Shrine of 'Ala al-din and Shams al-din (see **Appendix B, Plate 61**) by which it is dwarfed. Not only was Sultan 'Ala al-din Udauji, the second Sultan of Ma'bar, buried there, the shrine was also used as the final resting place for Sultan Shams al-din 'Adil Shah (r. CE 1356–72), the sixth sultan of the short-lived Ma'bar Sultanate. The shrine was constructed by Shams al-din and the *masjid* may have been constructed somewhat later. The *masjid* and the shrine do not form a *rauza* complex in the traditional sense — aligned towards Mecca with the *masjid* the closer of the two — since here the *masjid* is set to the north of the shrine. This arrangement is also encountered in Gujarat (see **Appendix B — Plate 66**).

Built upon a low platform, the *masjid* consists of a small, square *haram* and colonnaded, rectangular vestibule. The eastern porch is dominated by twin, octagonal, battered towers at the corners providing it with a militaristic appearance. The cella walls extend to the towers and enfold two ranks of two pillars. A small doorway is found in the southern wall of this space. Centred in the western wall is the entrance to the *haram* which is flanked by two windows. The square *haram*'s ceiling is supported by four columns forming a square. Centred in the north and south walls are two doors leading to the exterior. The *qiblā* holds a rectilinear, *en plan*, *mehrāb* which is flanked by two small windows. The exterior of the *qiblā* indicates the substantial *mehrāb*.

This small mosque falls within the **R1** design style (see **Figure 4 — R1**).

Plate 16 — Masjid 'Ala al-din, plan

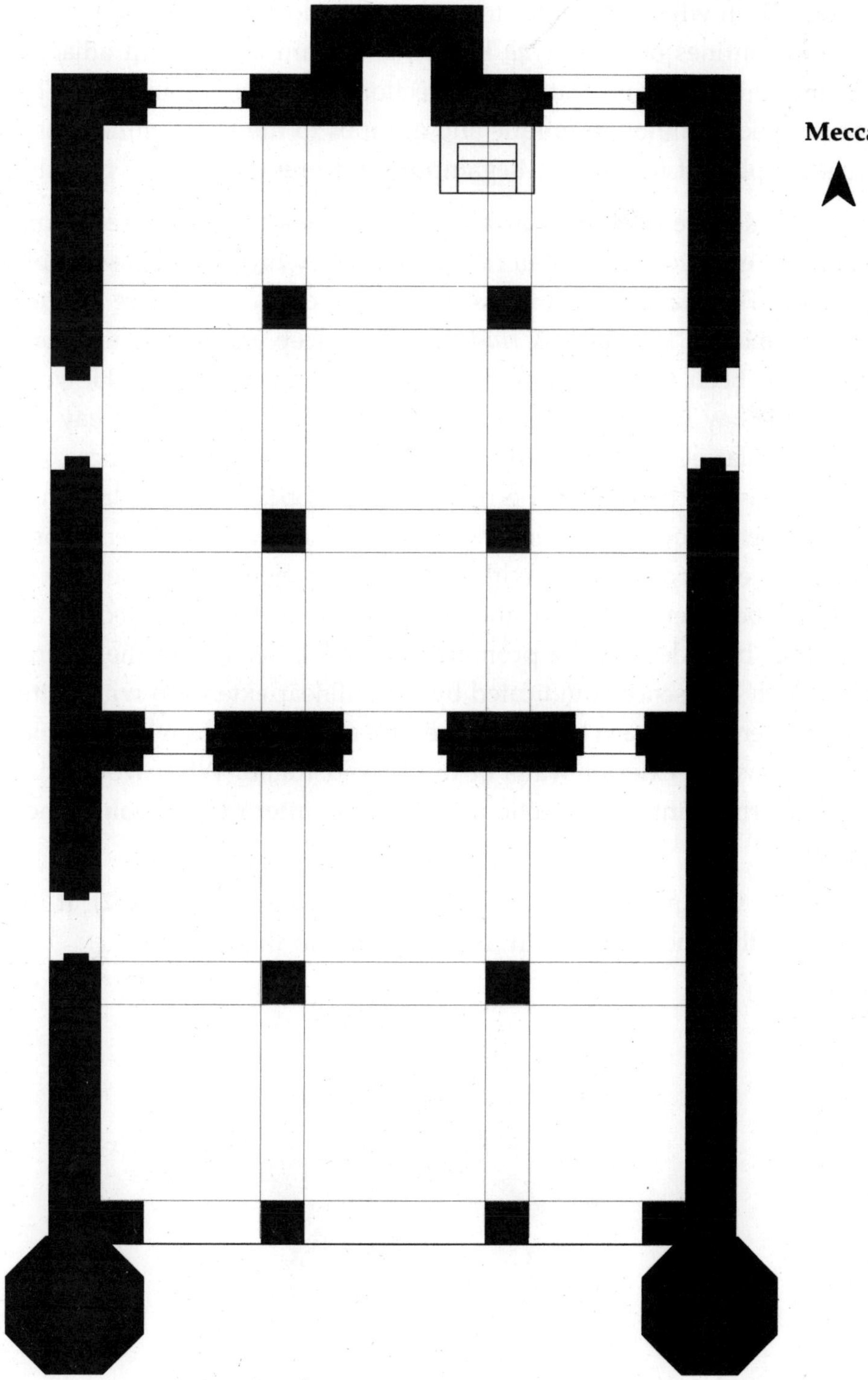

Masjid Kalan, Delhi (*c.* CE 1375)

One of the numerous *masjids* which were constructed under the reign of Firuz Shah Tughluq (r. CE 1351–88) (see **Appendix D**) in what some refer to as the "pseudo-militaristic style," is the Masjid Kalan. Set within the southern confines of the *dargāh* known as Nizam-ud-din and adjacent to the Tomb of Khan-i-Jahan Tilangani,[1] this *masjid* indicates the directions that the Sultan Firuz Shah was willing to take, but, one of the variations, although unique and apropos to the Delhi clime, was not repeated. The Masjid Kalan reflects the plan of the Masjid Begampuri and presages that of the Khiṛkī Masjid.

En plan, the *masjid* is square and hints at a cross-axial design with three prominent entrances, battered- towers guarding each corner, and all raised one storey high on a massive platform. However, here there is a difference. The Masjid Kalan is essentially based upon a square of one-hundred-twenty-one *pada* (or bays) — a Sthānīya Maṇḍala. A *riwāq*, one bay deep, surrounds the north, south and east sides of what would have been a traditional, rectangular, open court (*sahn*). However, here a domed and arcuated element, one bay wide, extends from the entrance — the central bay or the sixth *pada* — to the *haram*. Another, similar element runs from the north to the south entrances, centred on the fifth bay (*pada*) — from the eastern entrance. The resultant four open, rectangular court spaces are four bays by three bays or twelve square *pada* in area. The northern and southern portals of the Masjid Kalan mimic the massive eastern entrance with its extremely battered corner towers. Unlike earlier examples, the transition between the court and the *haram* is not punctuated by an obvious *haram*-screen. The *haram* is three bays deep and a prominent *mehrāb* is set within the central bay of the *qiblā*. On the exterior, the *mehrāb*'s presence is indicated by a rectilinear extension with battered towers at the corners of the extension. Centred in each bay along the *qiblā* are indentions which mimic the *jālī* windows of the north, south and eastern exterior walls of the Masjid Kalan. What would have been a simple cross-axial plan is transformed into an eclectic plan of some interest and points the way to the truly unique Khiṛkī Masjid.

The Masjid Kalan falls within the **SRc2** design style (see **Figure 3 — SRc2**). It hints at an implied cross-axial design, except that the north-south axis is shifted to the east.

1 This most important tomb is often viewed as the first octagonal, domed tomb in India. FWB 3, p. 52.

Plate 17 — Masjid Kalan, plan

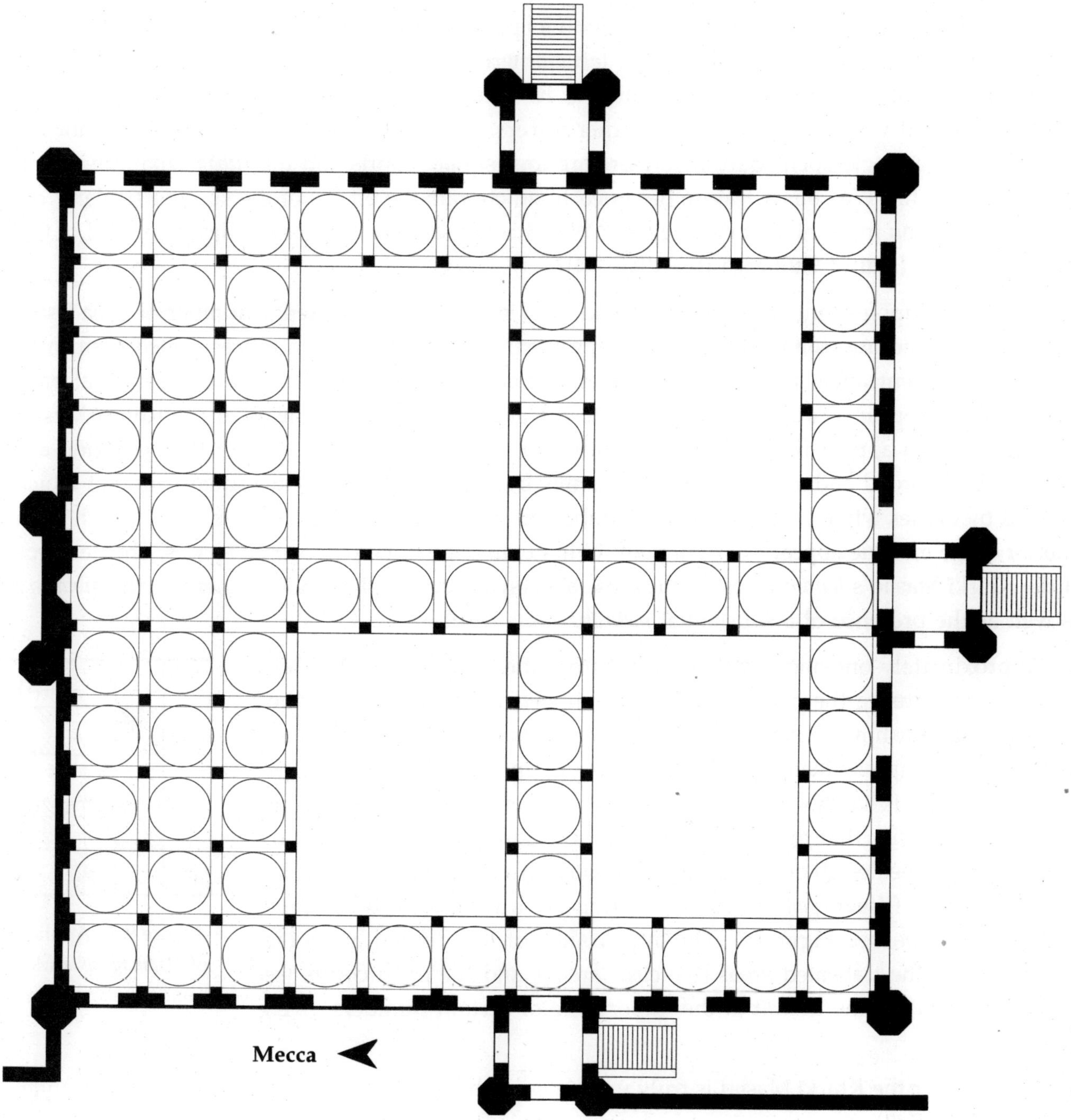

Khiṛkī Masjid, Delhi (*c.* CE 1375)

From its exterior, the Khiṛkī Masjid of Delhi exemplifies the "pseudo-militaristic style" of the Tughluqs. Indeed, it appears more citadel than mosque with its parapets, towers and massive character. Firuz Shah Tughluq (r. CE 1351–88) (see **Appendix D**) left numerous mosques in and around Delhi. The Khiṛkī Masjid follows the "Tughluq Style" inasmuch as it is cross-axial, *en plan*, built upon a raised platform, employs battered walls and bastion-like corner towers. However, it deviates in one significant feature — rather than a single open court, here there are four square courts and the *riwāq* separating them are of the same width. Was this a feature designed to ameliorate the effects of the sun, particularly during the hot-dry season in Delhi as some suggest?[1] Was this the same reason for the design of Rafi of Qazvin for the Masjid-i Jami of Gulbargā (see **Plate 14**)?

Being built upon a full storey high ground-level platform necessitated a number of broad steps to gain access to the imposing, almost forbidding north, south and east entrances which seem more as barbicans than entrances to a place of prayer.[2] At each of the four corners are substantial battered towers which appear as defensive additions to the *masjid*. The entrance areas of the Khiṛkī Masjid are lit by *jālī*s which appear more in keeping with a prison than a mosque. Rather than entering a *riwāq* surrounding a broad and spacious *sahn*, one is met by broad areas, nine bays square, nine of which are covered by domes while twelve are simply trabeated. There are four square open areas which from the interior of the mosque appear as bright pools of light amidst the darker covered spaces. The demarcation of the Khiṛkī Masjid's *haram* is lost in the cross-axial symmetry of the whole. However, the *qiblā* is clear as well as the presence of a substantial *mehrāb*.

Approximately one-and-a-half centuries from the founding of the Delhi Sultanate and during the period when other important Sultanates have their genesis — the Kashmiri Sultanate and the Bahmanī Sultanate — Islamic India had begun to impress their own distinctive style upon its monuments. Yet, the Hindu *sthapati*s had not been without their considerable influence. It would appear a possibility that their influence may be evident in the design of the Khiṛkī Masjid. The design may be seen to be related to a Padmagarbha Maṇḍala — a *maṇḍala* of fifteen *pada* in each direction for a total of two-hundred-twenty-five *pada* (see **Figure 9**). The appearance of the domed areas (see grayed areas), the trabeated areas (see clear areas), and the open courts (see darkened areas) seems to hint at the importance of certain numbers — e.g. nine and twelve.[3]

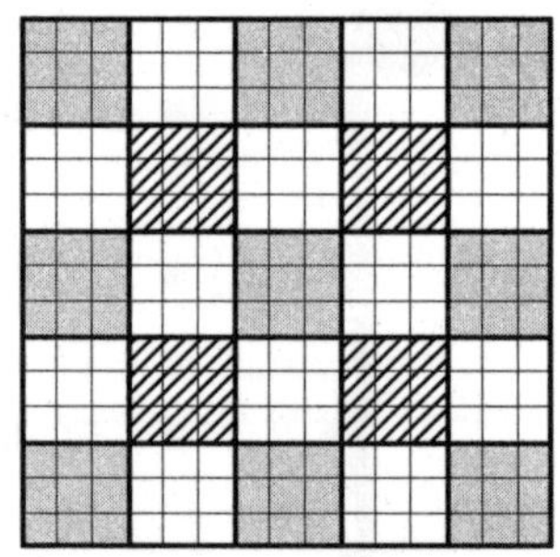

Figure 9 — Application of *Padmagarbha Mandala* upon the arrangement

The plan for the Khiṛkī Masjid is truly unique even though it is based upon an **Sc2** design style (see **Figure 3 — Sc2**).

1 SG, p. 32, states: ". . . Obviously the scorching sun of the long summers of India was the chief motivating force behind this new design." On the other hand, MF, p. 164, more precisely characterizes this *masjid* and the others of the Tughluq dynasty as exemplifying a century "marked by great creativity, eclecticism and experimentation in architecture."

2 This mock fortification feature of this *masjid* and many of the others of the Tughluq style are not unique to mosques nor is this meant to be a criticism. Albi Cathedral of southern France appears to be more citadel than cathedral.

3 Nine, referring to the number of *pada* in each of the squares, the number of domed areas and the number of squares which make up the area bounded by the open courts, is a number that is particularly sacred to the Hindus and Muslims alike. Twelve, referring to the number of trabeated areas, is also of universal importance.

Plate 18 — Khiṛkī Masjid, plan

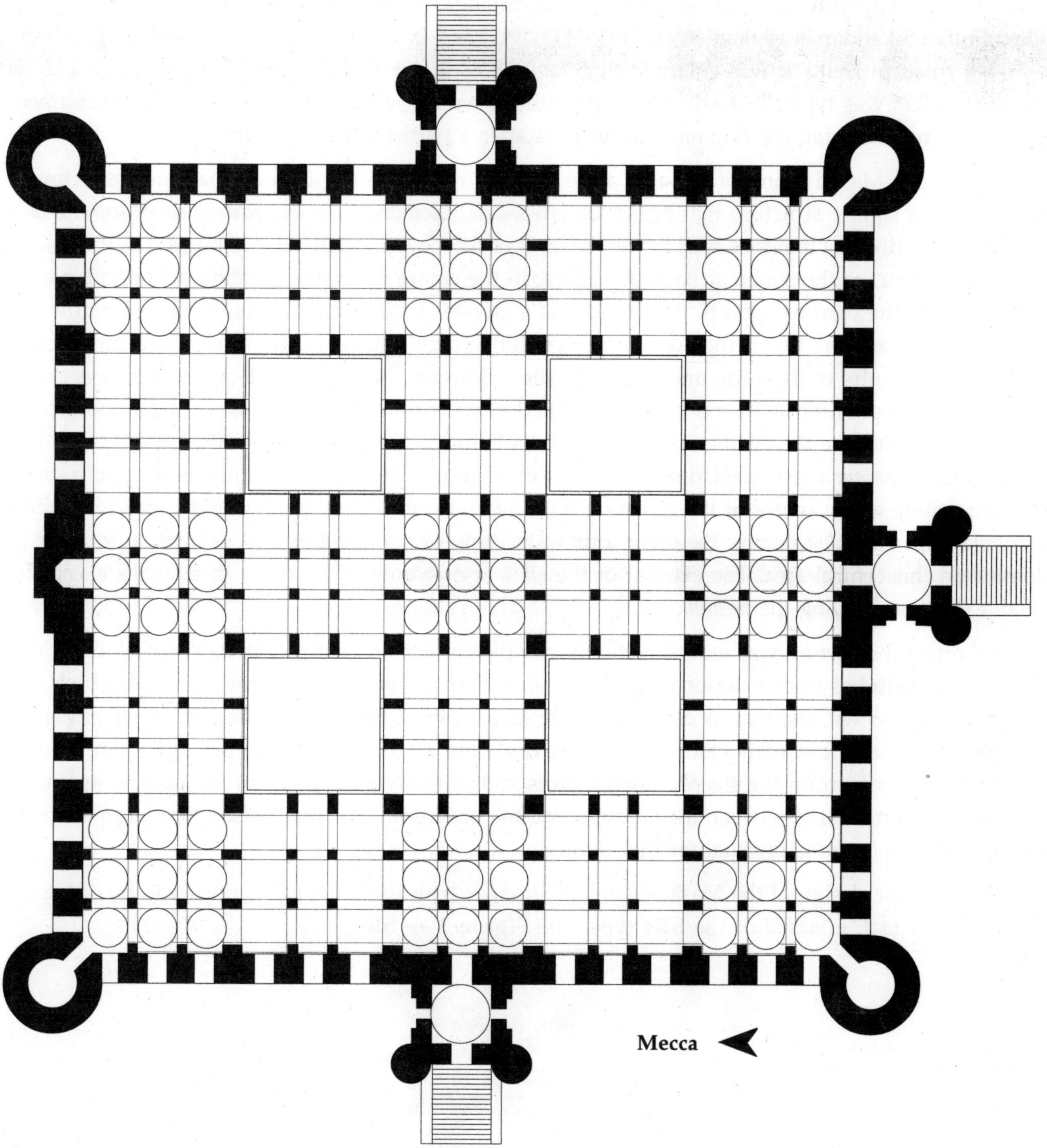

Masjid-i Jami, Srinagar (*c.* CE 1398 & 1674)

Kashmir had become an autonomous sultanate under Sultan Shah Mirza, Shams-ud-Din I (r. CE 1346–49) (see **Appendix D**). The Masjid-i Jami of Srinagar was initially constructed during the time when Sultan Sikandar Butshikan (r. CE 1393–1413) reigned in Kashmir and Firuz Shah Tughluq (r. CE 1351–88) ruled in Delhi. It was enlarged by Sikandar's son, the Sultan Zainal-'Abidin (r. CE 1420–70). Its construction was typically Kashmiri, being built of wood. Several times the mosque succumbed to fire. It was rebuilt using the original plan in 1674 after a particularly devastating fire.

En plan, the Masjid-i Jami of Srinagar appears to be related to the Tughluq, Jaunpur, and Imperial Styles. It is a square structure that possesses cross-axial elements. A near square *sahn* dominates the interior and is divided into four sections reminiscent of the Chahar-bagh, later to be seen in the Shalimar Bagh of Srinagar, or the Shalimar Bagh at Lahore. In the centre is a small pavilion set upon a platform with stairs at the cardinal points. To the east is a cloister (*riwāq*) three bays or aisles deep with an impressive, pyramidal, tiered roofed entrance pavilion (*ziarat*) at the centre. Two more similar *ziarat*s punctuate the centre of the north and south cloisters. However, here the cloisters are four bays or aisles deep. A fourth pavilion with monumental arched entrance dominates the west and announces the *haram*. The *haram*, like the north and south cloisters is four bays deep. The roofs of the three cloisters (*riwāq*) and the *haram* are stepped, double roofed forms. Four towering wooden pillars support a coffered wooden ceiling at the centre of the *haram's ziarat* and a sixteen-sided opening gives way to a wooden domelike-cap. The *qiblā* mimics the other four walls; however, a small *mehrāb*, set within a larger arch dominated this central area. The exterior of the *qiblā* also resembles the other three walls except for a small extension holding the *mehrāb*.

The original structure was almost certainly completely constructed of wood. The reworking of the 1674 *masjid* included brick exterior walls, but maintained the wooden interior and roof. Much of the structure, and, to wit, the plan is dictated by the geographical location. Srinagar is on such a latitude and elevation that the winters can become quite cool, and snow is not altogether unknown. This may be, in part, the reason for the steeply sloping roofs and certainly the reason for the narrow openings to the exterior, particularly between the cloisters and the open *sahn*. For that reason, the large opening in the *ziarat* of the *haram* is unusual for this clime.

Although the design of the Masjid-i Jami of Srinagar with its *chahar-bagh* appears to be of the **SRc2** type, it is, in fact, a *masjid* of the **SRc** type (see **Figure 3 — SRc**).

Plate 19 — Masjid-i Jami, plan

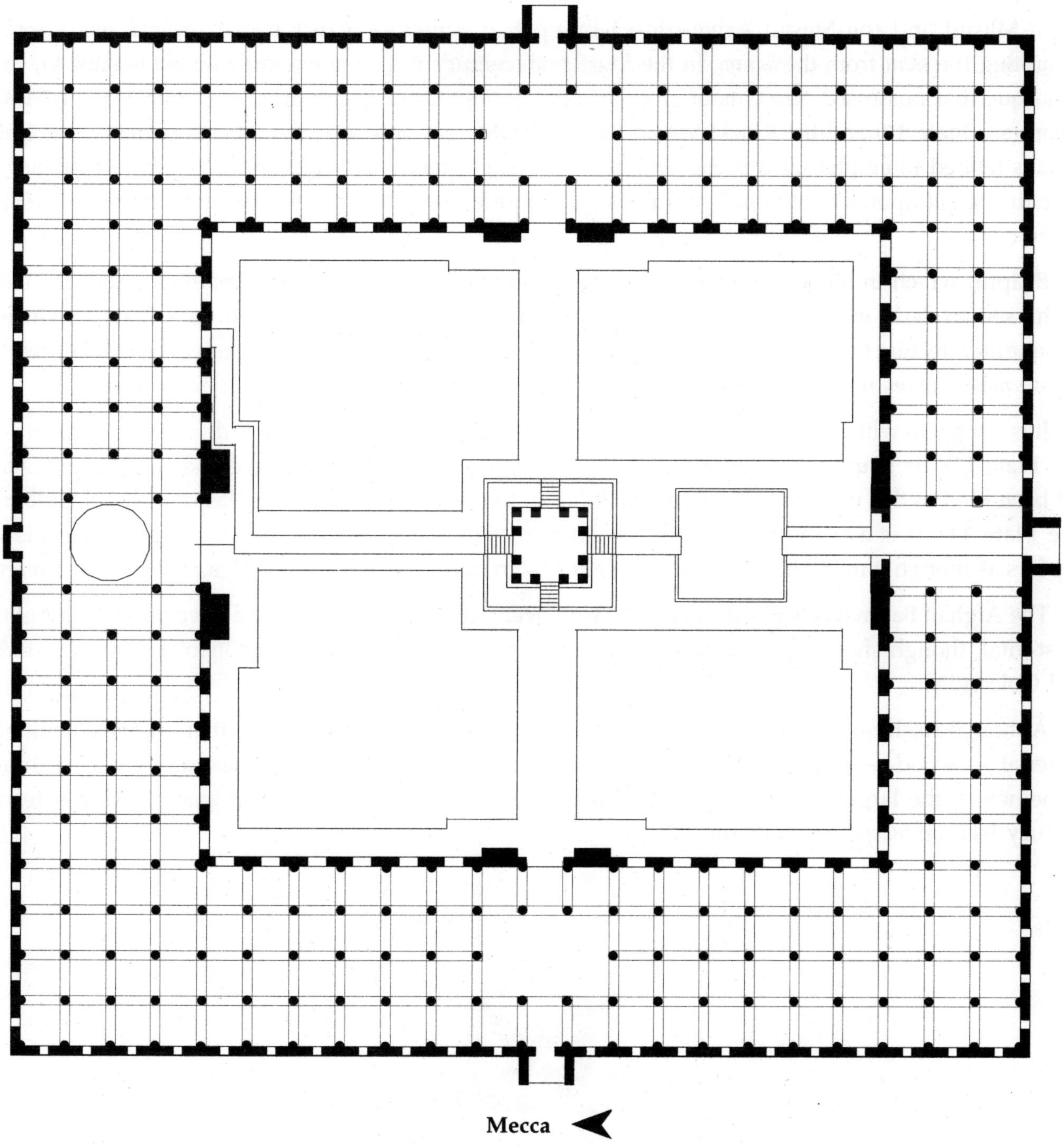

Fourteenth Century

The Imperial Delhi Sultanate had set certain standards in the design of the *masjid* with the Quwwat-ul-Islam Masjid and the Masjid Aṛhāī-din-kā-Jhoṅpṛā at Ajmer — a rectangular *masjid* and a screen separating the *sahn* from the *haram*. In the fourteenth century these parameters seemed to shift towards a mosque that possessed elements of cross-axiality — the Masjid Begampuri (see **Plate 15**), the Masjid Kalan (see **Plate 17**) and the Khiṛkī Masjid (see **Plate 18**). Not only a degree of cross-axiality, the Delhi Sultans tended to emphasize a pseudo-militaristic design quality. In addition, there was 'a tendency to raise the *masjid* upon a substantial podium which required an often impressive set of steps to enter the interior.

Bījāpur, which in the sixteenth and seventeenth centuries would achieve greatness under the 'Adil Shahi, see an early *masjid* form, interesting but undeveloped, mimicking Delhi (see **Plate 9**). Gujarat mosque architecture first makes a dramatic appearance at Cambay (see **Plate 10**). However, this impressive square *masjid* owes much to Delhi. The next century sees the fluorescence of Gujarātī design.

It is Bengal to which one must go to find a truly impressive *masjid*, and at Pandua is the Adina Masjid (see **Plate 13**). Its plan is unusual and the scale is massive. Unfortunately, time and the elements have not been kind to this impressive monument. South in the Deccan flowered the Masjid-i Jami at Gulbargā (see **Plate 14**). It is a paean to the dome. A large rectangular mosque which is completely enclosed appears as though it might have been a more apt design for the north or rainy regions. But here it reigns.

The Afghan Bahmanīs held this region for well over a century-and-a-half and gave birth to four of the most vital, though short-lived, Sultanates of central India — the Sultanates of Bījāpur, Gulbargā, Bidar and Golcoṇḍā.

Although Kashmir possessed a long line of sultans, their locale and especially their preferred building material — wood — did not allow for the development that is found in central and southern India. Nonetheless, the large Masjid-i Jami of Srinagar (see **Plate 19**) is an important example of fourteenth century Islamic *masjid* architecture.

The Mosques of the 15th Century

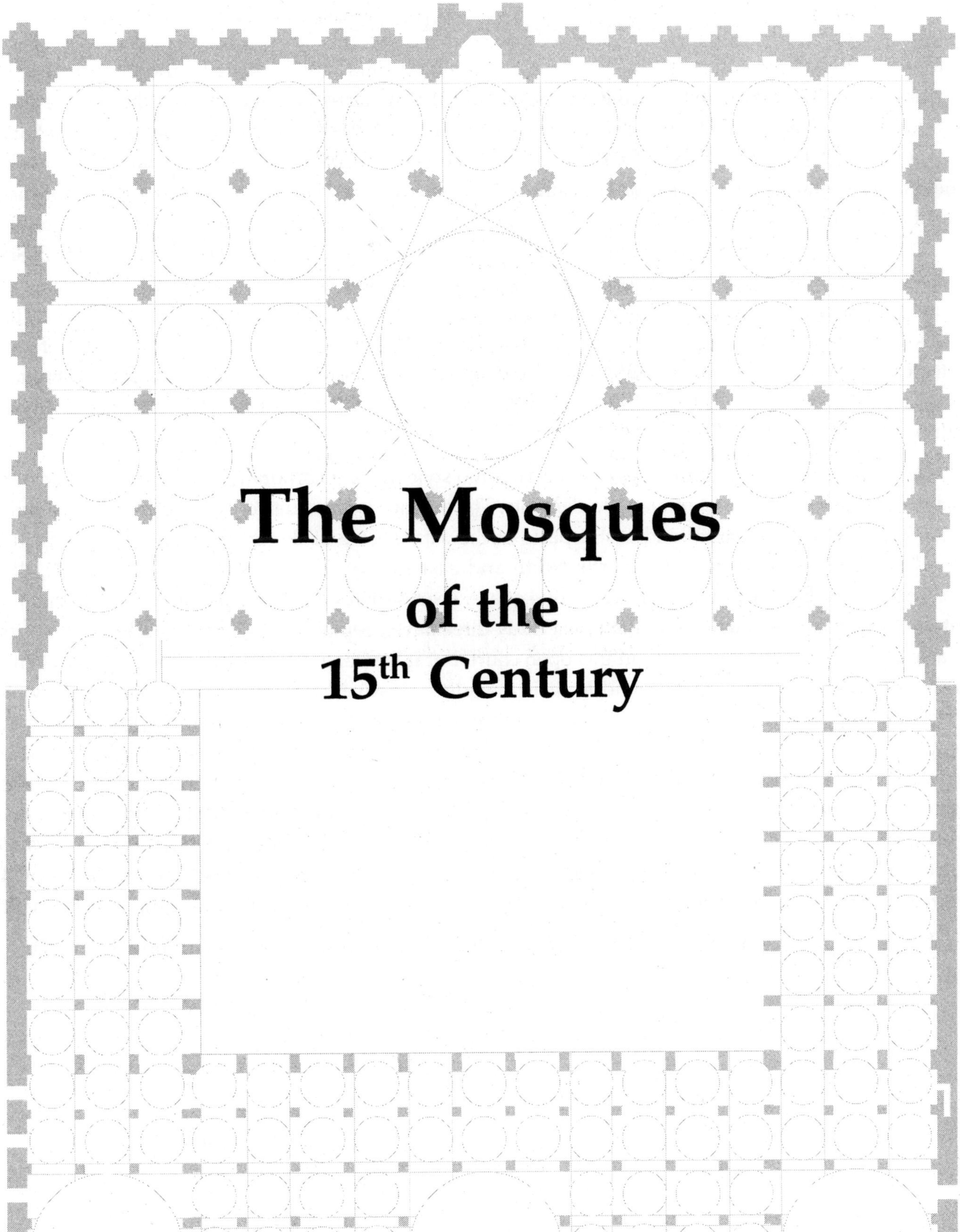

Atala Masjid, Jaunpur (*c.* CE 1408)

Jaunpur, it is said, was founded by Firuz Shah Tughluq around 1360. This city and environs were a territory of the Delhi Sultanate during the period of the important Tughluqs and at the decline of the Sayyid Dynasty. Jaunpur achieved its autonomy in 1394 under the Viceroy turned Sultan, Malik Sarvar Sharqi (r. CE 1394–99) (see **Appendix D**). In a sense, he was unique as he was an Indian born Muslim. The Sharqis of Jaunpur were vibrant and cultured rulers who expanded their capital to the point that it was the envy of many. The dramatic Atala Masjid was raised by the Sultan Shams-ud-Din Ibrahim Shah (r. CE 1402–40) soon after his ascension. It is said to have been built upon foundations laid by Firuz Shah and over a Hindu temple dedicated to Atala Devī. Not only did Sultan Ibrahim Shah create this and many other architectural monuments in his capital city, he also elevated that city's cultural level 'til it was known as the "Shiraz of India"[1] and the "refuge of sages and literati."[2] In 1476 the Lodis of Delhi defeated the overly ambitious Sultan Hussain Shah and commanded that all secular structures of note be razed to the ground. The exceptions were the sacred *masjid*. Hence, the brilliance that had once been Jaunpur was diminished.

The Atala Masjid owes certain debts to the Tughluq style in the incorporation of a multi-bayed cloister and the utilization of pseudo-militaristic elements. The exterior is punctuated by three, massive, identical entrances on the north, south and east aspects of the *masjid*. One of the truly unique features is to be found in the open bays along the north, south and east side of the exterior (see **Appendix C, Plate 88**). These open bays lead to small, generally square, spaces or rooms. After passing through the main entrance one is immediately confronted by a *riwāq* three bays deep along the north, south and east sides of a spacious *sahn*. A *haud* is found in this open court, but it is strangely off centre. The singular element of the *masjid* of Jaunpur is to be found in their towering, massive *haram* entrance (*haram*-screen) which are characterized by some as "pylons."[3] Indeed, these monumental gates do recall the pylons of Egyptian temples. Fronting the *haram* are three. The colossal, central propylon dwarfs the two flanking it. These *haram*-screen elements are rectilinear, *en plan*, with corner towers that are battered giving rise to the pseudo-militaristic characterization. The *haram*, which these three elements front, is three bays deep with domes obscured by the three towering elements. The unusually thick *qiblā* exhibits three *mehrābs*, corresponding with the pylons. The exterior of the *qiblā* indicates the presence and location of the *mehrāb* by rectilinear projections and circular towers. Towers also punctuate the corners of the *qiblā*.

This extraordinary, monumental *masjid* falls within the **Sc1** design type (see **Figure 3 — Sc1**).

1 Shiraz was known as the poetic capital of Persia (Iran).

2 SG, p. 44.

3 Ibid., p. 41.

Plate 20 — Atala Masjid, plan

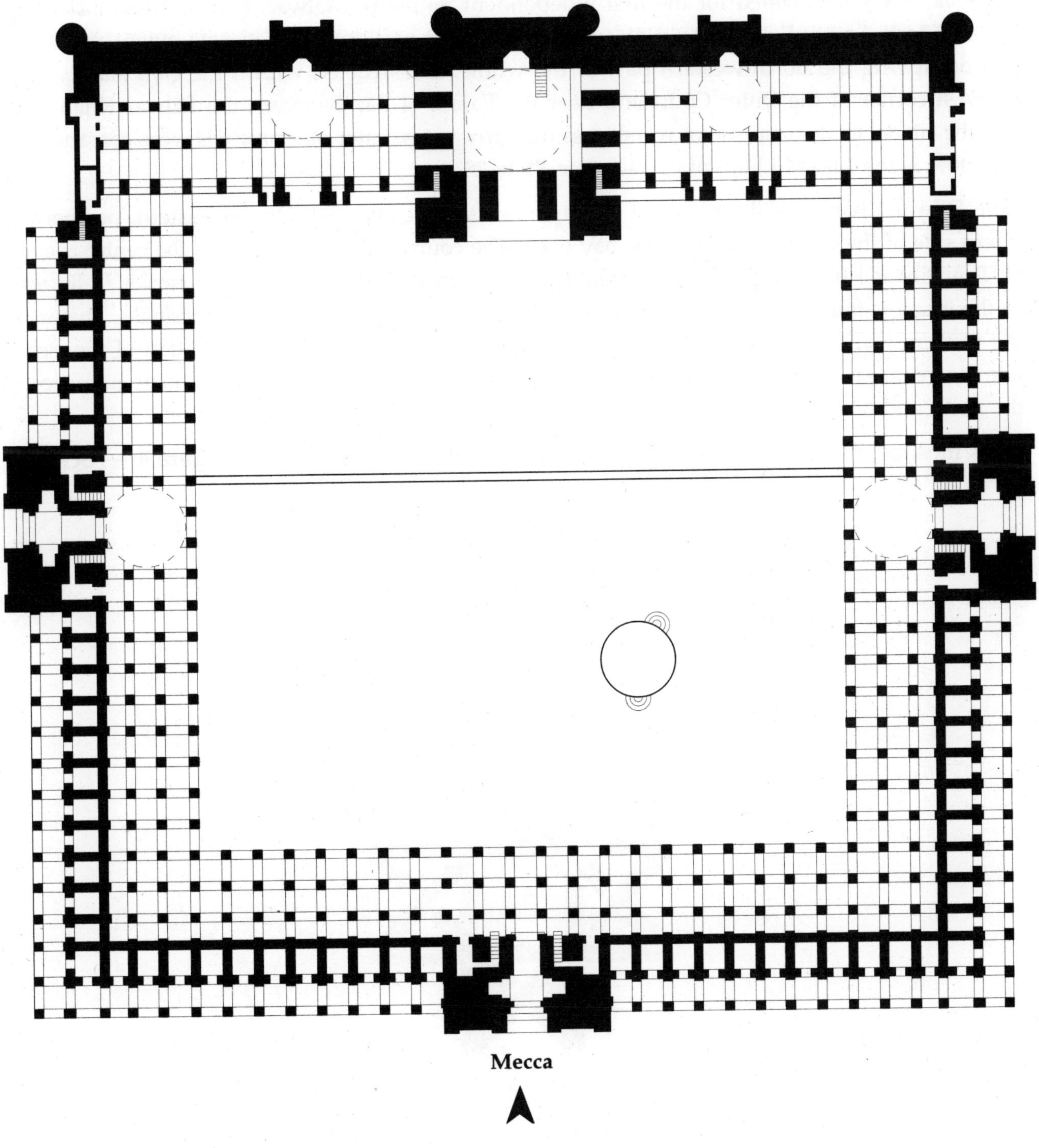

Dilwar Khan Masjid, Māṇḍu (*c.* CE 1410)

The Dilwar Khan Masjid was one of the earlier constructions of the Shadiabad of Māṇḍu (see **Appendix B, Plate 62 — D**) and named for the first independent Sultan of Malwar, Dilwar Khan Ghuri (r. CE 1392–1405) (see **Appendix D**). The plateau upon which it was constructed was extensive, the *gaṛh mahala* occupying the north-western part of the whole. Constructed within the *gaṛh mahala*, in the south-west corner of the Outer Court and near the Palace of Bāẓ Bahādur, the Dilwar Khan Masjid served the citadel as its main site of worship in the early years. Later other *masjid*s were constructed; of special note is the Masjid-i Jami of CE 1440 (see **Plate 28**).

The Dilwar Khan Masjid consists of a simple entrance to the east. On the eastern, northern and southern side of the *sahn* is a *riwāq* of one bay deep. The courtyard is ample and in the centre is a small *haud*. The Dilwar Khan Masjid does not exhibit a screen in the same mode as the earlier Delhi *masjid*. Here the *haram* is four bays deep, eleven wide and the *qiblā* supports but a single *mehrāb*s. The exterior of the western wall indicates a rectangular projection commensurate with the position of the *mehrāb*s. Beside the main, eastern entrance which leads to the large open court, there are two other entrances; one to the north and one to the south leading to the royal complex.

This mosque, the Dilwar Khan Masjid exhibits the **RSc** type design (see **Figure 4 — ScRSc 1**).

Plate 21 — Dilwar Khan Masjid, plan

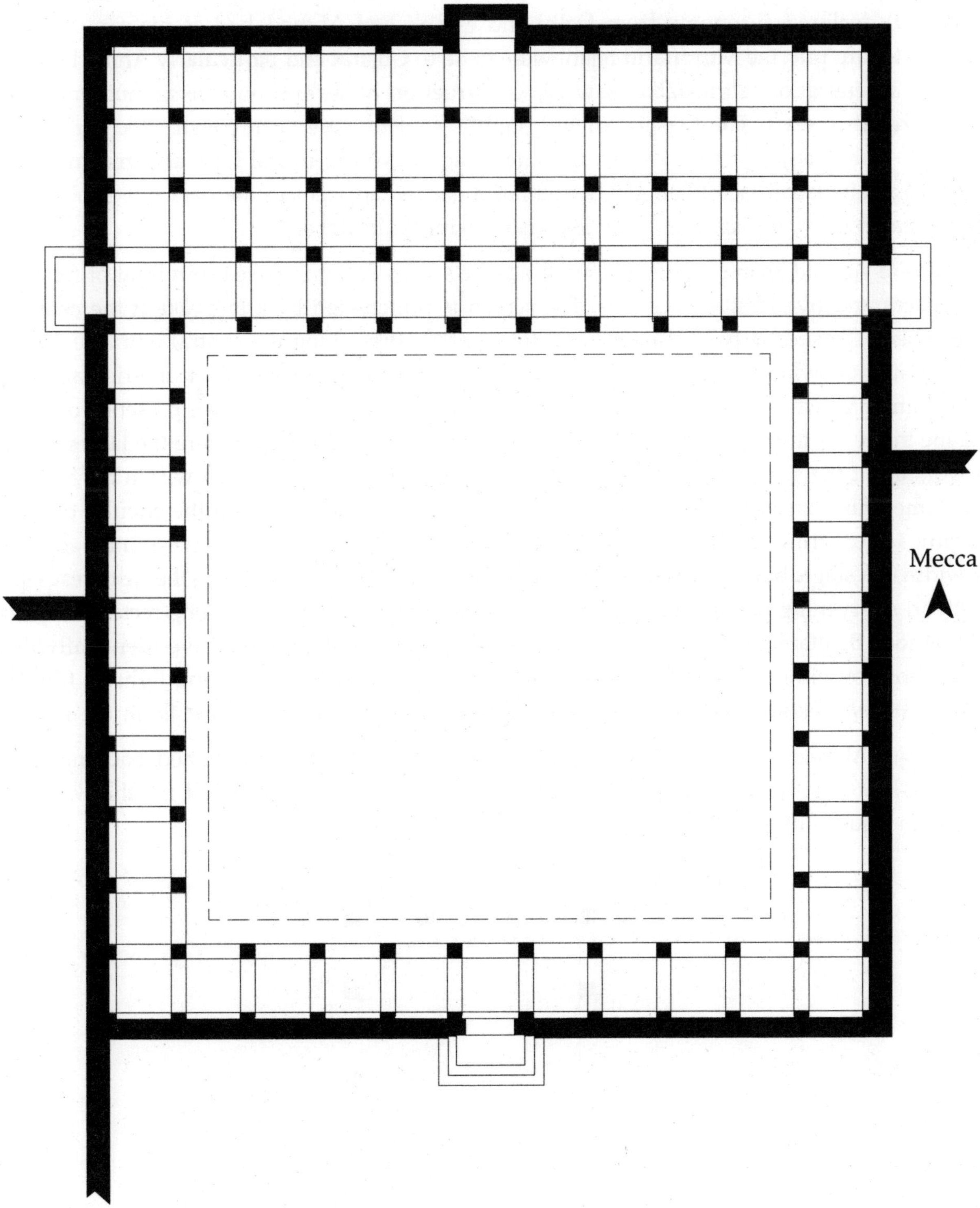

Masjid Ahmad Shah, Ahmedabad (*c.* CE 1411)

The first independent Sultan of Gujarat, Shams-ud-Din Muzaffar Ahmad Shah I (r. CE 1411–42) (see **Appendix D**) declared autonomy from Delhi and established Ahmedabad as his capital.[1] What the Sharqi were to Jaunpur, the Muzaffarid Shahi were to be to Gujarat and particularly Ahmedabad. Within the span of a generation Ahmedabad saw the construction of several notable monuments — *masjid*, *rauza*s and royal retreats. The Masjid Ahmad Shah is said to have been constructed for the Sultan's private use — the *masjid palatine* — like the later Nagina Masjid of Lal Qila at Agra and the Mothi Masjid of Shahjahanabad (see **Plate 47**). Set within a garden adjacent to the palace it establishes many of the hallmarks of style that were to be associated with Ahmedabad.

The Masjid Ahmad Shah consists of a Tughluq-like screen defining the eastern limit of the *haram*, ten domed spaces and five identical *mehrāb*s. The screen is punctuated by a *propylon* at the centre, which may have been flanked by two minarets[2] and four portals bracketing the central entrance. Eight small windows with *jālī* whose purpose was to allow light into the otherwise dark interior are also seen. Another feature which becomes *de rigueur* for the *masjid* of Ahmedabad is the presence of a screened mezzanine in the north-west corner with its own entrance from the exterior. Here the ladies of the court could worship at the same time as the men in complete seclusion — a *purdah* within the *masjid*. There are ten dome units consisting of twelve columns, an octagonal transition and the circular dome proper (see **Figure 10**) covering the *haram* of the Masjid Ahmad Shah. East to west, these units are separated by the width of a single bay. However, from north to south the separation is twice the east-west separation and with an intervening file of columns. This, of course, gives the *haram* its strong rectangular character (see **Appendix B, Plate 63**). The *qiblā* of the Masjid Ahmad Shah contains five identically designed *mehrāb*s. Those on either side of the central niche are flanked by *jālī*, allowing light to filter in. The exterior of the *qiblā* exhibits, via rectilinear projections, the presence of the *mehrāb* on the inside.

The Masjid Ahmad Shah, then, becomes a pattern for later mosques in Ahmedabad and Gujarat — a multi-bay *haram* with domes spaced across the width and a space reserved for the women of the court. The mosque is of the **R2** design style (see **Figure 4 — R2**).

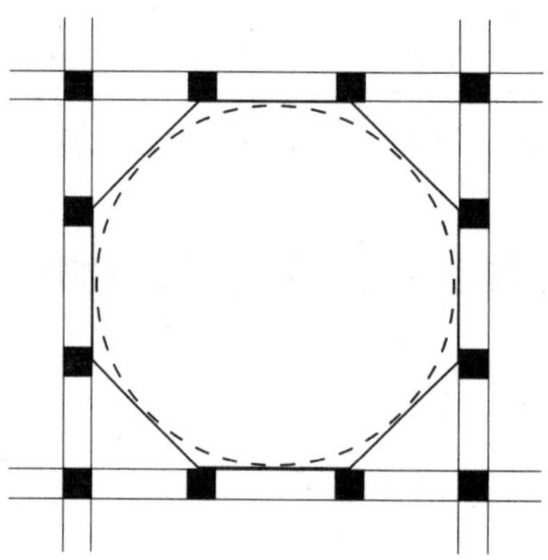

Figure 10 — Twelve columns with octagon and dome element

1 Ahmedabad was founded upon an older community area called Karṇavatī.

2 All that remains is the base to the roof line and stairways just inside the main portico.

Plate 22 — Masjid Ahmad Shah, plan

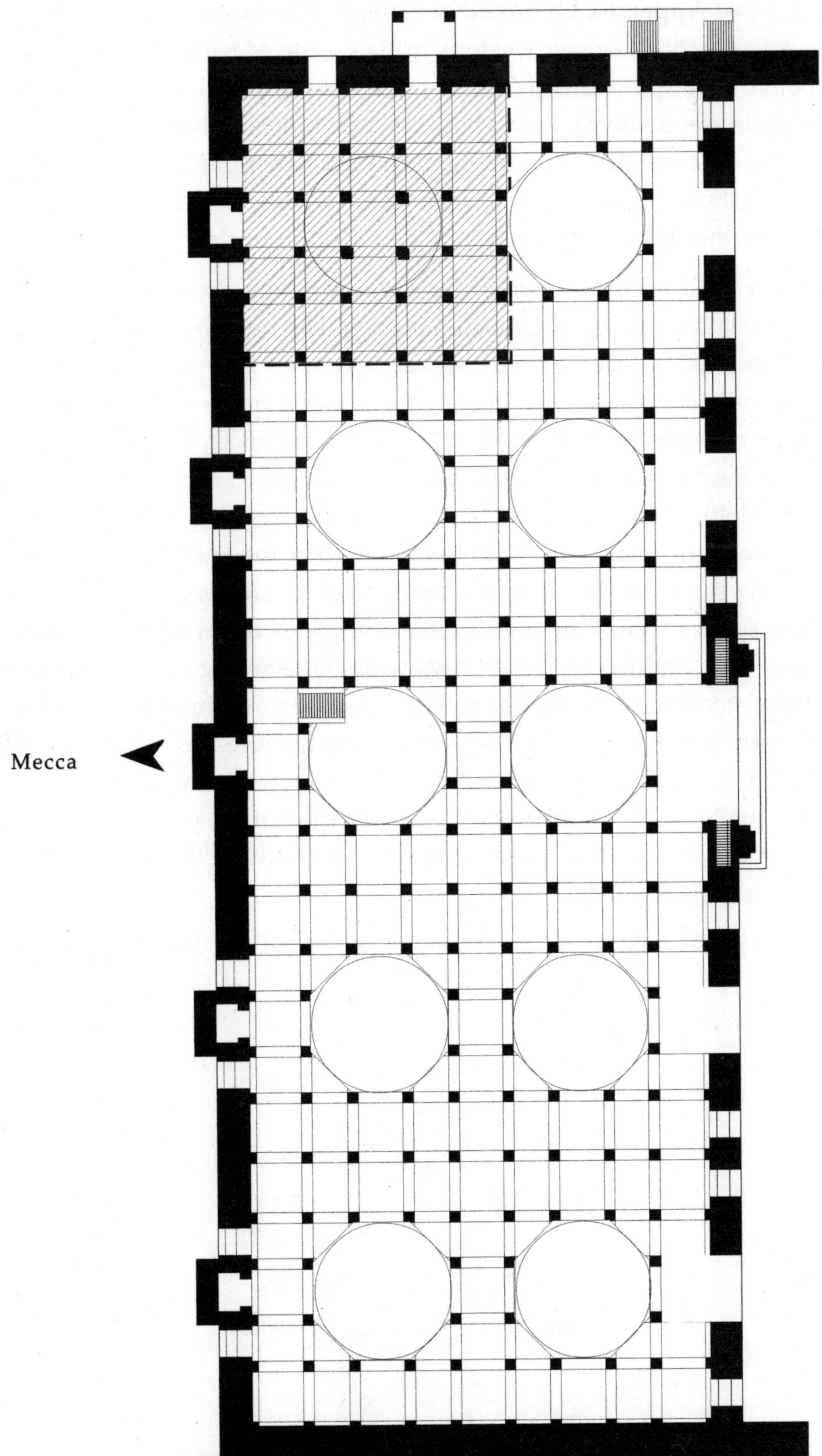

Masjid-i Jami, Ahmedabad (CE 1423)

Within a decade after the construction of the Masjid Ahmad Shah, Sultan Shams-ud-Din Muzaffar Ahmad Shah I (r. CE 1411–42) (see **Appendix D**) turned his attention to raising what would be seen by many as the epitome of mosque architecture in western India — the Masjid-i Jami. *En plan,* its sanctuary is related to that of both the Masjid-i Jami of Cambay (see **Plate 10**), and its *sahn* and *riwāq* to the Quwwat-ul-Islam Masjid in Delhi (see **Plate 8**). But, what was accomplished here and not totally realized in the plan was an explosion of space that was unique to Indian masjid architecture (see **Appendix C, Plate 89**). This was accomplished by composing a sanctuary of three storeys. The first storey consisted of unusually tall columns, the other two of columns more to the norm.

En plan, the main entrance to the Masjid-i Jami is centred on the south side of the *sahn.* A double staircase leads up to a relatively small, colonnaded portico. The small but elegant entrance gave no hint of what was to be encountered as one entered the *masjid* proper. Entrance was gained into the Masjid-i Jami by a single bay cloister which follows the south, east and north sides of the court. In the centre of the spacious *sahn* is a rectangular tank, the *haud.* Smaller entrances are centred in the north and east walls of the court. To the west is the majestic and extraordinary *haram*-screen. It consists of a central, soaring element (propylon), nearly seven bays wide and is bracketed by octagonal towers. This is flanked by a secondary element (propylon), one storey shorter than the soaring main portico. The flanking-element is, in turn, one storey higher than the main block of the *haram.* Finally, five openings to the north and five to the south of this flanking-element completes the western entrance to the *haram.* The *haram* is thirteen bays deep and twenty-seven bays wide. Fifteen large domes in three ranks of five are interspersed with fifty smaller cupola-like domes which cover the three levels of the *haram*'s roof. The *qiblā* of the Masjid-i Jami possesses five *mehrāb*s centred on the five files of domes. There are twelve *jālī* windows in bays 1, 3, 5, 8, 10, 12, 16, 18, 20, 23, 25 and 27 of the *qiblā* as well as six on the north and south walls of the *haram.* Finally, in the north-west corner of the haram is a mezzanine comprising thirty bays in area. Like that seen in the Masjid Ahmad Shah (see **Plate 22**), this area was for the women of the court and possessed its own entrance.

Related to the Masjid Ahmad Shah, the Masjid-i Jami is of the **RRc** type design (see **Figure 4 — RRc**).

Plate 23 — Masjid-i Jami, plan

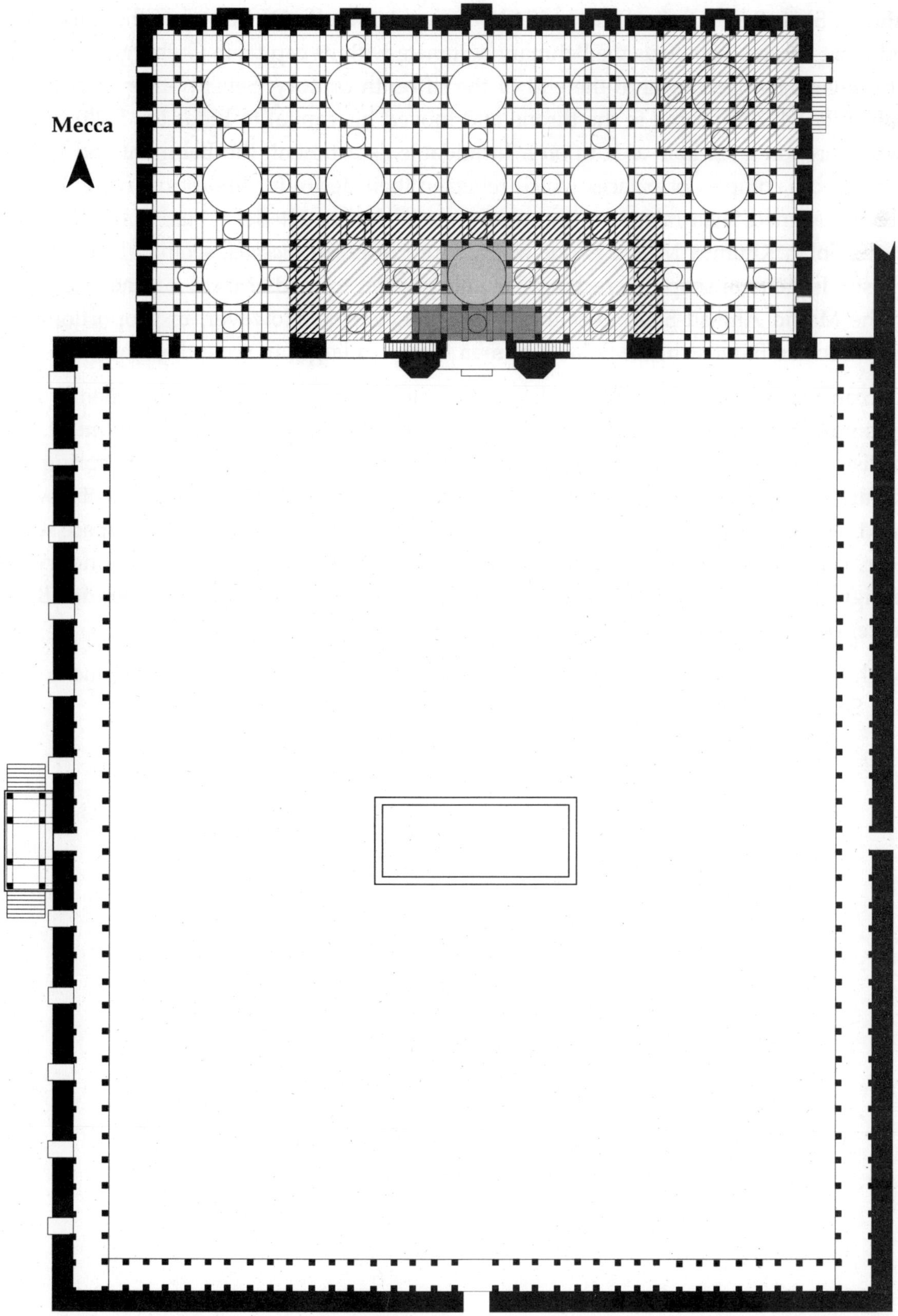

Solah Khumbā Masjid, Bīdar (*c.* CE 1424)

The Deccan had been a territory of tenuous loyalty to Imperial Delhi. In CE 1347, the then governor, Hasan Bahman Shah ('Ala-ud-din I) (r. CE 1347–58) (see **Appendix D**) threw off the imperial yoke and established what became known as the Bahmanī Sultanate with its capital in Gulbargā. It became a polity that was to govern the Deccan until the end of the fifteenth century. Seventy-five years after its birth, Amad Shah (r. CE 1422–35) came to the throne and moved his capital to Bīdar (CE 1429) (see **Appendix B, Plate 64**). Here, on a sizeable area upon a formidable escarpment, the Bahmanī and later the Barid Shahi constructed a complex of palaces which reflected their desire for luxurious living. Early, after the move to Bīdar, Ahmad Shah raised an impressive *masjid* for the citadel — the Solah Khumbā Masjid. However, the Solah Khumbā Masjid is one of the more reserved *masjids*, seemingly antithetical to the Bahmanī taste. In general shape — rectangular and parallel towards Mecca — and use, this *masjid* is related to the Masjid Ahmad Shah as both are palatine chapels. However, in proportion to the other structures within the Bīdargaṛh, the Solah Khumbā Masjid is larger in scale than the rest.

The Deccan was never an area where Islam took hold unconditionally, consequently much of the Bīdargaṛh is now in ruin. Nonetheless, the Solah Khumbā Masjid remains relatively intact. The eastern façade consists of eighteen square piers from which the nineteen arched openings spring. Sixty plain circular pillars in four ranks support seventy-five small cupola-like domes. Against the western wall, the *qiblā*, and within nine bays — files 9-11 — is found a rather massive, thick walled space serving as the *haram*. Here, centred within the *qiblā* is a semicircular *mehrāb* flanked by two secondary *mehrābs* of similar design. Over this space is found a large Gulbargā-type dome (see **Appendix B, Plates 83-85**). The exterior of the *qiblā* wall is flat with no indication of the *mehrāb*.

Although the **R2** (see **Figure 4 — R2**) style design is not unusual, it is rather unique here due to its scale in the Solah Khumbā Masjid.

Plate 24 — Solah Khumbā Masjid, plan

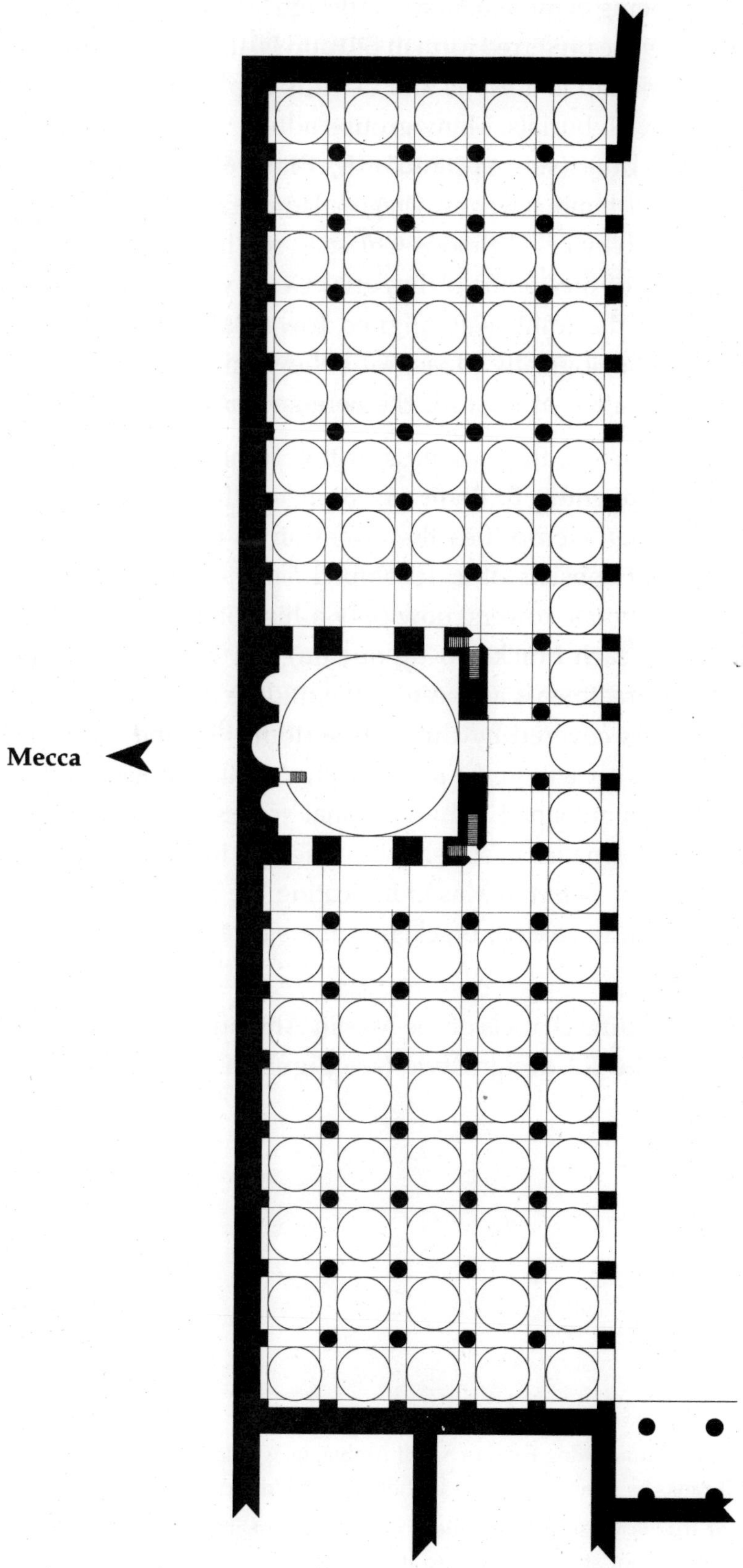

Rānī Rūpmatī Masjid, Ahmedabad (*c.* CE 1430)

The *rauza* — an architectural scheme which incorporates a tomb and a separate *masjid* which often "confront one another, and being complementary in design"[1] — is a form that finds numerous examples in Gujarat and later it becomes the preferred form in Bījāpur. Islam, traditionally, practises an egalitarianism that theoretically includes worship in a *masjid* and extends to places as well as types of burial. There is a Qur'anic reference against lavish burials. Many groups adhere to simple burial practice.[2] However, *circa* CE 892, the Qubba al-Sulaybiya (see **Appendix B, Plate 65** [top]) was constructed in Samarra, considered to be the first Islamic tomb. It was an octagonal tomb raised for the Calif Abu Dja'far Muhammad al-Muntasir Billah (r. CE 861–62) by his Orthodox Christian mother. This laid the foundation for more and more elaborate tombs. Many of the tombs of Imperial Delhi were of the Lodi Type (see **Appendix B, Plate 65** [bottom]) in which the tomb was aligned towards Mecca and a *qiblā* with a *mehrāb* was included. Although Islam, theologically, does not believe in the concept of "merit,"[3] there was the implication, if not for the hereafter, at least for the here-and-now.

Although not typically a *rauza*, the closeness of the Tomb of Rānī Rūpmatī to the Rānī Rūpmatī Masjid begs the issue (see **Appendix B, Plate 66**). Built for the remains of one of the Sultan's wives, a Princess of Dhar, this *masjid* exemplifies the attention to detail that was evident in the Gujarātī monuments. Here, the *masjid* consists of a developed *haram*-screen which is composed of a central major opening flanked by elaborate towers, now only a hint of their intended height. To the north and south are smaller doorways each bracketed by openings in the form of small, elegant balcony-like projections. Similar window treatments are seen in the middle of the north and south walls of the Rānī Rūpmatī Masjid. The *haram* is covered by three large domes in line with the eastern doors and also aligned with the three *mehrābs* set within the *qiblā*. Twelve small cupola-like domes are arranged around the larger domes. The *mehrābs* are small semi-octagonal spaces within the thickness of the *qiblā*. Three elaborate, stepped projections, smaller in scale, but mimicking the shape of the eastern towers, extend to the west of the *qiblā* of the Rānī Rūpmatī Masjid indicating the placement of the *mehrābs* within. Finally, four narror windows are equally spaced, bracketing the *mehrābs*, which allow additional light into the interior.

Related in form to the palatine chapels of the Masjid Ahmad Shah and the Solah Khumbā Masjid the Rānī Rūpmatī Masjid is of the **R2** design style (see **Figure 4 — R2**).

1 SG, p. 72.

2 In the recent burial of the former King Fahd of Saudi Arabia, he was laid to rest in a simply marked grave in a cemetery that was used by all ranks as practised by the Wahhabi of the kingdom.

3 "Merit" is a concept that is Buddhist and there is evidence of its practice in certain Judaeo-Christian societies, although Christianity does not strictly adhere to its precepts.

Plate 25 — Rānī Rūpmatī Masjid, plan

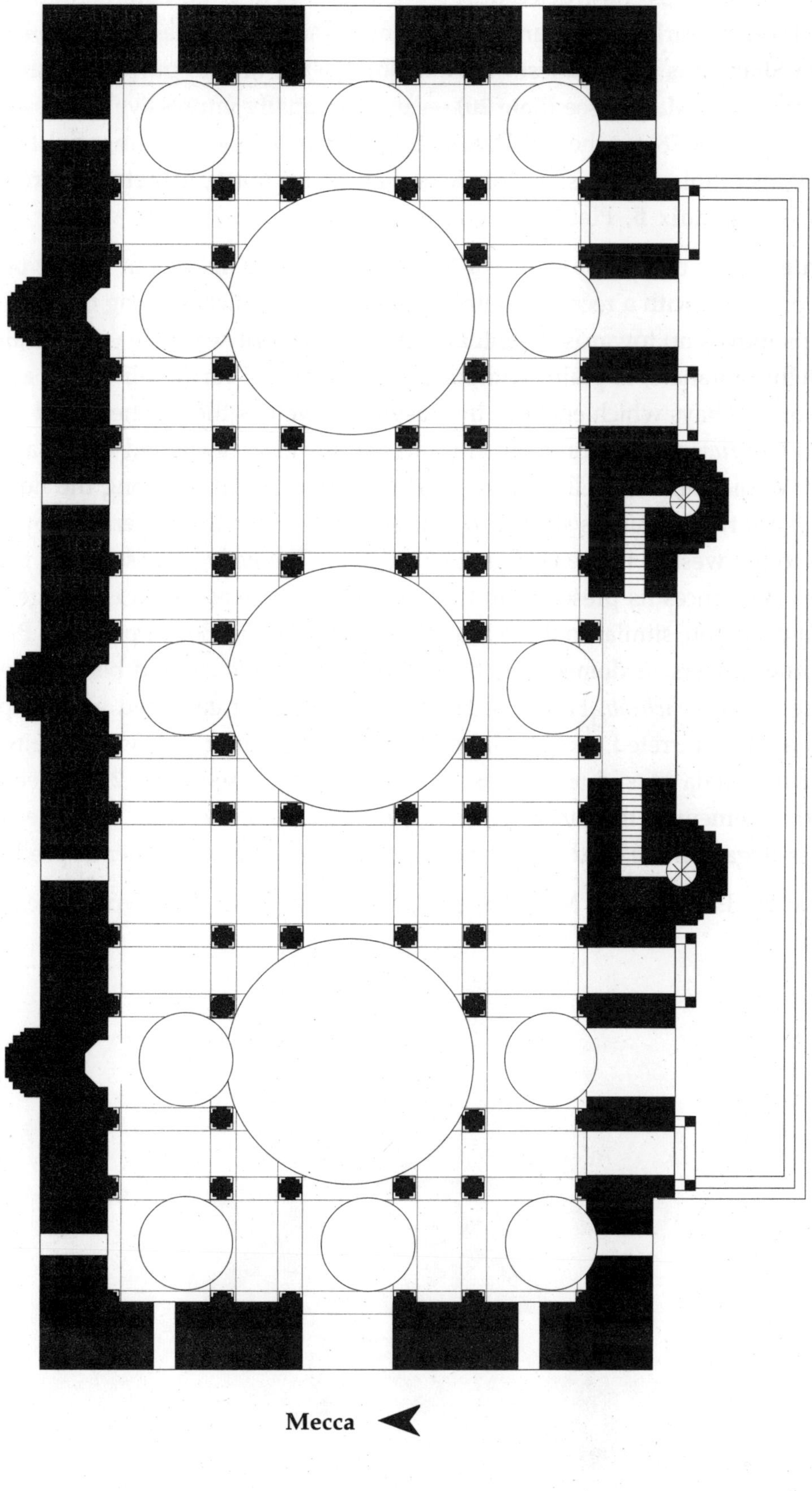

Mecca

Lāl Darwāẓa Masjid, Jaunpur (*c.* CE 1438)

The Lāl Darwāẓā Masjid was constructed during the reign of Nasir-ud-Din Mahmud Shah (r. CE 1440–57) (see **Appendix D**) and nearly forty years after the impressive Atala Masjid (*c.* CE 1408) of Sultan Shams-ud-Din Ibrahim Shah. It is the smallest of the major *masjids* of Jaunpur. Compared to its noteworthy predecessor — the Atala Masjid (see **Plate 20**) — and its equally impressive successor — the innovative Masjid-i Jami (*c.* CE 1438–78) — the Lāl Darwāẓā Masjid owes more to Imperial Delhi than any of the other Sharqi *masjids* of this city. It is also obvious that the far north, namely Samarqand, also influenced this mosque (see **Appendix B, Plate 57**), *en plan*.

The eastern entrance of the Lāl Darwāẓā Masjid is substantial, but can hardly be called impressive. It consists of a propylon with a recessed pointed arch and a smaller opening of like form. A broad flight of receding steps moves up towards the initial arch. The exterior wall, the girdle wall of this *masjid*, like those of the Delhi Sultanate, is plain, without penetration and fortress-like. A passageway leads to a cloister (*riwāq*) of two bays which encloses the eastern as well as the northern and southern sides of the *sahn*. This multi-bay *riwāq* with prominent entrances to the east, north and south, again finds parallel in the Samarqand Masjid Jami as well as those of Persia (Iran). Centred along the northern and southern sides of the *sahn* are two entrances similar to that encountered in the eastern propylon. An eccentrically shaped *haud* is to the west of the central area of the *sahn*. The *haram* is essentially four bays deep and a screen of arches announces its presence. In the centre of the *haram*-screen is a large, impressive, deeply recessed arched propylon, similar to those found at Delhi's Masjid Begampurī (see **Plate 15**), but without the battered corner towers. A domed area of nine bays square is centred behind the central pylon and emphasizes the *haram's mehrāb*. Here the *mehrāb* is somewhat enlarged and its presence is further emphasized by a large, turreted, rectangular extension on the outer *qiblā* wall. The relationship between this *masjid* and the Atala Masjid as well as the Masjid-i Ja'mi (see **Plate 27**) is seen in the impressive pylon-like central element of the *haram*-screen. However, unlike the other two, the Lāl Darwāẓā Masjid is somewhat less elegant, more solid and, certainly, less innovative than either its predecessor or successor.

Nonetheless, the Lāl Darwāẓa Masjid is an apt example of the **RRc** type of design (see **Figure 4 — RRc**).

Plate 26 — Lāl Darwāẓa Masjid, plan

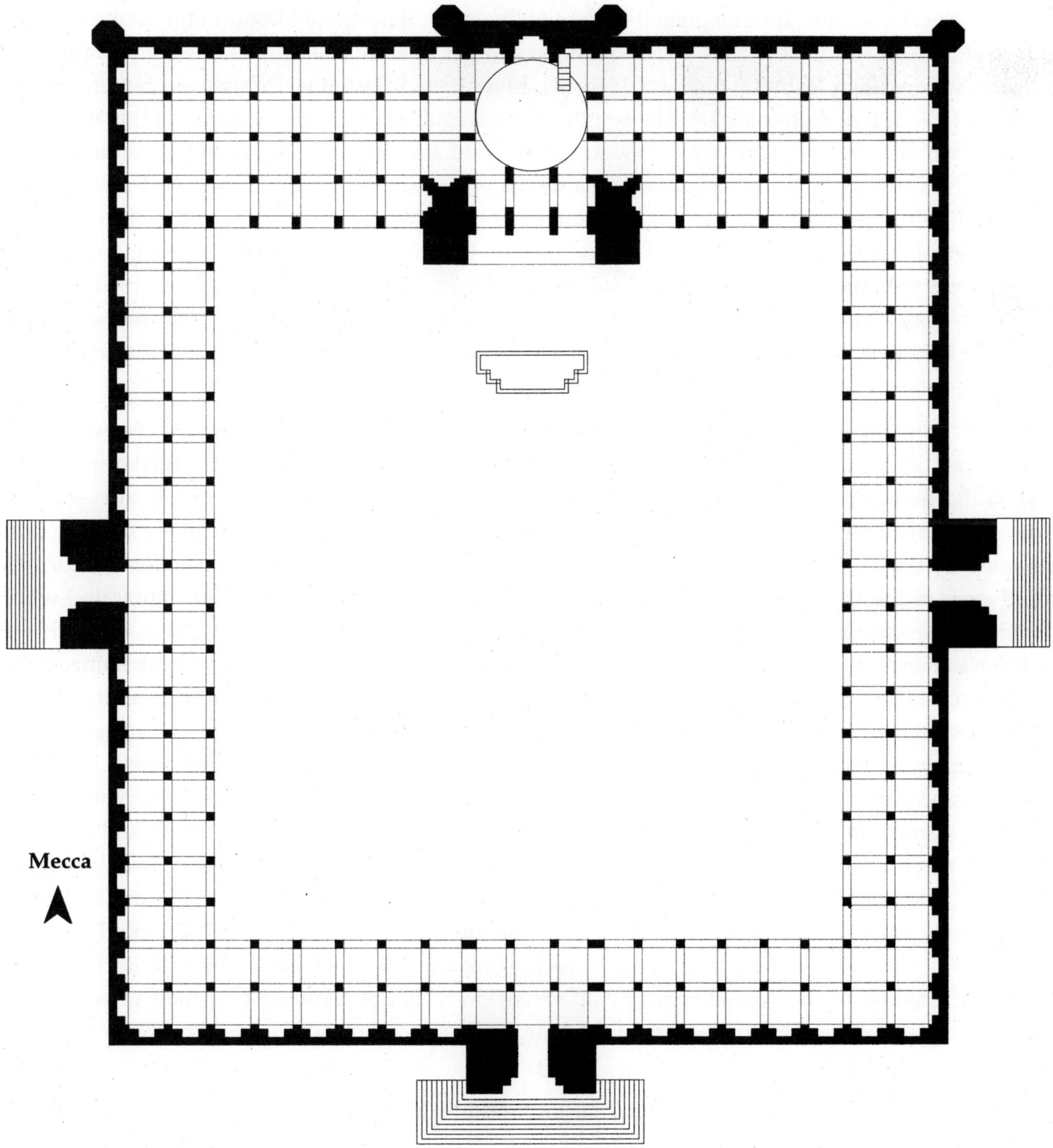

Masjid-i Jami, Jaunpur (*c.* CE 1438–78)

Begun in the same year as the completion of the Lāl Darwāẓa Masjid, the Masjid-i Jami took some forty years to complete — from late in the reign of Shams-ud-Din Ibrahim Shah (CE 1402–40) and through the reigns of Nasir-ud-Din Mahmud Shah (CE 1440–57), Muhammad Shah (CE 1457–58) and Husen (Husain) Shah (CE 1458–76) (see **Appendix D**). The length of time required in the construction of this monument is understandable. Its size, scale and innovations required this seemingly inordinate amount of time. "When the structurally more adventurous Muslim builders . . . set forth to build their next great mosque, they certainly succeeded in their grand constructional concepts but fared none too well in achieving equally great architectural effects."[1] Of this statement by Grover, exception must be taken. For example, the "architectural effect" of the open, two storied cloister juxtaposed to the massive, domed gateways with their soaring propylons, and all placed upon a grand, massive platform is not only spectacular visually, it is unique. In sheer scale it is impressive. The *sahn* alone is of such a size that the whole of the Atala Masjid (see **Plate 20**) could fit within its precincts.

Initially constructed on a platform of over 20 ft high, ingress to the Masjid-i Jami precincts, by necessity, need to be accomplished by stairs of considerable height. Three substantial gateways, fronted by propylons, masked the domes behind. The stairway to each of these — to the east, north and south — are the width of the elements, giving each an awesome detail. The square *sahn* is bordered along the east, north and south by open cloisters, two bays deep and two storeys high. These magnificent cloisters turn and enfold each of the three gates, thereby incorporating them and the cloister as an integrated whole. Centred in the *sahn* of the Masjid-i Jami is a large *haud*. As the splendid platform, the gates with their impressive stairs and the two storeyed cloister are unique, the *haram* of the Masjid-i Jami is unequalled! Centred in the *haram*-screen is a soaring, five storeyed pylon with a massive pointed arch enfolding three lesser arched doorways on the first level (see **Appendix C, Plate 88**). Behind is a spacious area surmounted by a large dome. Three passages lead to the north and south from this central space, into two low trabeated spaces. The areas above these spaces form a mezzanine in which the women of the court may partake in the worship. From these spaces three similar passages lead north and south into two of the most intriguing spaces of the whole Masjid-i Jami — two, large, open, barrel vaulted spaces. The combination of a large domed space flanked with low trabeated spaces which, in turn, are flanked by large, lofty barrel vaults is unprecedented and spatially nearly beyond comprehension. Each of the five spaces of the *haram* exhibit three *mehrāb*s each, sunk into the thick *qiblā*. The exterior of the *qiblā* indicates the width of the domed space by an extension which is cornered by round towers. Larger round towers are at the western corners of the haram. These four corners seem like strange references to the Delhi Sultanate style.

Of all the *masjid*s within this consideration the Masjid-i Jami is singular and easily represents the **RSc** design style (see **Figure 4 — RSc**).

1 SG, p. 42.

Plate 27 — Masjid-i Jami, plan

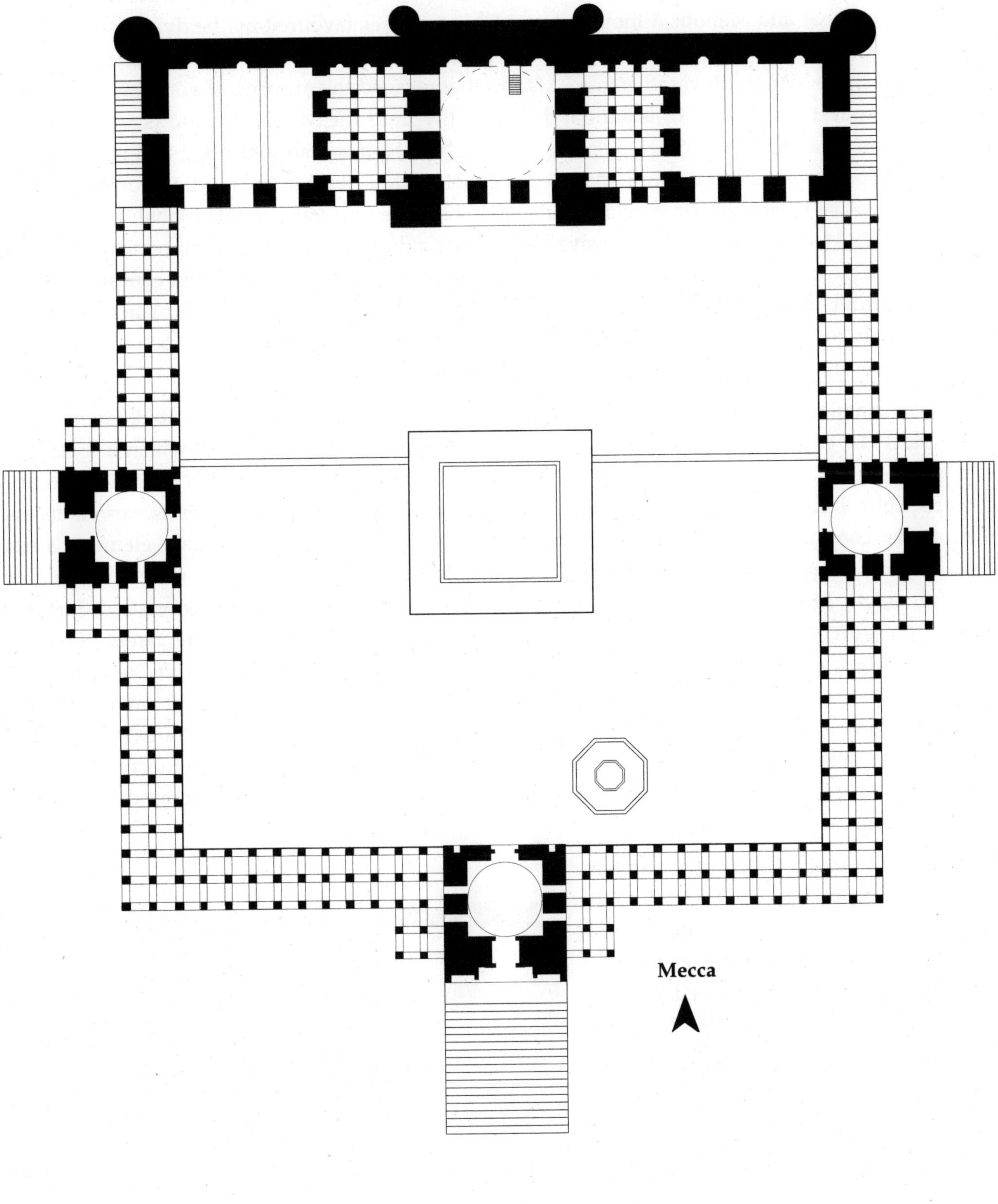

Masjid-i Jami, Māṇḍu (CE 1440)

Somewhat to the east of the vibrant Gujarātī Sultanate rose the equally brilliant Malwa Sultanate with the twin capitals of Dhar and Māṇḍu. Although it was Dhar that was favoured by the dynasty's founder — Dilvar Khan Ghuri (r. CE 1392–1405) — his son, Husam-ud-Din Hushang Shah (r. CE 1405–35) (see **Appendix D**) chose Māṇḍu. It was, therefore, Māṇḍu that gleaned the majority of notoriety. It possessed one of the grandest *gaṛh mahals* of Islamic India, certainly until the Mughal period (see **Appendix B, Plate 62**). In an area of twelve square miles, upon a high plateau, suitably fortified and geographically varied, the Sultans were allowed ample space to vent their architectural desires — the Mosque of Dilwar Khan, the extensive Palaces of Bāẓ Bahādur and Gada Shah, the unusual Hindola Mahal, the Lāl Mahal, the elegant Jahāẓ Mahal, as well as the extensive Muñja and Kaphur Talao. The most impressive monuments of Māṇḍu which were constructed upon the plateau, but somewhat south of the main complex, were the Masjid-i Jami built by Ghazni Khan, Muhammad Shah I (r. CE 1435–36) and the attached Tomb of Hushang Shah. Although not a *rauza* in the traditional sense the two structures complement each other and may be seen to present a single unit (see **Appendix B, Plate 69**).

Built upon a platform the Masjid-i Jami consists of a massive entrance giving way to the remainder of the complex. The entrance, rather a pylon-like form, is a domed cube, the entry of which is a trabeated doorway set within a pointed arch recess. A circular hall that matches the dome's diameter is centred within the cube. Inside this space is a variation on a theme of circles and semicircles as various recesses penetrate the core of the cube (see **Figure 11**). As one passes through this entrance element, a *riwāq* that is two aisles deep is first confronted and then a spacious *sahn*. Three aisles border both the north and south sides of this open court. There is an elegance about this court which consists of forty-four uninterrupted arched openings marching around the perimeter of the *sahn*. The *haram*, unlike the Delhi prototypes, or even the Jaunpur or Gujarat *masjid* is without a developed *haram*-screen or a pylon. The *haram* is five bays deep, seventeen bays wide and covered by fifty-eight small, secondary domes and three large domes. A large, rectilinear *mehrāb* is set within the *qiblā*. An extension on the exterior of the *qiblā* wall indicates the presence of the *mehrāb*. A small doorway set in the *qiblā* to the south of the *mehrāb* provides access to the large open square within which is centred the Tomb of Hushang Shah.

The Masjid-i Jami of Māṇḍu is a stately, understated monument that is related to the famed Sultan Hasan Bahman Shah's Masjid-i Jami at Gulbargā. Grover describes it as "grand and dignified"[1] and, indeed, it is that. The elegant Masjid-i Jami falls within the **SSc** design type (see **Figure 3 — SSc**).

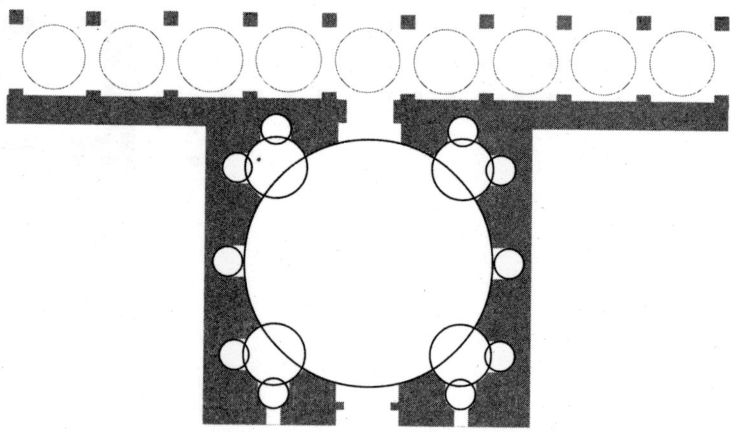

Figure 11 — Entrance block indicating profusion of circles

[1] SG, p. 47.

Plate 28 — Masjid-i Jami, plan

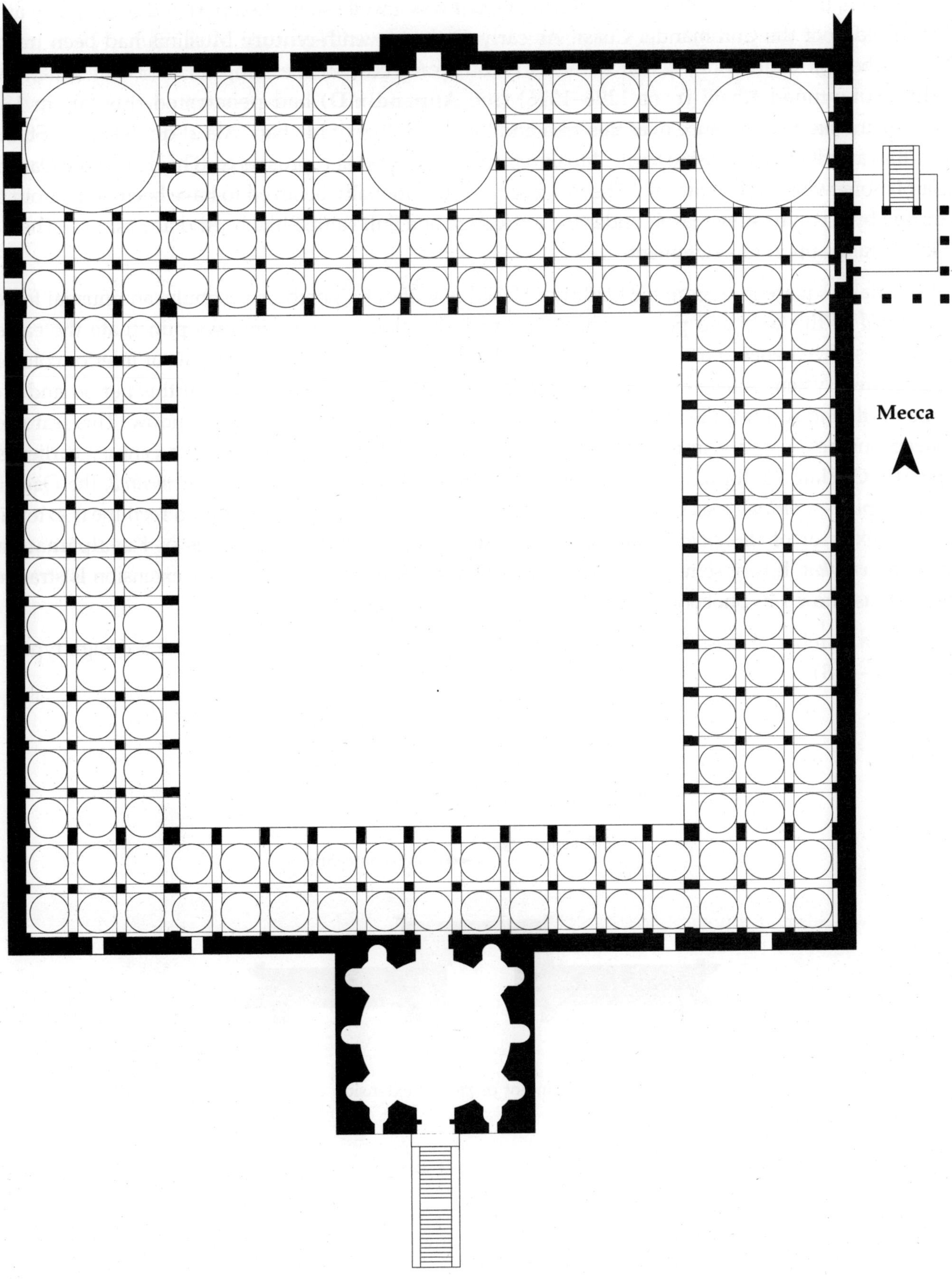

Qadiriya Masjid, Kayalpatnam (*c.* CE 1450)

Kayalpatnam, the ancient Kolkhoi, later Kayal or Qa'il was a well established port and trading city at the southern edge of the Coromandel Coast. As early as the eleventh-century Muslims had been trading here and there is some evidence that in the early fourteenth century the troops of the Delhi Sultan 'Ala-ud-din Muhammad Khalji (r. CE 1296–1316) (see **Appendix D**) had penetrated this far. In 1377, Vijayanagara exerted influence over this area and the last Sultan of Ma'bar, 'Ala al-din Sikandar Shah (r. 1377–78) was killed in a decisive battle. Muslim traders remained and prospered. The date of the Qadiriya Masjid is somewhat problematical. "The mosque . . . is traditionally believed to have been built about 650 years ago by a Hindu stonemason under the patronage of a Sūfī saint, Shaikh 'Abd al-Rashid."[1] The date *c.* 1450 is based upon this statement.

Essentially square in design, the Qadiriya Masjid is without a porch or vestibule, an unusual feature for a *masjid* of this area and period. Three doorways bracketing two windows punctuate the eastern façade. These five penetrations of the eastern wall denote the four files each of four of interior columns. The trabeated system is here employed as it was in most of the smaller *masjids* of this period and area. On the north and south walls two doors set within deep porches flank a single window. This feature — the deep porches — is a feature seen in the Ahmad Nainar Masjid (see **Plate 12**) a century earlier (see **Appendix C, Plate 90** [top]). Unlike the Ahmad Nainar Masjid with its rectilinear *mehrāb,* the Qadiriya Masjid displays a *mehrāb* that is a deep semicircular niche, *en plan,* and set within a rectilinear extension from the exterior of the *qiblā.* It is noteworthy that the majority of the *qiblās* of Kayalpatnam are rectilinear, *en plan.* It is of some interest and exceedingly curious that this exterior extension is strangely off centre as shown in Shokoohy[2] (see **Figure 12**; and **Plate 29**)!

Unlike a number of masjids in Kayalpatnam, the Qadiriya Masjid falls within the **S** design type (see **Figure 3 — S**).

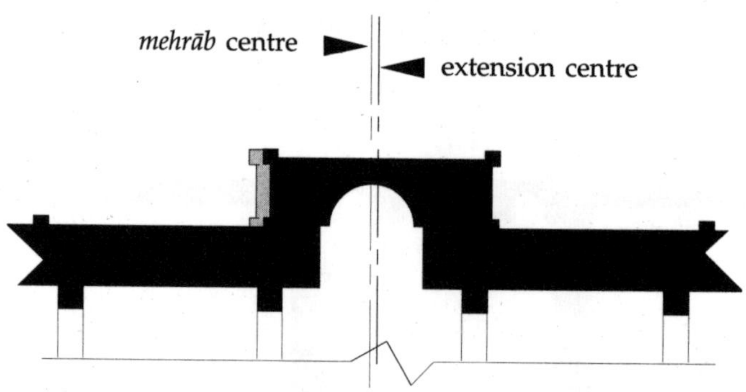

Figure 12 — Misalignment of *mehrāb* extension in the *qiblā*

[1] MS, p. 98.

[2] Ibid., p. 100.

Plate 29 — Qadiriya Masjid, plan

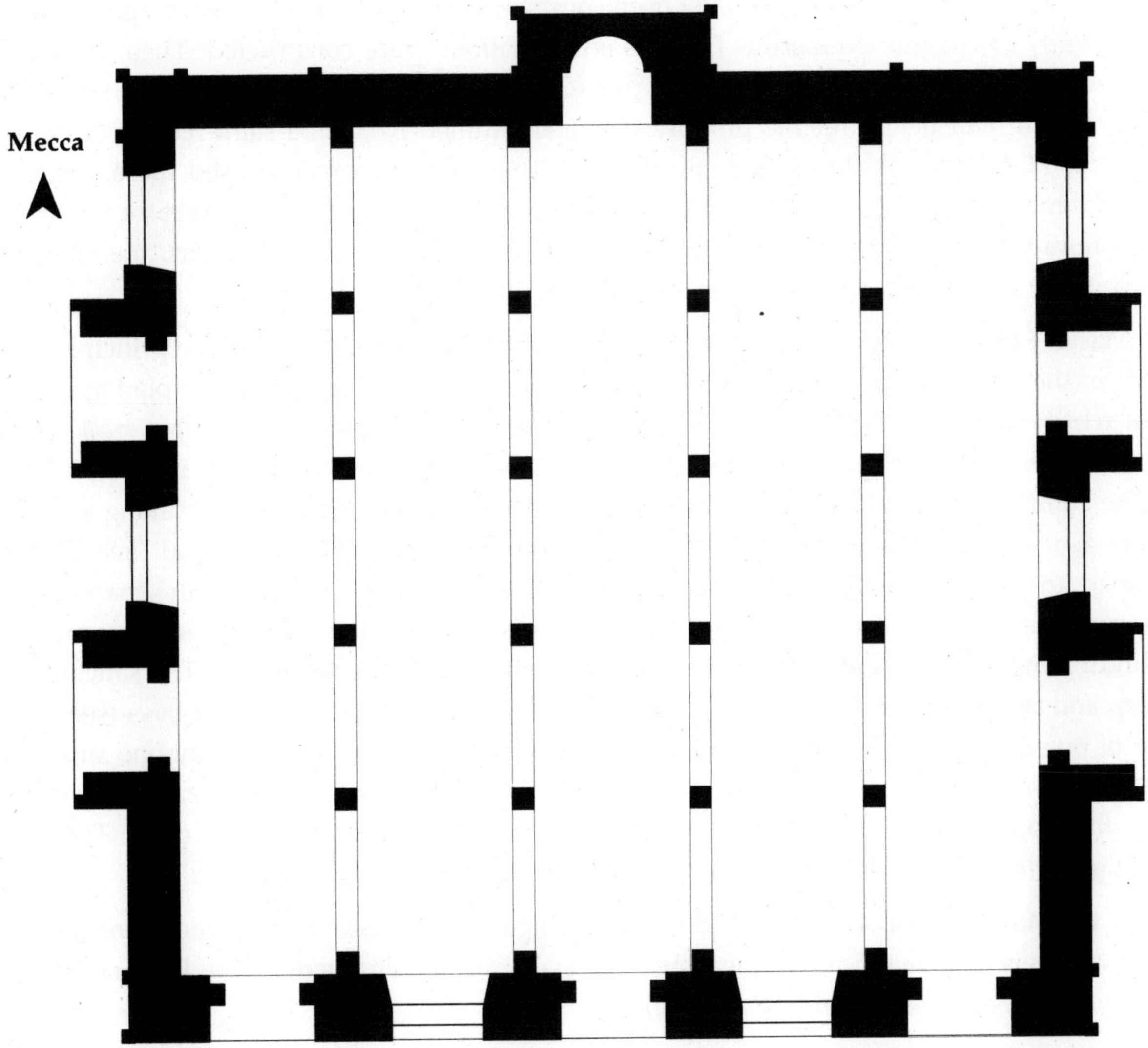

Masjid-i Jami, Sarkhej (*c.* CE 1451)

Constructed within a region and sultanate that produced a number of noteworthy monuments, the Masjid-i Jami at Sarkhej, a suburb of Ahmedabad, exemplifies yet another testimonial to this area's claim to aesthetic importance. Sarkhej had initially been conceived of as an area set aside as a garden retreat for the royal family of Gujarat. Numerous gardens and pavilions were constructed. Then, in 1441, Sultan Mohammad Karim Shah (r. CE 1442–51) (see **Appendix D**), out of piety, found this area suitable for the construction of a mausoleum for the prominent Sheikh Ahmed Khattri, a saint-recluse of Gujarat (see **Appendix B, Plate 70**). Subsequently, a number of other mausolea were raised there, including the Tomb of Mahmud Beghara (r. CE 1459–1511). Although Sarkhej still remained a retreat for the members of the royal family, its importance was supplanted by the mausolea. Nonetheless, the Masjid-i Jami overshadows by its sheer size the other monuments of this place.

The Masjid-i Jami at Sarkhej is large in scale, measuring some 225 by 157 ft. The principle entry is to the south of the whole, set towards the east of centre of the massive courtyard. Triple bays lead to the platform which is on level with the interior. As one enters, one is confronted with a *riwāq* that wraps around the southern, eastern and northern borders of the *sahn*. Every other bay is topped by a small dome. The columns of this cloister are somewhat thicker than those of the *haram* making an interesting variation. Unlike the Masjid Ahmad Shah (see **Plate 22**) or the Masjid-i Jami (see **Plate 23**) of Ahmedabad, the Masjid-i Jami at Sarkhej does not possess a developed *haram*-screen separating the *sahn* from the sanctuary area. Rather there are a series of sixteen slender columns, of differing design, scavenged from Hindu temples in the area, marching across the entrance to the sanctuary. The sanctuary is nine bays deep and twenty-one aisles wide alternating between square and rectangular bays (see **Figure 13**). A forest of one-hundred-eighty slender columns support ten large domes and fifty-one smaller domes within the *haram*. In the north-west corner of the *haram* is a raised floor, a mezzanine, sixteen bays square with its own exterior entrance. This is the prayer area for the women of the court. The *qiblā* holds five rectilinear *mehrābs* which are indicated on the exterior by similar projections.

Where the Masjid-i Jami of Ahmedabad is astounding in its multistoreyed, domed *haram*, the Masjid-i Jami at Sarkhej is amazing in its simple, single storeyed, multi-columned, *haram*. It represents the **RRc** style of *masjid* design (see **Figure 4 — RRc**).

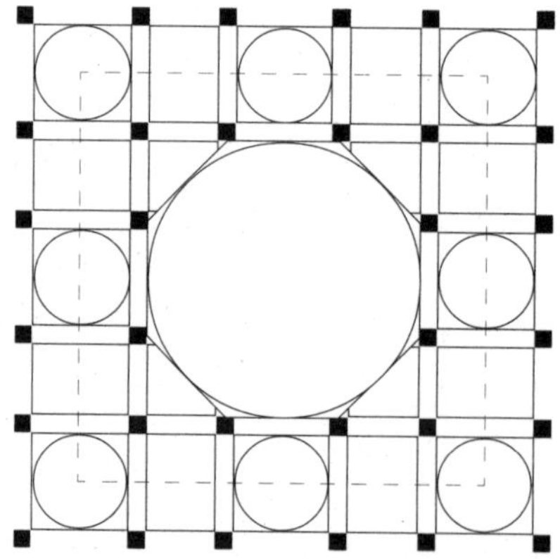

Figure 13 — Indicating square and rectangular bay arrangement with domes (- - - indicates a single unit)

Plate 30 — Masjid-i Jami, plan

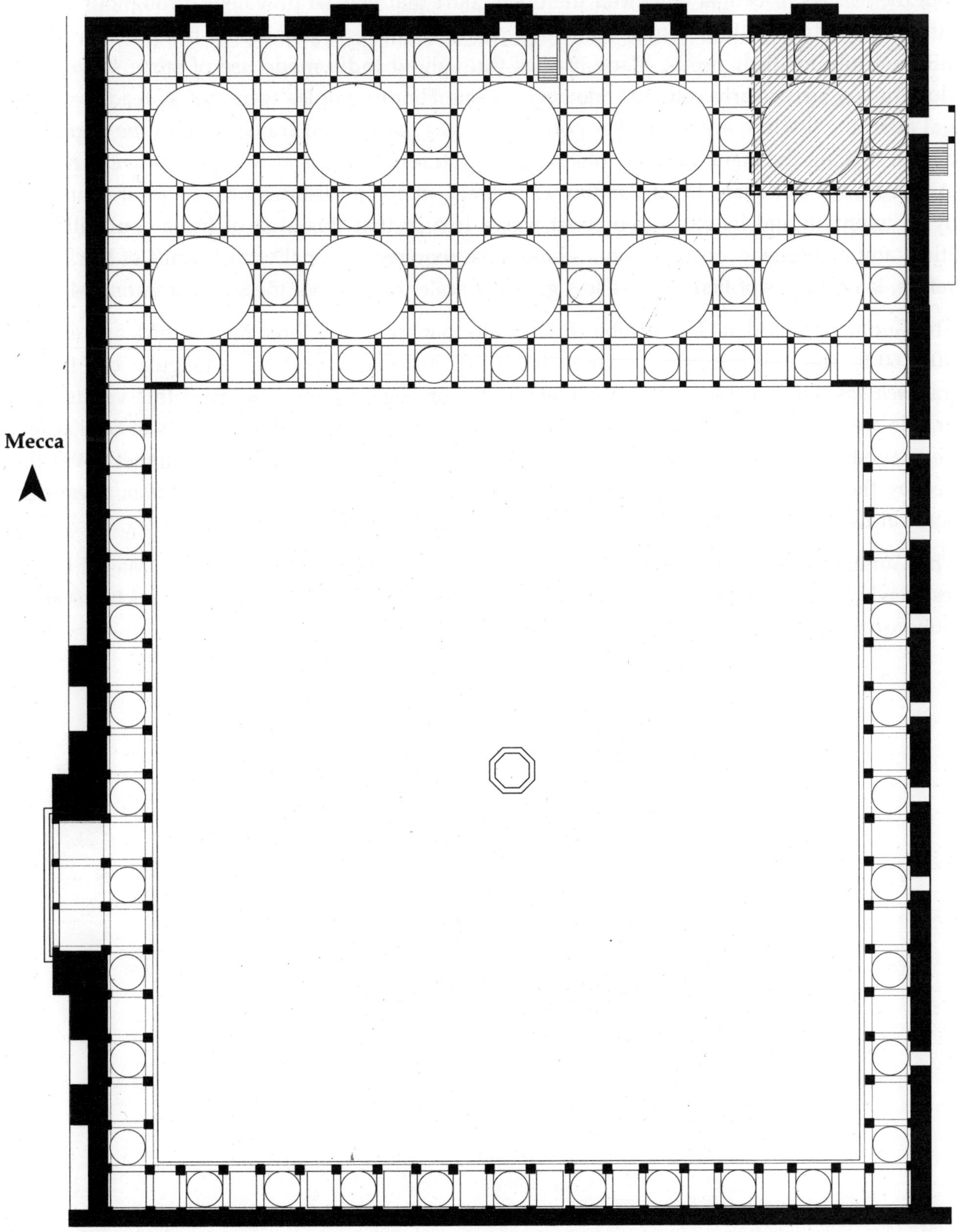

Gunmani Masjid, Gaur (CE 1484)

Constructed within an ecosystem where rain much of the year was a given, especially during the monsoon season, the *masjids* of Bengal eschewed the open court that was so prevalent throughout the western two-thirds of India. Further, Bengal craftsmen preferred the easily obtained brick which provided a plentiful supply for their needs. Many *masjids* throughout India made use of stone scavenged from Hindu temples, particularly columns. However, stone Hindu temples were not as readily available in Bengal as in the western areas. Furthermore, stone was too dear to transport into the region and the process of carving the many needed columns for the traditional *masjid* was prohibitive. An exception, the Adina Masjid (see **Plate 13**) at Pandua, as brilliant an accomplishment as it was, it simply was too costly to maintain and its vast open court was a luxury that this area of India could ill afford. In addition, any monument conceived on a grand scale required unusually thick walls of brick to realize. Therefore, later *masjids* of Bengal were less grand in scale than that of the singular Adina Masjid.

The Gunmani Masjid at Gaur exhibits brick walls that are nearly three metres thick and a dimension of 140 × 60 ft. The fully enclosed, rectangular *masjid* consists of a central, rectangular bay framing the central *mehrābs*. Four massive standing piers and four engaged piers support this vaulted bay. On either side are four aisles to the north and four to the south with secondary *mehrābs* in each aisle. These four east-west aisles are bisected by three north-south aisles. Twenty-four small domes cover the bays created by these aisles. Twelve standing columns punctuate these areas of the *haram* attesting to the economical use of stone columns.

The Gunmani Masjid stands as a transition from the exuberance of the Adina Masjid to the final throes seen in the Choṭā Sonā Masjid and the Qadam Rasul Masjid, both of Gaur. As such this *masjid* and the subsequent two are of the **R2** design type (see **Figure 4 — R2**).

Plate 31 — Gunmani Masjid, plan

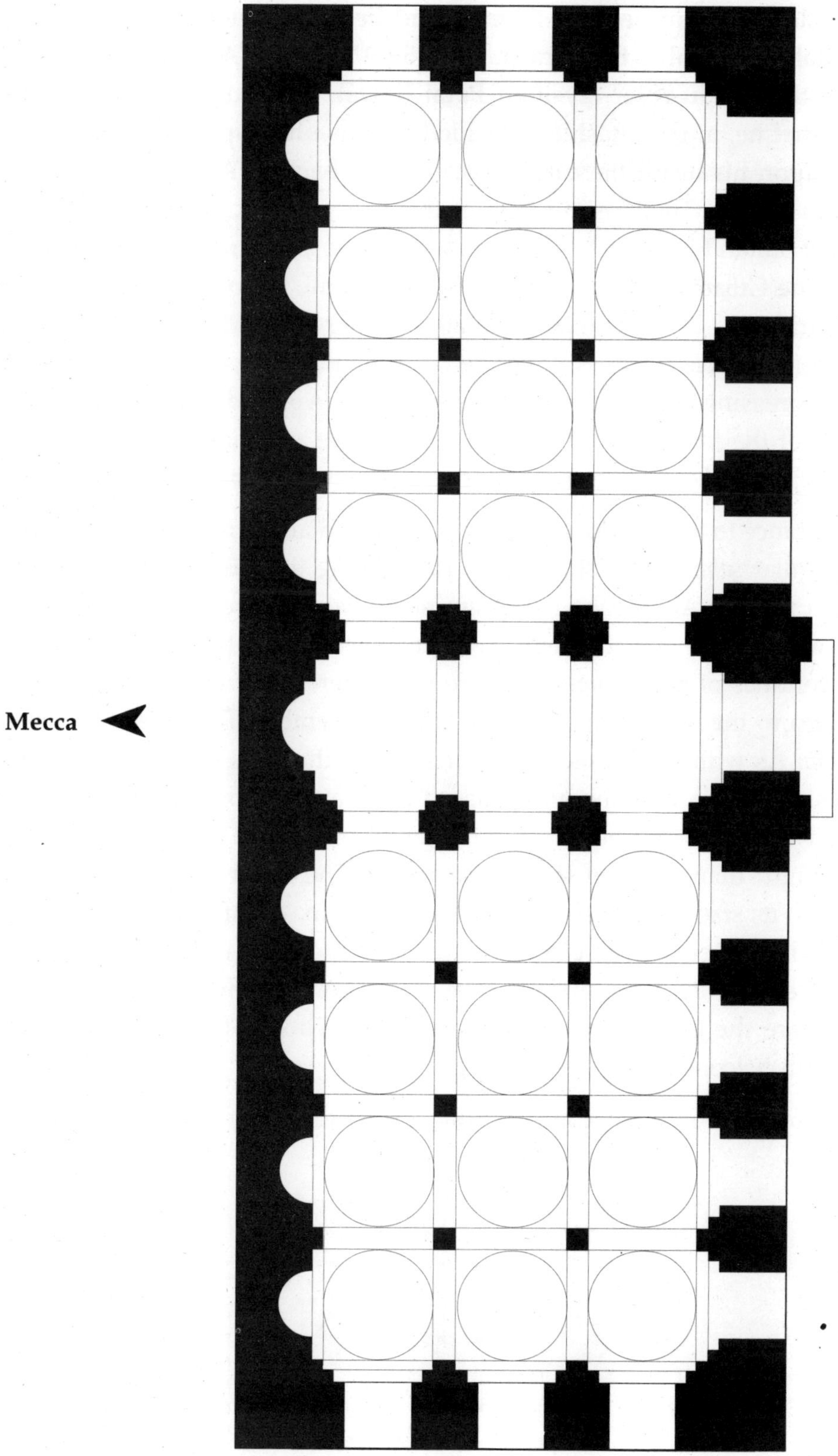

Masjid-i Jami, Campāner (*c.* CE 1485)

Some seventy miles south and east of Ahmedabad lies Campāner. The brilliant and powerful Sultan Nasir-ud-Din Mahmud Shah I Beghara (r. CE 1459–1511) (see **Appendix D**) captured the citadel of Campāner from the Hindu ruler Jaysingh Patai Rāwal. The sultan became so enamoured with this picturesque site that he, in royal fashion, decided to move his capital atop its 762 m plateau. Again, in typical fashion, upon his death the capital was moved back to Ahmedabad, but the glories of Sultan Mahmud Beghara remain. The Masjid-i Jami of this new capital city was a fitting addition, and the cap stone to the life of Sultan Mahmud Beghara, as well as the sister mosque, the Masjid-i Nagina. The three major *masjids* of the Gujarātī Sultanate — the Masjid-i Jami, Ahmedabad (C. CE 1423) (see **Plate 23**); the Masjid-i Jami, Sarkhej (*c.* CE 1451) (see **Plate 30**) and here, the Masjid-i Jami, Campāner — indicate a subtle shift in design, *en plan*. This is to be seen in the increasing emphasis placed upon the area of the *haram* and the decreasing emphasis upon the *sahn* (see **Appendix B, Plate 71**). There are, of course, similarities. Each of the three indicates a *riwāq* of a single aisle and each possesses a mezzanine in the north-west corner of the *haram* with an entrance to the north for the women of the court.

The major entrance to the Masjid-i Jami is via a pillared and screened, square porch. Immediately one enters the rectangular *sahn* with a single aisle *riwāq* along the east, north and south faces of the court. Like the Masjid-i Jami at Ahmedabad, a magnificent *haram*-screen separates the *sahn* from the *haram*. A *haram*-screen with a wide arched opening dominates the central portion. On either side of the portico, but within the confines of the *haram*-screen are tall towers, *minarets*. Four additional entrances, two to the north and two to the south, complete the screen ensemble. Twenty-three aisles, eleven bays deep, enclose the *haram*. As with the Masjid-i Jami at Sarkhej, the bays here are also made up of square and rectangular bays. However, here the unit is based upon an octagon (see **Figure 14**) rather than a square, as in the earlier two considered herein. The corners of the *haram* are punctuated by four towers which are shorter in height than those of the *haram*-screen. The main *mehrāb* of the Masjid-i Jami is given prominence due to its size and shape. On either side are six — three to the north and three to the south — with small rectilinear plans. The exterior of the *qiblā* indicates the placement of the *mehrāb* which are centred, east to west, on the large domes. These extensions are all semicircular, *en plan*. Numerous *jālī* windows punctuate the exterior of the *haram*'s walls. Those of the north and south are somewhat larger and are with balconies.

The Masjid-i Jami at Campāner falls within the **RRc** type of *masjid* design (see **Figure 4 — RRc**).

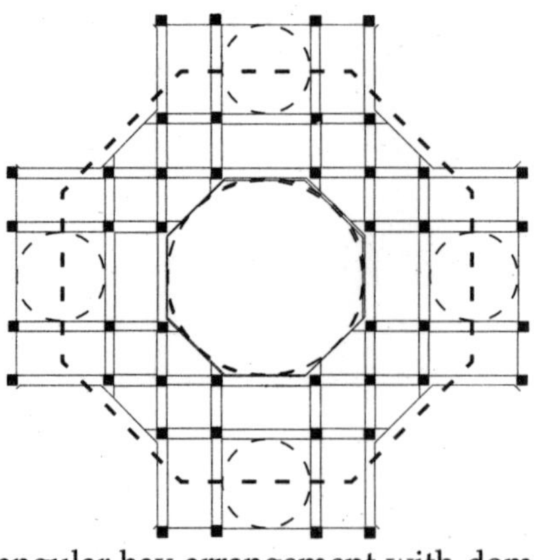

Figure 14 — Indicating square and rectangular bay arrangement with domes (- - - - indicates octagonal unit)

Plate 32 — Masjid-i Jami, plan

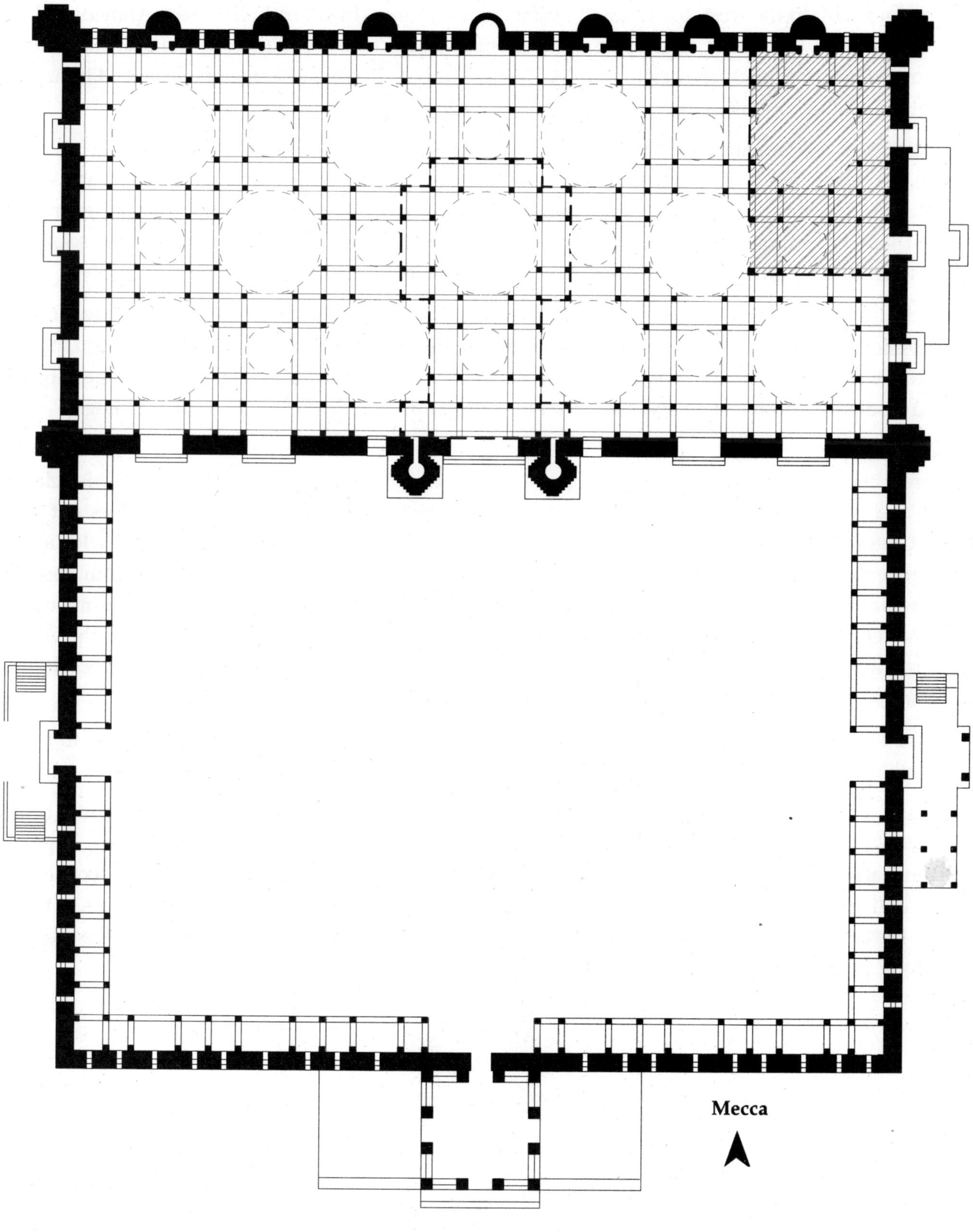

Fifteenth Century

The fifteenth century saw important developments in the mosque which were, in many ways, independent of Imperial Delhi. In the west, the Gujarātī Sultanate under the Muzaffarid Shahi saw Ahmedabad, then Sarkhej, and then Campāner raise spectacular *masjids*. Equal to the Gujarātī, in the east the Sharqi of Jaunpur took second place to none! Even Malwar's Ghuri & Khalji sultans embellished Māṇḍu which contributed to this vibrant century!

Changes in the treatment of the *riwāq* is seen, particularly in Jaunpur. There, the two-aisle *riwāq* became the norm. The Sharqi experimented with a double-storey cloister and a *riwāq* that was open to the exterior. The development of the *haram*-screen sees particular emphasis in Gujarat; even in the Masjid-i Jami of Sarkhej where they dispensed with it altogether. The proportions of the *sahn* to the *haram* shifted, dramatically, in Gujarat (see **Appendix B, Plate 71**).

Brick, the preferred building material of Bengal possesses both advantages and disadvantages. It was a building material that was readily available in the area and in seemingly endless quantity. Its initial cost was minimal. In the construction of smaller structures, brick finds its true advantage. However, there are potential problems in the employment of brick particularly in large-scale buildings.

The process of manufacturing brick requires that clay is suitably dried before it is fired in a kiln. Low-fired brick — fired well below a temperature where the material begins to vitrify — is relatively porous and will absorb water. High-fired brick, on the other hand, is non-porous and does not absorb water. Generally, in the employment of low-fired brick, the exterior surface is covered with a water proof material, frequently plaster or cement or stucco. This protects the porous brick from absorbing water which is deleterious to its permanence, but must be regularly maintained. The majority of monuments which employ brick in south and South-East Asia, use low-fired brick — the Ānanda Temple, Pagan, Burma (see **Appendix B, Plate 68**) or the Chedi Wat Chang Lom, Si Satchanalai, Thailand (see **Appendix B, Plate 69**).

Large-scale structures which employ brick require rather thick walls if the structure is to achieve any height. Vaulting large areas with brick is perilous unless high-fired brick is employed.

Finally, there is the possibility of severe, even irreparable damage to the environment if brick is exclusively employed. In the past wood was the exclusive fuel in firing a kiln. If numerous, large scale structures are to be raised, then enormous amounts of wood fuel is required. The rapid decline of the Pagan civilization is believed to a great extent to be due to the denuding of the region of trees to fuel the kilns in the never-ending construction of larger and larger temples and *pagoḍās*. This upset the ecosystem and a long period of drought occurred.

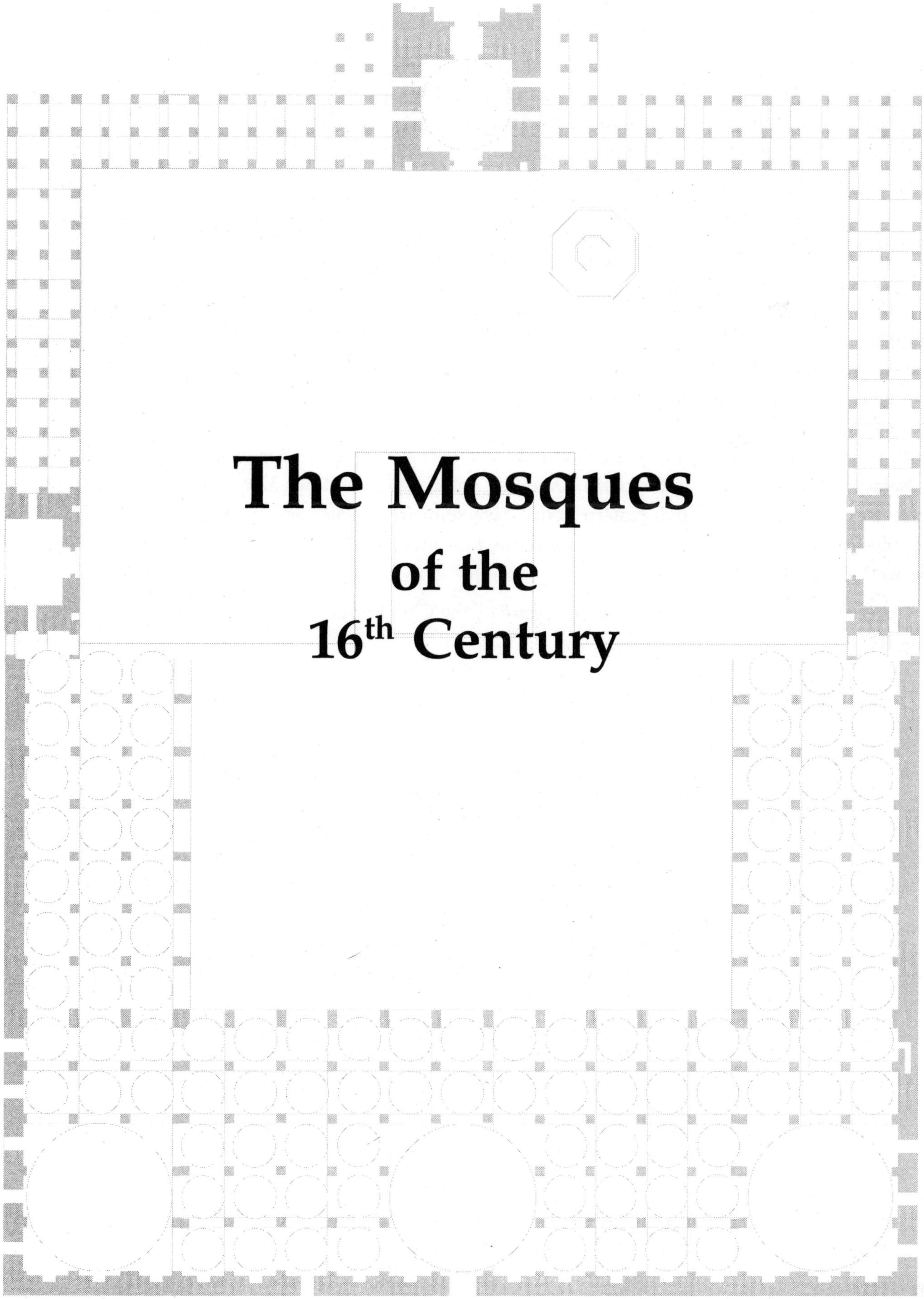

The Mosques
of the
16th Century

Choṭā Sonā Masjid, Gaur (CE 1510)

The Sultanate of Bengal is one of the longest lived sultanates in India — from the Iliyas Shahi Dynasty (see **Appendix D**) beginning in 1282 and through the Taj Karrani ending in 1576 with the take over by the Mughals. The short-lived Hussain-Shahi Dynasty (CE 1493–1538) with its capital at Gaur under the initial leadership of Alauddin Hussain Shah (r. CE 1493–1519) saw the construction of the Choṭā Sonā Masjid. Gaur and Pandua had seen the construction of a number of important monuments. The sixteenth century in Bengal was a period of turmoil and no single dynasty could achieve undeniable mastery or supremacy within the area. Consequently, the monuments reflect this cultural/dynastic malaise, and nothing of the greatness of the past was to be seen in this century.

The Choṭā Sonā Masjid is a typical Beṅgālī structure — thick brick walls, rectangular with the length perpendicular to Mecca, a roof-line reminiscent of the Ekalakhī Tomb,[1] and completely covered (see **Appendix C, Plate 90** [bottom]). Five arched doors allow ingress and egress into the domed interior, the *haram*. They are relatively narrow in comparison to other *masjids* to the west and south of Bengal. The *haram* consists of three ranks of five domes supported by two ranks of four columns each. In the north-west corner is a single bay, surrounded by *jālī*. This is reserved for the women of the court and possesses its own entrance to the north. On either end are *jālī*-windows allowing a sufficient amount of light, particularly with the five eastern doors. Five semicircular *mehrābs* in the *qiblā* are centred on the five files of domes. The central *mehrāb* is indicated on the exterior by a shallow rectilinear extension to the west.

As with most of the Bengal Sultanate's *masjids*, the Choṭā Sonā Masjid is of the **R2** type (see **Figure 4 — R2**).

1 The Ekalakhī Tomb (Thousand Lakh Tomb) was constructed by and for the Sultan Jalau-ud-din Mohammad Shah of the Gaṇeśa-Shāhī Dynasty (r. CE 1419-31).

Plate 33 — Choṭā Sonā Masjid, plan

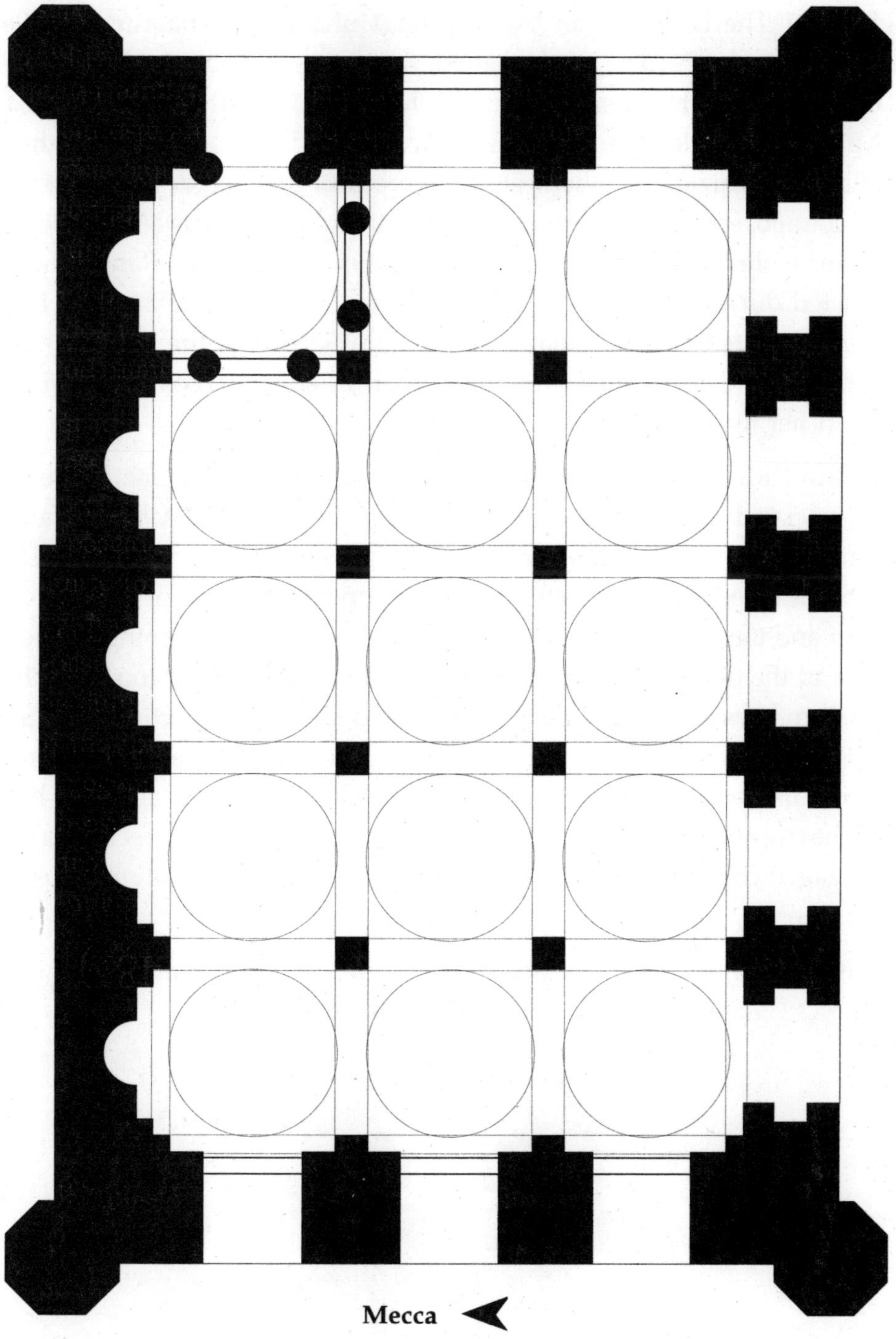

Rānī Siprī Rauza Masjid, Ahmedabad (*c.* CE 1514)

The location of the Gujarat sultanate on the sea provided the rulers with a seemingly unending source of income through trade. The Delhi Sultan 'Ala-ud-din Muhammad Khalji (r. CE 1296–1316) defeated Karṇadeva II Vaghelā (r. CE 1297–1304) of Karṇavatī, thereby establishing Islamic rule in this western region. Gujarat, therefore, became a satellite of Delhi, that is, until Muzaffar (Khan) Shah I (r. CE 1391–1411) (see **Appendix D**) declared independence in 1391 and established the vibrant Gujarat Sultanate. Early within the Muzaffarid Shahi Dynasty a burial practice developed known as the *rauza*. The *rauza* consists of a tomb, sometimes with a *birka* and an obligatory *masjid*. The elements complement each other and may be architecturally connected. The Rānī Siprī (aka *Separi*) Rauza Masjid (see **Appendix B, Plate 72**), constructed during the reign of Sultan Shams-ud-Din Muzaffar Shah II (r. CE 1511–26), is typical of the *masjid* associated with a Gujarat *rauza*. Rānī Siprī was the wife of the famed builder/administrator/general Sultan Nasir-ud-Din Mahmud Shāh I Begharā (r. CE 1459–1511), and her exalted position is reflected in her tomb and attendant mosque.

The Rānī Siprī Rauza Masjids is often referred to as the Masjid-i Nagina (Jewel of a mosque). As with most *masjid*s associated with a mausoleum (*rauza*), it is without a *sahn* or *riwāq*. The Rānī Siprī Rauza Masjid is a narrow rectangle with the long side oriented towards Mecca. The eastern façade consists of six pillars, doubled, front to back, and seven openings. Four of these spaces are narrower than the central space and those of files two and six. These three wider openings indicate the placement of the three *mehrāb*s and the domes. At each corner is a tall, narrow tower, too small to act as a *minaret*. There are six domes, two bays deep over files two, four and six. To the north and to the south there are two windows with *jālī*. The two windows to the south also possess pillared balconies. On either side of the central *mehrāb* are also two windows with *jālī* adding to the bright ambient lighting within the interior. The *mehrāb*s have a special setting in this *masjid*. They are essentially rectilinear, but are bracketed on the outside by engaged columns and also indicate two more engaged columns just to the inside (see **Figure 15**).

It reflects the basic design of a *masjid* associated with a tomb (see **Plate 25**) — of the **R2** type (see **Figure 4 — R2**).

Figure 15 — Plan of the *mehrāb* with engaged columns

Plate 34 — Rani Sipri Rauza Masjid, plan

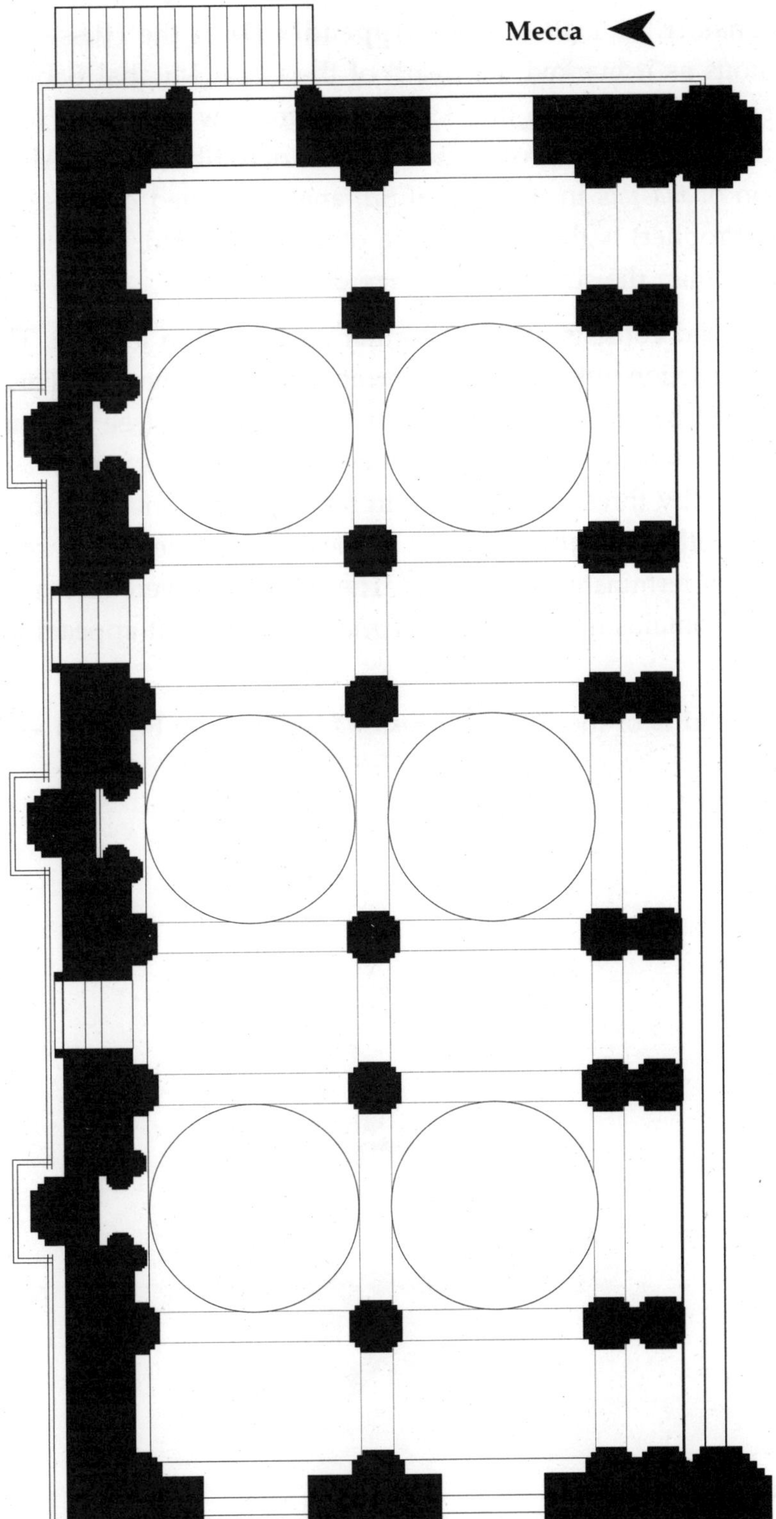

Qadam Rasul Masjid, Gaur (*c.* CE 1530)

Bengal had been going through a series of devastating political upheavals when Sultan Nasib Shah, Nasir-ud-Din Nusrat Shah (r. CE 1519–33) (see **Appendix D**) of the Hussain-Shahi ruled. The year 1530 was also momentous as it marked the death of the Great Mughal Babur and the on-again-off-again ascendancy of Humayun. In 1576 the Beṅgālī Sultanate would cease to exist falling under the yoke of Akbar the Great. Since the construction of the incredible Adina Masjid (see **Plate 13**), the design and construction of *masjids* in the Bengal Sultanate declined dramatically. The Qadam Rasul Masjid (the foot of the Prophet) is the last mosque of any note, and, frankly, a rather disappointing example being little more than the size of an average domicile.

The Qadam Rasul Masjid consists of a rectangular space within a space. The walls are unusually thick, befitting brick construction with the major entrance towards the east. This entrance-way consists of three openings separated by columns, two of which are engaged (see **Appendix C, Plate 91** [top]). To the north and south are two *jālī* windows. An inner room of the same rectangular shape serves as the *haram*. Ingress is gained by three doors — one to the west and one each to the north and south. A shallow *mehrāb* is found within the *qiblā*. At each corner of the outer wall are circular forms, neither towers nor minarets, which terminate at the eaves. The whole is covered by a typical *baṅgāladāra* roof. The Qadam Rasul Masjid contains neither *sahn*, nor *riwāq*, nor *haud*. It appears to be more a *surau* than a *masjid*.

The Qadam Rasul Masjid is of the **R2** type of *masjid* design (see **Figure 4 — R2**).

Plate 35 — Qadam Rasul Masjid, plan

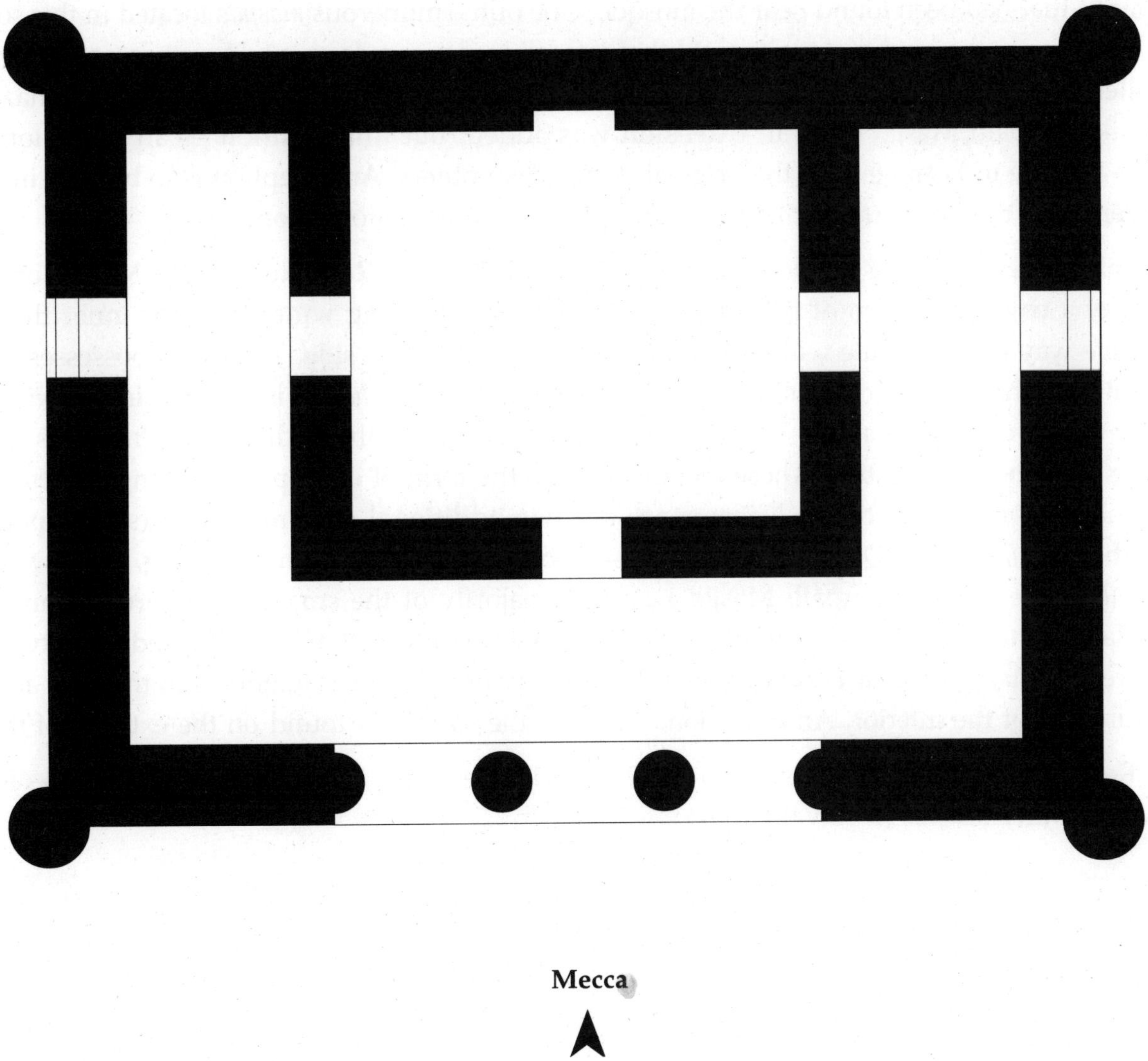

Rettaikulampalli Masjid, Kayalpatnam (*c.* CE 1550)

Rettaikulampalli Masjid is roughly translated as the "mosque with two ponds," referring to the two former tanks that had been found near the mosque. One of the numerous *masjids* located in this southern seaport, it indicates the kind of development that a small mosque underwent. However, as with many of the smaller *masjids*, extensions and additions were added over the years, some rather haphazard. In the Rettaikulampalli Masjid such an extension was added, but this addition — an extension of the portico — is more in keeping with the original design than others. An exception is to be seen in a small room inserted to the northern part of the original portico, now a store room.

Resembling, *en plan*, the Qadiriya Masjid (see **Plate 29**), the Rettaikulampalli Masjid originally consisted of a covered portico of five openings, the outer two being wider than the inner three. This portico gave way to a vestibule with an additional door on its south side. The *haram* possesses a single, central entry to the east which was flanked by two windows. The *haram* is divided into a wide nave-like space and two flanking aisles. This feature is rather unique as the width of the "nave" is achieved by a series of corbelled members. These members are in the form of eight piers, rectangular, *en plan*. To the north and to the south of the *haram* space are two additional entrances each (see **Appendix C, Plate 91** [bottom]). Like the Qadiriya Masjid, these doorways are set within extending, shallow porches. The *mehrāb* of the Rettaikulampalli Masjid is, as the majority of the smaller southern Indian *masjids*, rectangular in shape, but here it exhibits a rounded arch rather than the pointed variety usually encountered in Islamic structures. On either side of the *mehrāb* are small windows in the *qiblā* adding to the illumination of the interior. An extension, denoting the *mehrāb*, is found on the exterior of the *qiblā*.

The Rettaikulampalli Masjid is seen to be of the **R1** type of *masjid* design (see **Figure 4 — R1**) and indicative of other *masjids* in Kayalpatnam.

Plate 36 — Rettaikulampalli Masjid, plan

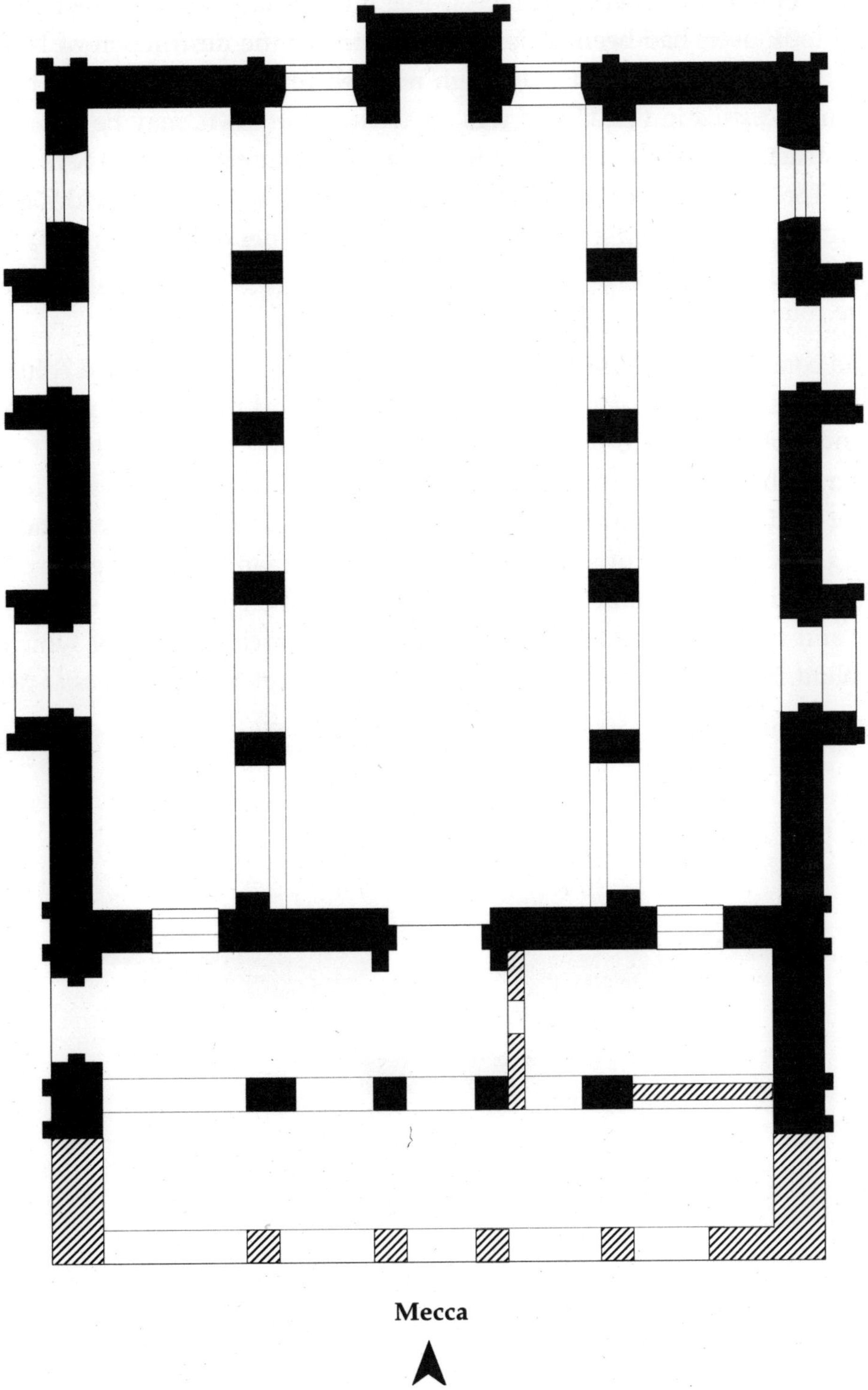

Safa Masjid, Ponda (*c.* CE 1550)

The Safa Masjid of Ponda, also known as Safa Shāhapurī or Safa Shahouri,[1] is in many ways a unique *masjid*. Certainly, one of the most interesting facts is that it is still in existence. The Portuguese Christians of Goa, when they took over, had been zealously dedicated to the destruction of Islamic structures in their enclave. Yet, the Safa Masjid stands, although restored in the nineteenth and twentieth centuries. That it was not a major *masjid* in Ponda and was away from the town, may be the reason for its being spared the total destruction by the Portuguese. Secondly, the uniqueness of the Safa Masjid is due to its plan and environs. The *masjid* proper sets to the north of a large and intricately designed tank, more in keeping with a Hindu temple than an Islamic *masjid* (see **Appendix B, Plate 73**). And, finally, the design of the Safa Masjid is most unusual as it consists of an enclosed space (*haram*) surrounded by a colonnade and the total was roofed, apparently (see **Appendix C, Plate 92**).

The Safa Masjid consists of a portico/porch in the form of four equally spaced columns. A colonnade also surrounds the whole structure, similar to a verandah. A broad flight of stairs mounts from the east, between the columns of the portico to the *haram* which sits atop a high podium. The *haram* has six windows, which may have originally contained *jālīs*. Two of the windows are found flanking the main, eastern door and two each on the north and south sides. The *qiblā* is without windows. The *mehrāb* is large in proportion and of a more intricate design than many others (see **Figure 16**). The *mehrāb*'s exterior extends well beyond the western surface of the *qiblā* and is suitably ornate, *en plan*. Both the exterior and the interior is adorned with numerous arches, some of which hold windows, while others are blind. This produces a plan of exceptional complexity for a *masjid* of this size.

The design of the Safa Masjid is seen to be an **R2** type (see **Figure 4, R2**).

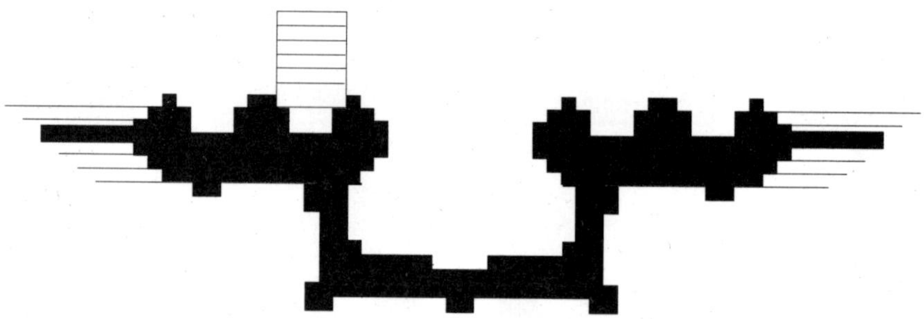

Figure 16 — Plan of the *mehrāb*

1 MS, p. 253.

Plate 37 — Safa Masjid, plan

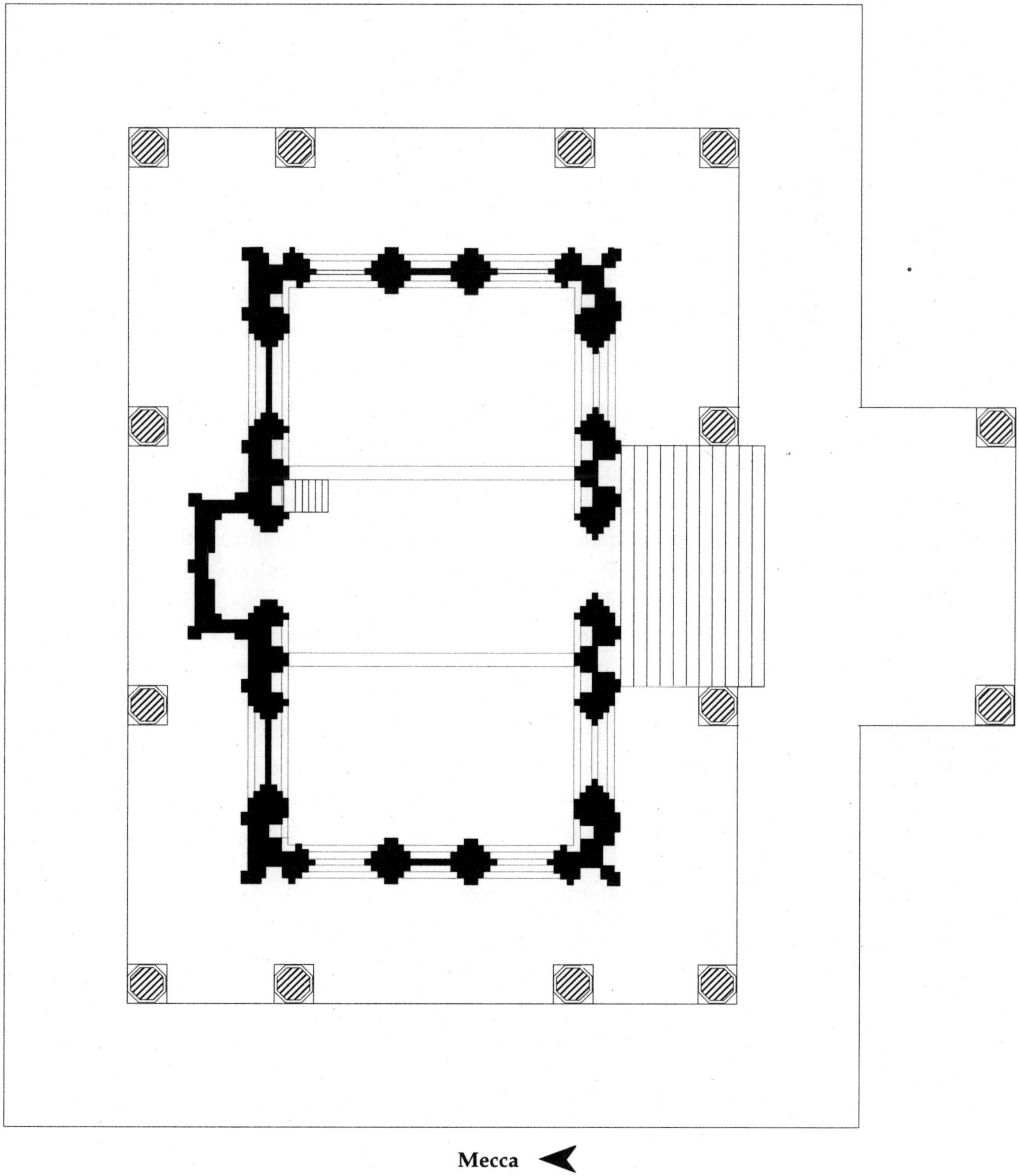

Masjid-i Jami, Bījāpur (*c.* CE 1560)

The Turkic 'Adil Shahi of Bījāpur, though not a particularly long-lived sultanate (CE 1489–1686), (see **Appendix D)** were vibrant, able administrators, extremely productive and raised a number of spectacular monuments of great importance — the Ibrahim Rauza (see **Plate 43**), Gol Gumbaz (see **Plate 44**), the Mehtar Mahal, Water Pavilion (Hammam) at Kumatagi and the various *rauzas* of the nobles. The monuments of Bījāpur were, in many instances, singularly unique in architectural detail, elevation and plan. The term "regional style" has been applied when describing these structures, the basis being the monuments of Delhi, giving them a slightly demeaning, tendentious slant. Yet, the 'Adil Shahi were a rather sophisticated dynasty with more than their share of capable rulers. They — the Qutab Shahi of Golconda, the 'Imad Shahi of Berar and the Nizam Shahi of Ahmednagar — ultimately fell to the vastly superior power of the Imperial Mughals. The incomplete Masjid-i Jami of Bījāpur, when compared to the earlier Karim-ud-Din Masjid of the same city, indicates the heights to which Bījāpur architecture climbed. Begun during the reign of Ali 'Adil Shah I (r. CE 1557–80) (see **Appendix D**) and never completely finished, the Masjid-i Jami, nonetheless, stands at the acme of Bījāpur architecture.

The eastern façade was never completed and a terrace of some 95 ft with a monumental *darwāẓā* was added by Augranzeb as well as the *musalla* divisions (see **Appendix B, Plate 77**). This addition, too, was left incomplete. Nonetheless, that which is intact and finished provides enough information to suggest that Bījāpur's Masjid-i Jami is, indeed, one of the great *masjid*s of India. A square *sahn* with a rectangular, stepped *haud* and major entrance to the north and south dominates the eastern aspect of the *masjid*. A single-aisled, domed *riwāq* to the north and south hints at its non-existent counterpart to the east. Neither a developed or simple *haram*-screen announces the sanctuary. On the other hand, a rank of seven elegant arches covered by a deep *chajjā* invites one into the interior. The *haram* consists of a rank of nine bays north to south and a file of five bays. Centred in the *haram* is a dome consisting of nine bays. It has been noted that this dome is somewhat unusual for Bījāpur as it is hemispherical in form (see **Appendix B, Plate 83**) rather than the "Saracenic"[1] dome that is often associated with this sultanate. The *qiblā* consists of arched recesses, mimicking the bays and the same feature is seen on the north and south inner walls of the *masjid*. The *mehrāb* of the Masjid-i Jami is substantial in dimension and octagonal, *en plan*. An elaborate extension on the exterior of the *qiblā* indicates the placement of the *mehrāb*. One additional feature of the Masjid-i Jami which makes it unique amongst the *masjid*s of the Indian subcontinent is to be found in the treatment of the north, south and western exterior walls. Rather than a plain, unadorned surface that is encountered in many *masjid*s, the walls here are treated with a blind arcade on the lower level and an arched clerestory on the second storey. What is of interest, however, is that this blind arcade does not correspond with the internal bays (see **Appendix B, Plate 77**). In both cases the exterior blind arches are one short of twice the number of bays — e.g. the *qiblā*: 17:9, and the north and south walls: 23:12.

The Masjid-i Jami of Bījāpur conforms to the **RSc** type of design (see **Figure 4 — RSc**).

1 HC, p. 58.

Plate 38 — Masjid-i Jami, plan

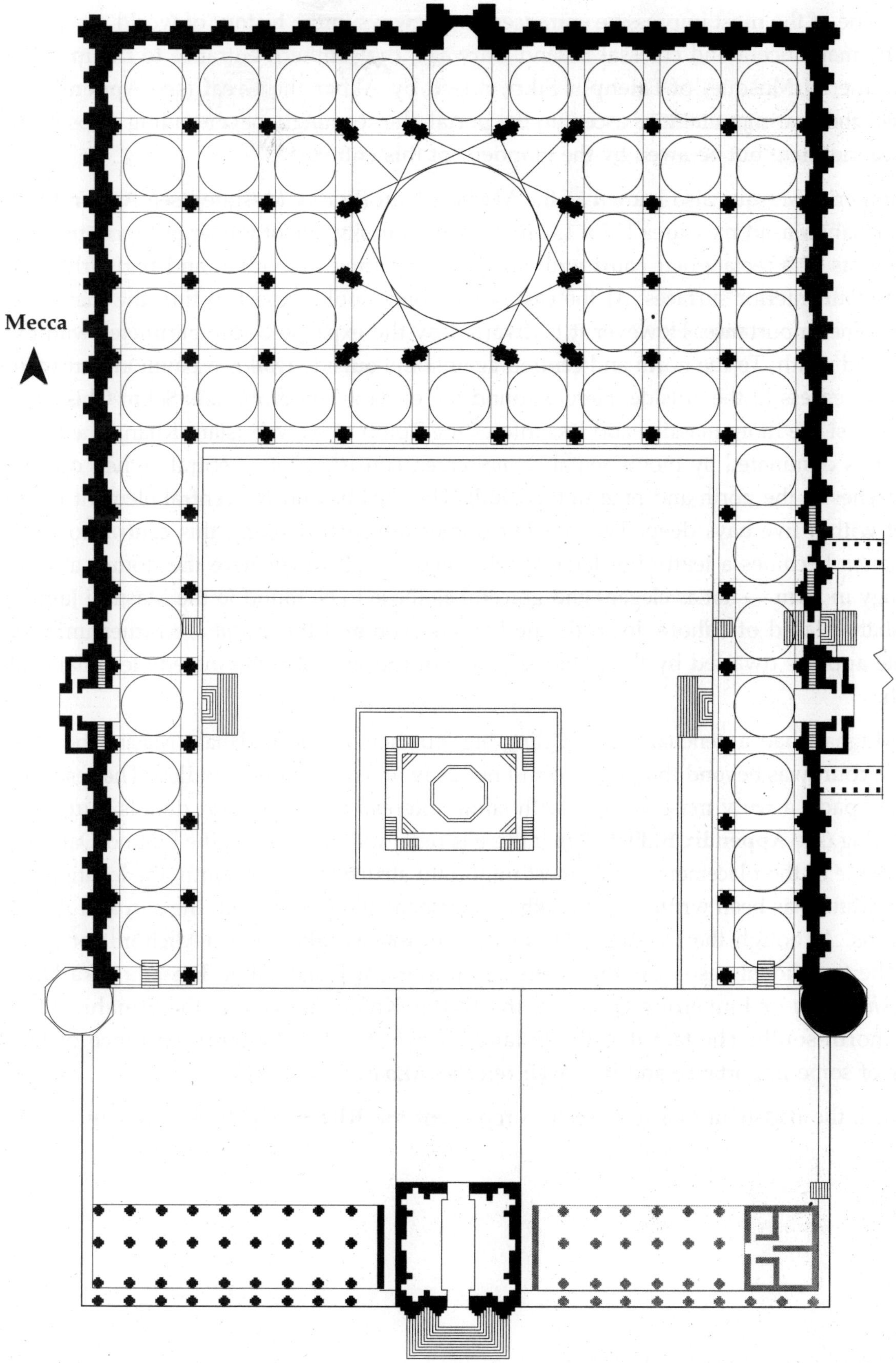

Bādshāhī Masjid, Fatehpur Sikri (*c.* CE 1568)

Certainly, one of the most impressive entrances or gateways in the history of world architecture is to be seen in the magnificent and colossal Buland Darwāẓā, the southern entrance to the massive Bādshāhī Masjid (Imperial Mosque) of Fatehpur Sikri, raised by Akbar the Great (see **Appendix D**). As one approaches the near mountainous ascent to the portal, the seemingly never-ending steps move upwards and one cannot help but be awed by the grandeur of this entrance.

The Imperial Mosque also known as the Masjid-i Jami (Friday Mosque) (see **Appendix B, Plate 81**) or the Bādshāhī Masjid measures 157 × 132 m, making it easily one of the largest mosques in India.[1] The *masjid* consists of a rectangular court with an arcade fronting individual and regularly spaced spaces around its four interior surfaces. At the east, where one would expect to find the main entrance, is a portal of some importance. However it is dwarfed by the expanse of the perimeter wall extending to the north and south. To the north and centred against the outside wall is a pavilion, but with no means of ingress or egress to the outside. Here is found the elegant Tomb of Sheik Selim Chistee, to the west and to the east the more massive and less interesting Tomb of Nawab Islam Khan. The western border of the *sahn* is dominated by monumental *haram*-screen consisting of a central arched opening, flanked by nine arches to the north and nine to the south. The area behind the central element is covered by a dome set within five bays deep. Two smaller domes are seen flanking this central form. This triple-domed *haram* becomes a feature of later Mughal *masjids*. However here the domes are massive and rather stogy in form — not as elegant and graceful as those to be found in the Masjid-i Jami of Delhi or the Bādshāhī Masjid of Lahore. In truth, the *haram*-screen and the *haram* are rather uninteresting and their scale appears dwarfed by the immense space of the *sahn* and the incredible Buland Darwāẓā to the south.

The Mughals had a penchant for building big, but here in the Bādshāhī Masjid the sheer size, the area of the court was beyond that which could be easily or satisfactorily handled. The resulting structure was a big space, a truly massive area with some interesting, even great details, but, *in toto*, rather disappointing (see **Appendix B, Plate 79**). If there is redemption — it is in the Buland Darwāẓā. Mention must be made of the placement of this most important structure — the south, the location of the sun at its zenith. Much has been written about Akbar's personal association with the sun and its iconographic implications. Although the Dīwān-ī-Ām and Dīwān-ī-Khās (aka Ankh-ī-Michoni) of Fatehpur Sikri were in the traditional east-west alignment, the important Ekastambha Prāsāda (aka Dīwān-ī-Khās) and the *khwābgāh* or Emperor's Quarters, the Daftar Khānā as well as the Sunahra Makan are all oriented north-south. The fact that the Buland. Darwāẓā is the southern entrance of the Bādshāhī Masjid is of some importance and may well refer to Akbar.

As such, the Bādshāhī Masjid is seen to represent the **RRc** type of *masjid* design (see **Figure 4 — RRc**).

1 The Masjid-i Jami of Delhi is but 99 m sq.

Plate 39 — Badshahi Masjid, plan

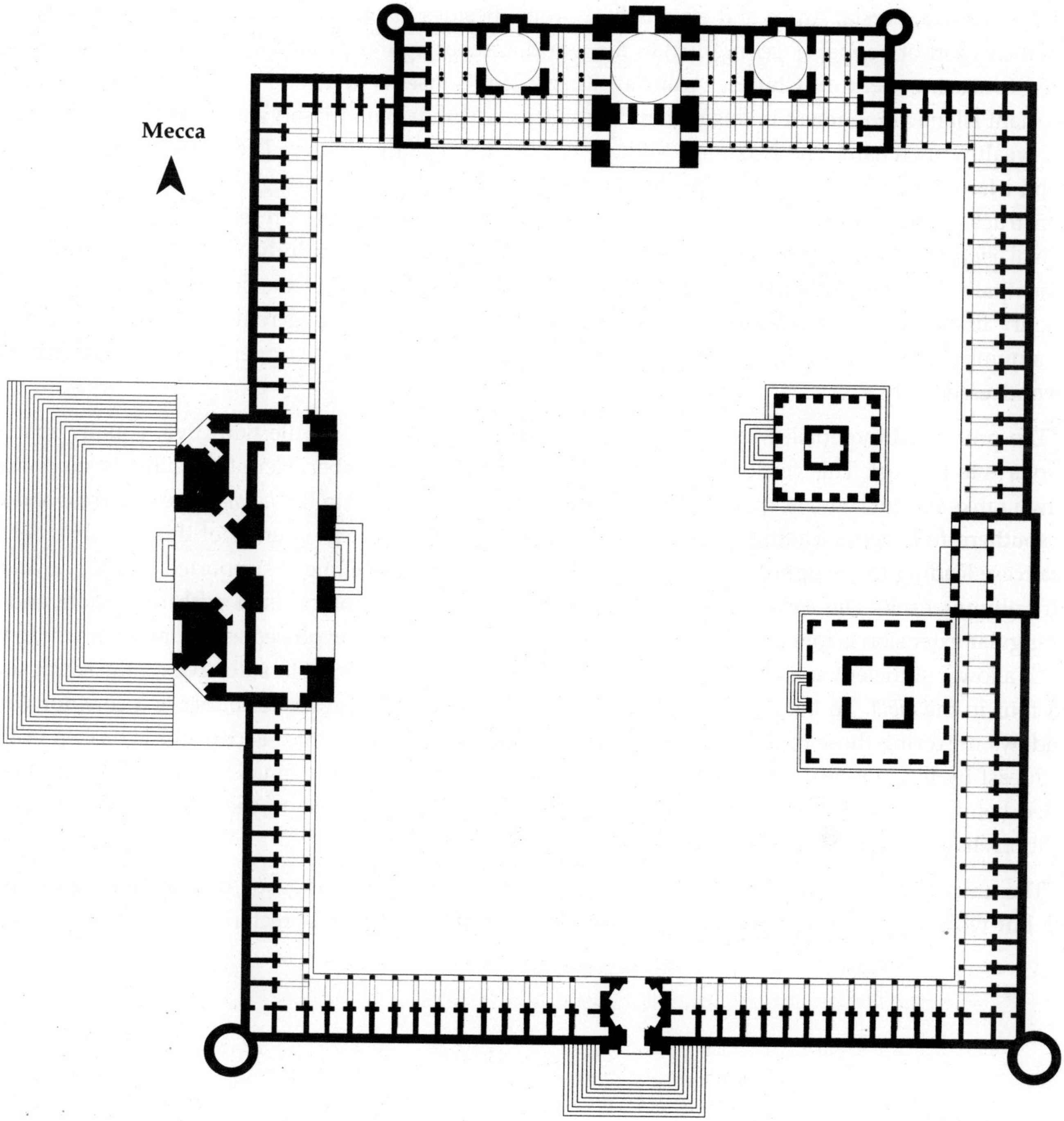

Mithqalpalli Masjid, Calicut (*c.* CE 1578)

Calicut was one of the most important ports along the Malabar Coast and, indeed, one of the most famous of the Indian Ocean. For centuries it was the terminus for trade goods from China, South-East Asia, the Arabia, Persia, Africa and eventually Europe. Besides external trade, much of its wealth came from the export of pepper (*Piper negrum*) to the world. Calicut figures prominently in the voyages of the famed fourteenth-century Chinese Admiral, Zheng He. Consequently, one would expect to find an important Islamic monument in this region. The spacious Mithqalpalli Masjid was originally constructed by a wealthy merchant, one Nakhuda Mithqal,[1] in the fourteenth century. Then it was known as the Masjid-i Jami. Later it was systematically torched by the overzealous Portuguese in CE 1510 and then reconstructed over a half century later — *c.* CE 1578. It is thought that the present *masjid* represents the original, *en plan*.[2] As such, it is one of the larger *masjids* raised in southern India in this early period. The Mithqalpalli Masjid is rather typical of the type of construction found in the south-west of India — a masonry first floor surmounted by a multi-levelled, rather steep, recessing roofs with deep overhangs and a number of storeys of decreasing size (see **Appendix C, Plate 93**). The upper stories are constructed of wood, essentially.

The present Mithqalpalli Masjid consists of a narrow entrance vestibule with five, equally spaced doorways to the east. This vestibule, in turn, leads to a large antechamber. Here the ceiling is supported by two ranks of four, widely spaced columns each. Four doors lead into the *haram*. These correspond to the southern four doors leading from the vestibule. In the north-western counter of this antechamber is a staircase leading to the upper storeys. The *haram* is square and its ceiling is supported by four ranks of four columns each. The *mehrāb*, semicircular, *en plan*, is small in comparison with the whole and a rectangular extension is found on the western side of the *qiblā*. The *haram* possesses a number of windows which allow a sufficient amount of light into the interior — five on the north side, five on the south side and four in the *qiblā*. To the north, south and east of the sanctuary and antechamber is a corridor with windows mirroring those of the *haram* and antechamber. The symmetry of this corridor is broken in the north-east by the modern addition of an ablution chamber. In addition a small storage room has been added behind the *mehrāb* in this surrounding corridor with an entrance to the south. Other modern additions have been made to the east.

The unique Mithqalpalli Masjid is seen to represent the **R1** type of mosque design (see **Figure 4 — R1**), but with the variation that the *haram* is square and the anteroom is rectangular.

1 MS, p, 154.

2 Ibid.

Plate 40 — Mithqalpalli Masjid, plan

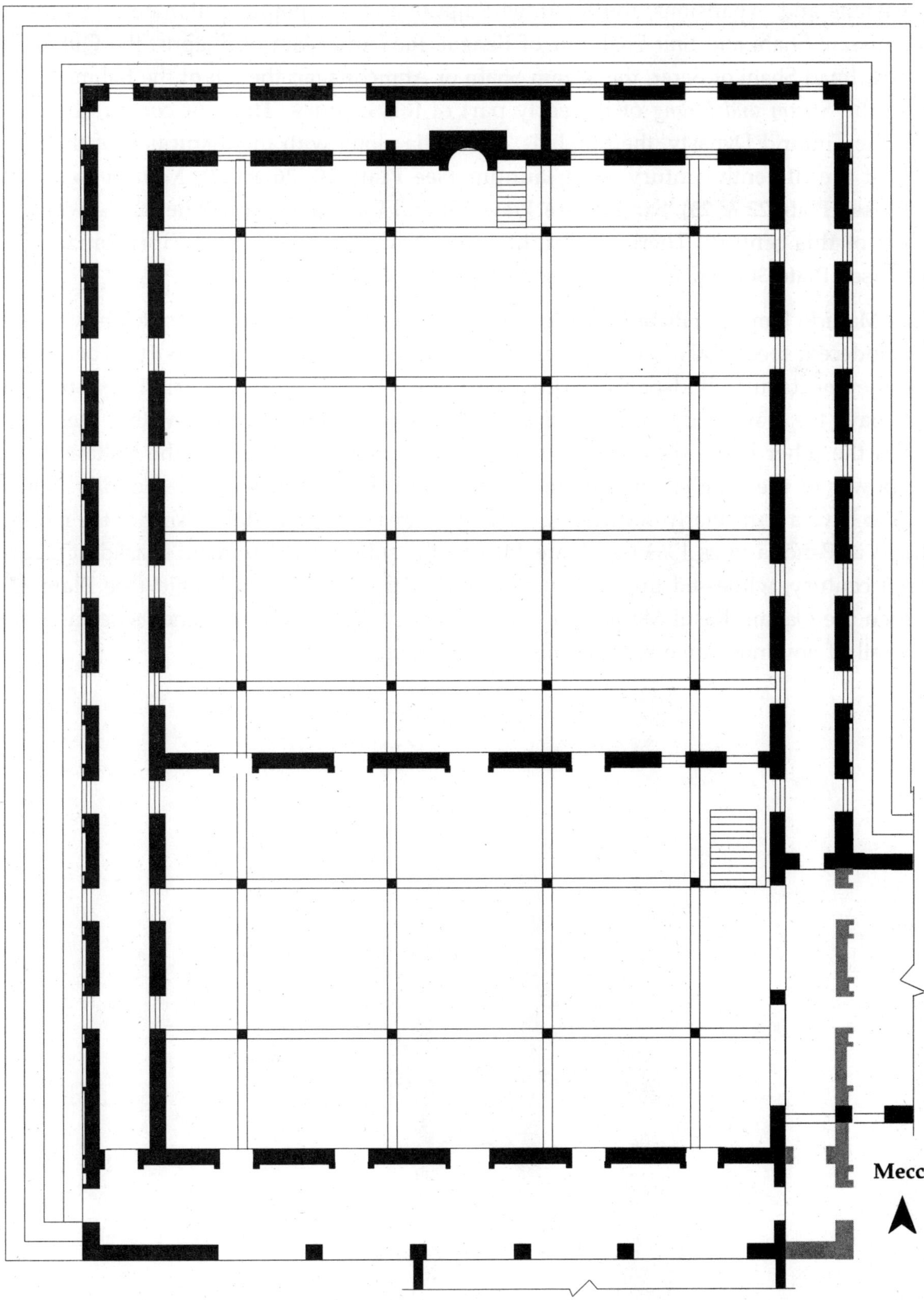

Sixteenth Century

The first half of the sixteenth century was a time of general turmoil throughout India. Numerous Islamic invasions and expansions, the fractious Rajputs and competing sultanates — the Lodi's of Delhi, the Hussain-Shahi and Shir Shah Sur of Bengal, the 'Adil Shah of Bījāpur, the Qutab Shahi of Golconda, the 'Imad Shahi of Berar, the Nizam Shahi of Ahmednagar, the fall of the Bahmanī Sultanate — added to the *Strum und Drang* of the early part of this century. Then, of course, there was the insertion of the Timurid Dynasty, the Mughals, into India along with the disruption of the Suris. The florescence of the fifteenth century — at Jaunpur (see **Plate 20, 26 & 27**), Mandu (see **Plate 28**), Ahmedabad (see **Plate 22 & 23**), Sarkhej (see **Plate 30**) and Campāner (see **Plate 32**) — was muted in the first half of this century. There are bright spots, however — the Rānī Siprī Rauza Masjid of Ahmedabad (see **Plate 30**) and the Safa Masjid of Ponda (see **Plate 37**).

Bījāpur's Masjid-i Jami (see **Plate 38**) begins the brilliance of this vibrant, but not long-lived sultanate. With almost indecent speed and incandescent greatness, Akbar the Great (r. CE 1556–1605) begins building and raises the spectacular Bādshāhī Masjid (see **Plate 39**) at Fatehpur Sikri. These two seminal monuments pave the way for the spectacular achievements of the next century within their respective domains. On the other hand, the constant warring and expansion between the Sultans before the coalescing power of the Mughals had its inevitable effect. In the north-east, especially Bengal, this turmoil was to have a particularly devastating effect. The area which saw the raising of the monumental Adina Masjid at Pandua in CE 1364 (see **Plate 13**) and the substantial Gunmani Masjid at Gaur of the late fifteenth century, witnessed the construction of first the Choṭā Sonā Masjid (see **Plate 33**) in CE 1510 and then the Qadam Rasul Masjid (see **Plate 35**) in CE 1530. Both monuments seemed to sound the death knell of any innovative brick architecture in Bengal.

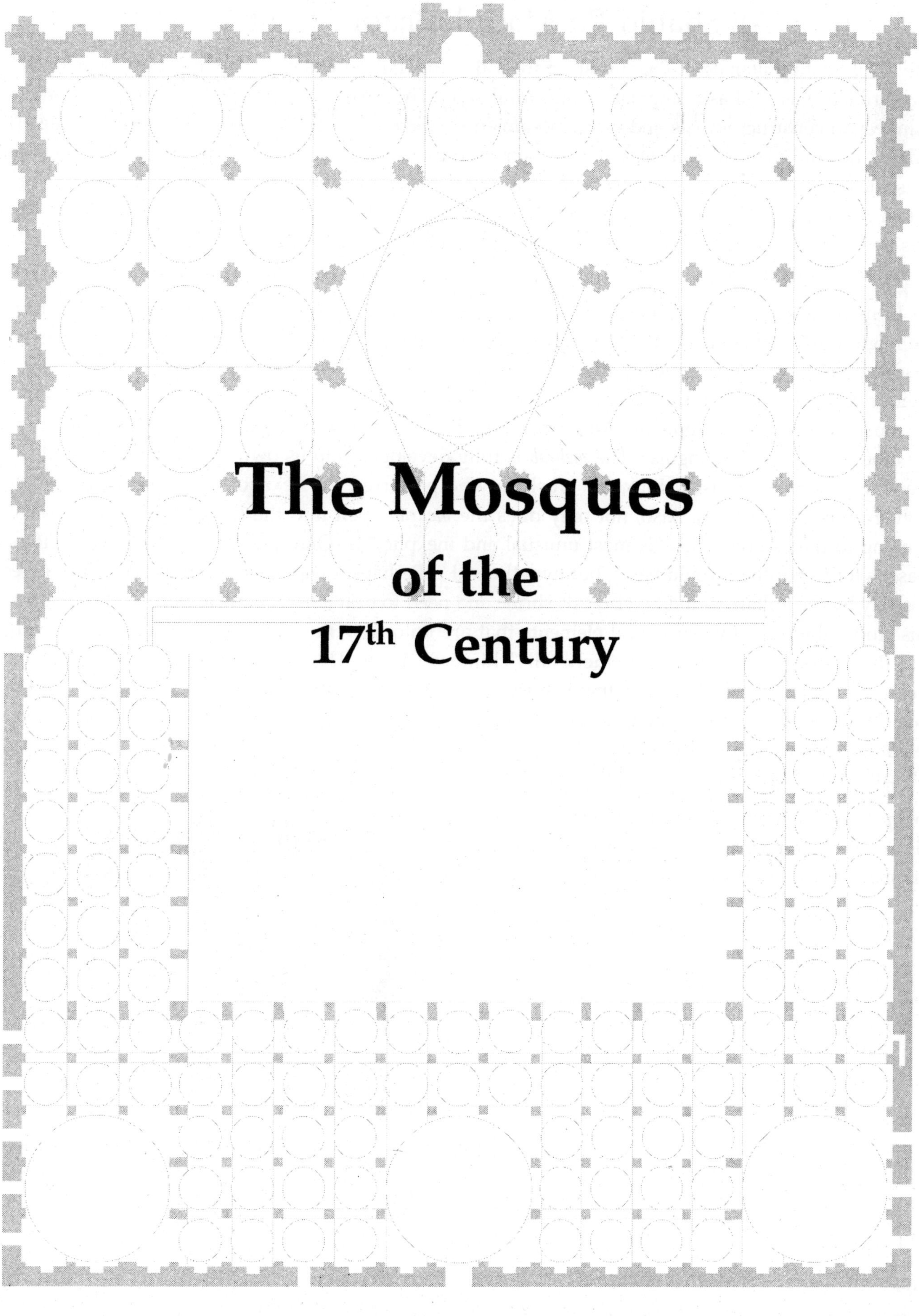

The Mosques of the 17th Century

Ali Shahid Pir Masjid, Bījāpur (*c.* CE 1600)

The 'Adil Shahi Sultanate of Bījāpur, apart from the Imperial centres of Delhi and Agra, developed its own brilliance as well as a singular architectural style. The wealth of this sultanate allowed numerous grandees to construct *masjids* and other monuments which added to the lustre of this small state. The Sultans not only constructed *masjids* for their own pleasure within the royal compound, they also constructed *masjids* in commemoration of important personages and/or events throughout the area. Sultan Ali I (r. CE 1557–80) (see **Appendix D**) caused the Ali Shahid Pir Masjid to be built. This mosque was dedicated to a local holy man, Hazrat Sayyid 'Ali Shahid Pir who was "martyred" (Arabic: *shahid*) in the area of Raylan.

In many ways the Ali Shahid Pir Masjid is rather typical of mosques found in Bījāpur built during the reign of the 'Adil Shahis. It is relatively compact, without a well-defined *sahn* or *riwāq*, three evenly spaced arched openings opposite the *qiblā* (see **Appendix C, Plate 94**), and an intricately designed interior. On the other hand, there are elements which make this *masjid* unique. Unlike the majority of the smaller *masjids* of Bījāpur, the Ali Shahid Pir Masjid is essentially square, *en plan*, where many of the other *masjids* are rectangular. The *mehrāb* is fully developed into its own space that is derived from a nonagon, a most unusual form for Muslims who preferred the hexagon or the octagon for their iconographic connections. Also, not only does the *mehrāb* open into the *haram*, it also has a second opening to the exterior. This "is most unusual and inexplicable. One might suggest a dozen different reasons for it, but they would be . . . but hypothetical."[1] Perhaps it was used as a means of quick egress, possibly by the Sultan should he visit this shrine and need to beat a hasty retreat. Beyond the concern of this study, there are two structural elements that are unique — the *haram* is covered by barrel vaults and the *mehrāb* possesses an extremely tall "chimney" vault. The three openings opposite the *qiblā* create a tripartite division, *en plan*, that is mirrored by a second tripartite division perpendicular to this axis. This establishes an implied internal division of nine areas (see **Figure 17**). This may be seen as relating to the nonagon of the *mehrāb*.

The unique Ali Shahid Pir Masjid is seen to represent the **S** type of mosque design (see **Figure 4 — S**), particularly as it applies to the main block, minus the *mehrāb*.

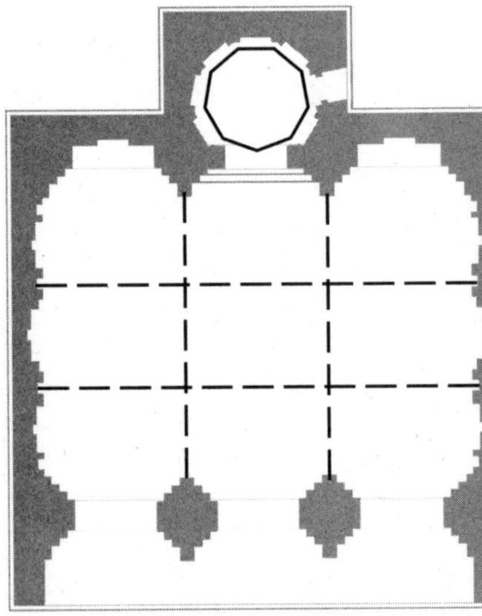

Figure 17 — Indicating the ninefold division & nonagon

1 HC, p, 62.

Plate 41 — Ali Shahid Pir Masjid, plan

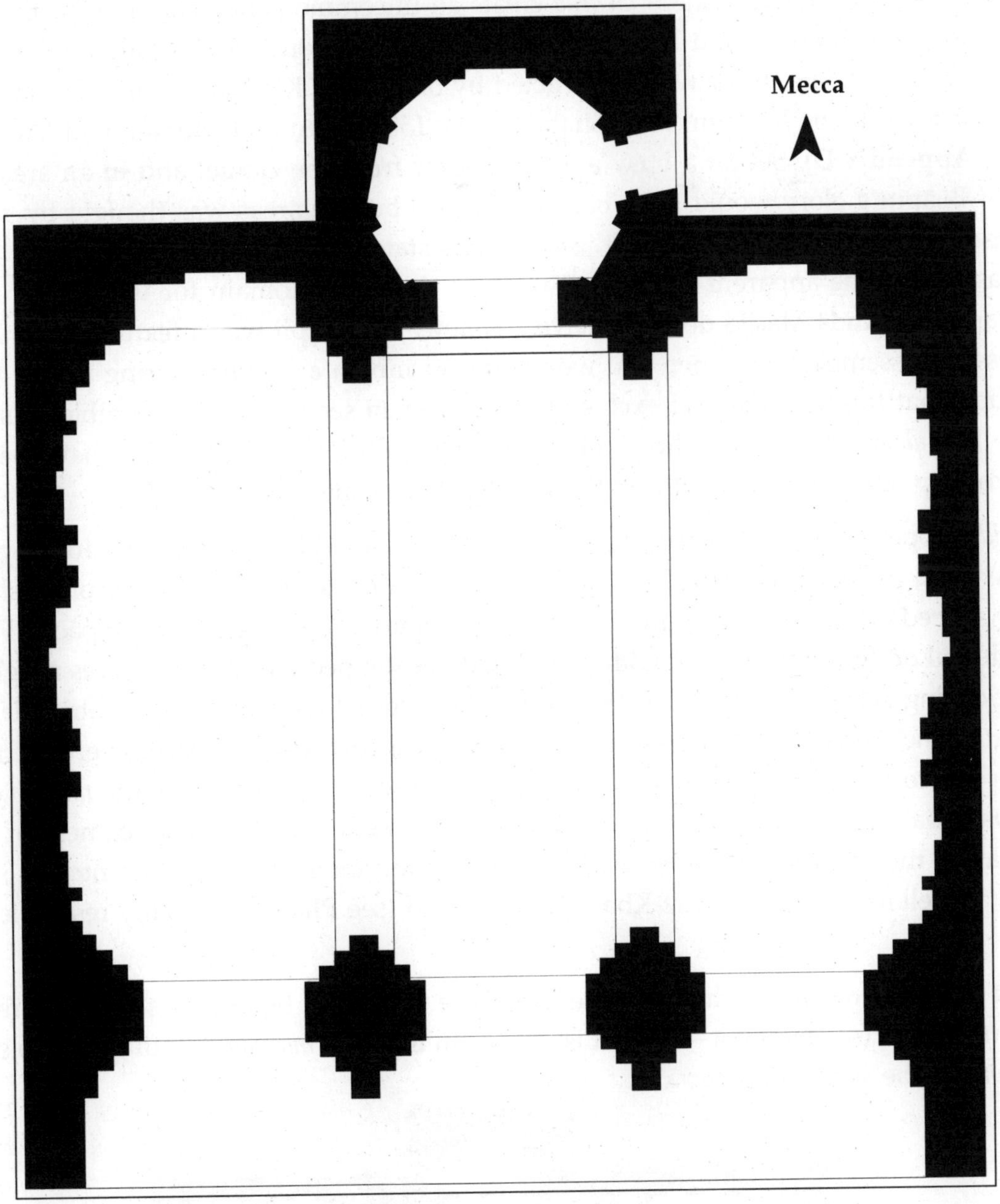

Aṇḍā Masjid, Bījāpur (CE 1608)

The frequently unique character of many of the Bījāpur *masjids* is mirrored in the Aṇḍā Masjid. Neither its rectilinear design, nor the prominent *mehrāb* create an uncommon character, but for the fact that the Aṇḍā Masjid does not sit on ground level, but is found on the second storey with a hall on the ground floor (see **Appendix C, Plate 95**). It was constructed by one I'tibar Khan in CE 1608, an important noble in the courts of the Sultans Ibrahim 'Adil Shah II (r. CE 1580–1626) and Muhammad 'Adil Shah (r. CE 1626–56) (see **Appendix D**). Set on a busy avenue not far from the citadel and in an area that during the apogee of Bījāpur's glory would have been one of the busiest areas was thought by some to have been the reason for its curious design. But, as Cousens states[1] the undoubted reason for this *masjid*'s elevation was due to the apparent fact that it was the exclusive domain for women. This he asserts partially because the Aṇḍā Masjid does not have a *minbar*. The pulpit was a feature by which the *imām* might address the assembled, and men and women never mix in a mosque during prayer time. Hence, the supposition that this was a *masjid* exclusively for women seems quite acceptable. Also the raised status of the *masjid* and the commodious, elevated and walled forecourt would have been ideal for women to worship and commune without the prying eyes of men.

The *masjid*, proper, consists of a rectangular *haram* with the width being approximately three times the depth. As with many of the *masjids* of Bījāpur the entrance to the *haram* is accomplished through three equally spaced arches. This then divided the interior into three roughly equal spaces. Furthermore, due to the internal design of the *masjid*, with niches that are stepped back, these spaces roughly conform to three interlocking octagons (see **Figure 18**). Unlike the external wall of the Ali Shahid Pir Masjid (see **Plate 41**), that of the Aṇḍā Masjid is broken by a series of narrow, evenly spaced, vertical ribs, creating a pleasing aspect from the exterior. As with many of the mosques of this region, the *mehrāb* of the Aṇḍā Masjid is substantial. Its exterior is rectilinear, whereas the interior consists of a segment of an octagon, thereby repeating the octagons of the *haram*. Only of passing interest is that the internal space of the Aṇḍā Masjid as well as the Shah Navaz Khan Rauza Masjid (see **Plate 53**) roughly resemble the outline of a crown.

The Aṇḍā Masjid dedicated to the exclusive use of the women of Bījāpur, is seen to represent the **R2** type of mosque design (see **Figure 4 — R2**). It is unique in that few *masjids* of India are two storeys high with the *haram* on the second storey.

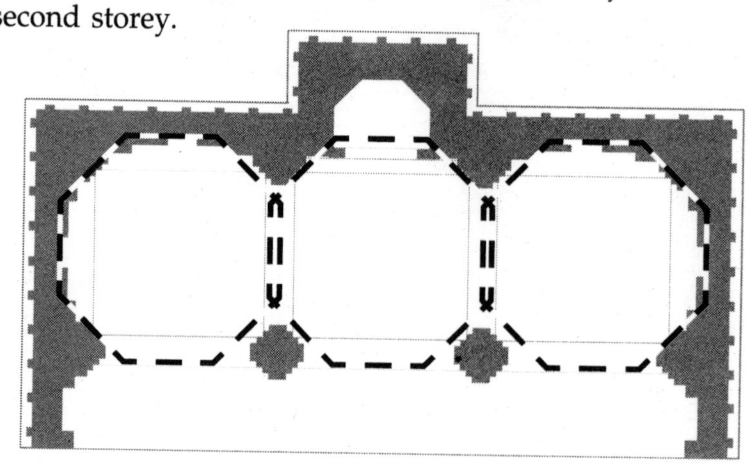

Figure 18 — Indicating overlapping octagons

1 HC, p, 78.

Plate 42 — Aṇḍā Masjid, plan

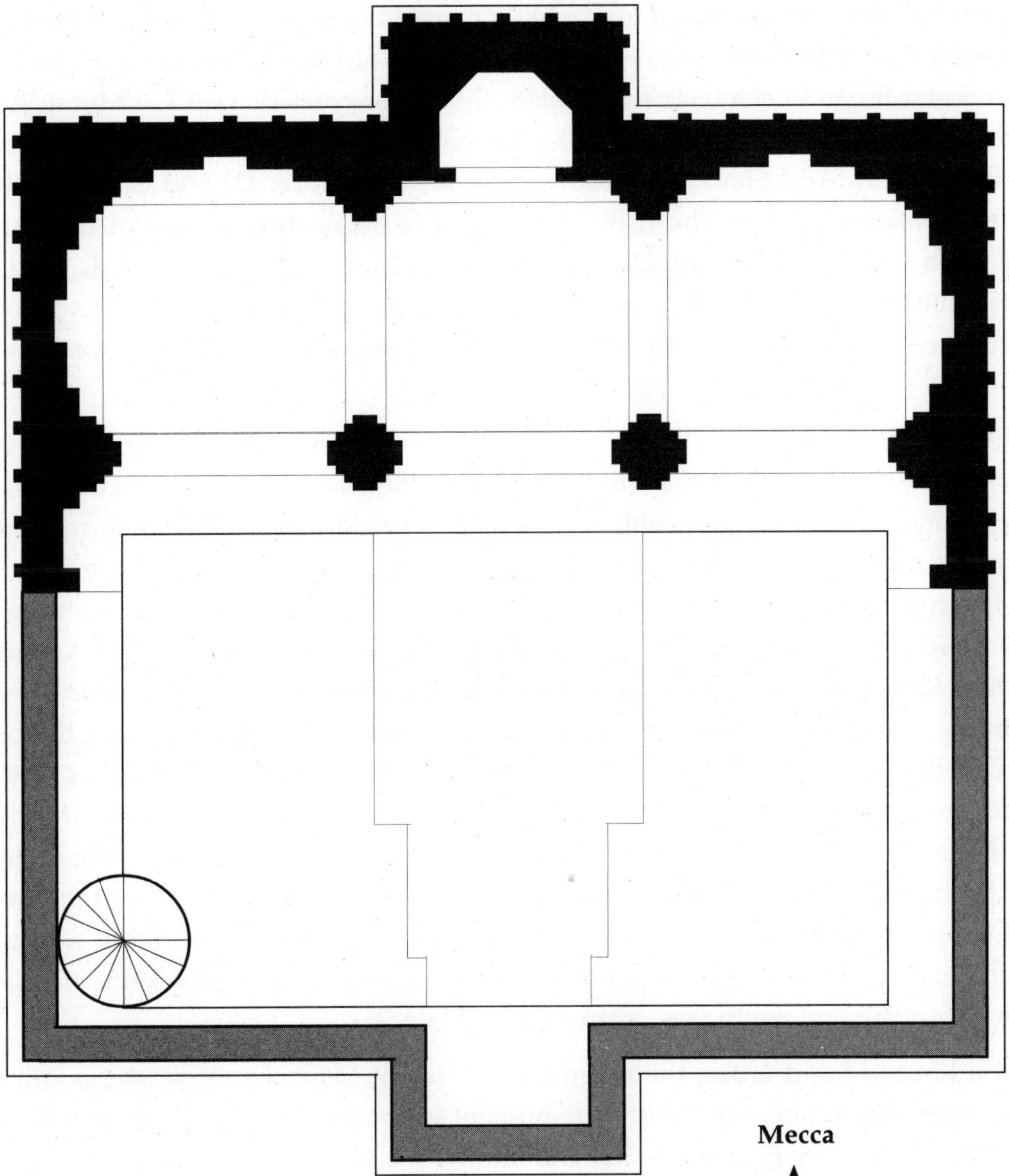

Ibrahim Rauza Masjid, Bījāpur (*c.* CE 1615)

A Turkic prince and brother of the Ottoman Sultan Mehmet II (r. CE 1451–81), established the brilliant 'Adil Shahi Sultanate in Bījāpur. On the death of his father, the Ottoman Sultan Murat II (r. CE 1421–51), Yusuf al Murat had been spirited away from the fratricidal court of the Ottomans by his mother and ultimately found his way to Bīdar. There he was accepted into the Bahmanī Court as a retainer and grandee, and his star began to climb. The displaced prince was created: Yusuf al Murat 'Adil Khan and made governor of Bījāpur. With the decline of the Bahmanī Sultanate, Yusuf declared independence and took the name of Yusuf 'Adil Shah (r. CE 1489–1512) (see **Appendix D**) and established the brilliant 'Adil Shahi Sultanate in Bījāpur. The fifth 'Adil Shahi to sit on the *masnad* of Bījāpur was Sultan Ibrahim 'Adil Shah II (r. CE 1580–1626). He was the son of the brother of Sultan Ali 'Adil Shah I (r. CE 1557–80), one Tahmasp 'Adil Shah. Ibrahim rose to unparalleled brilliance, but not without numerous attempts to displace him. Midway in his long reign he began construction of his tomb — the Ibrahim Rauza.

The Ibrahim Rauza followed an established pattern — a generally square mausoleum facing a rectangular *masjid* (see **Appendix B, Plate 75**). As was the norm, the mausoleum was larger, and frequently its decorations were considerably more lavish. Here, the proportional norm is exhibited. Yet, in the Ibrahim Rauza Masjid the façade is generally duplicated in the mausoleum, except, in the latter, the dome is in proportion considerably increased and there are seven arched openings of varying widths, while there are only five equal width arches across the *masjid's* façade (see **Appendix C, Plate 96**). The Ibrahim Rauza Masjid is three bays deep and the width of one bay extends westward. The *haram* is relatively spacious and there are eight equally spaced columns supporting the upper terrace. As with many of the Bījāpur *masjids*, the *mehrāb* is not contained within the thickness of the *qiblā* wall, but extends beyond, creating its own viable space, *en plan*. As with the Ali Shahid Pir Masjid, here the *mehrāb* is of a nonagon design with niches in each of the exposed sides. Centred in the easternmost bays are openings to the exterior with balconies. Of these two, and embedded within the thickness of the northern and southern walls are stairways to a roof terrace. The whole ensemble — the mausoleum and the accompanying *masjid* — rests upon an elevated terrace (see **Figure 19**) which is reached by broad stairs to the north and south (see **Appendix B, Plate 75**).

The *I*brahim Rauza Masjid facing the magnificent Ibrahim Mausoleum, *in toto*, is considered to be one, if not, the most important architectural monument in Bījāpur. Further, it is seen to represent the **R2** type of mosque design (see **Figure 4 — R2**) and follows the pattern for this brilliant, though relatively short-lived, sultanate.

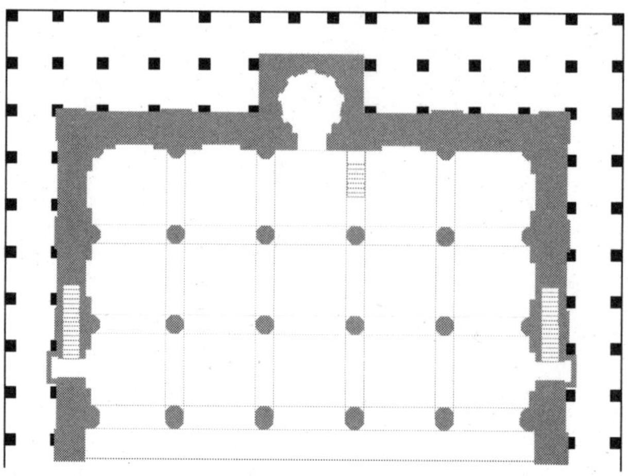

Figure 19 — Indicating the placement of the piers supporting the terrace

Plate 43 — Ibrahim Rauza Masjid, plan

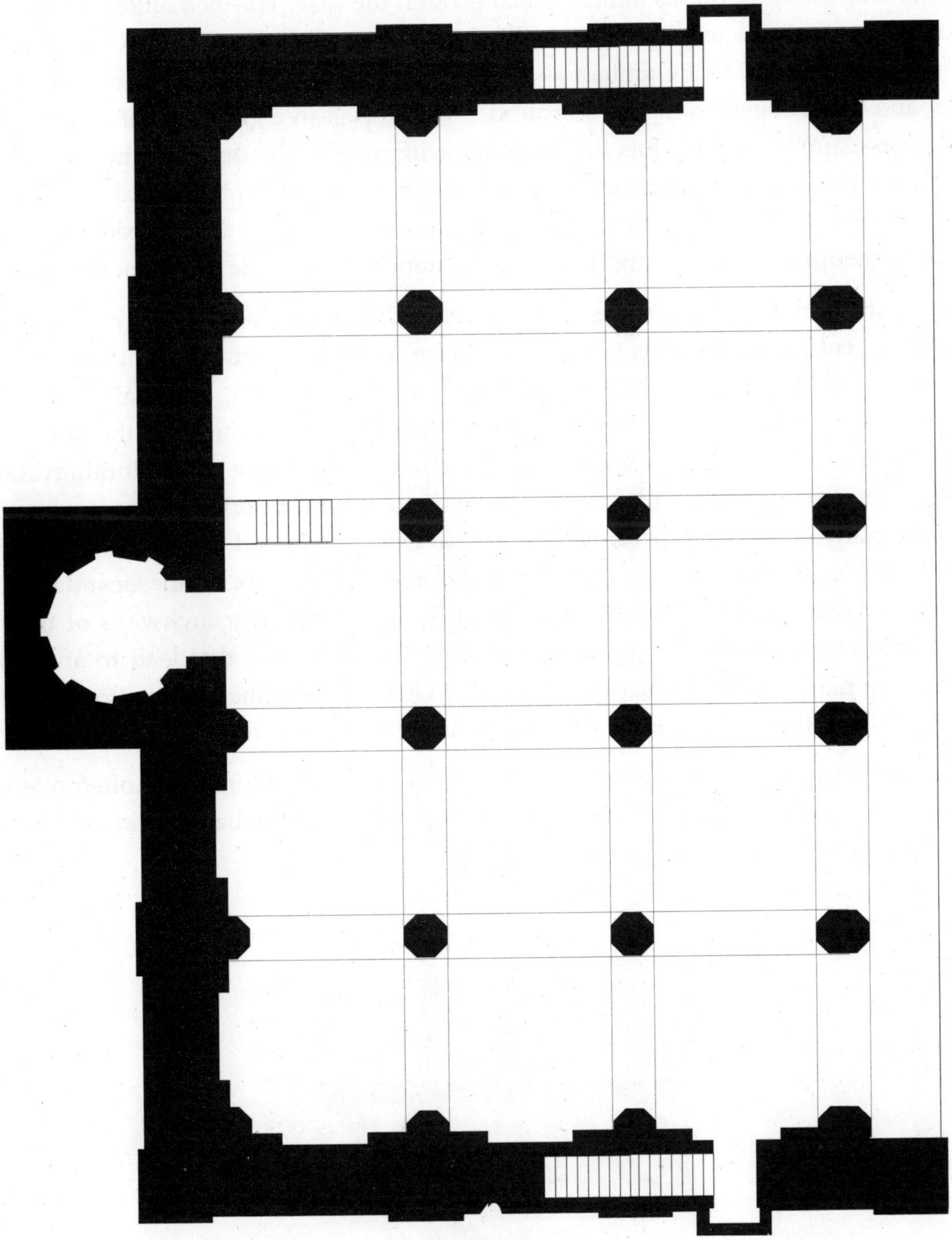

Mecca ◀

Gol Gumbaz Masjid, Bījāpur (*c.* CE 1626)

The son of Ibrahim 'Adil Shah II (r. CE 1580–1626), Sultan Muhammad 'Adil Shah (r. CE 1626–56) (see **Appendix D**) attempted to outdo his father, which is often the case. This is manifest in the construction and design of his own mausoleum. Whereas the Ibrahim Rauza was refined and elegant, the mausoleum of Sultan Muhammad — the Gol Gumbaz — was daring and monumental in scale. It dominates its surroundings and can be seen from miles around. "The impressive grandeur of the building and its imponderable mass simply overwhelms the spectator with awe."[1] The dome of the Gol Gumbaz is the largest in Asia and it covers the largest unimpeded area of any dome in the world — over 18,000 sq ft. However, the *masjid* of this *rauza* literally pales in size and significance.[2] It is considerably smaller than the massive mausoleum in elevation and plan (see **Appendix B — Plate 76**; **Appendix C — Plate 97**).

Set to the west of the mausoleum, the Gol Gumbaz Masjid is approached by a flight of stairs as wide as the monument itself and leads to a broad terrace. From this terrace, five arched openings lead into the *haram*. The northern two archways and the southern two are of equal width. The central opening is wider. Above these arches is a wide, well proportioned cornice. At the north-eastern and south-eastern corners are tall elegant spires or *minarets* recalling those of the Ibrahim Rauza. Three bays deep, the interior is punctuated by twelve pillars and a hemispherical dome crowns the central, square bay. Like many of the Bījāpur *masjid*, the *mehrāb* extends beyond the *qiblā* in a rectilinear plan. Unlike the Ibrahim Rauza, this *mehrāb*'s interior is heptagonal, *en plan*. Four secondary *mehrābs* are found in the *qiblā*, corresponding to the openings of the four narrower archways of the façade. Set within the thickness of the northern and southern walls are stairways that lead to an upper terrace. Whether or not the masterbuilder (*sthapati*) of the Gol Gumbaz was the same who designed the Gol Gumbaz Masjid, is not known.[3] But here a talented hand can be seen in all its details.

The Gol Gumbaz Masjid facing the imposing, overwhelming Gol Gumbaz is often overlooked and considered secondary to its appended mausoleum. Further, the Gol Gumbaz Masjid is seen to represent the **R2** type of mosque design (see **Figure 4 — R2**).

1 HC, p, 99.

2 Ibid., pp. 98-104. Cousens devotes seven pages to the Gol Gumbaz and a mere thirteen lines to the Gol Gumbaz Masjid.

3 It is conjectured that masterbuilder may have been Yaqut of Dabul; SG, p. 100.

Plate 44 — Gol Gumbaz Masjid, plan

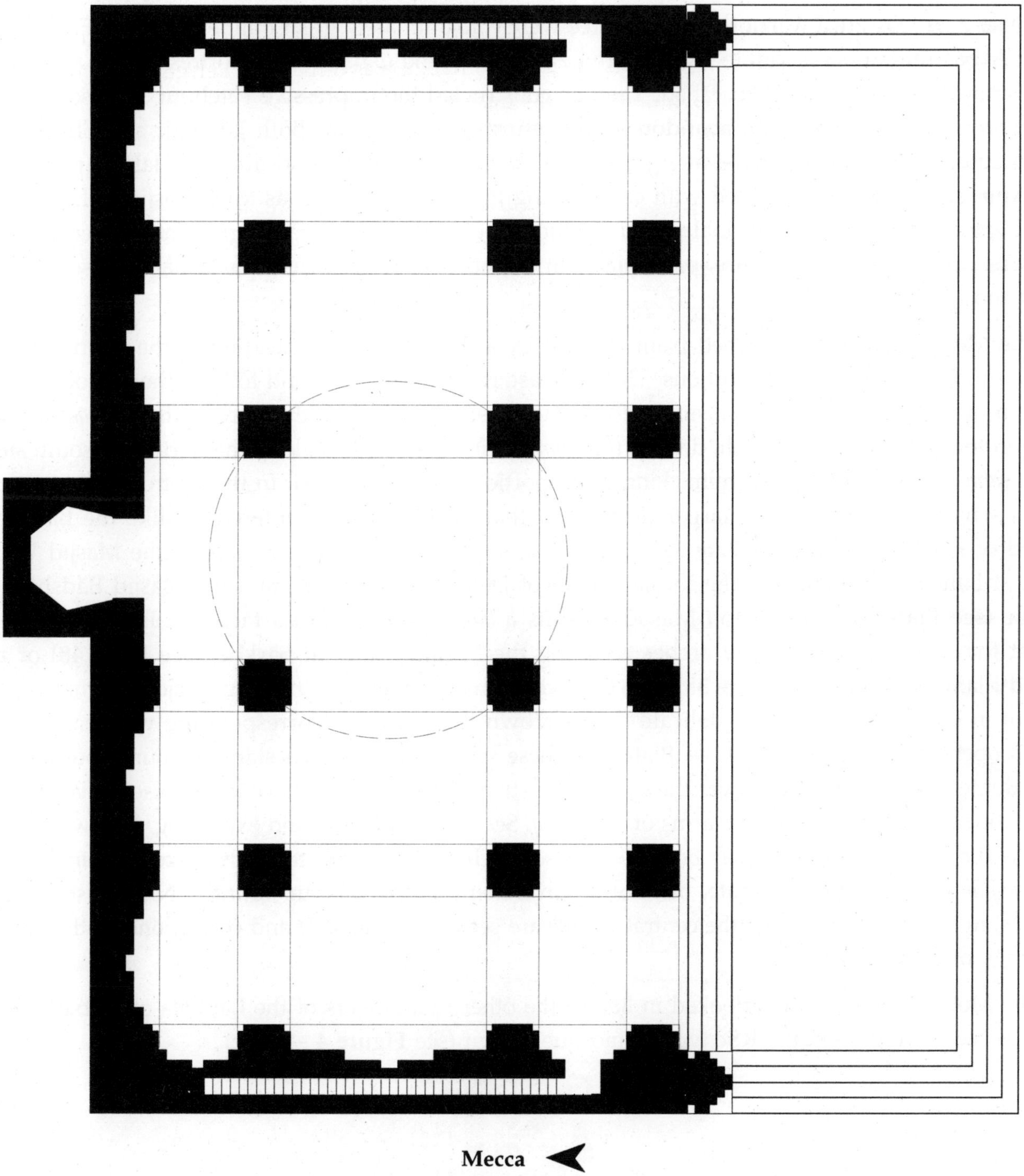

Motī Masjid, Lal Qila, Agra (*c.* CE 1628)

The Great Mughals — Babur, Humayun, Akbar, Jahangir, and Shah Jahan — were not only great administrators and great warriors, the last three were consummately great builders as well. Early in his reign, Akbar shifted his capital to Agra, there he improved and expanded the fortress which would become known as Lal Qila or Akbarābād. Then he constructed the impressive Fatehpur Sikri some miles to the west and north, only to abandon it and return to Akbarābād. Both Jahangir and Shah Jahan added substantially to the citadel at Agra. It was the Emperor Shihab-ud-din Shah Jahan (r. 1628-66) (see **Appendix D**) who is credited with constructing the mosque known as Motī Masjid at Lal Qila or Akbarābād. It became the principal *masjid* for the Imperial Capital city at Agra. The influence of the Mughals upon *masjid* architecture, particularly in the north, was immense, particularly as seen in the larger mosques.

The Motī Masjid is approached from the east by a double staircase leading to the main entrance with a propylon of modest proportions. This staircase is relatively wide and follows the contours of the western façade, presenting an unusual entrance, to be sure. A square courtyard, with a *riwāq* one bay deep on the east, north and south, defines the *sahn*. Centred in the middle of the north and south sides of the *sahn* are small propylons mimicking in proportion that of the west. In the centre of all is a tank, a *haud* which is proportionally larger than many that have been encountered. Unlike the Bādshāhī Masjid of Fatehpur Sikri (see **Plate 39**), and unlike subsequent Mughal *masjids* — the Masjid Wazir Khan at Lahore (see **Plate 46**), the Masjid-i Jami of Delhi (see **Plate 48**), and the Masjid Bādshāhī of Lahore (see **Plate 54**) — the Motī Masjid exhibits a *haram*-screen with a face that is uninterrupted except for seven equally spaced arches recalling the Masjid-i Jami at Sarkhej (see **Plate 48**) or the Masjid-i Jami of Bījāpur (see **Plate 38**). The tall pylons that characterize the other major Mughal *masjids* are not in evidence here. Seven delicate *chatrīs* crown the roof line, corresponding with each of the arched openings (see **Appendix C — Plate 98**). These small domed kiosks stand in counterpoint to the three domes which are centred over the second, fourth and sixth bays. The *haram* is raised several steps above the *sahn* and the bracketing arms of the *riwāq*. Set within the *qiblā* and extending, step-wise to the west, is the *mehrāb*. *En plan*, it may be said to be somewhat substantial, certainly more so than those of the *masjids* of the Delhi Sultanate, but not as prominent as the Bījāpur *mehrābs*. Niches, secondary *mehrābs*, mirroring the width of the central *mehrāb* are set within the *qiblā* and correspond to the arched openings of *haram's* façade.

The Motī Masjid, often overlooked in lieu of the other monuments of the Lal Qila or Akbarābād of Agra, is seen to represent the **RSc** type of mosque design (see **Figure 4 — RSc**).

Plate 45 — Mothi Masjid, plan

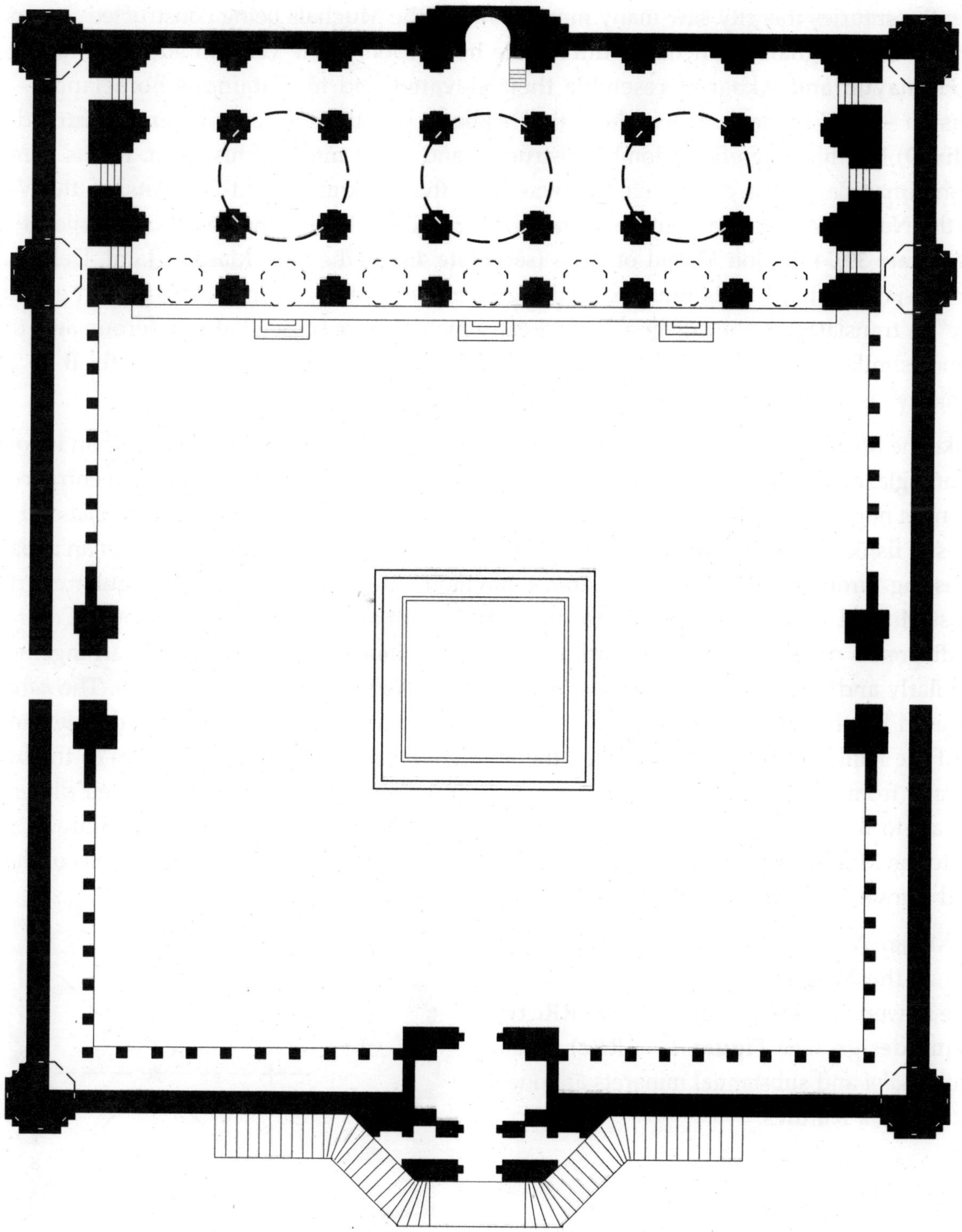

Masjid Wazir Khan, Lahore (CE 1634)

Far to the north-west of Agra, in modern-day Pakistan, is the city of Lahore. During the sixteenth and seventeenth centuries this city saw many monuments of the Mughals being constructed. It was a locale favoured by the Mughals, particularly during the hot season of the year. In addition, it was seen by Babur, Humayun and Akbar to resemble their elevated and mountainous homeland — modern Afghanistan — of Ferghana. It was here that Akbar's son the Emperor Jahangir-Nur-ud-din (see **Appendix D**) had his magnificent tomb constructed and spent much of his reign. It was here that the famed Shalimar Bagh was constructed. It was here that Hakim Ilm-ud-Din Ansari, the Viceroy of Punjab, the Nawab Wazir Khan built the Masjid Wazir Khan. Unlike the Bādshāhī Masjid at Fatehpur Sikri (see **Plate 39**), the Motī Masjid of Agra (see **Plate 45**) or the later Masjid-i Jami, Delhi (see **Plate 48**), the Masjid Wazir Khan is unusual in design, *en plan*, primarily in its solidity. In elevation this "solidity" is translated in the octagonal minarets which appear somewhat ponderous and the use of low domes similar to the Bīdar/Gulbargā Solah Khambā Masjid type (see **Appendix B — Plate 83**). This "solidity" is often referred to as the "Provincial Mughal" style.[1]

Unlike the Mughal mosques of Delhi, Agra and Fatehpur Sikri, the Masjid Wazir Khan is constructed of brick and glazed tile in the Persian style. This mosque consists of a large, thick-walled entrance pavilion which, on its north-south axis, bridges a narrow passage running the width of the *masjid* and made up of a series of flanking shops. This bazaar enclosed within the confines of a mosque is not an usual feature. Upon passing through this substantial entrance pavilion, one enters a large, rectangular courtyard. As with most Mughal *sahns*, a *riwāq* surrounds the north, south and east sides of the court. Centred on the eastern diagonals of the *sahn* are the north and south pavilions and the *haud*. This arrangement is not seen regularly and adds to the uniqueness of the Masjid Wazir Khan (see **Figure 20**). The *haram*-screen of the Masjid Wazir Khan may be viewed as conforming to Mughal standards with the elevated central mass and the flanking archways. However, the flanking *minarets* and the five domes of the *haram* veer dramatically from the "standard." The four minarets of the mosque are unwieldy in their dimension and out of scale to the *haram*-screen. The four flanking domes of the Masjid Wazir Khan are in no way a referent to the Mughal-style domes of Delhi or Agra, but recall the squat Gulbargā domes of the Deccan, as noted above (see **Appendix C — Plate 99**).

The Masjid Wazir Khan is a mosque that reflects the rule of the Mughals, yet mirrors a regional influence as well. It is seen to represent the **RRc** type of mosque design (see **Figure 4 — RRc**) and its rectangular *sahn* and substantial minarets are one of its most unusual features.

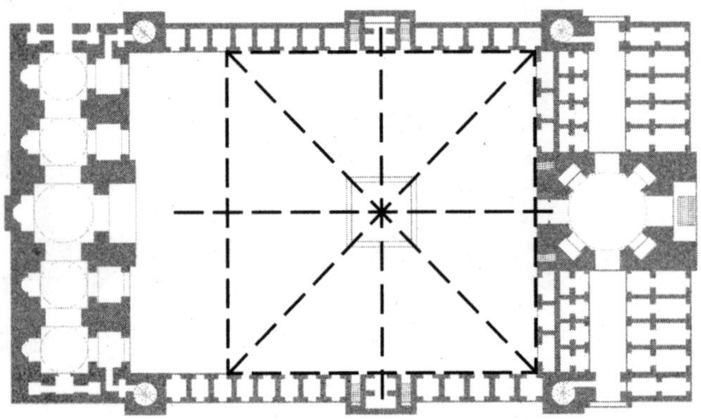

Figure 20 — Indicating the square orientation of the *haud* and the north and south pavilions

1 MF, p, 171.

Plate 46 — Masjid Wazir Khan, plan

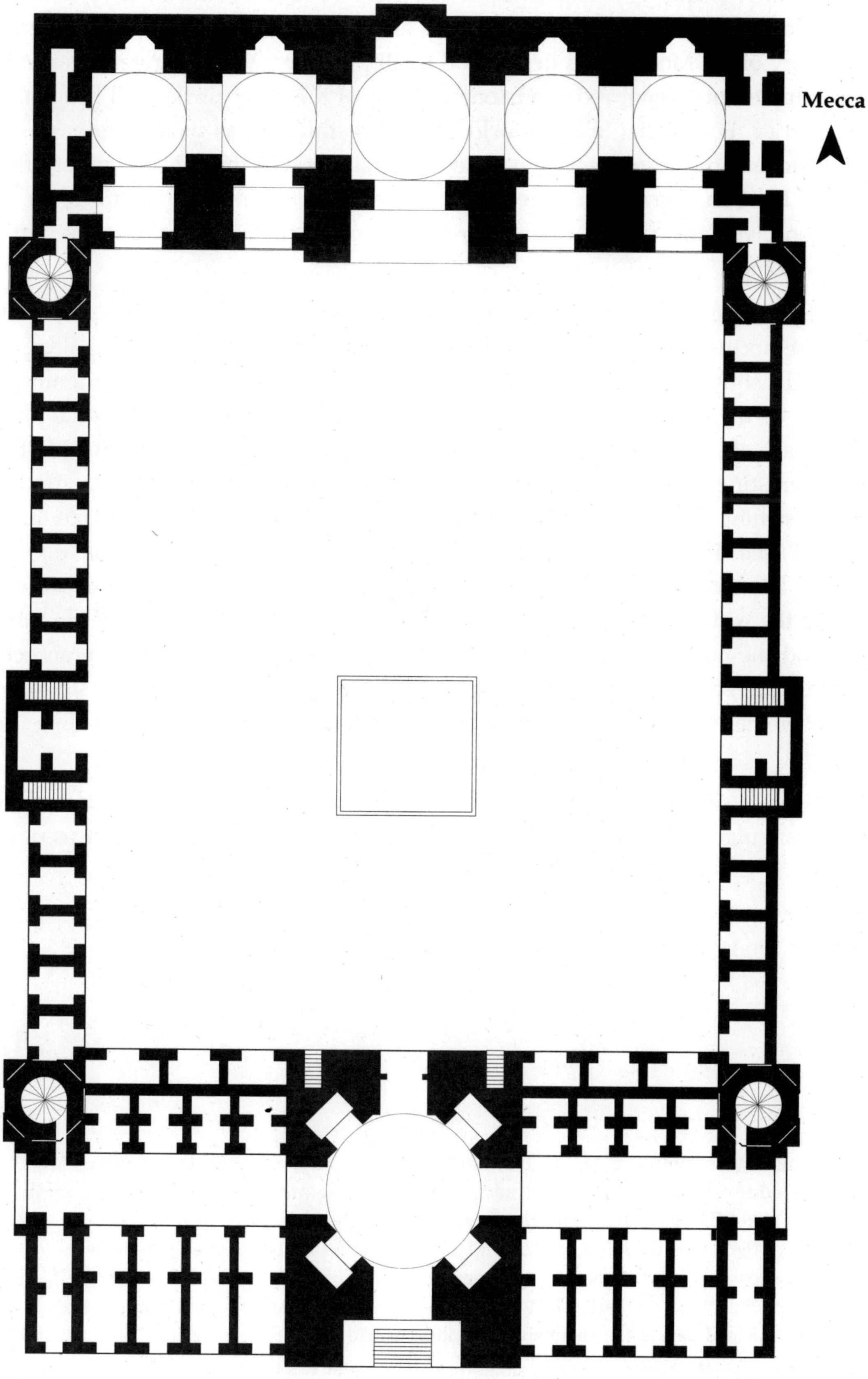

Motī Masjid, Shāhjahānabād, Delhi (*c.* CE 1639)[1]

The Motī Masjid (Pearl Mosque) of Shāhjahānabād (Lal Qila), Delhi, is a pearl! Set deep within the imperial confines of the citadel, adjacent to the Dīwān-ī-Khās and the imperial *hammam* and other architectural gems, the true glory of the Motī Masjid lies behind a tall protective wall, a protective shell. It is truly a jewel box. The simple but elegant red sandstone exterior of the high girdle wall belies the glistening, white marble interior. Few sights in this world are as breathtaking as when one passes through the modest red sandstone entrance and step into the ephemeral world of this small place of prayer. Like the Masjid Nagina of Lal Qila, Agra, tucked deep within the restricted imperial confines, the *Mothi Masjid* was obviously conceived as a private chapel[2] for the person of the Emperor. It is truly matchless as a private area of worship.

The Motī Masjid consists of a thick, high girdle wall that surrounds and screens the whole. This wall is aligned with the north-south axis of the imperial precincts within the citadel and along the Yamunā. However, the slight shift in the placement of the *qiblā* required that the interior alignment be rotated slightly from that of the exterior — the Mecca alignment as opposed to the imperial alignment. The thickness of the walls of the Motī Masjid allowed for this slight shift or readjustment and, if nothing else, makes for an interesting albeit erratic plan. Upon entering the inner confines, one finds themselves within a small glistening court with walls and floor covered by brilliant white marble. In the centre of the *sahn* is a small *haud*. The placement of this ablution tank (*haud*) is symbolic as the Motī Masjid is just to the west of the imperial *hammām*. The *haram* of the *masjid* is three bays wide and two deep with the central bay being the widest. The *mehrāb* sinks into the mass of the western wall of the *masjid* and does not extend beyond the normal limits of that wall. Its form, *en plan*, is derived from an octagon. Three domes herald the three bays and their proportional size. To the north of the *sahn* is a stairway leading up to a roof terrace. Similarly, to the north of the eastern entrance is also a stairway leading up to the roof terrace.

The Motī Masjid is seen to represent the **RRc** type of mosque design (see **Figure 4 — RRc**). Here, however, the rectangular *sahn* is parallel to the *qiblā*, rather than perpendicular as was observed in the Masjid Wazir Khan.

---

1 The problem of date is confusing. SG, p. 173, illustrates this monument with the caption: "Motī Masjid built by Aurangzeb, Delhi, CE 1622." 1622 would have placed the beginning dates during the reign of Nur-ud-din Jahangir (r. CE 1606-27). MF, p. 165, dates the mosque during the early reign of Muhiy-ud-din Aurangzeb (r. CE CE 1658–1707) — CE 1662 — as does GM, p. 270. GM II, p. 119, specifically assigns the date as CE 1659, one year after Aurangzeb's usurpation of the throne. On the other hand, AM, pp. 146-48, states that the *masjid* was most probably started a. 1653 by Shihab-ud-din Shah Jahan (r. CE 1628–58, d. CE 1666) and finished during the early reign of his son. Since the acknowledged date of the beginning of Shāhjahānabād is CE 1639, "*c.* CE 1639" is used above.

2 The term "chapel" is used here to denote a small, private place of worship.

Plate 47 — Mothi Masjid, plan

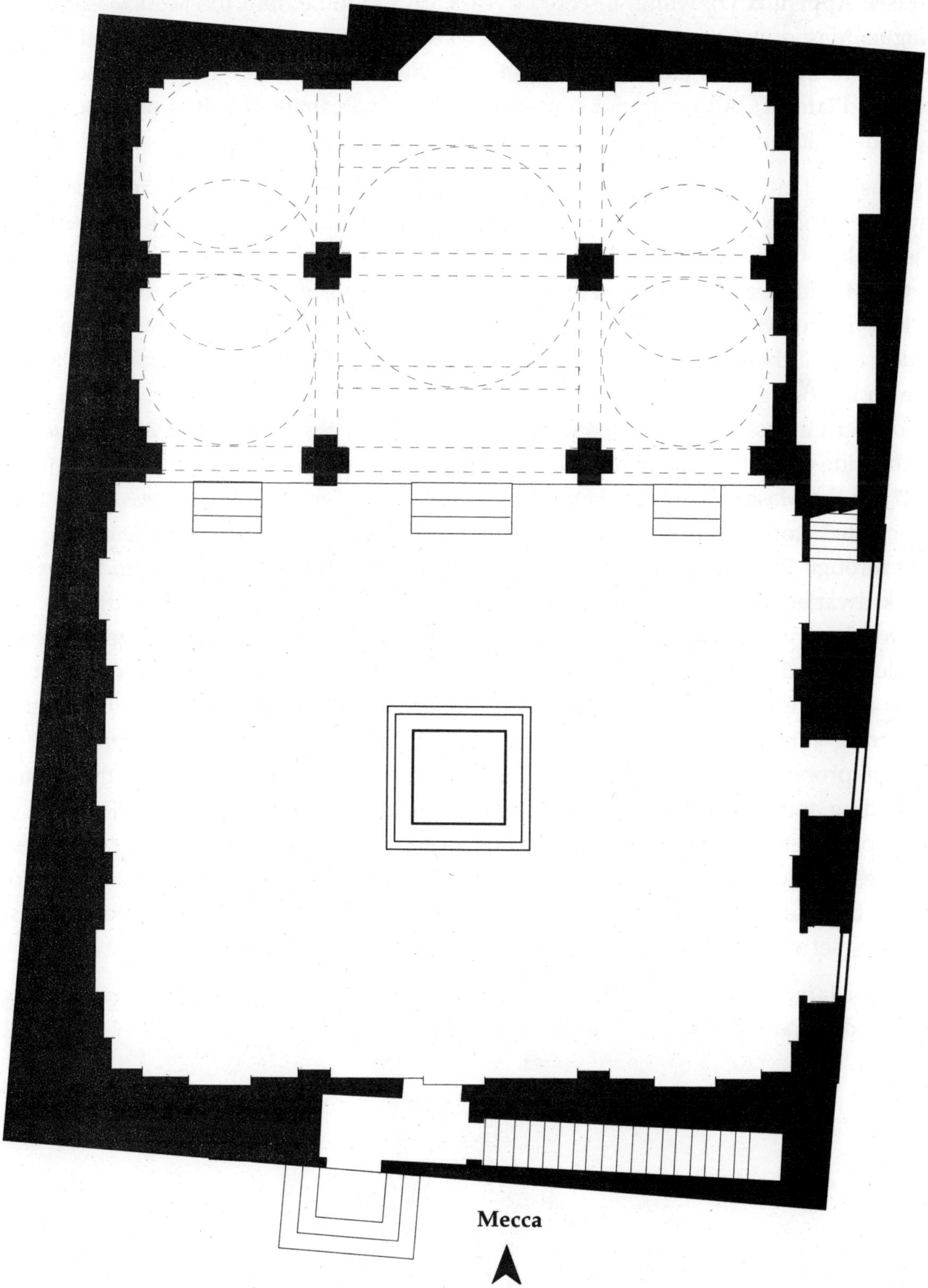

Masjid-i Jami, Delhi (*c.* CE 1644)

Constructing more mosques than any other Mughal Emperor, Shihab-ud-din Shah Jahan (r. 1628-58, d. CE 1666) (see **Appendix D**), within a score of years, caused to be built the Motī Masjid (see **Plate 45**) and the Nagīnā Masjid in Agra as well as the Motī Masjid (see **Plate 47**) and the Masjid-i Jami in Delhi. The latter is acknowledged as one of the largest in modern day India — over 9,000 sq m in area (see **Appendix B — Plate 81**). Although not contained within Shāhjahānabād, it is nonetheless considered to be the "Friday Mosque" (Masjid-i Jami) for that imperial palace/city.

Delhi's Masjid-i Jami is considered to be the epitome of Shah Jahan's elegant and luxurious classical style. Many of its attributes find their genesis in earlier Islamic monuments of India. Initially it is constructed upon a raised platform, a referent to the "Tughluq Style" (see the Masjid Begampurī and **Plate 15**). As is seen in the Masjid Begampurī, three stairways lead to/from the north, south and east entrances. However, here in the Masjid-i Jami the stairs fan out as they descend from the substantial entrance blocks, or *darwāẓā*, of the north and south and the truly monumental eastern *darwāẓā*. These mounting steps create an imposing, even awesome approach to these three portals/gateways. They resemble the dramatic, southern access to the Bādshāhī Masjid of Fatehpur Sikri (see **Plate 39**). The eastern portal dominates this side of the façade and recalls the imposing entrance blocks of the Masjid-i Jami at Jaunpur (see **Plate 27**) or the Masjid-i Jami of Māṇḍu (see **Plate 28**). The main entrance mass rises to the height of three articulated storeys, topped with a wide architrave and small towers at the corners (see **Figure 21**). Moving through the arched door, one then moves into a huge *sahn* — 67 sq m. In the centre is an ablution tank dwarfed by the size and scope of the whole. Bordering the open court is a colonnaded *riwāq* one bay deep with corner pavilions topped by *chatrī*. The *haram* is a large space with three substantial domes and a massive *pishtaq*, mirroring the eastern entrance. On either side of the central portal are ten arched entrances into the interior of the *haram* — five to the north and five to the south — and tall, tapering *minarets* at the north-eastern and south-eastern corners (see **Appendix C — Plate 100**). The *haram* proper consists of two lateral bays — the open area to the east and the separate spaces to the west ending at the *qiblā*. Whereas the eastern façade of the sanctuary block indicates an elevenfold division, the spaces terminating at the *qiblā* are but seven. The three domes rise over the second, fourth and sixth spaces. The Masjid-i Jami's mehrāb follows the pattern long established in the north of India — set within the thickness of the *qiblā* wall. Each of the other six, flanking spaces possess a secondary *mehrāb* similarly set within the thickness of the *qiblā*.

The Masjid-i Jami of Delhi is seen to represent the **Sc1** type of mosque design (see **Figure 4 — Sc1**). Its size and scope make it, truly, an Imperial *masjid*.

Figure 21 — Simplified proportional elevation of eastern *darwāẓā*

Plate 48 — Masjid-i Jami, plan

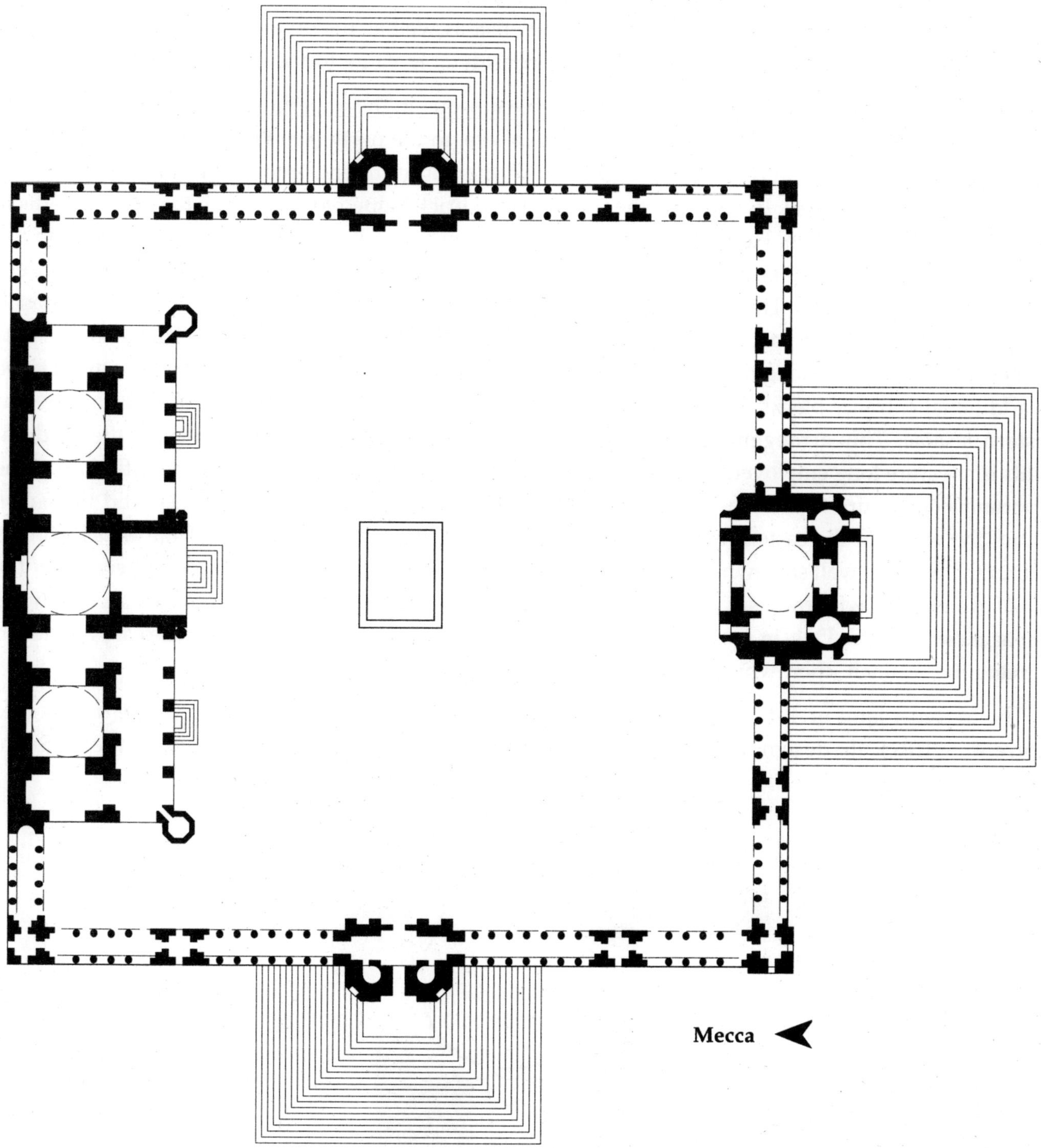

Masjid-i Jami, Tatta (CE 1644)

In the west of his realm, in modern-day Pakistan, Emperor Shihab-ud-din Shah Jahan (r. CE 1628–58, d. 1666) (see **Appendix D**), caused to be constructed in Tatta the Masjid-i Jami. This he did to commemorate his stay in that Sind city. Rather than impose his Imperial will on the design and construction of the *masjid*, he apparently acquiesced to regional taste and influence of this valued hub. The importance of Tatta as a trade centre between northern India and Persia as well as the other Arab states and the west was recognized. Its commercial importance was of considerable value to the Empire.

Rather than construct an essentially square, marble mosque in the imperial style, the Masjid-i Jami at Tatta follows the plan of the Masjid Wazir Khan in Lahore, to the north (see **Plate 46**). Brick and glazed brick was the building material. Here in the west of the subcontinent, frequent rainfall was not the problem as occurs in Bengal. In addition, the use of glazed brick helped to ameliorate the negative effects during the monsoon season. Here in Tatta a rectangular plan was followed with a major entrance in the east. Later in CE 1658, this entrance was extended further eastward and ablution pools (*haud*) were added in their own courts. This also followed the extended and developed entrance area of the Masjid Wazir Khan, but was not part of the original design. The *sahn* is rectangular and bordered by a *riwāq* which is two bays deep along the east, north and south. Midway, along the northern and southern *riwāq* are additional entrance blocks, but considerably more abbreviated in size and scale than the eastern and western *pishtaq*. This arrangement — a rectangular *sahn* with *liwan* and/or *pishtaq* at the cardinal points is a feature long employed by the Persians. The use of glazed tile is also seen as an influence of the important neighbours to the west. The western section of the *riwāq* is three bays deep and the *haram* mimics the width of the eastern block — approximately two bays wide. The *qiblā* of the *haram* extends beyond the western wall somewhat. The *mehrāb* is set within the width of that wall. On either side of the *mehrāb* are two *jālī* windows, set at floor level and a narrow window within the *mehrāb* proper. This is seen as most unusual. Due, in part, to the brick construction, a complex network of arches are employed to create the squinch upon which the dome rests (see **Figure 22**).

The Masjid-i Jami of Tatta is seen as being representative of the **RRc** type of mosque design (see **Figure 4 — RRc**). Its design and construction reflects Shah Jahan's ability to adapt to the different tastes of his realm.

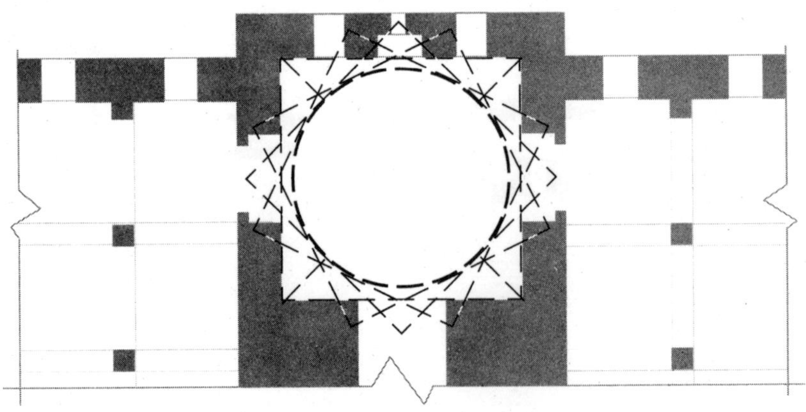

Figure 22 — *Mehrāb* dome support system

Plate 49 — Masjid-i Jami, plan

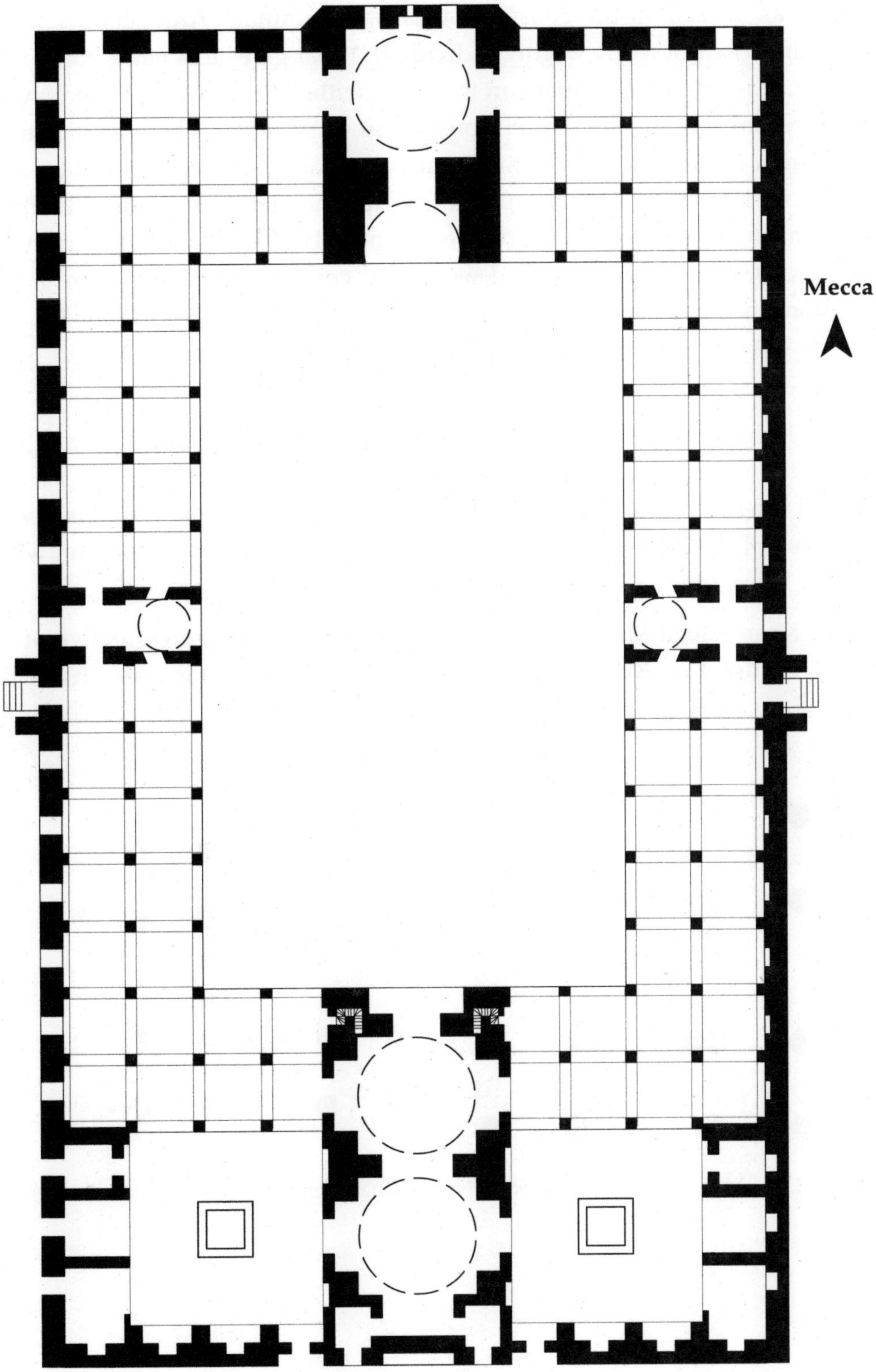

Shah Navaz Khan Rauza Masjid, Bījāpur (*c.* CE 1647)

Shah Navaz Khan was a *wazīr* in the court of Sultan Muhammad 'Adil Shah (r. CE 1626–56) (see **Appendix D**), but otherwise not a noteworthy individual. What gives this name some importance is to be found in his *rauza*. It is small by comparison to others within the area but Shah Navaz Khan Rauza Masjid has much to recommend it. Cousens curiously states that it is "of little architectural merit, (but) is interesting as giving a general idea, on a small scale, of what Jahan Begam's tomb . . . was probably intended to be like."[1] An interesting assessment, but far from the mark (see **Figure 23**). The mausoleum's elevation may be considered out of proportion (see **Appendix C — Plate 101**) but the *masjid* is not.[2] What makes this *rauza's masjid* interesting and worthy of consideration is its plan. It is considerably smaller, in proportion, than the mausoleum to the east (see **Appendix B — Plate 77**). One only finds this disparity within Bījāpur between the Gol Gumbaz and the Gol Gumbaz Masjid (see **Appendix B — Plate 76**).

The Shah Navaz Khan Rauza Masjid consists of three deep rectangular bays and an interior that seems to undulate with numerous niches and indentations. It appears that what this *masjid* lacks in size, it makes up for in its interior configuration. The *qiblā* of this small mosque contains a *mehrāb* that is as unusual as the interior of the *haram*. The *mehrāb* finds its basic design in a decagon with seven small niches in its exposed sides, unique in the Indian subcontinent.

The Shah Navaz Khan Rauza Masjid near Bījāpur is seen as being representative of the **R2** type of mosque design (see **Figure 4 — R2**). Its design reflects the architectural concerns of this important Sultanate.

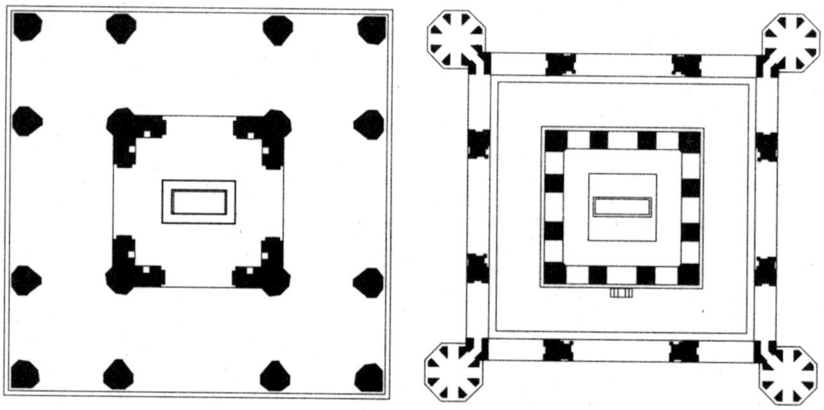

Figure 23 — Mausoleum plans of Shah Navaz Khan (left) and Jahan Begam (right)

1 HC, p. 111.

2 The proportion of the Shah Navaz Khan Mausoleum is 1:1.75 (see **Appendix C — Plate 101**), making it exceedingly high in proportion to its base. On the other hand the proportion of the Afzal Khan Mausoleum is 1:1 (see **Appendix C — Plate 102**) — a more pleasing proportion.

Plate 50 — Shah Navaz Khan Rauza Masjid, plan

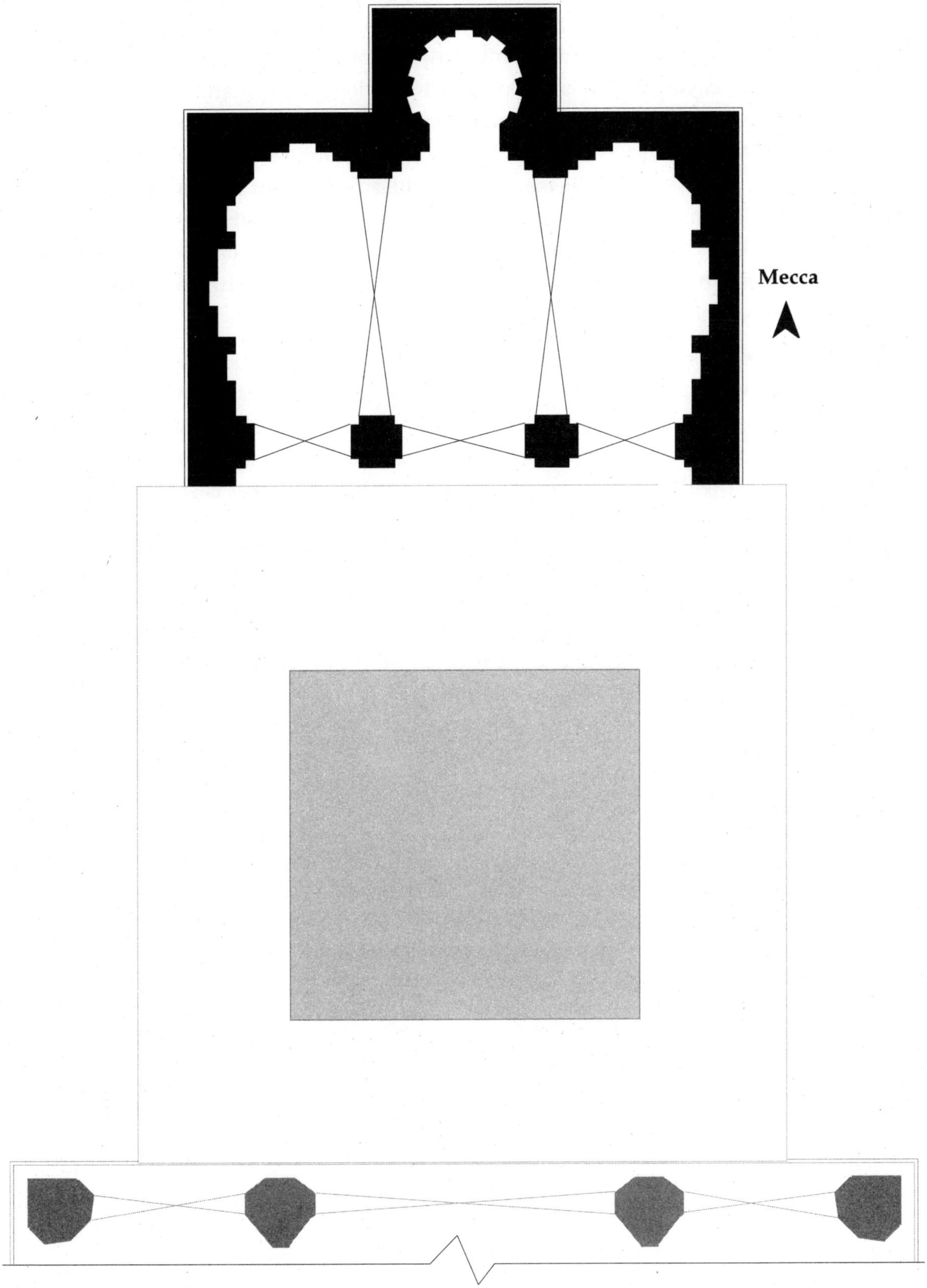

Marakkayarpalli (Masjid), Kayalpatnam (*c.* CE 1650)

While impressive mosques were being constructed throughout the Mughal Empire, far to the south, at the tip of the subcontinent, a wealthy merchant, possibly one Musaliyar Pillai Marakkayar, built a small mosque, the Marakkayarpalli.[1] It was dedicated to a local holy man, Shaikh Sulaiman, whose mausoleum lies near the *masjid*. Kayalpatnam and much of this region, including a good part of Tamil Nadu, Kerala and part of Karnataka — most of the older Coḷa empire — remained fiercely independent and unconquered. Here flourished Islamic merchants amidst a dominant Hindu culture. The merchants were more interested in commerce and enlarging their substantial coffers than proselytizing. The *masjids* that they built were for the small number of faithful and did not require large or expansive structures. Cooled by the trade winds of the Indian Ocean, Kayalpatnam could, nevertheless, become quite warm, and during the monsoon, the rain drove everyone inside.

The Marakkayarpalli (Masjid) consists of only a prayer hall or *haram*. The walls of thick masonry tend to keep the interior somewhat cooler than the exterior. The enclosed area is divided into nine bays by four supporting pillars. To the east, the main entrance is a door flanked by two windows. The same arrangement is encountered in the north and south sides as well. However, the north and, originally, the south doorways were set within projecting porches. A rectilinear *mehrāb* is set within the *qiblā* wall. Two niches are set within the *qiblā* of the outer two bays. As is generally seen within the smaller *masjids* of south India, including Bījāpur, the exterior of the *qiblā* is punctuated with a form announcing the *mehrāb*. Here a semicircle or half cylinder defines the rectilinear *mehrāb*.

The Marakkayarpalli (Masjid) of Kayalpatnam is seen to represent the **R2** type of mosque design (see **Figure 4 — R2**). It is essentially not unlike many of the other smaller *masjids* of this region dominated by the Hindu but with a viable, small Muslim population.

1 The term Marakkayar is an appellation assumed by many of the important Muslim sea traders of the region and refers to an owner of ships and/or horses.

Plate 51 — Marakkayarpalli (Masjid), plan

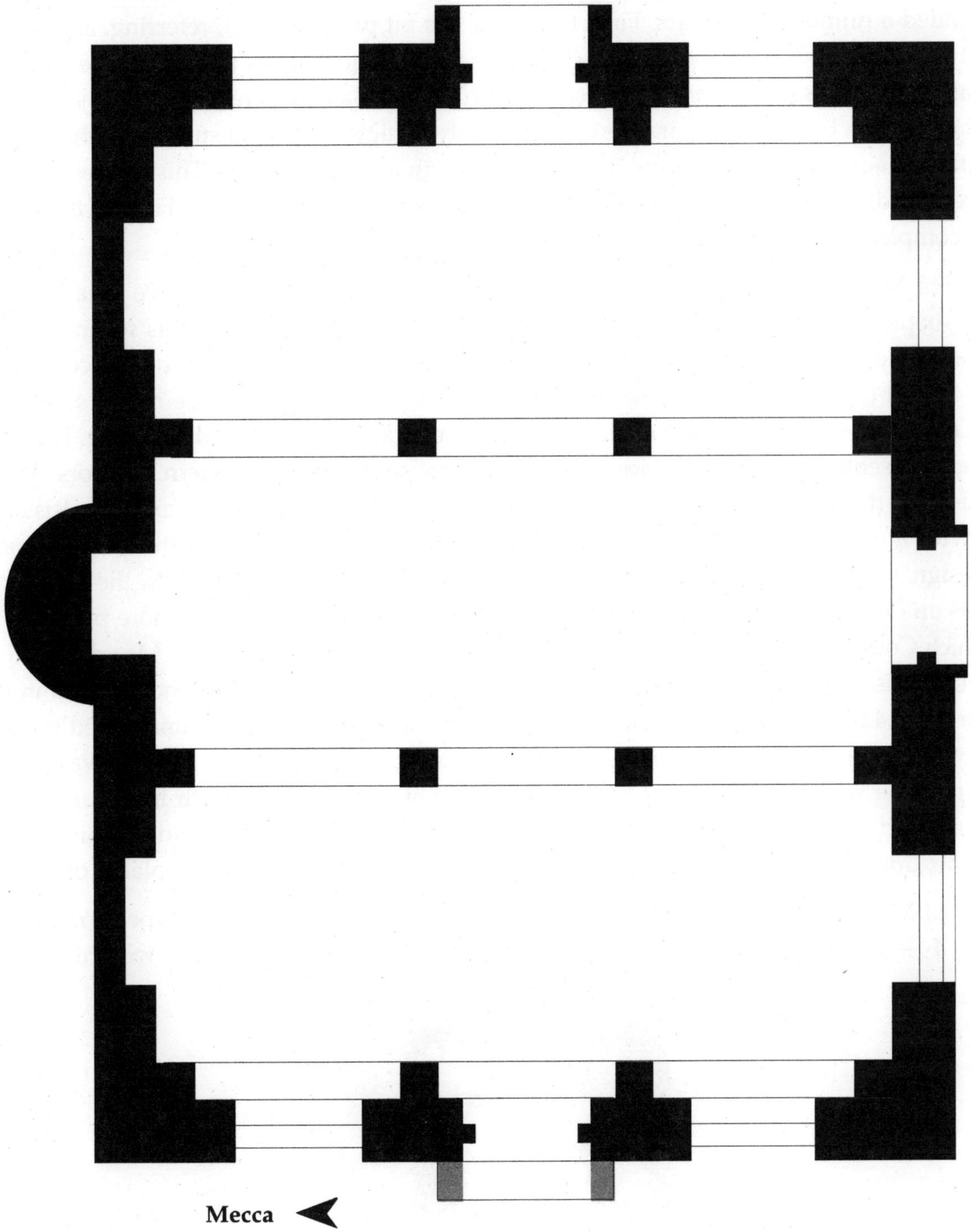

Mecca Masjid, Bījāpur (*c.* CE 1650)

The Mecca Masjid (Makkā Masjid)[1] of Bījāpur is viewed by many as a gem, albeit a minor one, amidst the rich assemblage of important monuments within this city. Located in the citadel, this small *masjid* has confounded a number of scholars. First, the name is a bit problematical, referring, as it does, to the Masjid al-Haram of the holy city of Mecca. The only true relationship is seen in the rectangular *sahn*. One may also view the square *haram* of Mecca Masjid (Makkā Masjid) as relating to the square Ka'ba of the Masjid al-Haram, but here the parallels end! Secondly, a high, solid wall surrounds the *masjid* on the north, south and east sides with narrow doors on the north and south walls. This creates a fortress-like atmosphere. Thirdly, the *haram* is a completely separate structure, not attached. Finally, the eastern end was never completed and the planned solution is lost.

The Mecca Masjid (Makkā Masjid) consists of an unfinished eastern entrance area in which one encounters six piers creating seven means of ingress.To the north and south of this seven-part entry are the remains of older minarets which evidently had been incorporated into the newer construction. In the Mecca Masjid (Makkā Masjid) the *sahn* has a *riwāq* completely enclosing the north, south and west confines. Centred in the western area of the *sahn* is the separate and independent *haram*. It too, like the exterior wall, presents unadorned surfaces to the northern, southern and western exteriors. The eastern entrance displays five equally spaced arched openings into the interior. The inner area consists of twenty-five bays with a dome over the central nine bays (see **Figure 24**). Set within the *qiblā* is a *mehrāb* of unusual design — resembling a Tau cross. As with the majority of Bījāpur *masjids*, the exterior wall of the *qiblā* has an extension corresponding with the *mehrāb*. There is one factor, or more precisely the lack thereof, which Cousens sees as the solution to many of the unique features of the Mecca Masjid (Makkā Masjid) and that is: the *haram* lacks a *minbar* — a pulpit. The same feature was encountered in the *Anda* Masjid (see **Plate 42**). Quite probably, the simple high, girdle wall, the curious unfinished entrance and the lack of a *minbar* may point to the possibility that the Mecca Masjid (Makkā Masjid) was reserved for the worship of the women of the court. Unlike the Court at Ahmedabad which incorporated separate, elevated, enclosed areas — the Masjid Ahmad Shah (see **Plate 22**) or the Masjid-i Jami (see **Plate 23**) — the Bījāpur Court apparently preferred to provide their women with separate places of worship.

The Mecca Masjid (Makkā Masjid) of Bījāpur is seen to represent the **RRcS** type of mosque design (see **Figure 4 — RRcS**). It is also indicative of other *masjids* dedicated to the worship by women, primarily.

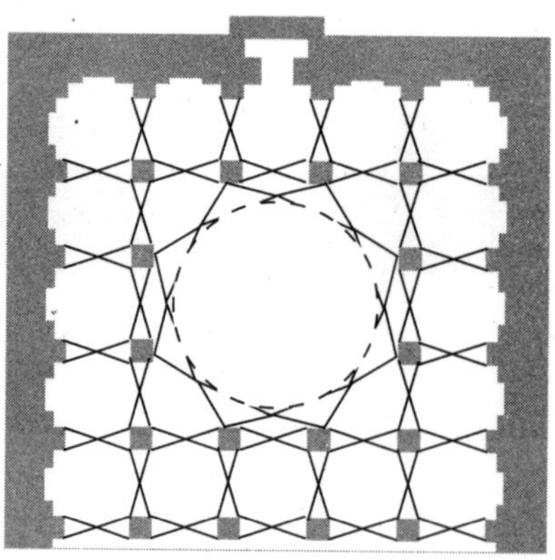

Figure 24 — *Haram* indicating support system

1 The spelling used by HC, pp. 110-11.

Plate 52 — Mecca Masjid, plan

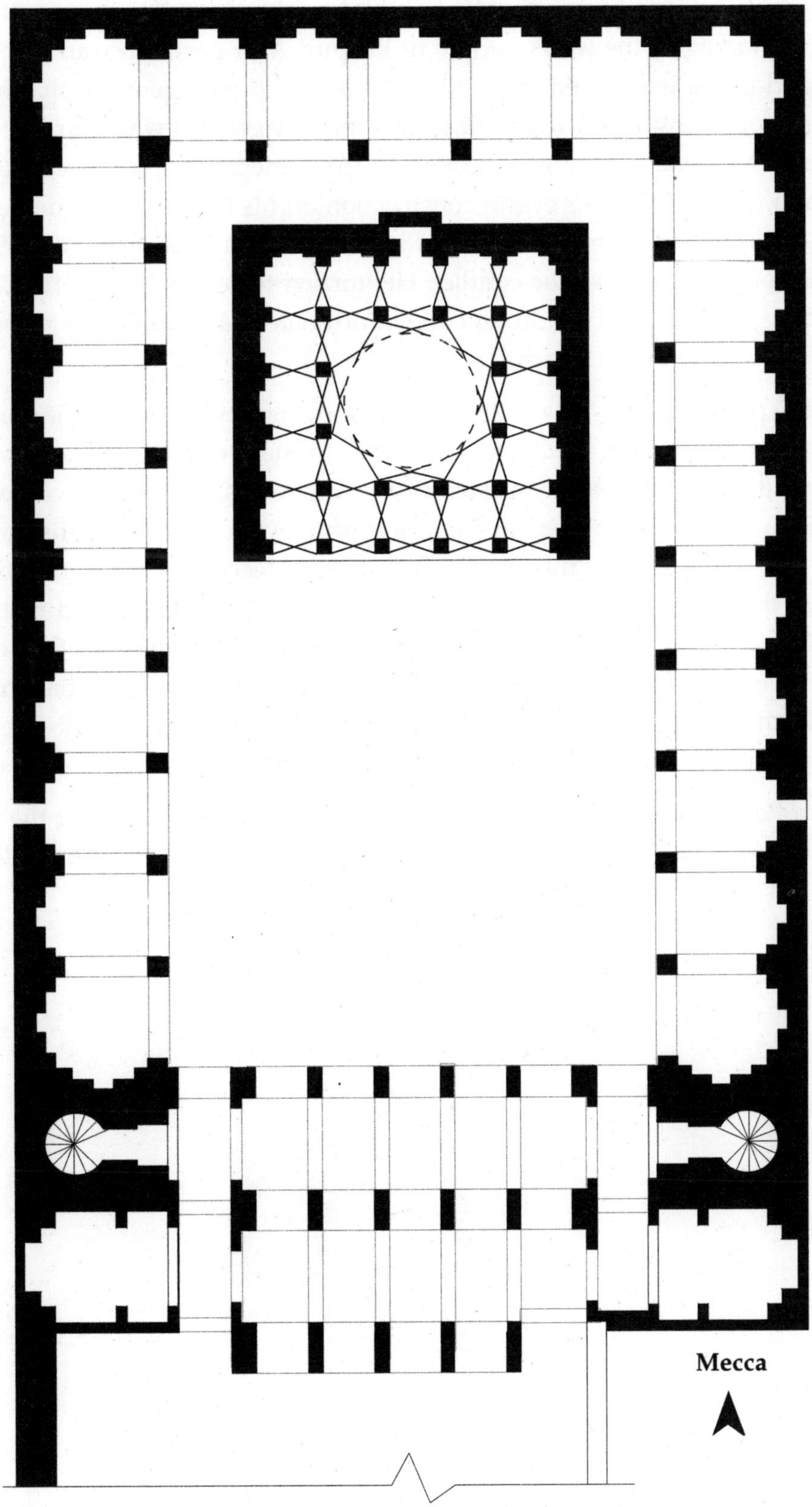

Afzal Khan Rauza Masjid, Bījāpur (*c.* CE 1653)

Afzal Khan was the *wazīr* and general for both Sultan Muhammad 'Adil Shah (r. CE 1626–56) and Ali 'Adil Shah II (r. CE 1656–72) (see **Appendix D**). As a high ranking courtier, he was the builder/engineer who oversaw the upgrading of the water supply to Bījāpur. As a partial reward for a job well done, he was put in command of the troops sent to subdue the Marāṭhā insurgent, Śivājī. This turned out to be a disaster both for Bījāpur and Afzal Khan. Bījāpur's courtier-general was murdered by Śivājī under a flag of truce and the Sultanate's army was decimated. As a member of the royal court and apparently a man of vast wealth, Afzal Khan had begun construction on his tomb some time before CE 1653. It was nearly completed when he took command of the ill-fated army of Bījāpur in CE 1659. He was told by a soothsayer that he would not survive the conflict. He hurried to set his life in order, and, in so doing, it is said that he had his sixty-four wives drowned.[1] Unfortunately, his tomb was not completely finished and Afzal Khan was buried in Partagaṛh.

The *rauza* (see **Appendix B — Plate 78**) was of a design typical for Bījāpur. It consisted of a square mausoleum, an intervening *haud* and the *masjid* to the west. The Afzal Khan Rauza Masjid is rectangular, *en plan*. Its eastern façade consisted of five archways, the outer two being wider than the middle three. This division is mimicked in the northern elevation of the mausoleum (see **Appendix C, Plate 102**). The *masjid* divisions — five bays wide and two deep — is rather traditional. An octagonal *mehrāb* is set within the thickness of the *qiblā* wall of the third bay. Similarly, a rectilinear extension to the west of the *qiblā's* exterior defines the *mehrāb*. Set within the thickness of the southern wall of the *masjid* is a staircase leading to a second storey. A most unusual feature is that this second storey is identical, *en plan*, to the first storey, but without a *minbar*. It is surmised that this second storey was the *masjid* for the women of Afzal Khan's family.

The Afzal Khan Rauza Masjid of Bījāpur is seen as being a representative of the **R2** type of mosque design (see **Figure 4 — R2**). The whole *rauza* reflects the high position that could be attained by a noble courtier as well as the brilliance of the Sultanate.

1 HC, p. 97. This is incorrect. As a Muslim, Afzal Khan was allowed but four wives at any one time. Obviously, the other sixty "wives" were concubines and/or mistresses — a state that was frequently practised.

Plate 53 — Afzal Khan Rauza Masjid, plan

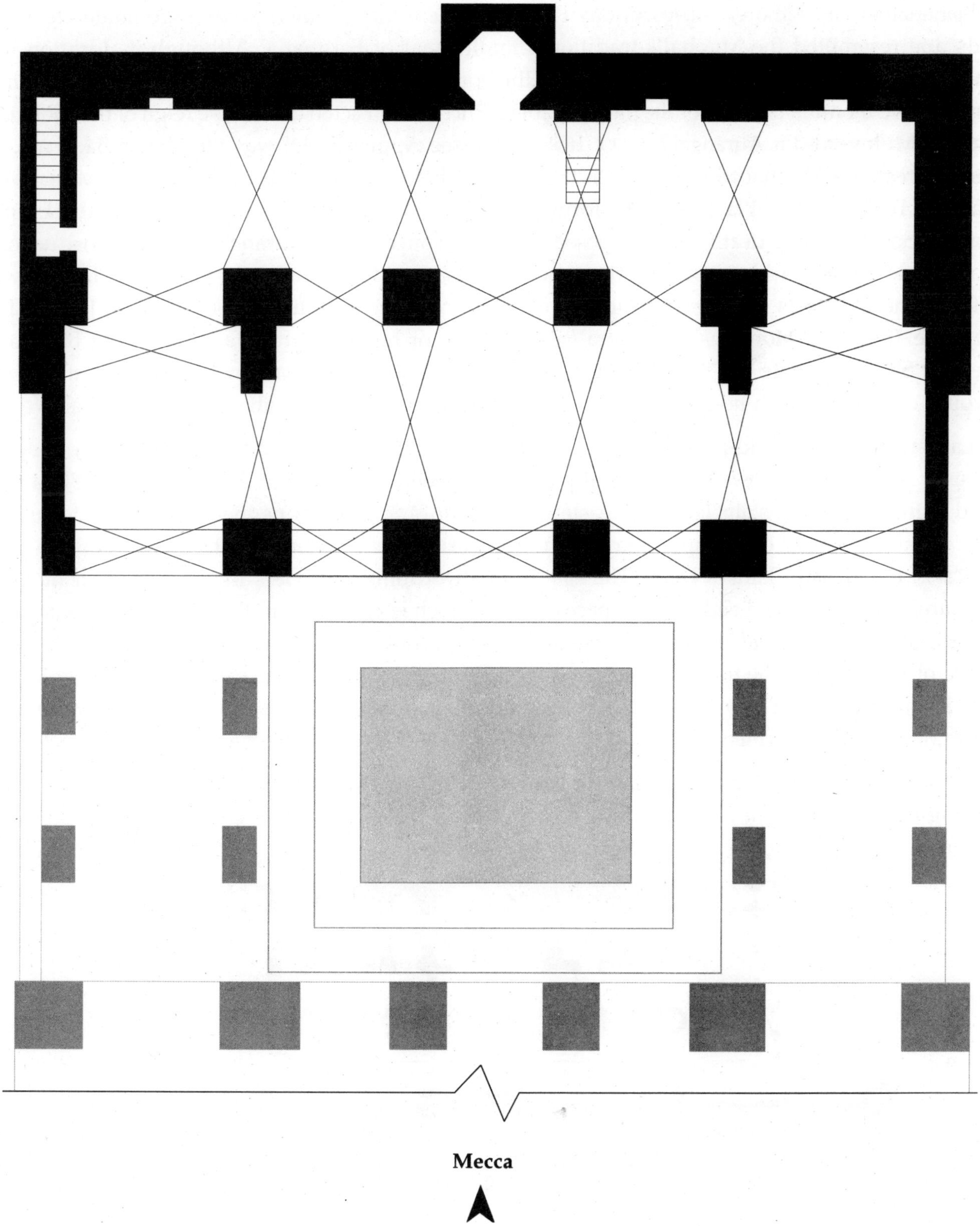

Masjid Bādshāhī, Lahore (CE 1673)

The Mughals possessed three capitals — Agra with its Lal Qila or Akbarābād, Delhi with its Lal Qila or Shāhjahānābād and Lahore, in present-day Pakistan, where the summers were more moderate and the landscape resembled the Mughal's traditional family seat of Ferghana. Although its location made Lahore easy prey to invaders, particularly from the north-west, it, nonetheless, was the site for a number of impressive monuments. One of the most notable edifices constructed during the reign of the contentious Emperor Muhiy-ud-din Aurangzeb (r. CE 1658–1707) (see **Appendix D**) was the Masjid Bādshāhī. This mosque created a Mughal trio along with the Begum Shāhī Masjid (CE 1611–14) and the Masjid Wazir Khan (CE 1634–35) (see **Plate 46**). The former monument was built by the mother of the Emperor Jahangir. Soon after the death of his deposed and imprisoned father Aurangzeb began construction on what was to be one of his most important monuments, the Masjid Bādshāhī in Lahore. Lahore was a perfectly chosen site as Aurangzeb's mosque need not compete with his father's Masjid-i Jami in Delhi (see **Plate 48**) or the Motī Masjid in Agra (see **Plate 45**) or his great-grandfather's Masjid Bādshāhī at Fatehpur Sikri (see **Plate 39**). The Masjid Bādshāhī of Lahore is an impressive structure, but truthfully it would come out fourth best when compared with the three Great Mughal *masjids* noted above.

Larger than the Masjid-i Jami of Delhi would be the Masjid Bādshāhī's main claim to fame! The Emperor Aurangzeb followed the general plan of the Delhi mosque (see **Appendix B — Plate 81**). A broad flight of receding stairs led to the eastern *masjid-darwāẓā*, which is neither as large nor as imposing as the Buland Darwāẓā of Fatehpur Sikri, nor as impressive as the eastern, northern and southern *masjid-darwāẓā* of the Masjid-i Jami of Delhi. The *sahn* is, in a word, gigantic. Here the *riwāq* consists of a series of square, rectangular and eight-sided spaces, all with arched entrances to the *sahn*. In the centre of the *sahn* is a commodious *haud*, dwarfed by its surroundings. As with the Masjid-i Jami of Delhi, the central feature of the whole is the triple-domed sanctuary. The general plan of the sanctuary is nearly identical to its Delhi counterpart (see **Figure 25**). The significant difference here is that the eastern *minarets* are shorter, less elegant. Further, the Masjid Bādshāhī sees a plethora of towers — eight to be exact.

As an expanded version of the Masjid-i Jami of Delhi, the Masjid Bādshāhī is seen to be of the **SSc** (see **Figure 4 — SSc**). *In toto*, it is less pleasing than the large *masjid* constructed by the father. Certainly, it is the last great mosque built by the Mughals.

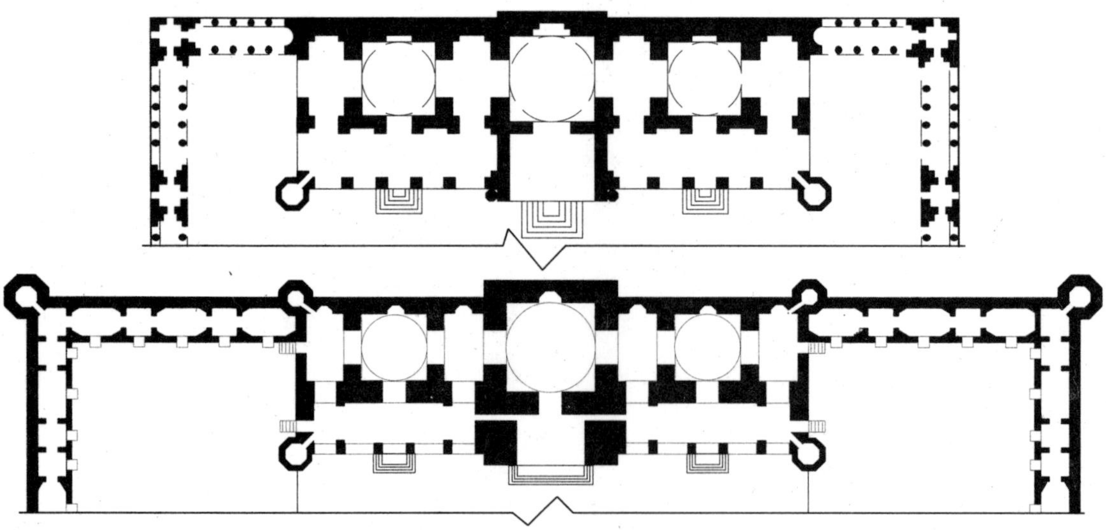

Figure 25 — *Haram* of Masjid-i Jami, Delhi (top) & Masjid Bādshāhī, Lahore (bottom) (not to scale)

Plate 54 — Masjid Bādshāhī, plan

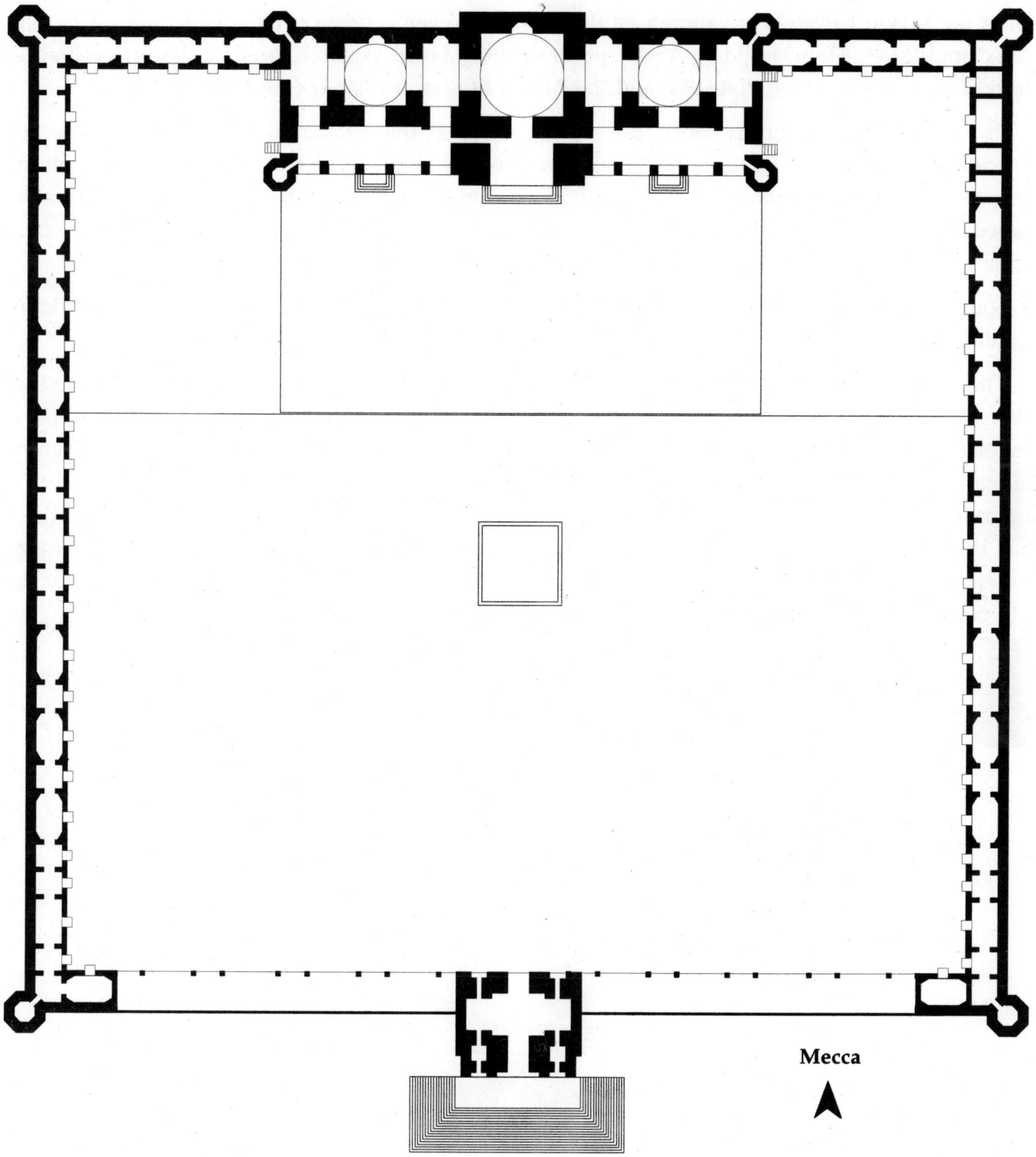

Seventeenth Century

The Seventeenth century sees the culmination of a series of approaches to the design of mosques in the Indian subcontinent. Imperial Mughal *masjids* tended to be square — Masjid-i Jami at Delhi (see **Plate 48**), or the Masjid Bādshāhī in Lahore (see **Plate 54**). However, numerically the larger *masjids* tended to be rectangular — Motī Masjid at Agra (see **Plate 45**), Masjid Wazir Khan of Lahore (see **Plate 46**), Masjid-i Jami in Tatta (see **Plate 49**), and the Mecca Masjid at Bījāpur (see **Plate 51**).

In virtually all cases noted above, the eastern entrance, the *darwāẓā,* tended to be the focal point, particularly of the exterior façade with a prominent masonry block. Those that enjoyed Imperial patronage were generally elevated above the surrounding area on a platform as in the Tughluq tradition. Size, particularly in the Masjid-i Jami of Delhi and the Masjid Bādshāhī in Lahore, appears to have been a prime concern.

South of the Imperial Court in Agra/Delhi rose the brilliant 'Adil Shahi Dynasty at Bījāpur. Both the Ibrahim Rauza and Gol Gumbaz are monuments of the first order.

The latter half of the seventeenth century brought irrevocable changes across the face of the Indian subcontinent. The open approach to the faith of his subjects that was practised by Akbar the Great and the relatively similar reigns of Jahangir and Shah Jahan were negated by the narrow minded bigotry of Aurangzeb. But, it was not merely Aurangzeb's character and approach that sounded the knell to any important architectural achievement in the subcontinent. The Masjid Bādshāhī of Lahore was the last truly important *masjid*. The decline of the Mughal Empire saw numerous petty princes vying for power in their areas. No longer did relative large kingdoms coalesce under a singly dynasty, but petty states with petty rulers grew up, not unlike Germany at the end of the nineteenth century.

Considerations

The considerations of architecture and regional architecture within India have seen numerous studies throughout the years. However the vast majority of these considerations have dealt with architectural detail and "style." Some are incredibly detailed, focusing on the myriad mouldings which go to make up the unbelievably detailed temples. Few, if any, have concentrated on the plans.[1] The focused consideration upon Islamic India's *masjid's* plans in India is even rarer.

Square or Rectangular

When considering the "Appearance of *masjid* types within this study" (see **Figure 6**) it is patently evident that the vast majority of *masjids* within India are of the rectangular type. This is understandable. When one peruses the various plans of mosques throughout the Islamic world, it is quite evident that the rectangle holds an elemental allure both in the broad expanse of the Islamic world, and India which is not outside the pale. Of the fifty-four, randomly selected *masjids*, forty-two are rectangular (see **Figure 26**). This would seem to cause one to state that the Indian Muslims preferred rectangular *masjids*. Of the forty-two, four are rectangular but with a square *haram*. Twelve of the selected *masjids* are square. Considering the twelve square *masjids* and the four with a square *haram*, it may be said that the square enjoyed some, but limited popularity. However, if one considers the major *masjids*, then the numeric difference between the square and the rectangle appears closer — thirteen major rectangular *masjids* and eleven which are square or have a square *haram*.

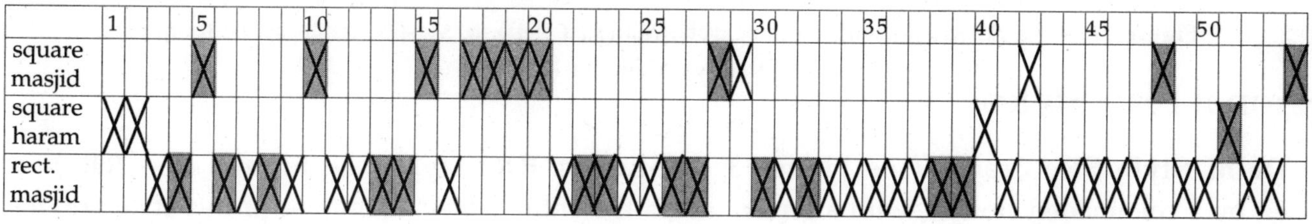

Figure 26 — Distribution of square *masjids*, square *haram* and rectangular *masjids*, (▇ = major masjids)

The square is not alien to Islam; a number of Islamic tombs exhibit a square plan (see **Appendix B — Plate 80**), although, the octagon seems more to their liking (see **Appendix B — Plate 65**). On the other hand, the rectangle was preserved for their *masjids*. The use of the square as the basic design element for a mosque was unusual, especially outside of India. However, a small number of important Indian *masjids* which are essentially square are found particularly in the northern half of India and before the mid-fifteenth century.

From the earliest Islamic incursions into India, it is believed that the local *sthapatis* were often employed in the construction and possibly certain design elements of the *masjids* of India. As with the Hindu temples, Islamic *masjids* had rather specific parameters. These conditions regarded orientation and certain required spaces — *qiblā, mehrāb* and *haram*. They were not concerned with construction techniques — the dome on pendentive and/or squinch was common in Persia, Syria and Turkey, while the corbelled dome was more often than not employed early in Islamic India (see **Appendix B — Plate 82**).

1 HC and MS are excellent in their narrow focus in dealing with Islamic architecture. Krishna Deva, *Temples of India*, New Delhi: 1995, is one of the finest in an overview of Hindu temples, although there are some important areas that he neglects — temples of south India.

Considerations (Continued)

Construction techniques and elemental design are not necessarily intertwined. The early square *masjids* — the Masjid Aṛhāi-din-kā-Jhoṅpṛā at Ajmer, the Masjid-i Jami of Cambay, the Masjids Begampurī, Kalan and Khiṛkī in Delhi, and the Masjid-i Jami of Srinagar — may be square, but to apply the Hindu *maṇḍala*, a basic Hindu design element, to these *masjids* is fraught with problems. The Masjid Aṛhāī-din-kā-Jhoṅpṛā and the Khiṛkī Masjid may generally appear to be related to the Sthānīya and Padmagarbha Maṇḍalas, at least as far as the *sahn* and *haram* are concerned (see **Figure 27**). But, the relationship of a *maṇḍala* and the whole is not possible, it would seem.

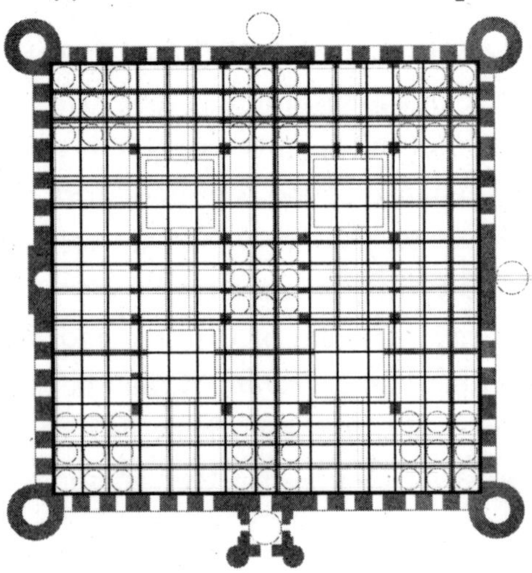

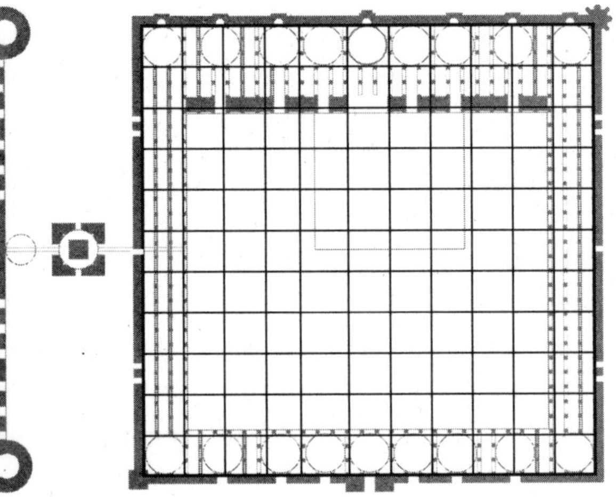

Figure 27 — Khiṛkī Masjid with Padmagarbha Maṇḍala (left), & Masjid Aṛhāī-din-kā-Jhoṅpṛā with Sthānīya Maṇḍala (right)

Regional Plan Styles

The **Delhi Style SRc** design (see **Figure 3 — SRc**) or **RRc** style (see **Figure 4 — RRc**), is typified by a colonnaded cloister, with a screen across the entire *haram*. Examples of this style are: the Quwwat-ul-Islam Masjid (see **Plate 39**) and the Masjid Aṛhāi-din-kā-Jhoṅpṛā, Ajmer (see **Plate 5**) (see **Figure 28**), as well as the Masjid-i Jami, Cambay (see **Plate 10**).

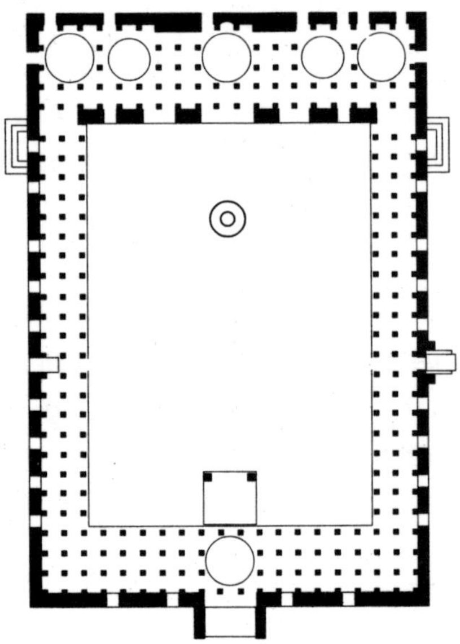

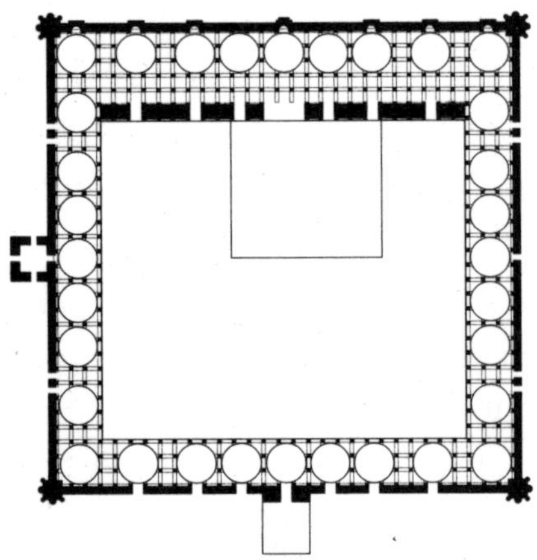

Figure 28 — Delhi Style, Quwwat-ul-Islam Masjid (left), Masjid Aṛhāī-din-kā-Jhoṅpṛā (right)

Considerations (Continued)

The **Delhi/Tughluq Style** is generally seen to be cross axial, *en plan* — **Sc2** design (see **Figure 3 — Sc2**) — built upon a substantial raised platform, employs battered walls for the entrance pavilions and bastion-like corner towers. Of note are the following: the Masjid Begampurī (see **Plate 15**) (see **Figure 29**), the Masjid Kalan (see **Plate 17**), the Khiṛkī Masjid (see **Plate 18**), and the Masjid-i Jami, Srinagar (see **Plate 19**).

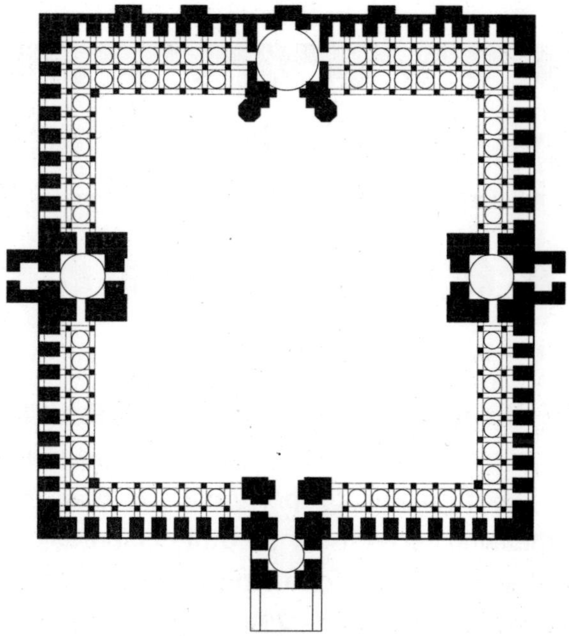

Figure 29 — Delhi/Tughluq Style, Masjid Begampurī

Jaunpur Style is related to the Delhi/Tughluq Style, and tends to be quite large. The *masjid*s are generally square and cross axial They possess monumental entrances or *darwāẓā* with massive and battered *haram*-screens resembling a pylon (propylon). They have deep, multi-aisle cloisters (*riwāq*) which are sometimes two storeys in height. Exemplars of this style being: Atala Masjid (see **Plate 20**) (see **Figure 30**), and the Masjid-i Jami (see **Plate 27**).

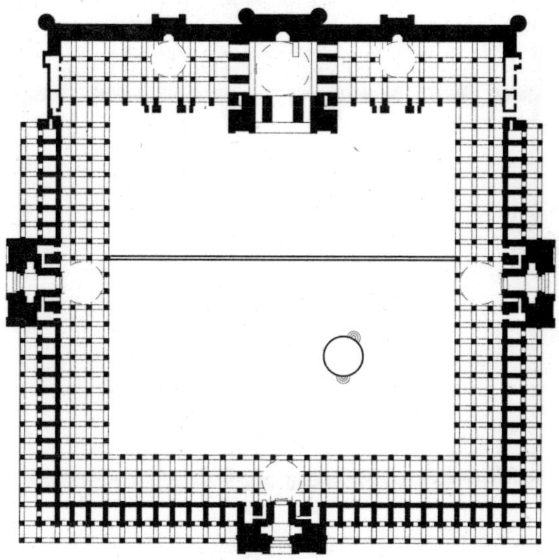

Figure 30 — Jaunpur Style, Atala Masjid

Considerations (Continued)

Pandua/Gaur/Beṅgālī Style is generally **R2** in design (see **Figure 4 — R2**). The *masjids* are constructed of brick and, therefore, tend to have thicker walls. Their bays are generally domed and later examples — after the Adina Masjid of Pandua — are without a *sahn*. Some examples of this style are: the Adina Masjid (See: **Plate 13**), the Gunmani Masjid (see **Plate 31**) (see **Figure 31**), and the Choṭā Sonā Masjid (see **Plate 33**).

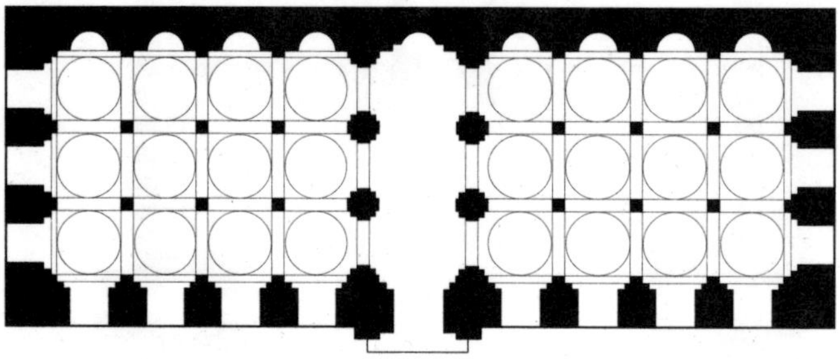

Figure 31 — Pandua/Gaur/Bengal Style, Gunmani Masjid

The **Gujarat Style** is generally **RRc** in design (see **Figure 4 — RRc**). The mosques frequently exhibit colonnaded *riwāq* and *haram* that consists of several deep bays and with multiple domes in various arrangements. The *haram* tends to be of greater, proportional size than found in other *masjids* of India (see **Appendix B, Plate 72**) and the *haram*-screen my be quite elaborate. The Gujarātī *rauza* displays a domed *haram* but separated from the tomb. The following are examples: the Masjid Ahmad Shah (see **Plate 22**), the Masjid-i Jami, Ahmedabad (see **Plate 23**), the Rānī Separī Rauza Masjid (see **Plate 25**), the Rānī Rūpmatī Masjid (see **Plate 26**), the Masjid Ahmad Shah, Sarkhej (see **Plate 30**), the Masjid-i Jami, Campāner (see **Plate 32**) (see **Figure 32**).

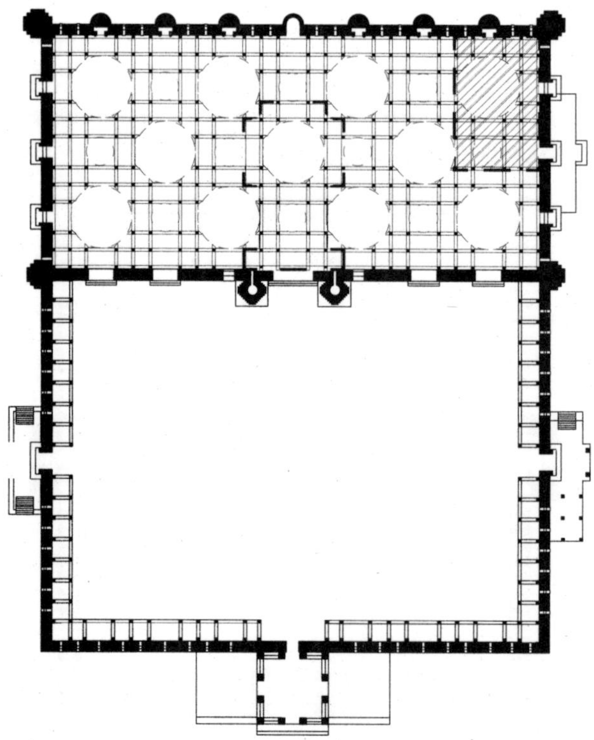

Figure 32 — Gujarātī Style, Masjid-i Jami, Campāner

Considerations (Continued)

The **Bījāpur Style** is generally an **R2** design (see **Figure 4 — R2**). It is often of a smaller scale and may be attached to a tomb creating a *rauza*. Symbolic of this style are: the Ibrahim Rauza Masjid (see **Plate 39**) (see **Figure 33**), the Ali Shahid Pir Masjid (see **Plate 40**), the Aṇḍā Masjid (see **Plate 41**), the Gol Gumbaz Masjid (see **Plate 42**), the Afzal Khan Rauza Masjid (see **Plate 49**), and the Shah Navaz Khan Rauza Masjid (see **Plate 50**).

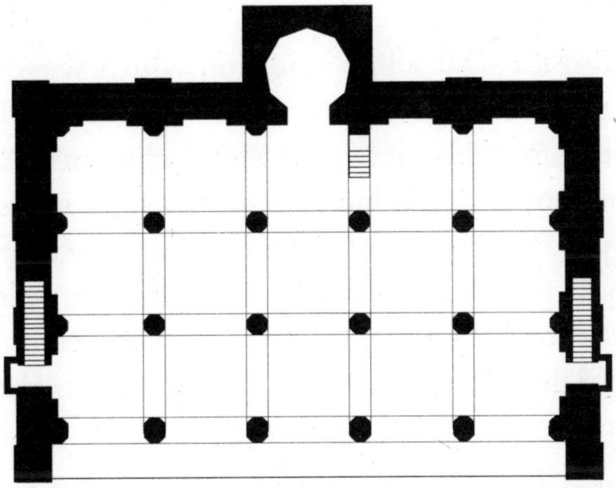

Figure 33 — Bījāpur Style, Ibrahim Rauza Masjid

Imperial Mughal Style emphasizes size and grandeur. The mosque is often square, set upon a raised platform, and with a monumental *darwāẓā*(s) accessed by broad flights of receding stairs. The cloisters (*riwāq*) are colonnaded with a multistoried *haram* consisting of three or five domes often extending into the *sahn* (see **Appendix B — Plate 85**). Examples of this style are: Bādshāhī Masjid, Fatehpur Sikri (see **Plate 37**), the Masjid-i Jami, Delhi (see **Plate 45**) (see **Figure 34**), and the Masjid Bādshāhī, Lahore (see **Plate 51**).

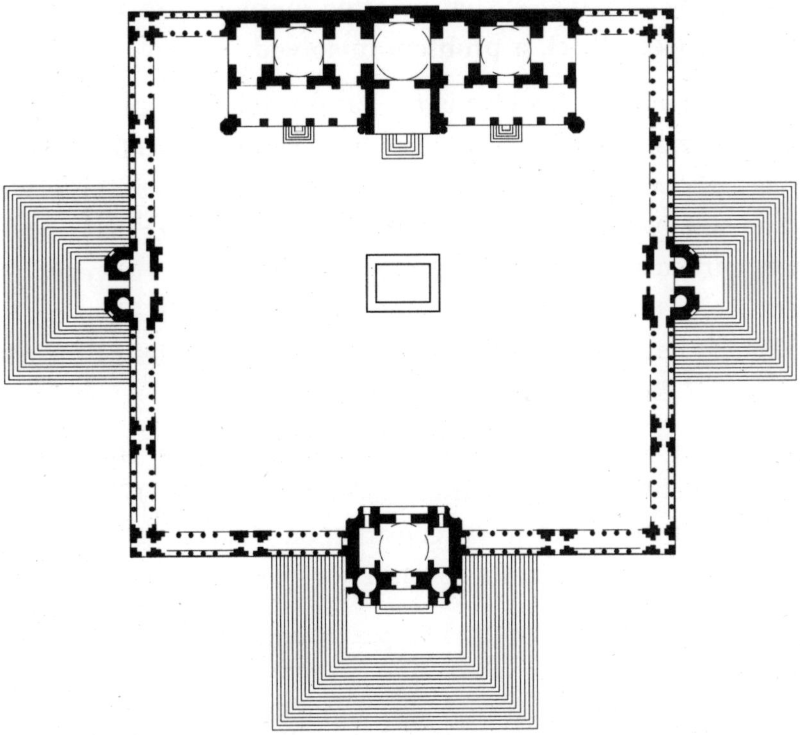

Figure 34 — Imperial Mughal Style, Masjid-Jami, Delhi

Considerations (Continued)

Material and Design

Stone, Brick or Wood

Stone architecture within India, whether additive or subtractive, had been practised for two millennia prior the coming of Islam to its shores. The Turkic, Afghani and Mughal invaders brought with them not only a religious tradition, but also a construction tradition which was largely trans-Indus or trans-Hindu-Kush and much of it rooted in eastern Mediterranean techniques. The clash came, not so much in building techniques, particularly stone, but in basic design techniques. Although the arcuated system of construction would have been known to the Indian *sthapati*s since early Persian times and certainly since the time of Alexander, they chose to employ the trabeated system instead. They were masters of the trabeated system and true masters of the monolithic or subtractive system of stone architecture. To fault the Buddhist/Hindu *sthapati*s for not employing the arcuated technique would be as ludicrous as faulting the Greeks for their use of the trabeated system. The Buddhist/Hindu builders of India simply preferred the use of post and lintel over the arch and dome.

Stone was suited to the trabeated system with the obvious caveat that one could only span so far with a stone lintel. Neither the Buddhist, nor Hindu faiths required large areas for weekly worship — they were not congregational. Trabeated stone architecture served their purpose. Further, there were adequate supplies of suitable stone for construction in India with the exception of Bengal and the Ganges basin.

Brick architecture in India, or the employment of brick certainly is ancient. However, the major extant Hindu temples are of stone. Buddhist builders employed brick frequently in their early monuments, but later works tend to be of stone or brick and stone. Brick architecture may be trabeated if the lintel is of wood or stone. However, the arcuated system is often employed in major structures. Brick had advantages and disadvantages (see "**Brick a problem unsolved**," below).

Of all the available building materials, wood is the easiest to access, prepare and employ. Its main disadvantage is that unlike stone, it degrades quickly — it is susceptible to fire, rot and a host of insects. Only teak (*Tectona grandis verbenaceae*) and bubinga (*Guibourtia leguminosa*) are woods available that were resistant to insects and suitable for construction. It is an accepted fact that many cultures employed wood in their construction, particularly of smaller domestic architecture. However, the transitory nature of wood means that there are virtually no examples except those which have been constructed in the near past. The brilliant Khmers have left numerous architectural examples of their temples and temple mounts. Their wooden palaces? Nothing remains!

However there are examples of wood architecture in India that are noteworthy. The Padmanābhapuram Palace of Kanyakumari District in Tamil Nadu (CE 1729–58) is a prime example. Much of this complex is wood or stone and wood construction. And, of course the Mithqalpalli Masjid of Calicut employed a great deal of wood in its construction (see **Plate 40**).

Considerations (Continued)

Brick, a Problem Unsolved

Brick architecture possesses many advantages. First, clay, the basic material needed for the making of bricks, is generally available throughout the vast subcontinent. Second, bricks are easily made and require only low-tech preparation. Third, the techniques for laying brick are easily learned. And, four, brick construction progresses rather rapidly. However, there are downsides! Wood, which in those days was the only readily available material needed in the firing process, was plentiful, but the renewal of that natural resource took years to replenish. Famed Pagan built hundreds of temples of low-fired brick and it is surmised that part of its decline was spawned by the razing of the surrounding forests eventually creating major ecological problems. If the bricks were to be high-fired more wood was required, and high-fired bricks are impervious to water. It was far easier and more economical, though inherently more problematical, to produce low-fired bricks which, unfortunately, were not waterproof and would eventually deteriorate from the effect of being directly exposed to water. However, the problematical low-fired bricks could have been employed and easily maintained if the surfaces were protected from the inevitable rain, particularly of the Bengal area. This could be achieved by applying waterproofing to the interior and exterior such as stucco. But this would not be enough! The base of the structure would have to be elevated and constructed of material, such as stone, which would not be affected by ground water or standing water. Finally the whole would have to be protected by a roof-form that would carry rain away from the walls and base of the structure. The *baṅgāladāra* roof may be seen as one attempt, but it was woefully inadequate. All Bengal needed to do was to look south — FAR south. Both the Safa Masjid (see **Plate 37**; and **Appendix C — Plate 90**) at Ponda or the Mithqalpalli Masjid (see **Plate 40**; and **Appendix C — Plate 92**) of Calicut provided a solution — high pitched roofs with wide overhanging eaves to direct the rain water away from the walls. Alas, this was not done.

To Cover or Not to Cover

Grover, referring to the Masjid-i Jami of Gulbargā, asserts that "To the great egalitarian brotherhood" of Islam where congregational worship was the pivotal ritual, this 'compartmentalization' of the faithful at prayer was psychologically more difficult to tolerate than the hot Indian sun."[1] He further asserts that a mosque which is completely covered is, likewise, "psychologically more difficult to tolerate." But then goes on to infer that the Turkic exemplar of an "uninterrupted huge domed space" was the only other choice to an open *sahn*. Where does that put other *masjid*s which are completely covered — the Masjid al-Aqsa at Jerusalem, the Great Mosque of Cordoba, or Fez' Masjid Qarawiyyin, Tanzania's Masjid Kilwa Kisiwani, or Malaysia's Masjid Kampung Laut? Quite simply, a covered mosque, whether trabeated or arcuated has never been an impediment to the world of Islam. The eclectic Khiṛkī Masjid of Delhi, the Jami' al-Kabir or Khutba Perriapalli at Kayalpatnam, the Masjid-i Jami of Gulbargā, the Masjid Ahmad Shah of Gujarat, the Solah Khumbā Masjid in Bīdar, the diminutive Qadiriya Masjid at Kayalpatnam, Gunmani Masjid and the Choṭa Sonā Masjid in Gaur, the impressive Mithqalpalli Masjid at Calicut, and the various *rauza masjid*s were enclosed without apparent undue psychological or theological problems to the worshippers. Furthermore, virtually all the converts to Islam in India were either Hindu or Buddhist who had for centuries worshipped in small, dark, confined spaces.

1 SG, p, 32.

Considerations (Continued)

Islam is an "egalitarian brotherhood", to be sure. Within a mosque, during the assigned prayers, all are equal. Originally, the *maqsura* was a raised platform with screens set apart for the safety of the Calif or other high ranking worshippers. This was soon done away with as it elevated literally and theologically the ones who used it. This was unacceptable. Furthermore, in most countries, those who attend prayers in a *masjid*, divest themselves of anything denoting wealth, particularly gold.[1] Even the former King of Morocco, when he prayed at Friday prayers with his countrymen/subjects, did so sitting on the same level, in a simple white garment and without his gold Rolex.

An Accommodation to the Women

Islam, in many areas, separates men and women. Within palaces and larger domiciles, there are separate areas for the women of the household. Within the faith, neither the Qur'an nor the Sunna prohibit women from entering a mosque, but there are guidelines on how they are to act. In many countries men and women worship separately. In some areas women are not allowed into mosques to worship and, generally, women do not attend the *solat jumaat*.

Among the many elements which make the Adina Masjid of Pandua most interesting is the inclusion of a mezzanine to the north of the main *mehrāb* for the ladies of the court (see **Plate 13**). This feature was not generally found in the major *masjids* of India prior to this time. On the other hand, the major *masjids* of Gujarat, beginning with the Masjid Ahmad Shah at Ahmedabad (see **Plate 22**) and continuing with the Masjid Ahmad Shah of Sultan Shams-ud-Din Muzaffar Ahmad Shah I (see **Plate 23**), as well as the Masjid-i Jami at Sarkhej (see **Plate 30**), the Masjid-i Jami of Campāner (see **Plate 32**) and finally Choṭā Sonā Masjid of Gaur (see **Plate 30**) all provided an elevated and/or screened enclosure for the women of the court. Bījāpur, on the other hand, approached the problem a bit differently. There, they constructed *masjids* specifically for women — the Aṇḍā Masjid (see **Plate 42**), the Mecca Masjid (Makkā Masjid) (see **Plate 52**) and the Afzal Khan Rauza Masjid (see **Plate 53**).

1 Many Muslims will not allow gold crowns or inlays on their teeth for this very reason.

Bibliography

Bibliography

Acharya, P.K., *An Encyclopaedia of Hindu Architecture*, London: 1927-1946.

———, *Architecture of Manasara*, translated from the original Sanskrit, London: 1932.

Ahmad, Mabel L., *The Secret Power of Names and Numbers: A Guide to your Destiny*, Bombay: 1991.

Alfieri, Bianca Maria, *Islamic Architecture of the Indian Subcontinent*, London: 2000.

———, and Vivat Temiyabandha, *Northern Thai Domestic Architecture and Rituals in House-Building*, Bangkok: 1978.

Asher, Catherine B, *Architecture of Mughal India*, New Delhi: 1995.

Atmadi, Parmono, *Some Architectural Design Principles of Temples in Java*, Yogyakarta: 1994.

Auboyer, Jeannine et al., *Oriental Art: A Handbook of Styles and Forms*, trans. Elizabeth and Richard Bartlett, New York: 1980.

Banerje, Jitendranath N., *The Development of Hindu Iconography*, 2nd edn., Calcutta: 1956.

Banerjee, P. et al., *Buddhist Iconography*, New Delhi: 1989.

Bary, Theodore de, *Sources of Indian Tradition*, vol. I, New York: 1958.

Batley, C., *Design Development of Indian Architecture*, Bombay: 1934

Bell, Eric T., *Numerology*, Baltimore: 1933.

Bhattacharyya, Benoytosh, *The Indian Buddhist Iconography Mainly Based on the Sadhanamala and other Cognate Tantric Texts of Rituals*, Calcutta: 1958.

Bhattacharyya, Dipak Chandra, *Studies in Buddhist Iconography*, New Delhi: 1978.

Bhattacharya, K., "Les religions brahmaniques dan l'ancien Cambodge, d'après l'èpigraphie et l'iconographie," *Cahiers de l'ècole Française d'Extrême-Orient*; XLIX, Hanoi: 1961.

Bhiarsri, Silpa, *Thai Buddhist Art (Architecture)*, Bangkok: 1988.

Brown, Percy, *Indian Architecture* (*Buddhist and Hindu Periods*), Bombay: n. d.

———, *Indian Architecture* (*Islamic Period*), Bombay: (1965-1968).

Brunes, Tons, *The Secrets of Ancient Geometry and Its Use*, vols. I-II, Copenhagen: 1967.

Bunce, Fredrick W., *A Dictionary of Buddhist and Hindu Iconography — Illustrated — Objects, Devices, Concepts, Rites and Related Terms*, New Delhi: 1996.

———, *Numbers Found in Buddhist & Hindu Practices: an Iconographic Consideration*, New Delhi: 2002.

———, *The Iconography of Plans: A Study of the Influence of Buddhism and Hinduism on Architectural Plans of South and South-East Asia*, New Delhi: 2002.

———, *The Yantras of Deities and Their Numerological Foundations: An Iconographic Consideration*, New Delhi: 2000.

Burgess, J., *Muhammadan Architecture in Gujarat*, Varanasi: 1971.

Bussagli, Mario; John Shepley, trans, *Oriental Architecture/ 1: India, Indonesia, Indochina*, New York: 1989.

Carr, Stephen, *Archaeology and Monumental Remains of Delhi*, Allahabad: 1967.

Chandra, Lokesh, *Buddhist Iconography*, New Delhi: 1991.

Charernsupkul, Anuvit, *The Elements of Thai Architecture*, Bangkok: 1978.

Chopra, P.N., T.K. Ravindran, N. Subrahmanian, *History of South India*, 3 vols., New Delhi: 1979.

Coedès, George, *The Indianized States of South-East Asia*, Honolulu: 1968.

———, "Les Etats hindouises d'Indochine et d'Indonesie," *Histoire du Monde*, vol. III, Paris: 1948.

———, "Arte dell'Indonesia," *Civiltā dell'Oriente*, vol. IV, Rome: 1962.

Commissariat, Manekshah Sorabshah, *A History of Gujarat: Including a Survey of its Chief Architectural Monuments and Inscriptions*, Bombay: 1938.

Coomaraswamy, Ananda Kentish, "Symbolism of the Dome," *Indian Historical Quarterly*; XIV, Calcutta: 1938, pp. 1-56.

Cousens, Henry, *Bījāpur and Its Architectural Remains: With an Historical Outline of the Adil Shahi Dynasty*; (Archeological Survey of India, vol. XXXVIII, Imperial Series), reprint, Delhi: 1996.

Creswell, K.A.C., *A Short Account of Early Muslim Architecture*, Beirut: 1958.

Critchlow, Keith, *Islamic Patterns: An Analytical and Cosmological Approach*, London and New York: 1976.

Crump, Thomas, *The Anthropology of Numbers*, Cambridge: 1990.

Dagens, Bruno, ed. & trans., *Mayamata, Traite Sanskrit d'architecture, Premiere Partie*, Paris (?): 1970.

———, ed. & tr., *Mayamata, Traite Sanskrit d'architecture, Deuxeme Partie*, Paris (?): 1970.

Bibliography (Continued)

———, ed. & trans, *Mayamatam, Treatise of Housing, Architecture & Iconography* (2 Vols.), New Delhi: 1994.

de Bary, Wm, Theodore (ed.) et al., *Sources of Indian Tradition*, vol. I, New York: 1958.

Deva, Krishna, *Temples of India*, 2 vols., New Delhi: 1995.

Dieulafoy, M, *L'art antique de la Perse*, Paris: 1884-1885.

Fergusson, James, et al., *History of Indian and Eastern Architecture*, 2 vols., Delhi: 1967.

Frishman, Martin J., and Hasan-Uddin Khan, eds., *The Mosque, History, Architectural Development & Regional Diversity*, London: 1994.

Goodwin, Godfrey, *A History of Ottoman Architecture*, London: 1971.

Govinda (Lama), Anagarika, *Psycho-cosmic Symbolism of the Buddhist Stupa*, Emeryville: 1976.

Grover, Satish, *Islamic Architecture in India*, New Delhi: 1981.

Grube, Ernst, et al., ed., *Architecture of the Islamic World: Its History and Social Meaning*, London: 1978.

Haig, Wolseley, ed., *The Cambridge History of India*, Delhi: 1958.

Hara, O. Hashnu, *Number, Name and Colour: As Applied to Character and Fate*, New Delhi: 1995.

Havell, E.B., *Encyclopaedia of Architecture in the Indian Subcontinent*, reprint, New Delhi: 2000.

Hill, D. and O. Grabar, *Islamic Architecture and Its Decoration*, CE *800-1500*, Chicago: 1964.

Hillenbrand, Robert, *Islamic Art and Architecture*, London: 1999.

———, *Islamic Architecture: Form, Function & Meaning*, Edinburgh: 1994.

Hoag, John D, *Islamic Architecture*, Milan: 1975.

Husain, A.B.M., *Fatehpur-Sikri and its Architecture*, Dacca: 1970.

Intralib, Sonthiwan, *An Outline of the History of Religious Architecture in Thailand*, s.l., (Bangkok?): 1987.

Issam El-Said and Ayse Parman, *Geometric Concepts in Islamic Art*, London: 1976.

Jung, C.G., *Mandala Symbolism*, tr. R.F.C. Hull, Princeton: 1973.

Khan, Mohammad Waliullah, *Lahore and its Important Monuments*, Karachi: 1973.

Waliullah Khan, Mohammad, *Lahore and its Important Monuments*, Karachi: 1973.

Koch, Ebba, *Mughal Architecture: An Outline of Its History and Development 1526-1858*, London: 1991.

Kramrisch, S., *The Hindu Temple*: Calcutta: 1946.

———, "The Temple as Purusha," *Studies in Indian Temple Architecture*; ed. Pramod Chandra, Benares: 1975, pp. 40-47.

Kumar, Ravindra, *Secrets of Numerology: A Complete Guide for the Layman to Know the Past, Present and Future*, New Delhi: n.d.

Lalou, M., *Iconographie des etoffes peintes d'apres le Manjusrimulakalpa*, Paris: 1930.

Leksukhum, Santi, *The Redented Added-Angled Chedis and the Rabbeted-Angled Chedis of the Ayutthaya Period*, Bangkok: 1986, (BE 2529).

Liebert, G., *Iconographic Dictionary of the Indian Religions*, Leyden: 1976.

Luce, G.H., *Old Burma, Early Pagan*, 3 vols., New York: 1969.

———, "The Greater Temples of Pagan; The Smaller Temples of Pagan; Fu-kan-tu-lu; The Tan and the Ngai; Countries Neighboring Burma; The Ancient Pyu; Economic Life of the Early Burman." *Burma Research Society*, Fiftieth Anniversary Publication, no. 2. Rangoon: 1960.

Mahapatra, Sthapaka Miranjana, *Śilparatnakośa: A Glossary of Orissan Temple Architecture*, New Delhi: 1994.

Majumdar, R.C., ed., *The Delhi Sultanate*, Bombay: 1960.

———, *An Advanced History of India*, London: 1960.

Mani, Vettam, *Purāṇic Encyclopaedia*, Delhi: 1996.

March, Lionel, et al., *The Geometry of Environment*, Cambridge: 1974.

Marchal, H., *L'Architecture comparèe dans l'Inde et l'Extrême-Orient*, Paris: 1944.

Mehta, Rustam, *Masterpieces of Indo-Islamic Architecture*, Bombay: 1976.

Micell, G., ed., *Architcture of the Islamic World*, London: 1978.

Mohammad al-Asad, et al., eds., *The Mosque: History, Architectural Development & Regional Diversity*, London: 1994.

Morgan, W.S., *Kisah Tanah Melayu*, Singapore: 1949.

Muhammad Rabi 'ibn Muhammad Ibrahim, *The Ship of Sulaiman*, New York: 1972.

Mukherji, Anisha Shekhar, *The Red Fort of Shahjahanabad*, New Delhi: 2003.

Naqoi, S.A.A., *Humayun's Tomb and Adjacent Buildings*, Delhi: 1947.

Nath, R., *Fatehpur Sikri and its Monuments*, Agra: 2000.

Bibliography (Continued)

———, *History of Mughal Architecture*, New Delhi: 1985.

———, *History of Sultanate Architecture*, New Delhi: 1978.

———, *Islamic Architecture & Style in India*, New Delhi (?): 1982.

Nayeem, M.A., *The Splendour of Hyderabad : The Last Phase of an Oriental Culture (CE 1591-1948)*, reprint, Hyderabad: 2002.

Nilakanta Sastri, *South India Influences in the Far East*, s. l., : 1949.

Parmentier, H., *L'Art khmer primitif*, Paris, 1927.

———, *L'Art khmer classique*, Paris: 1939.

———, *L'Art architectural hindou dans l'inde et en Extreme-Orient*, Paris: 1948.

Pereira, Jose, *Islamic Sacred Architecture: A Stylistic History*, New Delhi: 1994.

Prabhakar Apte, June, "Vastu-Purusha Mandala: Dramatic Architectural and Artistic Study of Vastu-Purusha Mandala in Vastu-Vedic, Agamic and Puranic Tradition with Special Reference to Mayamata," *1993 Seminar on Mayonic Science & Technology*, Madras (unpublished: Library of the American Institute of Indian Studies, Gurgaon, Haryana).

Prochazka, Amjad Bohumil, *Architecture of the Islamic Cultural Sphere*, Zurich: 1986.

Raja Bahrin Shah bin Raja Ahmad Shah, *The Terengganu Timber Malay House*, s. l. (Kuala Lumpur): (1981).

Rapson, E.J., et al. (eds.), *The Cambridge History of India*, 6 vols., Delhi: 1955.

Rowland, Benjamin, *The Art and Architecture of India: Hindu, Buddhist, Jain*, Baltimore: 1967.

Safrani, Shehbaz H., *Golconda and Hyderabad*, Bombay: 1992.

Sartono Kartodirdjo, ed., *700 Tahun Majapahit (1293-1993) Suatu Bunga Rampai*, Surabaya: 1993.

Sarkar, H., *Some Contributions of India to the Ancient Civilization of Indonesia and Malaysia*, Calcutta: 1970.

———, *Studies in Early Buddhist Architecture of India*, Delhi: 1966.

Sevcenko, Margaret, ed., *Theories and Principles of Design in the Architecture of Islamic Societies*, Cambridge: 1988.

Sharma, P.K., *Mughal Architecture of Delhi*, New Delhi: 2000.

Sinclair, W.B., "Monasteries of Pagan," *Burma Research Society*, Fiftieth Anniversary Publication, no. 2, Rangoon: 1960.

Sivaramamurti, C., *The Art of India*, New York: 1977.

———, *Le Stupa de Barobudur*, Paris: 1960.

Smith, Edmond W., *Akbar's Tomb.*, n.d.

Snodgrass, A., *The Symbolism of the Stupa*, Ithaca: 1985.

Soucek, Pricilla P., *Content and Context of Visual Arts in the Islamic World*, University Park: 1988.

Soundara Rajan, K.V., *Ahmedabad*, New Delhi: 1980.

———, *Islam Builds in India*, Delhi: 1983

Stierlin, Henri, ed., *Architecture of the World: India*, Lausanne: n. d.

———, *Architecture of the World: Islamic India*, Lausanne: n. d.

Strachan, Paul, *Imperial Pagan: Art and Architecture of Burma*, Honolulu: 1989.

Stuart, C.M. Villiers, *Gardens of the Great Mughals*, New Delhi: 1983.

Tewari, S.P., *Hindu Iconography*, New Delhi: 1979.

Thapar, Binda, *Introduction to Indian Architecture*, Singapore: 2004.

Tillotson, G.H.R., *Mughal India*, London: 1990.

Vatsyayan, Kapila, *Buddhist Iconography*, New Delhi: 1989.

———, *The Square and the Circle of the Indian Arts*, New Delhi: 1983.

Volwahsen, A., *Living Architecture: Islamic-Indian*, London: 1970.

Williams, C.A.S., *Outlines of Chinese Symbolism and Art Motives*, New York: 1976.

Wilson, G., et al., *Geometry for Architects*, Champaigne: 1962.

Yazdani, Ghulam, *Bīdar, Its History and Monuments*, London: 1947.

Appendix A

Glossary

Glossary

ablaq — (Arab.) The term refers to two-toned marble or stone decoration. Literally means "piebald."

amīr — (Arab.) The term refers to a commander or prince of the Islamic world.

aṇḍā — (Indic: aka *dhātu-garbha, garbha, gaeba*) The term refers to an egg-shape, more specifically to the hemispherical form of a *stūpa*. It is also referred to as: *garbha* and *gaeba*.

atabeg — (Arab.) The term refers to a governor or a guardian of a prince.

axiality — The symmetrical arrangement of the elements of a plan along a given axis. If that axis is east-west, then the northern half is a duplicate of the southern half.

bagh — (Arab.) The term refers to a garden, usually square or made up of square components. It may also refer to a pleasure palace.

baṅgāladāra — (Indic) The term refers to a bowed roof-line, typical of thatched roofs of the region, but later applied to masonry roofs of the same shape. (see **Appendix B, Plate 55**)

baraka — (Arab.) The term refers to "blessed one" or divine grace. It may also refer to the intangible spirit emanating from a holy man, or spiritual power.

birka — (Arab.: aka *fisqiya, haud, saqaya, sihrij*) The term refers to an ablution tank that is normally found within the confines of a *masjid*.

Brāhmanic — Here, referring to the religious practice which includes both Vedic and post-Vedic or Hindu practices.

brahmasthāna — (Indic) The term refers to the central area of a Hindu *maṇḍala* in which the prime deity resides.

buq'a — (Arab.) The term refers to a monastic retreat.

calif — (Arab.) The term refers to a successor of the Prophet Mohammad, from the Arabic *khalifa*.

cami — (Turkish: aka *masjid*) The term refers to a mosque particularly one in which great numbers gather for Friday prayers.

canopy tombs — (Eng.) The term refers to an octagonal, *en plan*, tomb which has a roofed verandah around the whole of the central chamber. The form of this central (octagonal) chamber extends above the level of the surrounding verandah as a podium for a culminating dome.

caravanserai — (Arab.; Turk.: *han*) The term refers to a resting place for travellers or caravans. Generally found on trade routes and may be fortified to protect the travellers and their goods.

cardak — (Arab.) The term refers to a reception room generally employed during the summer months.

chahar-bagh — (Arab.) The term refers to a plot of land, generally square, that is divided into four equal sections.

caitya — (Indic: aka *cetiya, stūpa*) Another term for *stūpa*. As in a *caitya* hall, the *stūpa* here tends to be carved from solid rock as a memorial.

chajjā — (Indic: aka *cajjā*) The term refers to the overhanging eaves-stone that generally encircles a temple or mausoleum above the level of the doors.

caṇḍī — (Indon.: aka *caṇḍī*) The term is attached to a temple or temple complex in Indonesia — *Chaṇḍī Sewu*. It may be derived from or refer to: *chedi*, or *Chaṇḍī* (goddess of death).

chatrī — (Indic) The term refers to a kiosk with a dome usually supported by four or eight pillars.

cedi — (Thai: aka *caitya, stūpa, zeidi*) The term refers to the Thai equivalent of a *stūpa*. Its form is greatly elongated into a tall thin form and may contain holy relics, ashes of monarchs, saints or other meritorious persons. In the later periods it loses its circular shape and becomes more angular.

cetiya — (Pāli: aka *caitya*) See: *caitya*.

cloister — (Eng; Arab.: *riwāq*) Although a term that is normally applied to Christian architecture, it is herein used to describe a court in which a covered or arcaded area is found around the perimeter of the court and is open towards the court. Generally it is found on all four sides, but, herein it is used to describe those courts (*sahn*) within a mosque in which a covered walkway is found on three sides of the open court.

cross-axiality — The symmetrical arrangement of the elements of a plan along both axes, precisely duplicating each quadrant. This term is not applied to rectangular plans. The north-south and east-west axes divide the form. The north-west quadrant is a duplicate of the north-east, south-west and south-east quadrants. This quadrant can either be mirrored in any of the other three, or rotated 90°, 180°, and 270° to achieve the whole.

Glossary (Continued)

dagaba — (Java.: aka *dagobā, dhātu-garbha, pagoḍā, stūpa*) The term refers to a *stūpa*, as in the *dagabā* of Borobudur. See *stūpa*.

dagoba — (Indic: aka *dagaba, pagoḍā*) A variant spelling for the term *dagaba*, see *dagaba*.

dargāh — (Arab.) The term refers to precinct that is set aside as a shrine, often for a holy man. It also refers to an entrance or portal (see **Introduction**).

darih — (Arab.) The term refers to a tomb.

darwāẓā — (Persian) The term refers to a gate, generally of monumental chatacter.

dergah — (Persia.) The term refers to a royal court.

dhātu-garbha — (Indic: aka *aṇḍā, garbha, gaeba*) A variant term for *aṇḍā*. See *aṇḍā*.

dikka — (Arab.) The term refers to a raised platform in line with the *mehrāb* where the *qadi* repeats the postures of the imam and responses to the prayers.

dīwān — (Arab.) The term refers to a royal reception chamber or enclosure — *Dīwān-ī-Ām* (Hall of Public Audience) or *Dīwān-ī-Khās* (Hall of Private Audience). It may also refer to a ministry of the government.

file — (Eng.) The term as used refers to a line of things, one behind the other. It also refers to the line, front to back, of a group of evenly spaced objects. See *rank*.

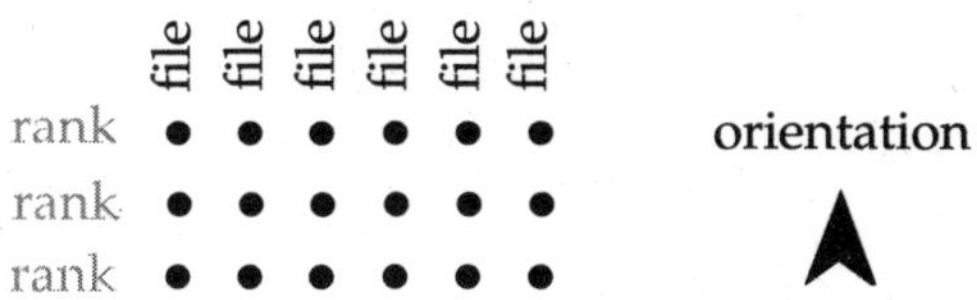

fisqiya — (Arab.: aka *birka, haud, saqaya, sihrij*) The term refers to an ablution tank that is normally found within the confines of a *masjid*.

funduq — (Arab.) The term refers to an inn or warehouse.

gaeba — (Sinhalese: aka *garbha, aṇḍā*) A variant term for *aṇḍā*. See *aṇḍā*.

garbha — (Indic: aka *aṇḍā, gaeba*) A variant term for *aṇḍā*. See *aṇḍā*.

garbhagṛha — (Indic) The term refers to the sanctuary, specifically of a Hindu temple. It is the place where the image of the main or presiding deity is housed and the access to it is limited to the priesthood. It is the *sanctum sanctorum* and the term refers to the womb room.

gaṛh mahal — (Indic) The term that is employed herein to refer to any palace or royal residence that is within and/or part of a fort or fortified, defensive structure.

ghazi — (Arab.) The term refers to a holy warrior, one who defends the faith.

girdle wall — The term refers to a wall enclosing a structure or compound.

gunbad — (Arab.: aka *gumbad, qubba*) The term refers to a dome.

han — (Turk.; Arab.: *caravanserai*) The Turkish equivalent for *caravanserai*. See *caravanserai*.

haram — (Arab.: aka *liwan*) The term refers to anything that is prohibited or forbidden by Shariah. The term also refers to private quarters in a home or the sanctuary of a mosque, or a sacred place of prayer. See: *liwan* (See **Introduction**).

haram-screen — A series of arches or propylon fronting the *haram*.

hasht bihisht — (Arab.) The term refers to the eight paradises. In architecture it refers to the eight rooms or areas around a central space. See also *muthamman baghdadi*.

haud — (Arab.: aka *birka, fisqiya, saqaya, sihrij*) The term refers to an ablution tank found in a *sahn*. (See p. 10)

hujra — (Arab.) The term refers to a small chamber or cell.

imām — (Arab.) The term refers to a leader of prayer, a spiritual leader analogous to a minister or priest.

imām khatib — (Arab.) The term refers to a preacher and prayer leader.

imām ratib — (Arab.) The term refers specifically to a prayer leader.

intarsia — (Ital.: aka *pietra dura*) See *pietra dura*.

iwan — (Arab.) The term refers to a roofed hall exposed at one end. Generally, it is a form that is found in Persian (Iranian) architecture

jabāna — (Arab.: aka *maqbara*; Persia.: *qabrstan*) The term refers to a cemetery.

jālī — (Arab./Ind.) The term refers to a thin, stone screen with a perforated design. See also *mashrabiya*.

jama'a — (Arab.) The term refers to a congregation.

jami' — (Arab.) The term refers to a large mosque where Friday prayers are held and a sermon is preached.

Glossary (Continued)

jihād — (Arab.) The term refers to "holy war," or a war to defend the faith.

Jum'at — (Arab.) The term refers to Friday *zuhur* prayer.

khan — (Arab.) The term refers to a man of high rank, either a lord or a prince.

khānaqāh — (Arab.) The term refers to a monastic-like structure that may also contain a mausoleum.

kiosk — (Turk.) The term refers to a summer house or a pavilion of open construction. It also refers to a small, often domed architectural form supported by pillars that appears as a major ornamental unit, usually at the corners of larger structures. See *chatrī*.

kotla — The term refers to a royal citadel or fortification.

ksar — (Arab.) The term refers to a fortified village.

kursi — (Arab.) The term refers to a lectern. (See p. 10)

lahd — (Arab.) The term refers to a burial vault. It may also refer to a niche. See also *madfam*.

liwan — (Arab.: aka *haram*) The term refers to a vaulted hall often associated with a mosque (*masjid*). It sometimes refers to the prayer hall of a *masjid*. See *haram*.

ma'adhdhana — (Arab.: aka *manara, minaret, sawma'a*) The term refers to a *minaret*. See *minaret*.

mabkhara — (Arab.) The term refers to a censor. It also refers to any *minaret* top which resembles a censor.

madfam — (Arab.: aka *lahd*) The term refers to a burial vault or mausoleum.

madrasa — (Arab.) The term refers to a Muslim school or institution in which orthodox sciences are taught, generally associated with a *masjid*.

maidan — (Arab.) The term refers to a square or plaza or ceremonial enclosure.

mamluk — (Arab.) The term refers to a slave.

manabhat-kari — (Indic) The term refers to stone inlay or *pietra dura*.

manara — (Arab.: aka *ma'adhdhana, minaret, sawma'a*) The term refers to a *minaret*. See *minaret*.

maṇḍala — (Indic) The term refers to a sacred Buddhist/Hindu diagram. Certain *maṇḍalas* were employed as the basis for architectural plans. The two preferred forms for temple designs were the Maṇḍūka Maṇḍala with sixty-four *pada* and the Paramaśayika Maṇḍala with eighty-one *pada*.

Maṇḍūka Maṇḍala — (Indic) The term refers to a *mandala* of sixty-four *pada* — eight in either direction. See *maṇḍala*.

maqbarā — (Arab.: aka *jabana;* Persia.: *qabrstan*) The term refers to a cemetery.

maqsura — (Arab.) The term refers to a screen which protects. It may be a pierced stone screen which protects an important tomb. Within a *masjid* is screened area to protect the Caliph or sultan or prince. In modern *masjid*, this feature does not exist.

marmas — (Indic) The term refers to the perpendicular crossing of lines within a *mandala*, created by the conjunction of four or more *pada*. In the Hindu tradition, it is considered inauspicious for any line delineating the form of the structure to fall upon a *marmas*. See *maṇḍala*.

mashhad — (Arab.) The term refers to a tomb or mausoleum for a martyr.

mashrabiya — (Arab.) The term refers to a grilled window or screen usually of wood. See also *jālī*.

masjid — (Arabic: aka *mosjid, cami*) The term refers to a mosque; literally "a place of prostration."

masjid-i jami' — (Arab.) The term refers to a mosque specifically for Friday prayers.

maẓār — (Arab.) The term refers to a mausoleum.

merlon — (Fr.) The term refers to a solid element often on a battlement between two openings (crenels). Within Indo-Islamic architecture these tend to be more decorative than functional.

mehrāb — (Arabic: aka *mikhrab*) A variant of *mikhrab*. See *mikhrab*..

mikhrab — (Arabic: aka *mehrāb*) The term refers to the "prayer niche" found in mosques in the wall facing Mecca (*qiblā*). The *imam* preaches or recites the Qur'an from the *minbar* adjacent to the *mikhrab* during the prayers.

minaret — (Arab.: aka *ma'adhdhana, manara,* ***sawma'a***) The term refers to a tall, slender tower(s) connected to a *masjid* from where the faithful are called to prayer.

minbar — (Arab.) The term refers to a raised pulpit adjacent to the *mikhrab* from where the *imam* recites the Qur'an and delivers the sermon.

mosjid — (Arabic: aka *masjid*) The term refers to a

Glossary (Continued)

variation on the term *masjid*. See *masjid*.

muqarnas — (Arab.) The term refers to small vaults, part of a larger vault that resemble honeycombs or stalactites.

musalla — (Arab.) The term refers to a compartment or space for prayer — the area on the floor that corresponds to the space needed for an individual to pray.

muthamman baghdadi — (Arab/Mughal) The term refers to a square plan to which the corners have been sheared off forming an irregular octagon. See also *hasht bihisht*.

pada — (Indic) The term refers to a single square found within a *maṇḍala*. See *maṇḍala*.

pagoḍā — (Burmese: aka *dagaba, dagoba, dhātu-garbha*) A variant term for *dagaba*. See *dagaba*.

pañcaratha — (Indic) The term refers to two separate extensions, generally in the middle portion of the surface of a wall, creating five surfaces per face. See *ratha* & *triratha*.

Paramaśayika Maṇḍala — (Indic) The term refers to a *maṇḍala* of eighty-one *pada* — nine in either direction. See *maṇḍala*.

Paṭhān — The term frequently refers to a style of Indo-Islamic architecture which finds its roots in Afghanistan (Pashtun tribe) and Iran (Persia).

pendentive — The term refers to an inverted triangle which is the transition from a square space to a dome. See squinch.

pietra dura — (Ital.: aka *intarsia*) The term refers to the inlaying or fitting of small, often complexly formed, pieces of stone, both precious and semi-precious, into a larger stone matrix which has been carefully carved out to receive the smaller pieces. It differs from the technique employed in an inlaid stone floor in which larger pieces of stone are fitted together in a pattern and set in concrete or other cementing agent.

pishtaq — (Arab.) The term refers to a tall arch which frames an *iwan*. It may also refer to a large, impressive portal.

propylon — The term refers to an entrance element or the feature of a *maqsura* which takes the form of a pylon — straight or stepped or slightly battered sides based upon a narrow rectangular plan and with an arched opening.

purdah — (Arab.) The term refers to being veiled, screened or separated. It may refer to an area or it may refer to a garment in which only the eyes are exposed.

qabr — (Arab.) The term refers to a grave.

qabrstan — (Persia.; Arab.: *jabana, maqbarā*) The term refers to a cemetery.

qadi — (Arab.) The term refers to an official of the *masjid* who repeats the postures and responses of the *imam* to the prayers, particularly in a large *masjid*.

qasabā — (Arab.) The term refers to a citadel or capital.

qasr — (Arab.) The term refers to a fortified residence, castle or a palace.

qiblā — (Arab.) The term refers to a wall which is perpendicular to the direction in which prayers are offered — always towards the Ka'ba in Mecca.

qubba — (Arab.: aka *gunbad*) The term refers to a dome. It may also refer to a mausoleum.

Qur'an — (Arab.; Eng.: Koran) The term refers to the holy book of Islam which was written down by the Prophet (Nabi) Mohammed.

rank — (Eng.) The term as used refers to a regular row or line — soldiers standing abreast. It also refers to the line, side to side, of a group of evenly spaced objects. See: *file*.

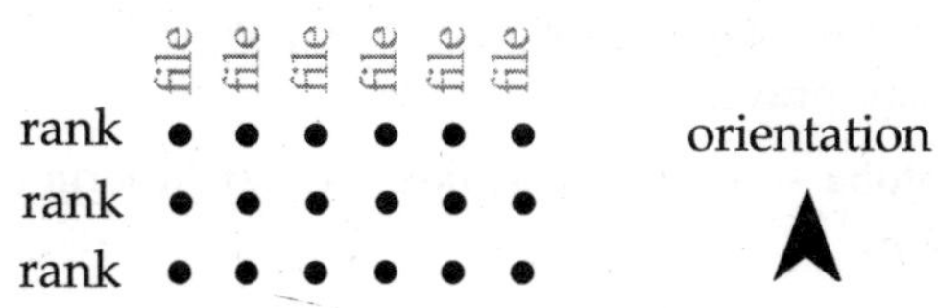

ratha — (Indic: aka *puṣpaka*) The term refers to an extension of a wall surface, generally on all four sides. If there is a single extension, the form is called *triratha* — creating three surfaces per face. If there are two extensions, the form is called *pañcaratha* — creating five surfaces per face. See: *pañcaratha* & *triratha*. Also, a variant of the term *puṣpaka*. See *puṣpaka*.

rauza — (Arab./Ind.) The term refers to an arrangement of a tomb, *birka* and *masjid*. The tomb confronts the *masjid* and the *birka* is between the two.

ribat — (Arab.) The term refers to a fortified Islamic monastery or hermitage. It may also refer to a frontier settlement.

riwāq — (Arab.) The term refers to the colonnaded arcade that surrounds the courtyard (*sahn*) of a *masjid*. (See *cloister*).

Glossary (Continued)

sahn — (Arab.) The term refers to a court within a *masjid.*

sawma'a — (Arab.: aka *minaret, ma'adhdhana, manara*) The term refers to a *minaret*. See *minaret.*

serai — (Arab.) The term refers to a pavilion, often open on four sides and is used for relaxation and other pleasurable activities.

shafá'a — (Arab.) The term refers to the concept of intercession and respect for a holy person such as a martyr (*śahīd*) or saint (*wilaya*). It is related to *baraka* which emanates from the tomb of a holy person.

shaikh — (Arab.: aka *sheik*) The term refers to a leader, usually a tribal chief.

shari'a — (Arab.) The term refers to Islamic law or code.

śikhara — (Indic) The term refers to a towerlike superstructure over the *garbha-gṛha* of a temple or any part thereof. It is made up of various sculptural devices and its form can vary.

sihrij — (Arab.: aka *saqaya, birka, haud, fisqiya*) The term refers to an ablution tank that is normally found within the confines of a *masjid.*

simurgh — (Arab.) The term refers to a phoenix, the mythical bird of countless legends.

solat jumaat — (Arab.: aka *solat jum'at*) The term refers to Friday prayers.

sotoba — (Japan: aka *stūpa*) A variant term for *stūpa.* See *stūpa.*

squinch — (Arab.) The term refers to an arch-like transition from a square chamber to an octagon to the surmounting dome.

sthapati — (Indic.) The term refers to an architect-builder, who in the Indian Hindu tradition was what the "master builder" was to the European Medieval tradition.

suffa — (Arab.) The term refers to a stone platform usually as a base for tombs.

sultan — (Arab.) The term refers to an Islamic ruler with the rank equivalent to a king, although, a *sultan* is referred to as "His Highness" rather than "His Majesty."

surau — (Arabic: aka *musalla*) The term refers to an area or small structure utilized by Muslims for the daily prayers. It is not a mosque, but may be equated with a chapel in the Christian world — a place of worship to which a cleric is not permanently attached.

triratha — (Indic) The term refers to a single extension, generally in the middle portion of the surface of a wall, creating three surfaces per face. See *ratha* & *pañcaratha.*

turba — (Arab.) The term refers to a mausoleum

turbe — (Turk.) The term refers to a mausoleum.

visier — (Arab.: aka *visir*) An alternate spelling for *visir*. See *visir.*

visir — (Arab.: aka *wazir*) See *waẓīr.*

waẓir — (Arab.: aka *visir*) The term refers to a high governmental official, a Minister of State.

zedi — (Burmese) A variant of *Zeidi*. See Zeidi;

zeidi — (Burman) The term refers to a *stūpa* (Thai: *chedi*).

ziārat — (Ind.) The term refers to a village shrine frequently encountered in Kashmir. It consists of a square, wooden structure with symmetrical verandahs or balconies and a pyramidal roof. It also refers to a square pavilion with pyramidal, tiered roofs topped by a narrow flesche-like spire.

ziyara — (Arab.) The term refers to a tomb.

zuhur — (Arab.) The term refers to the noon prayer.

Appendix B

Miscellaneous Plans

Plate 55 — Great Mosque of Damascus (CE 707-714)

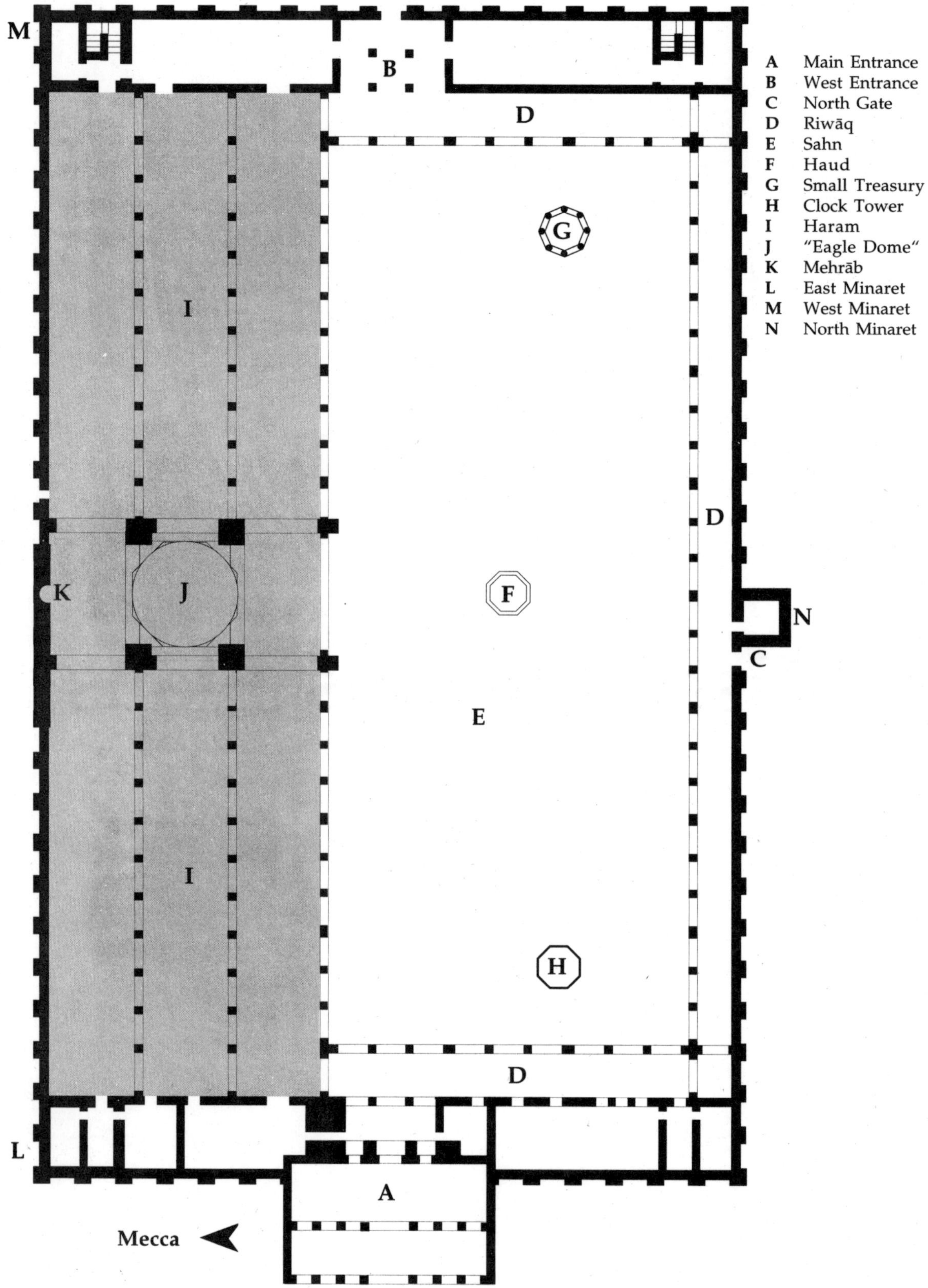

Plate 56 — Great Mosque of Cordoba (CE 785-987)

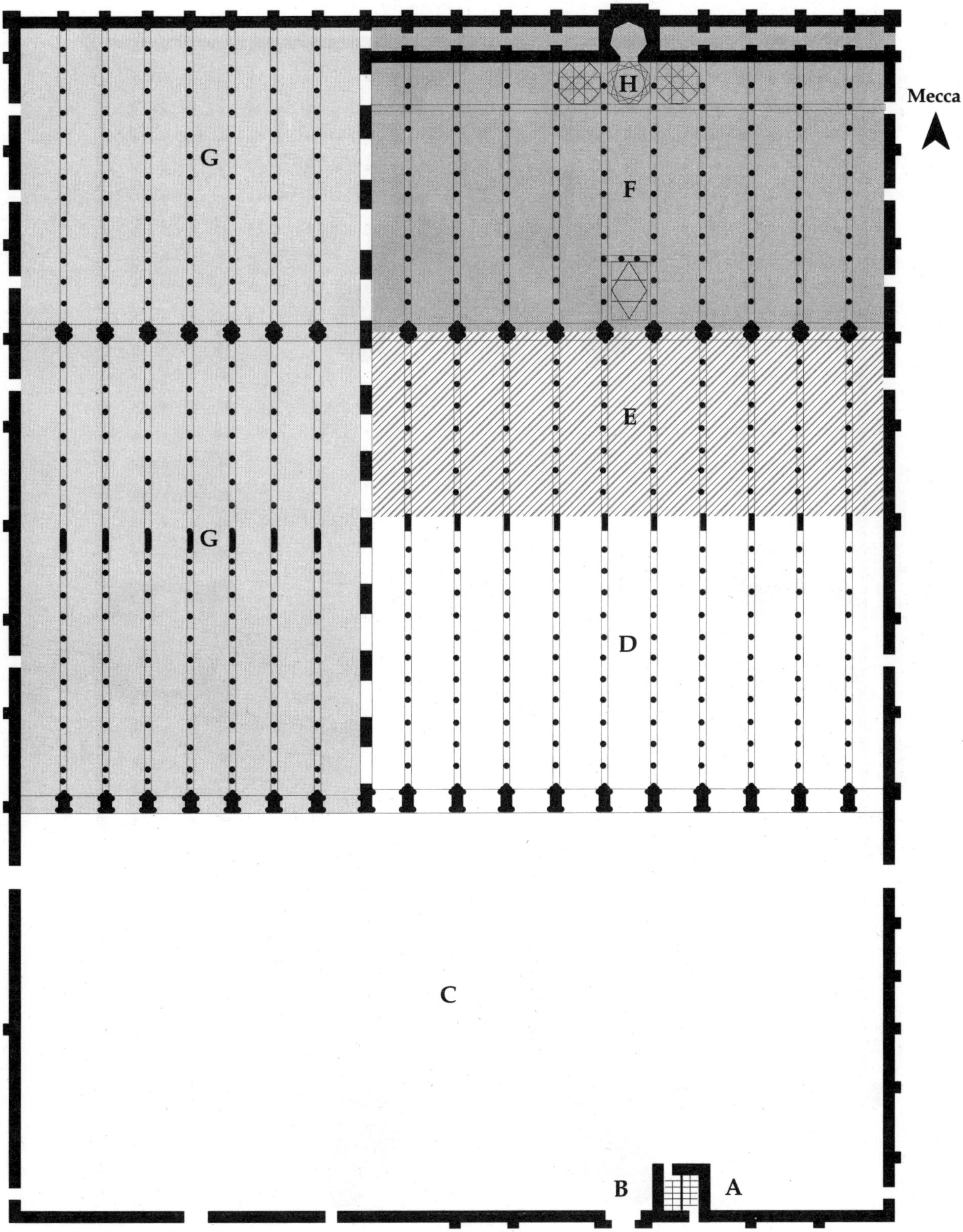

A	Minaret	**F**	Haram of 929
B	Main Entrance	**G**	Haram of 987
C	Sahn	**H**	Maqsura & Mehrāb of 961
D	Haram of 785		
E	Haram of 832		

Plate 57 — Masjid Jami, Samarqand (CE 1398-1405)

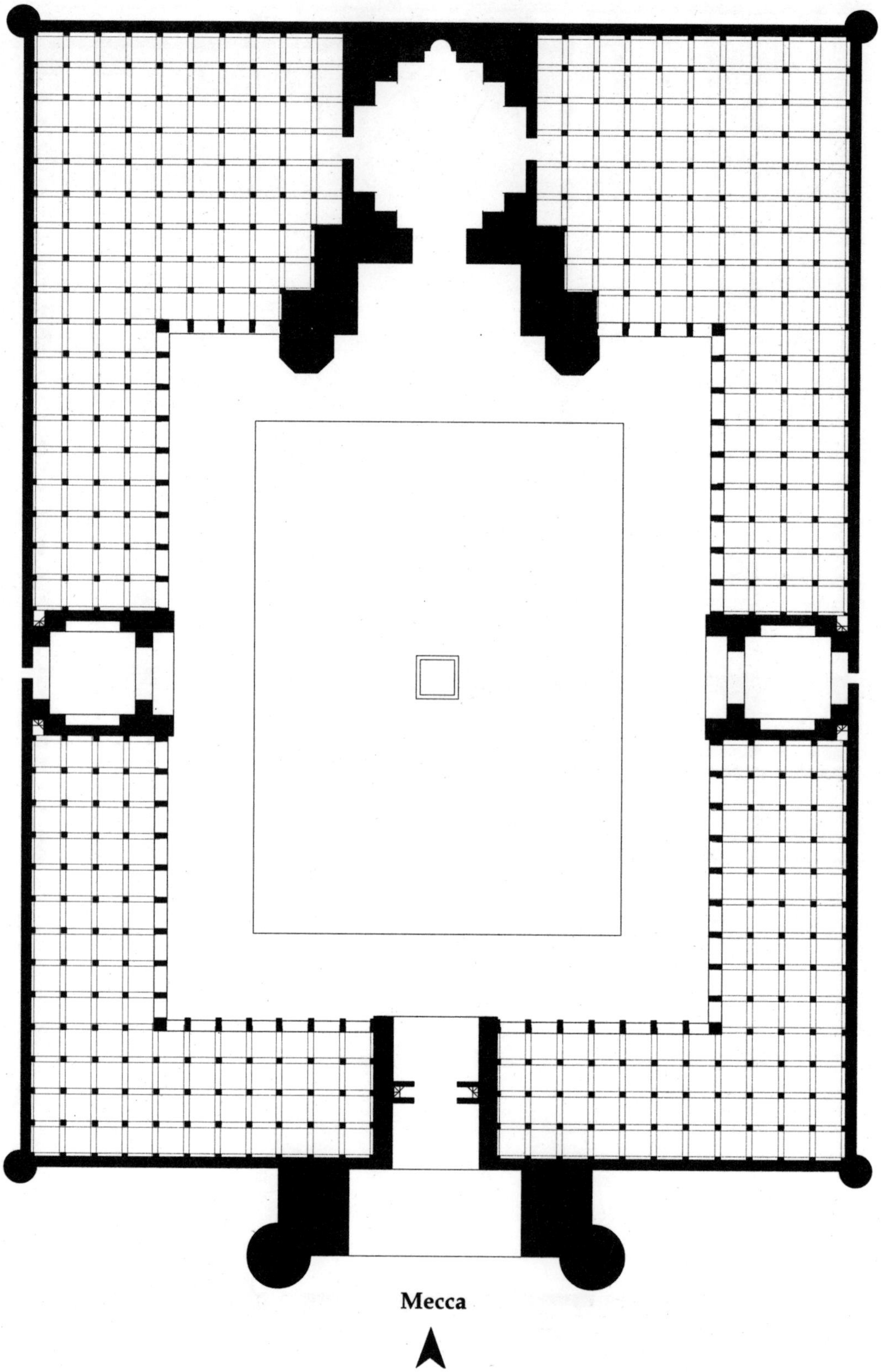

Plate 58 — Sehzade Mehmet Masjid, Istanbul (c.CE 1550)

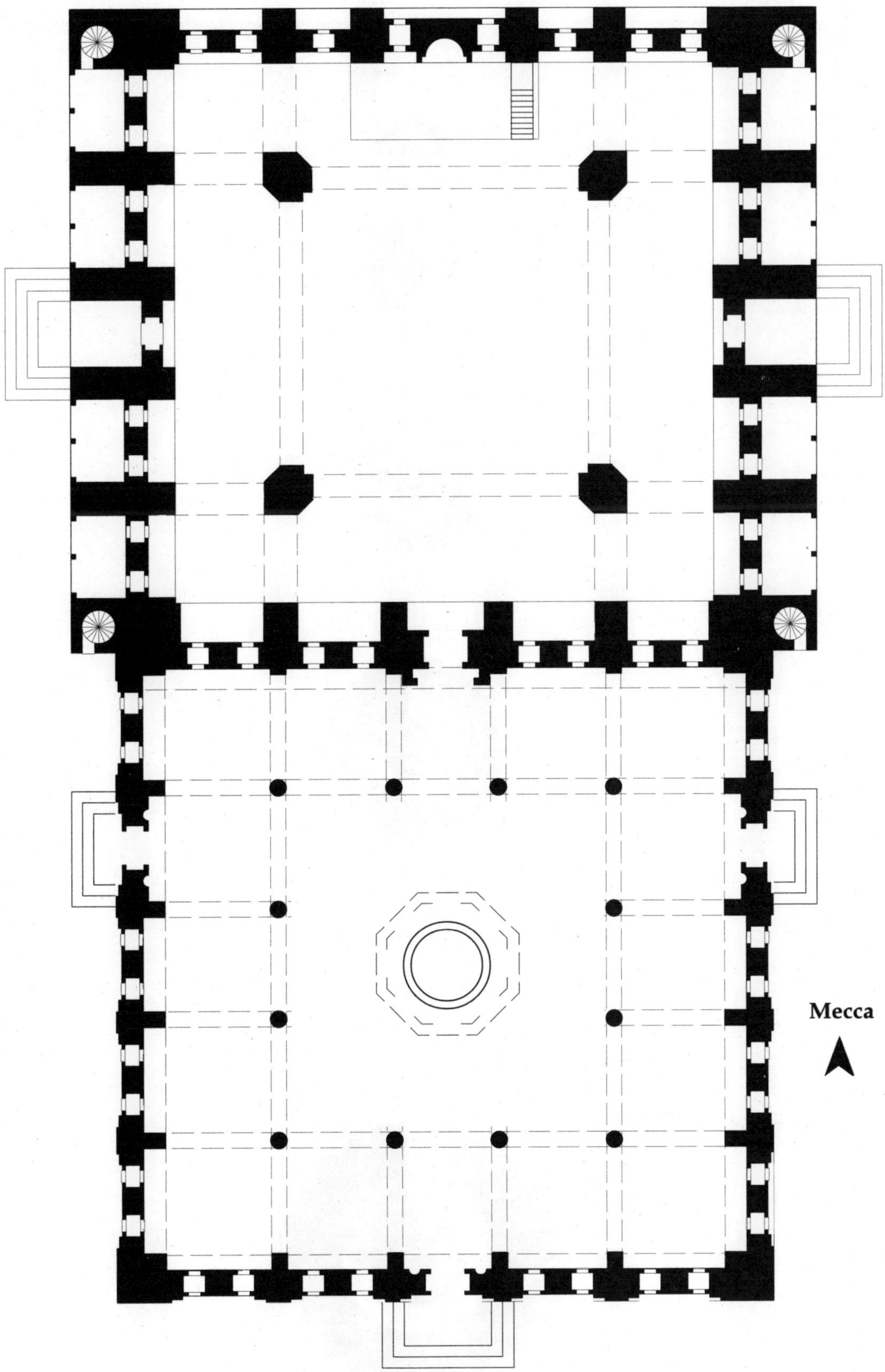

Plate 59 — Qutb Minar, storey plan

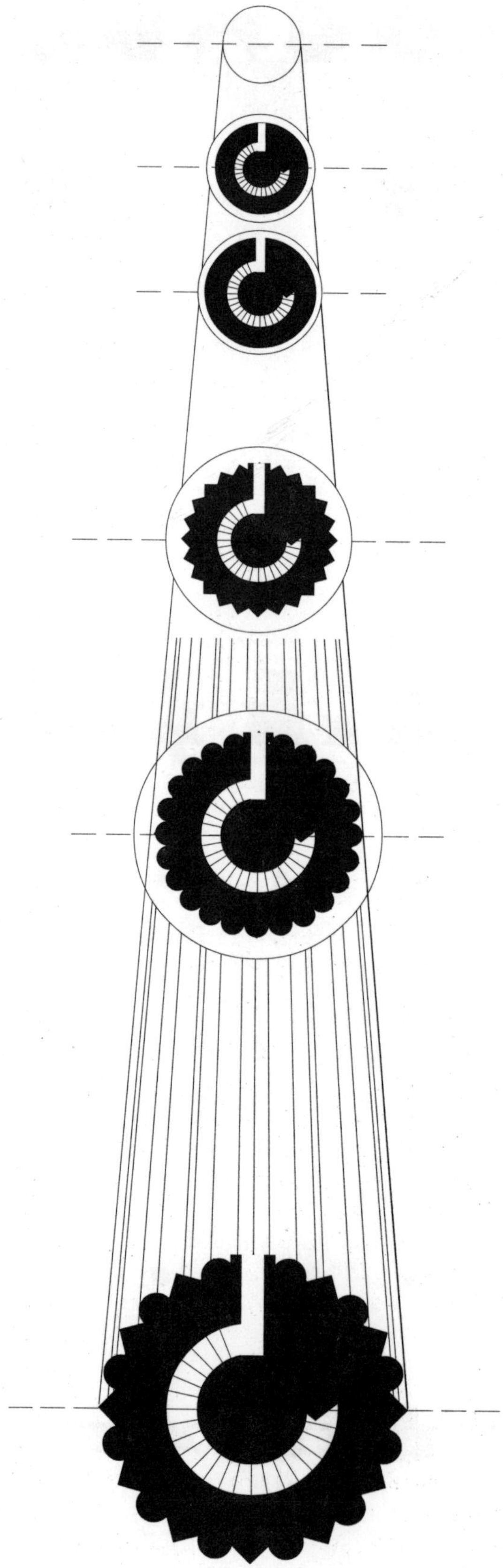

Plate 60 — Alai Darwāẓā, elevation & plan

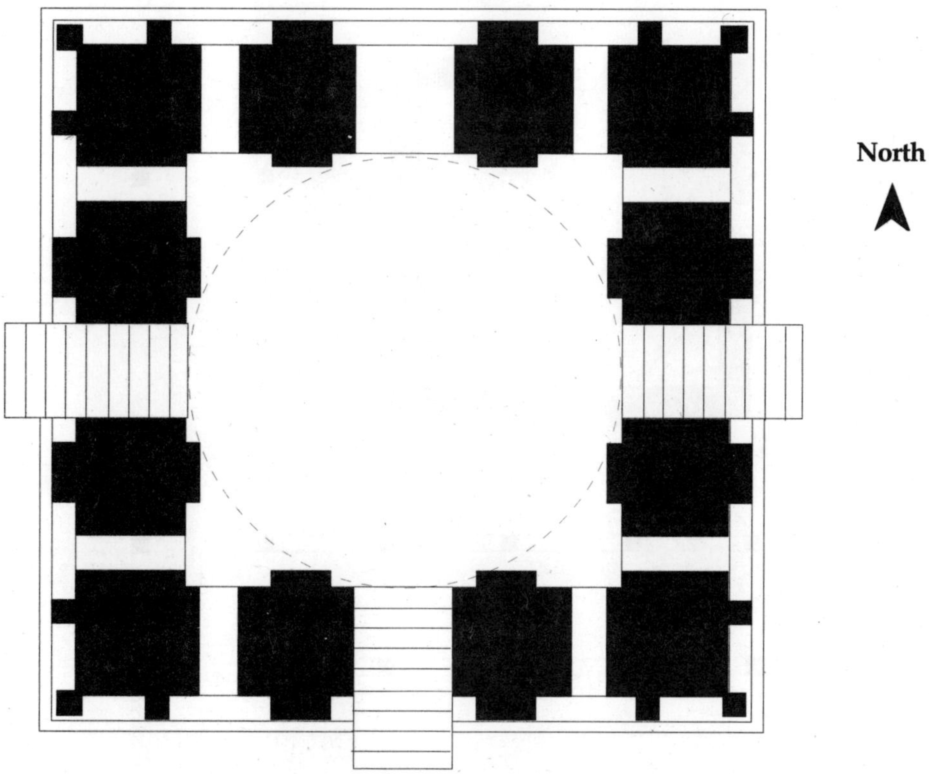

Plate 61 — Shrine of 'Ala al-din & Shams al-din and Masjid 'Ala al-din, scale

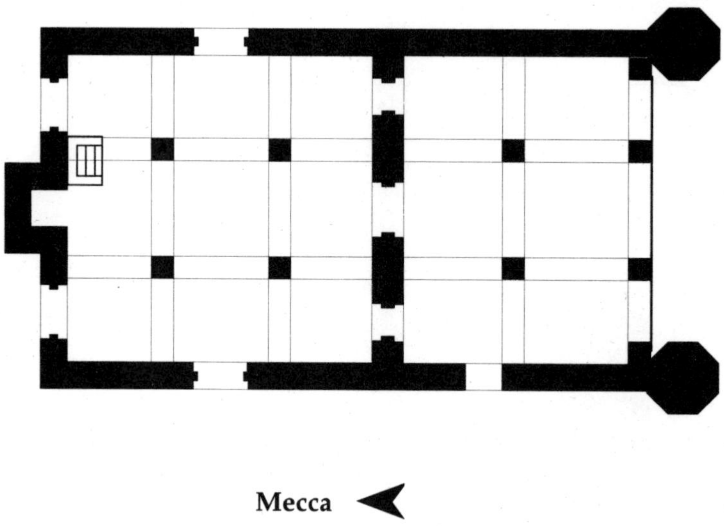

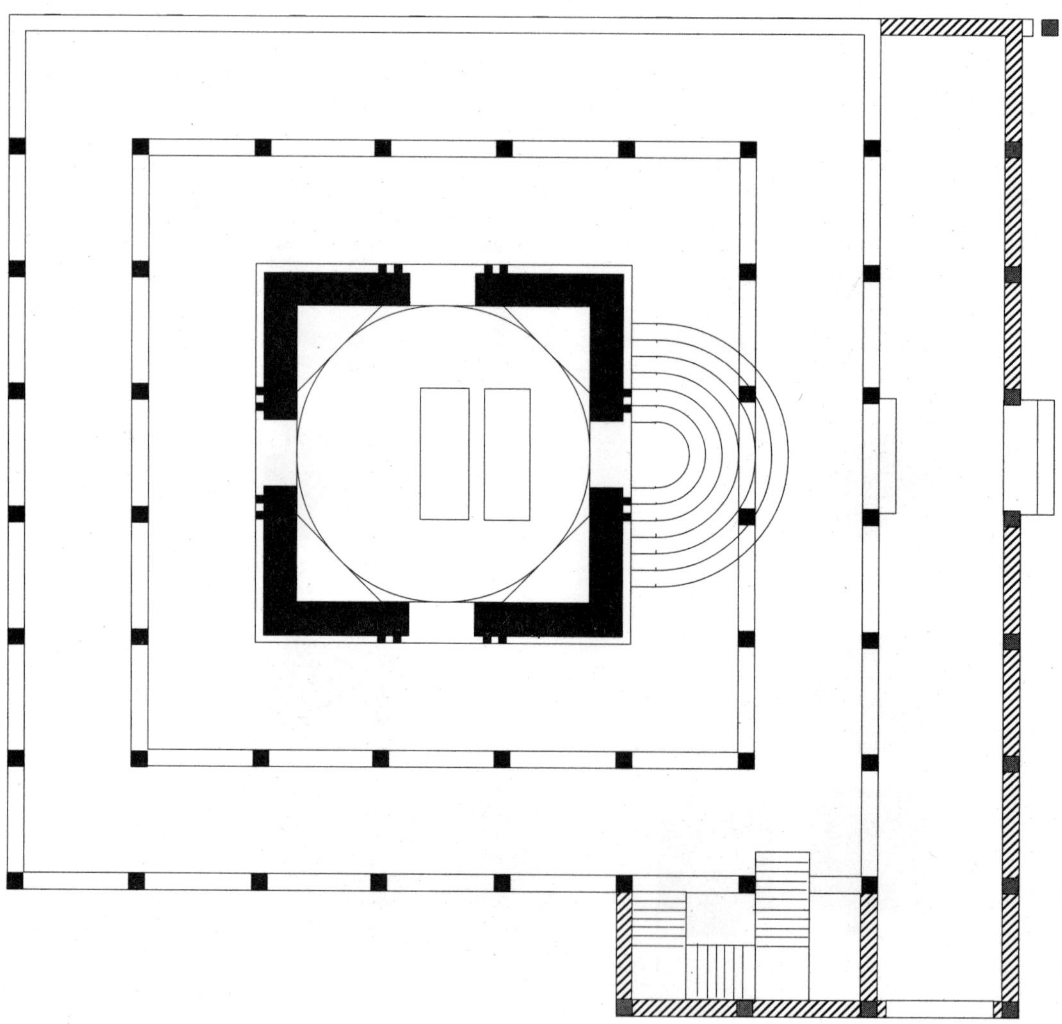

Plate 62 — Shadiabad Mandir, Māṇḍu, main compound

A	Delhi Darwāza
B	Hāthī Pol
C	Outer Court
D	Mosque of Dilwar Khan
E	Palace of BāḤ Bahādur
F	Palace of Gada Shah
G	Hindola Mahal
H	Lāl Mahal
I	JahāḤ Mahal
J	Inner Court
K	Muñja Talāo
L	Kaphur Talāo

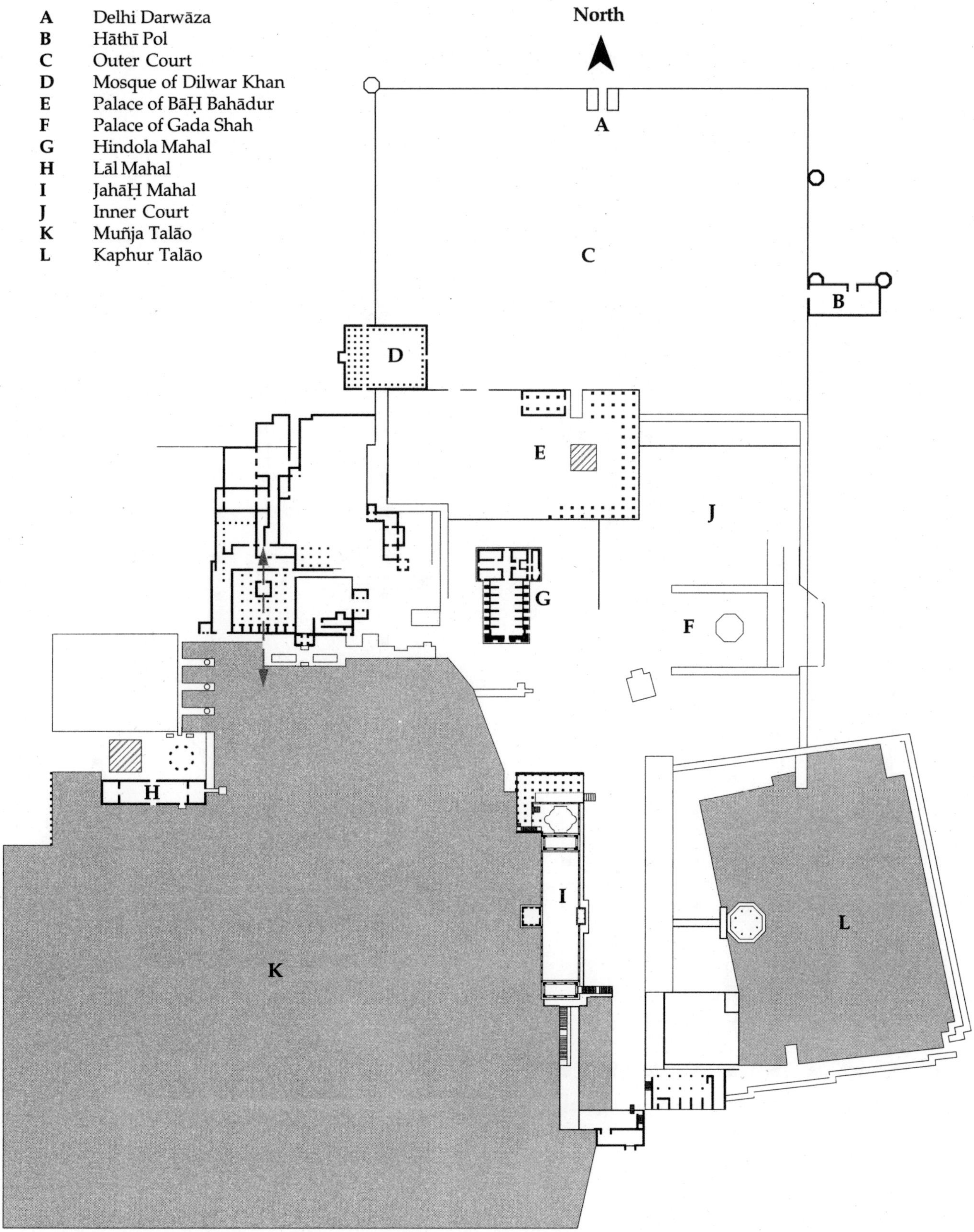

Plate 63 — Dome element proportions (*Masjid Ahmad Shah*)

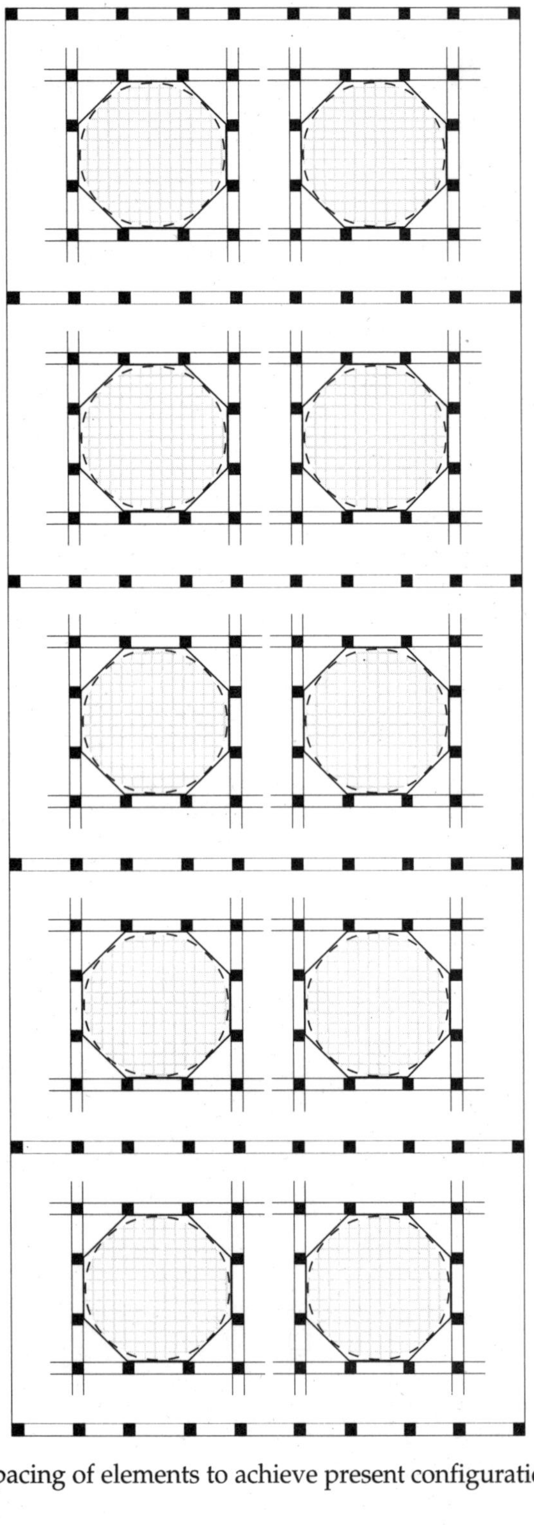

Spacing of elements to achieve present configuration

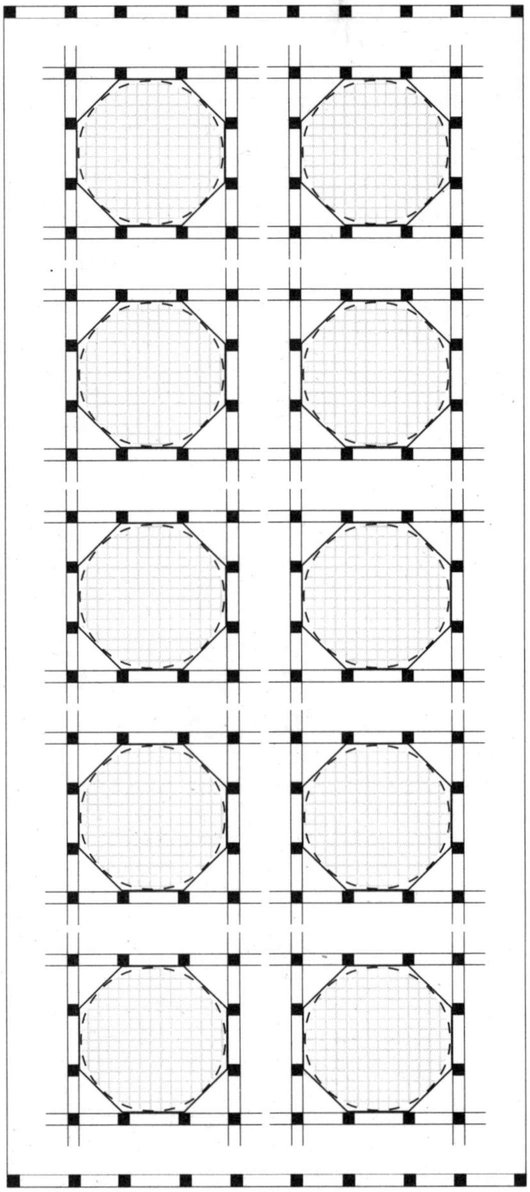

Configuration of equally spaced elements

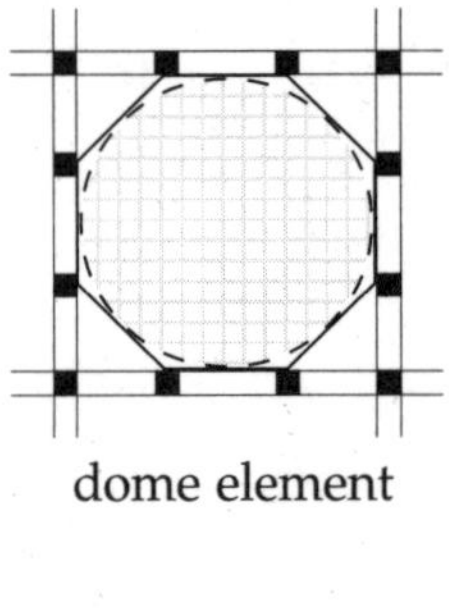

dome element

Plate 64 — Bīdar Koṭila & Mandir, Plan (Partial)

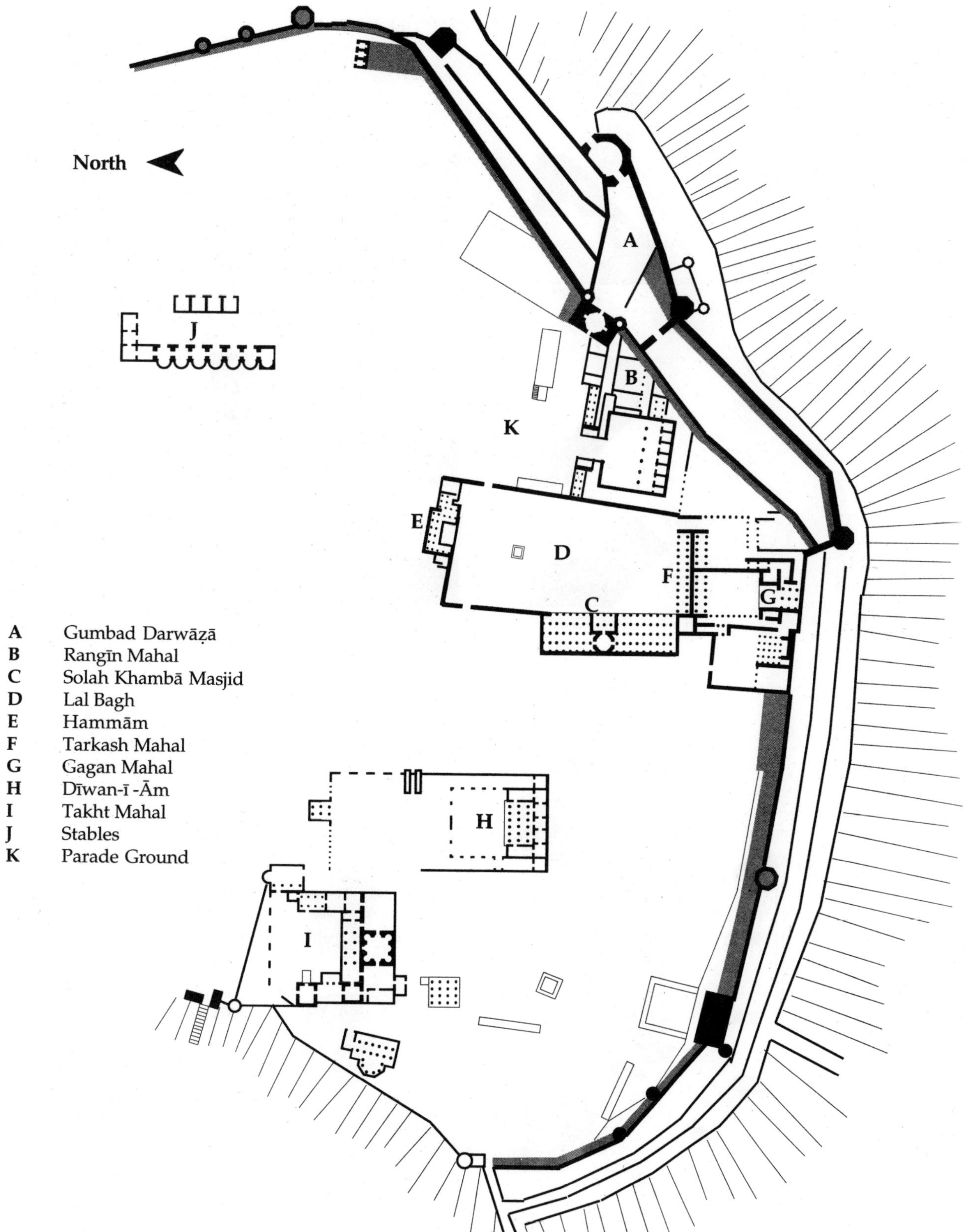

Plate 65 — Plans, Qubba al-Sulaybiya, Samarra (c.CE 892) (top) & Tomb of Sikandar Lodi, Delhi (c.CE 1518)

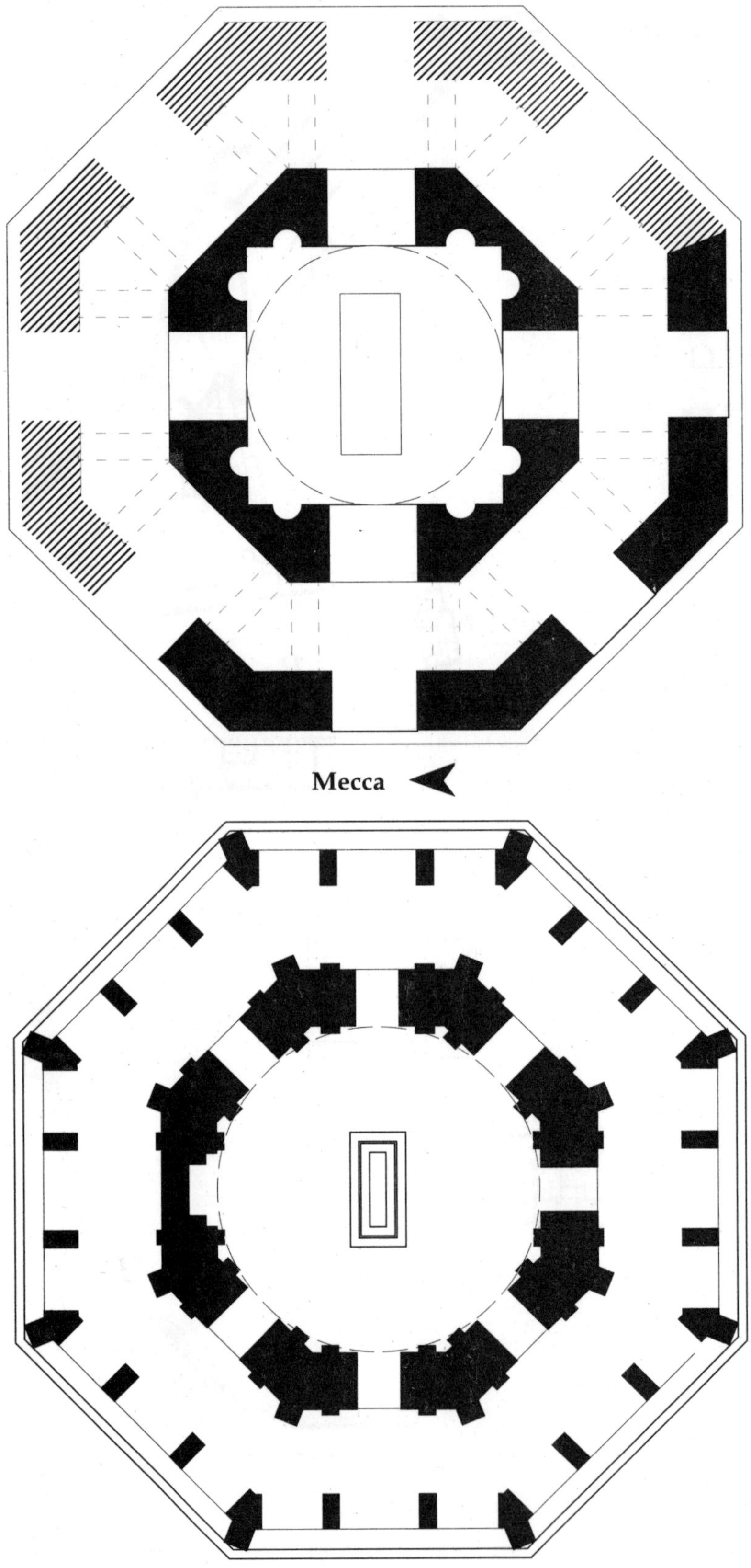

Plate 66 — Rani Rupmati Rauza, plan

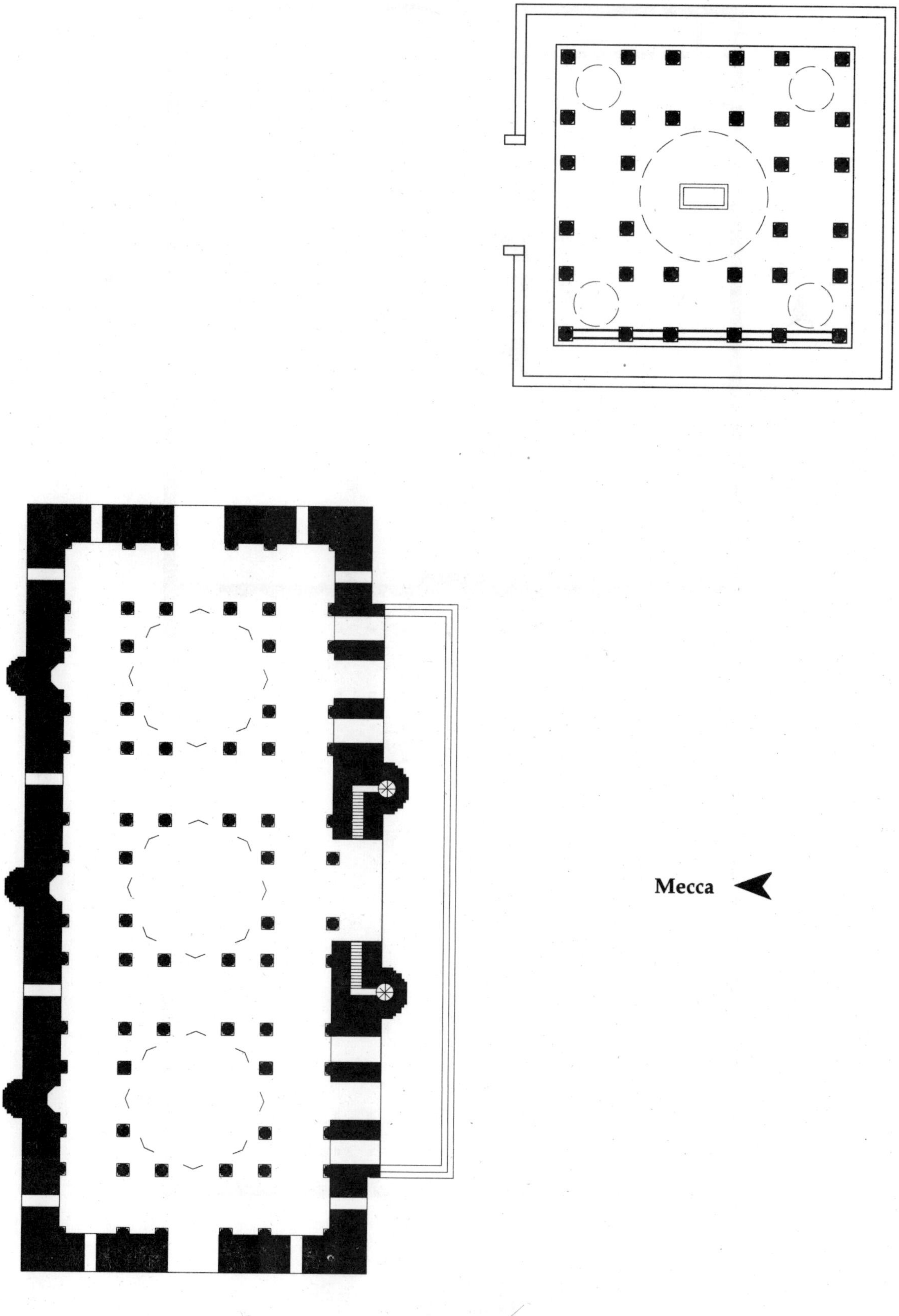

Plate 67 — Masjid-i Jami & Hushang Shah's Tomb, plan

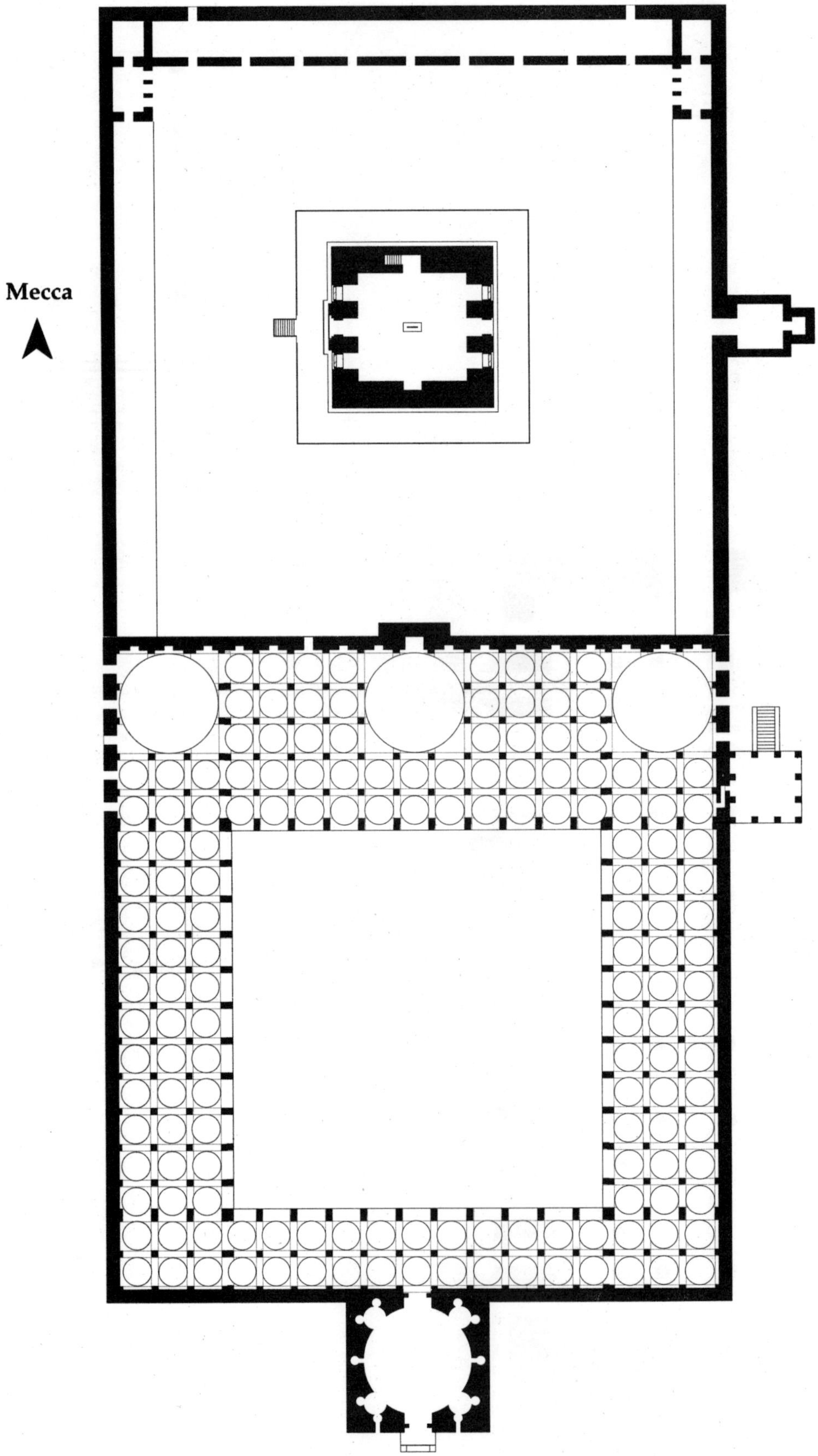

Plate 68 — Ananda Temple, Pagan, Burma

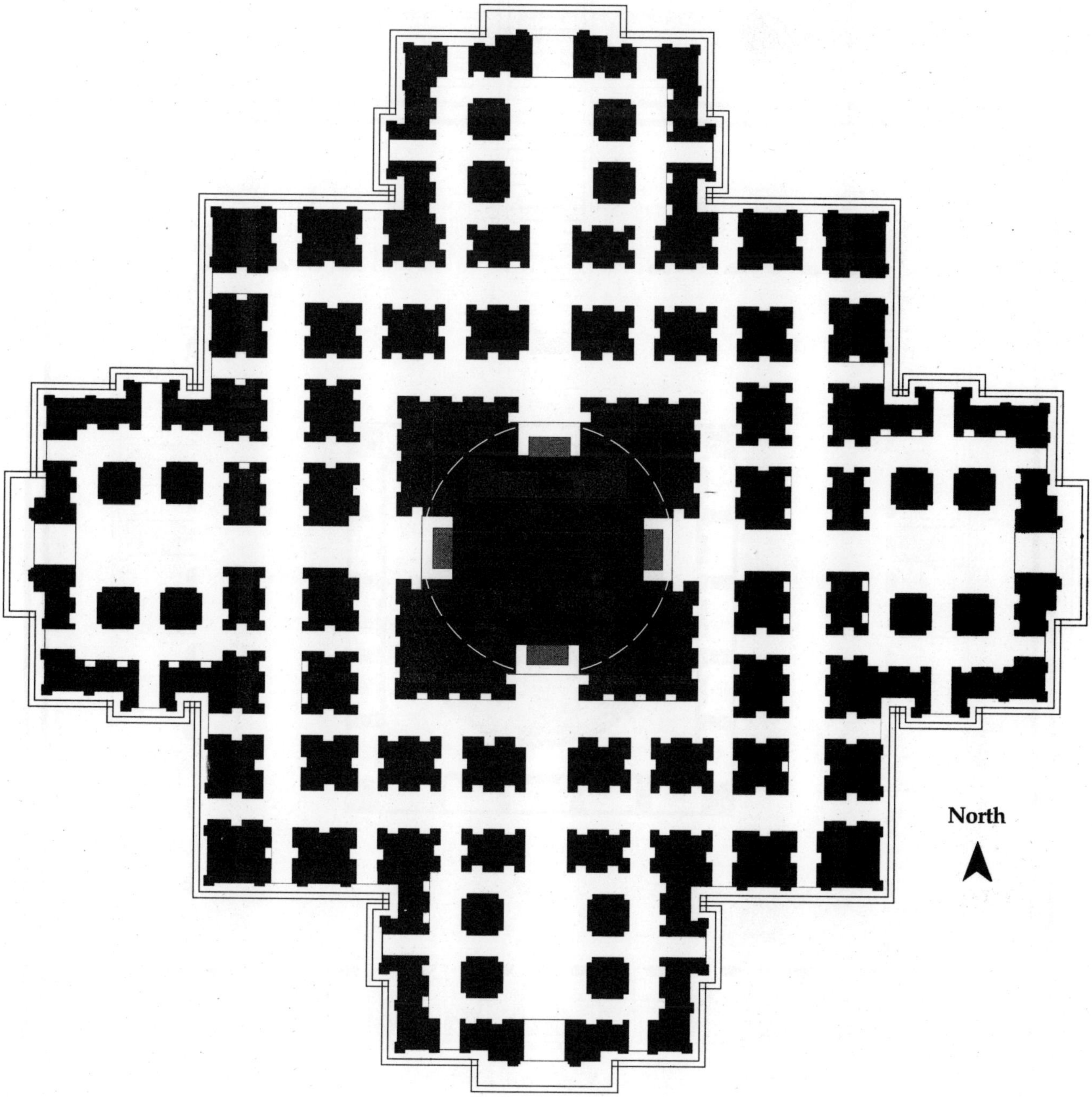

Plate 69 — Chedi Wat Chang Lom, Si Satchanalai (*c.*CE 1275)

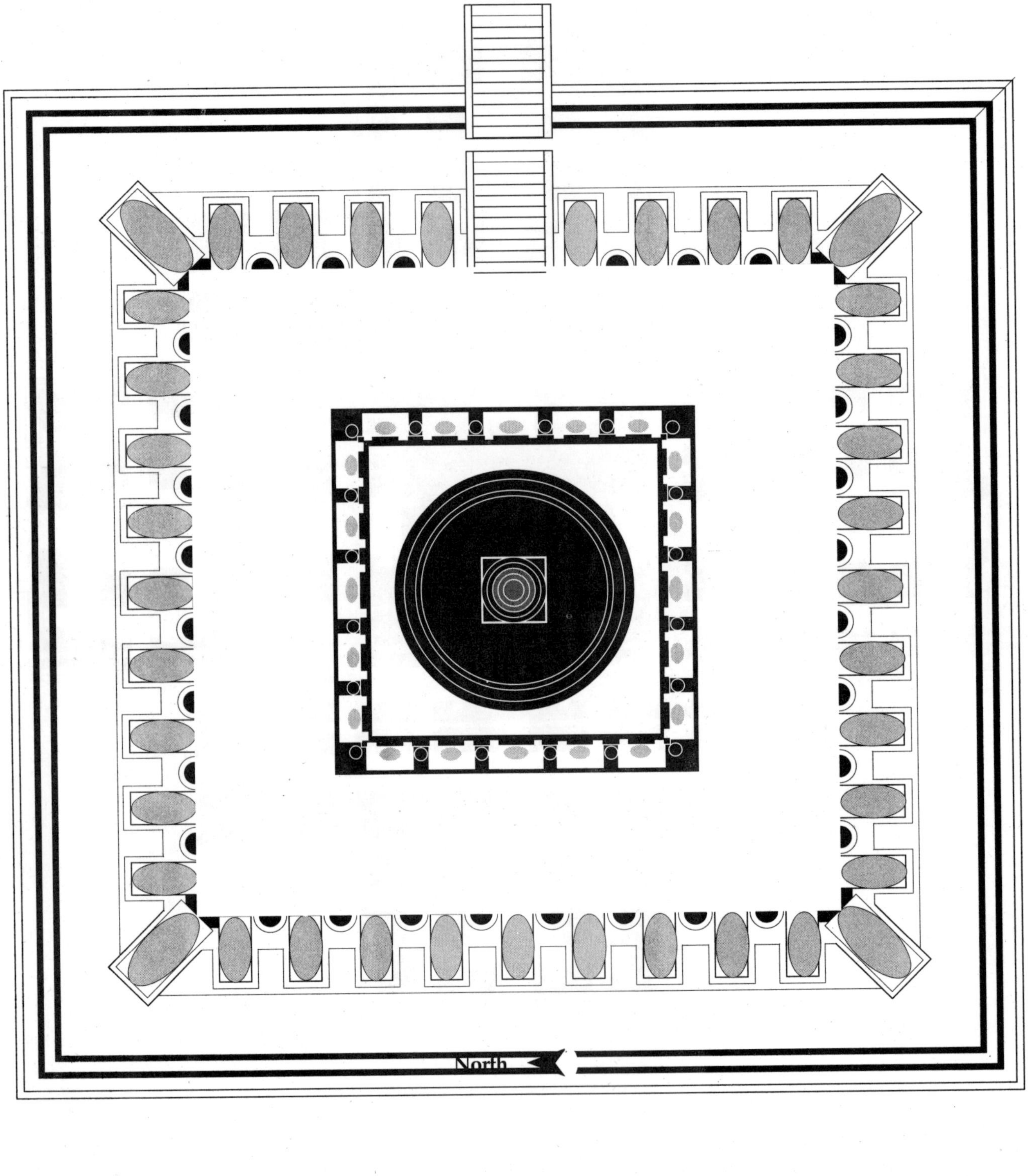

Plate 70 — Tomb of Sheikh Ahmed Khattri, Sarkhej (*c.* CE 1441)

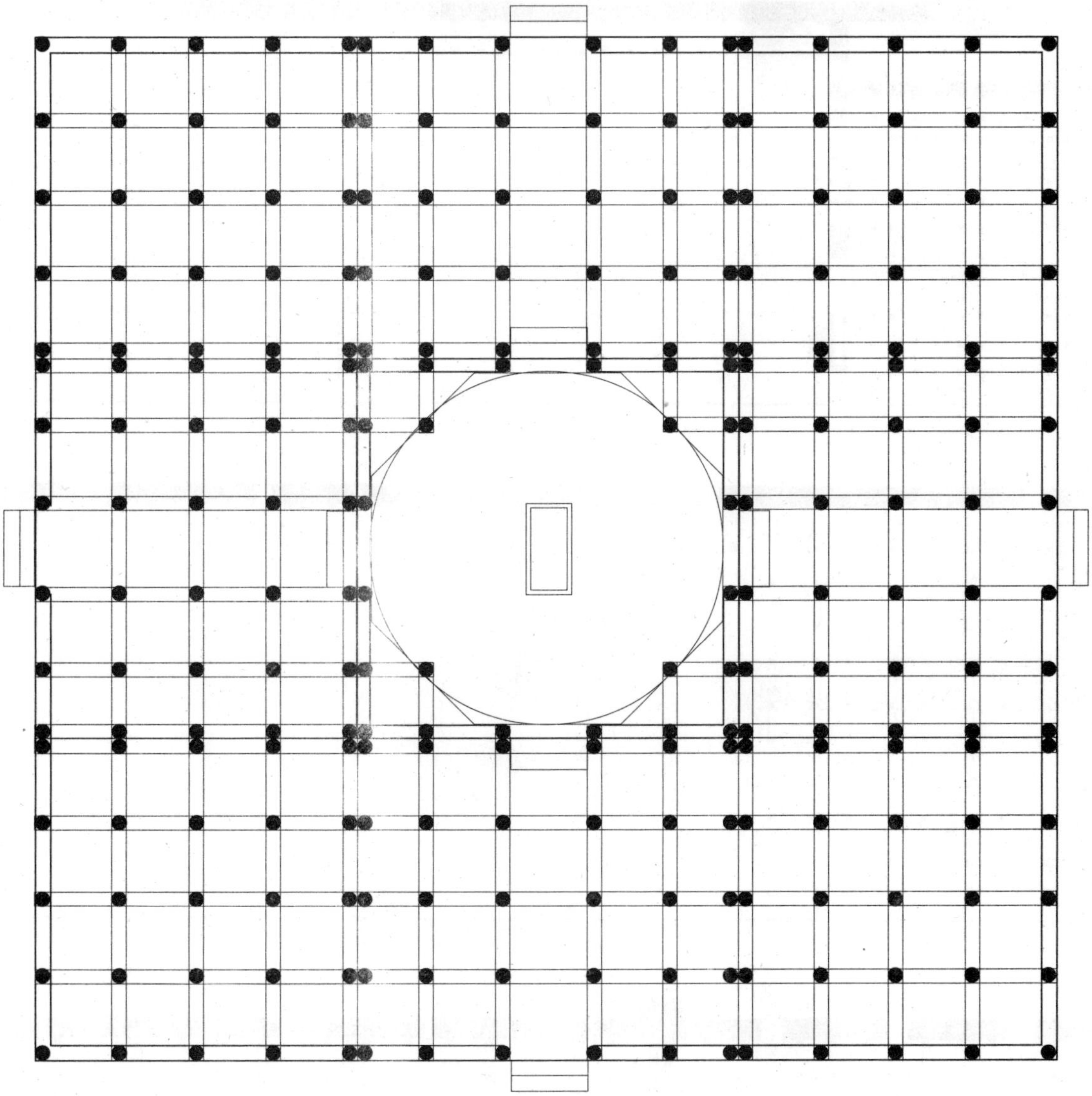

Mecca

Plate 71 — proportions of *sahn* and *haram*

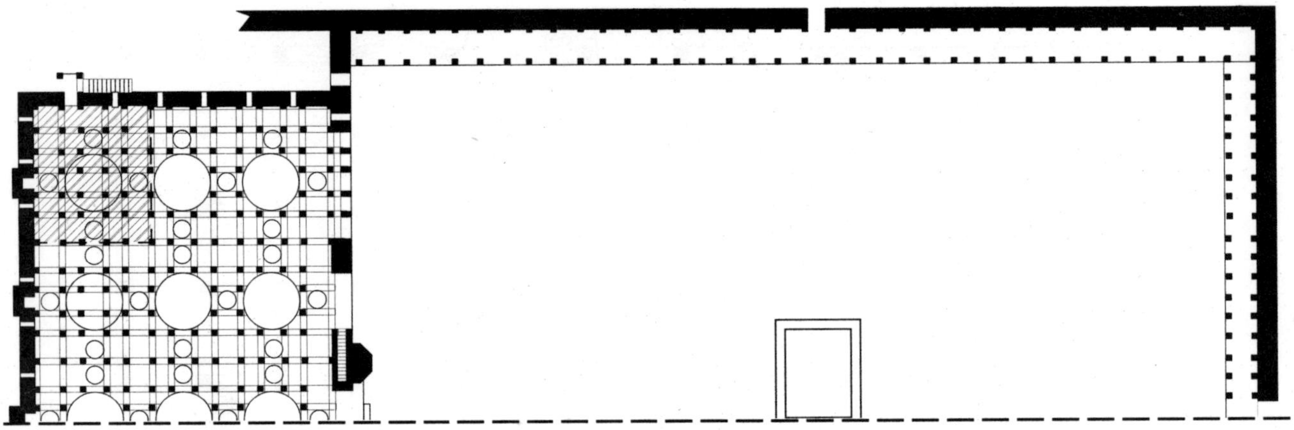

Masjid-i Jami, Ahmedabad

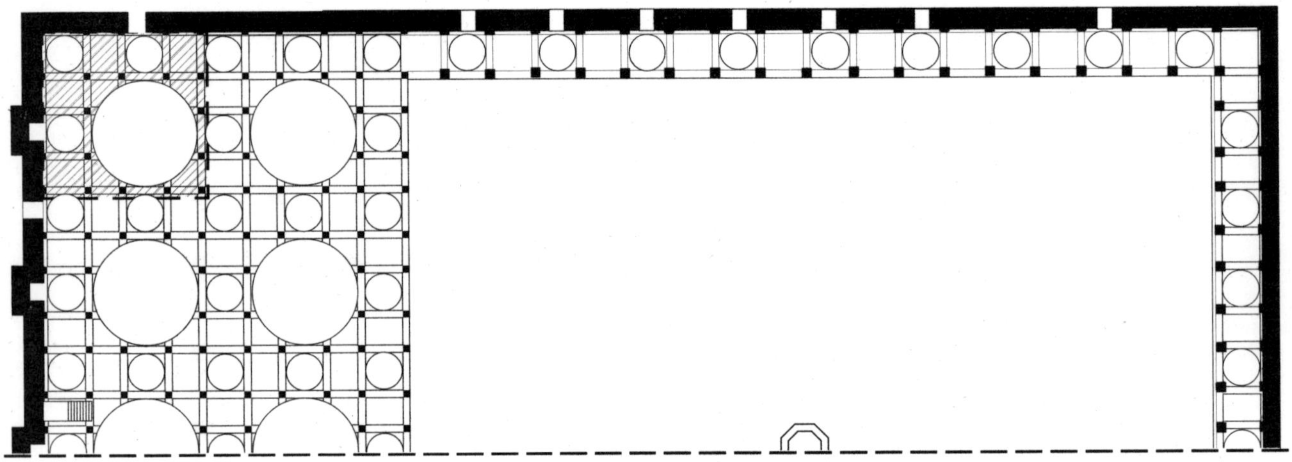

Masjid-i Jami, Sarkhej

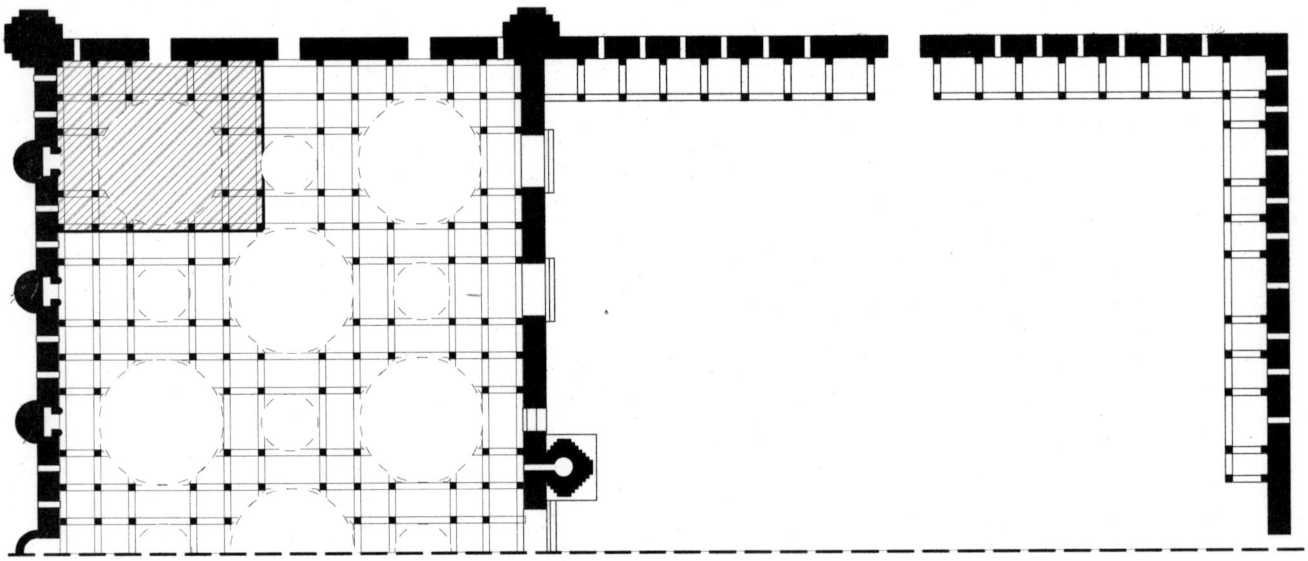

Masjid-i Jami, Campāner

Plate 72 — Rani Sipri Rauza, Ahmedabad, masjid & tomb

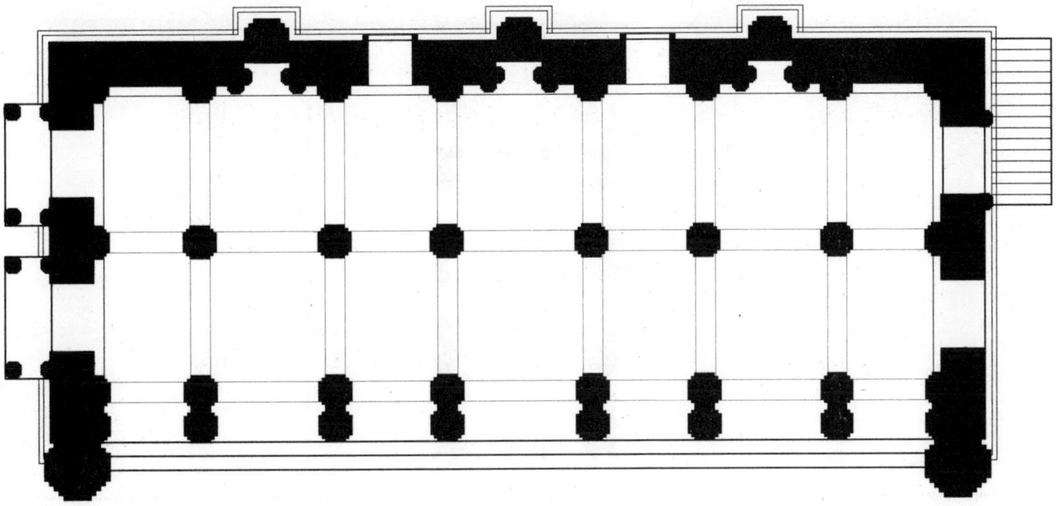

Mecca

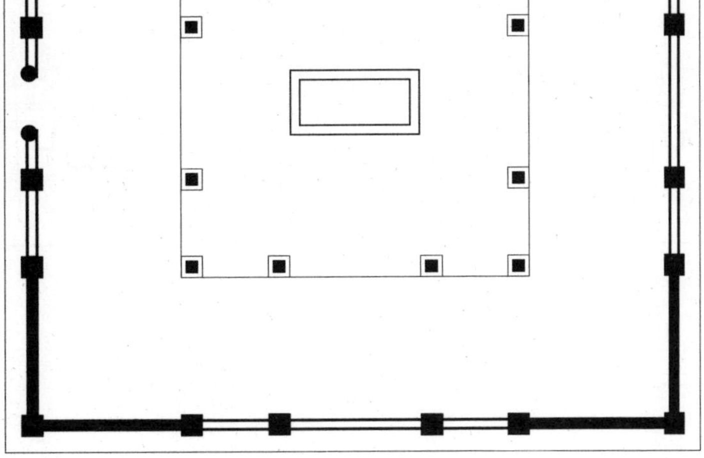

Plate 73 — Safa Masjid (with tank and niches)

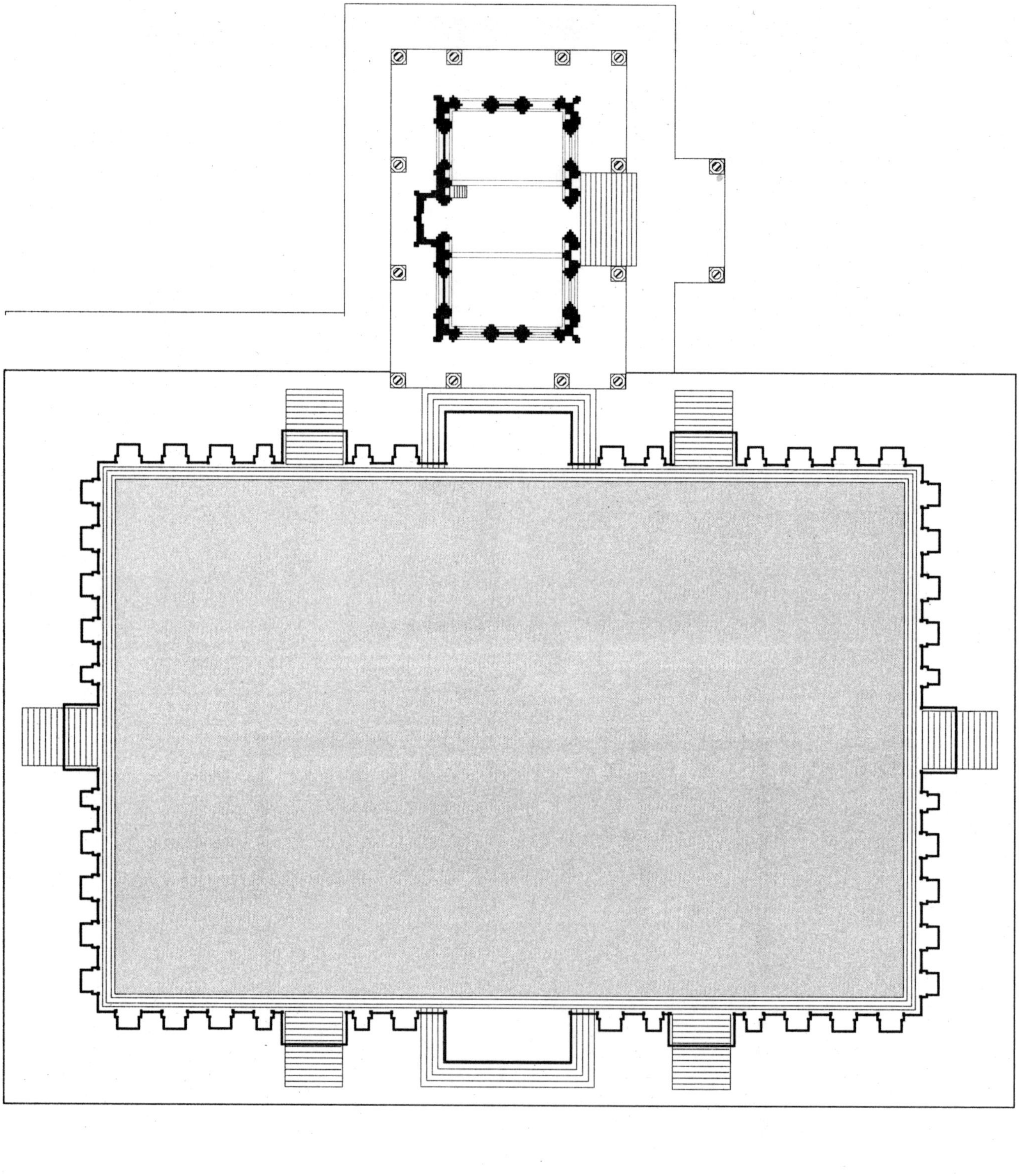

Plate 74 — Masjid-i Jami, Bījāpur (variations)

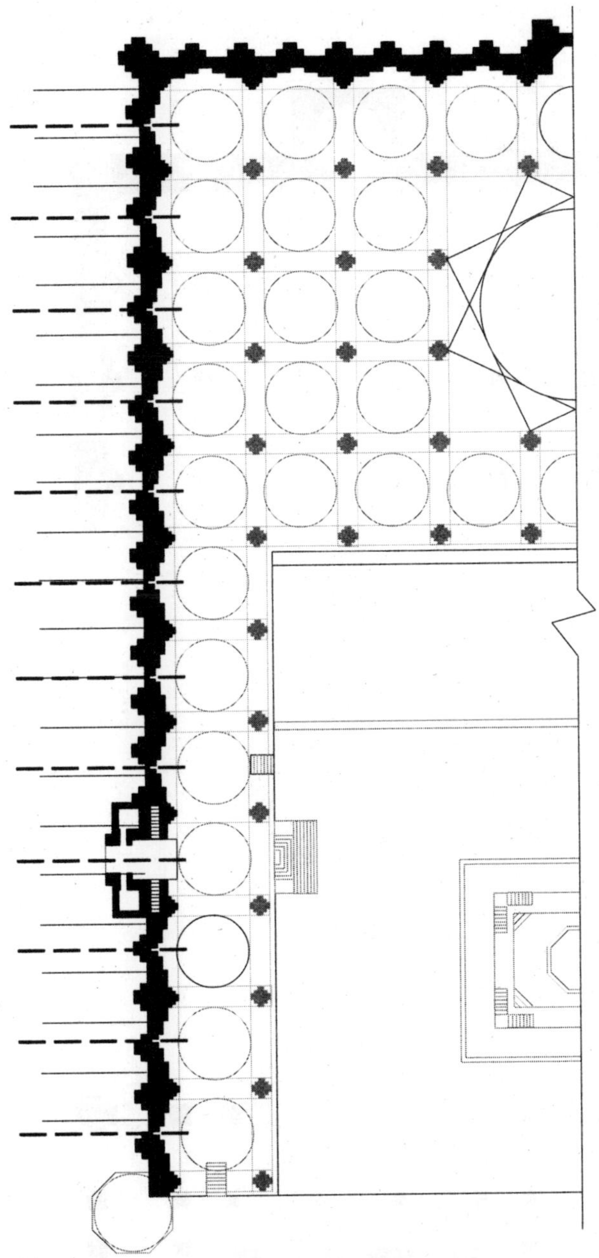

dome/bay centres (– – – – – – –), blind arcade centres (————)

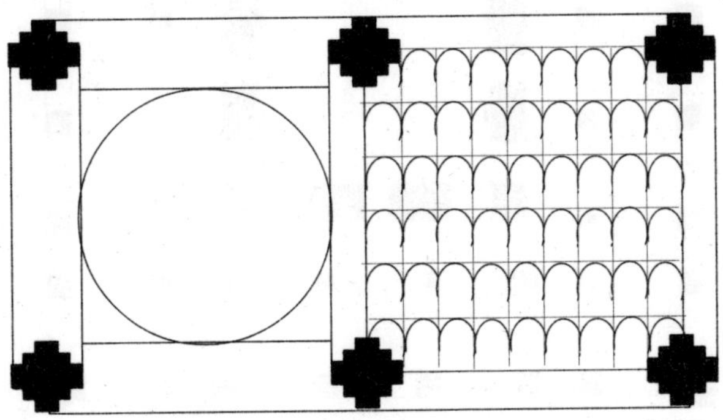

division of bays into 54 *musallas*

Plate 75 — Ibrahim Rauza

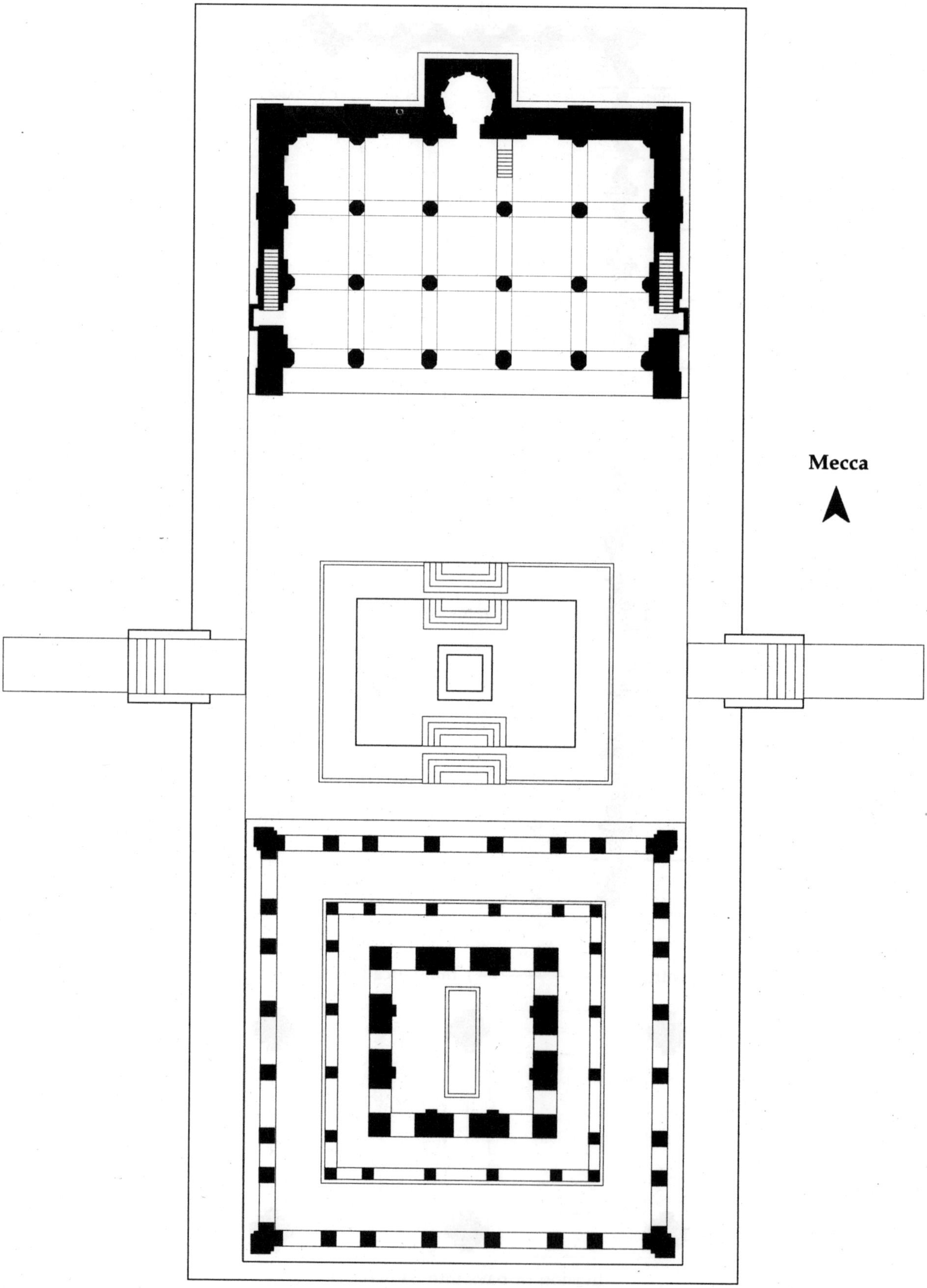

Plate 76 — Tomb (Gol Gumbaz) and Masjid of Muhammad 'Adil Shah

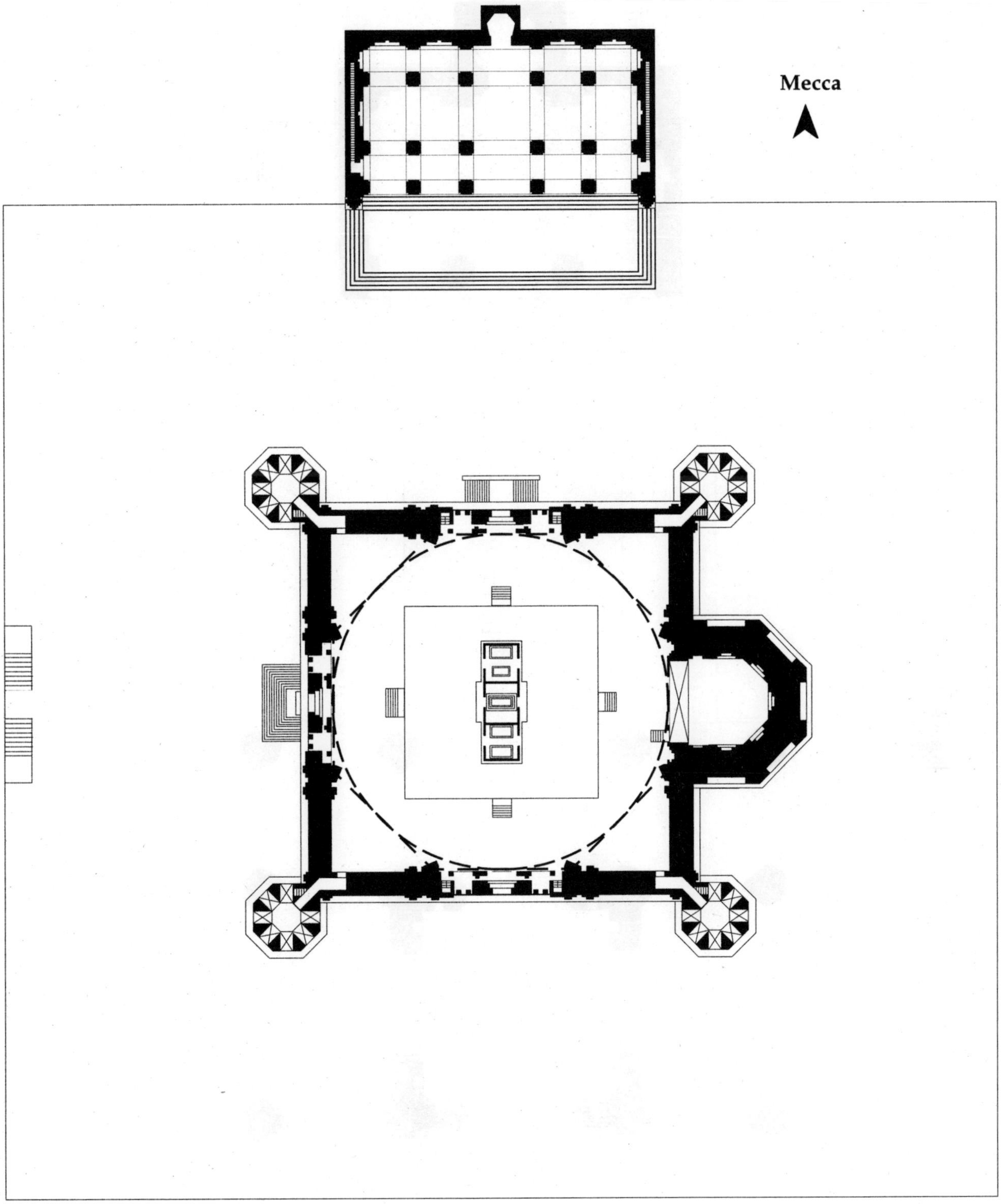

Plate 77 — Shah Navaz Khan Rauza (Plan)

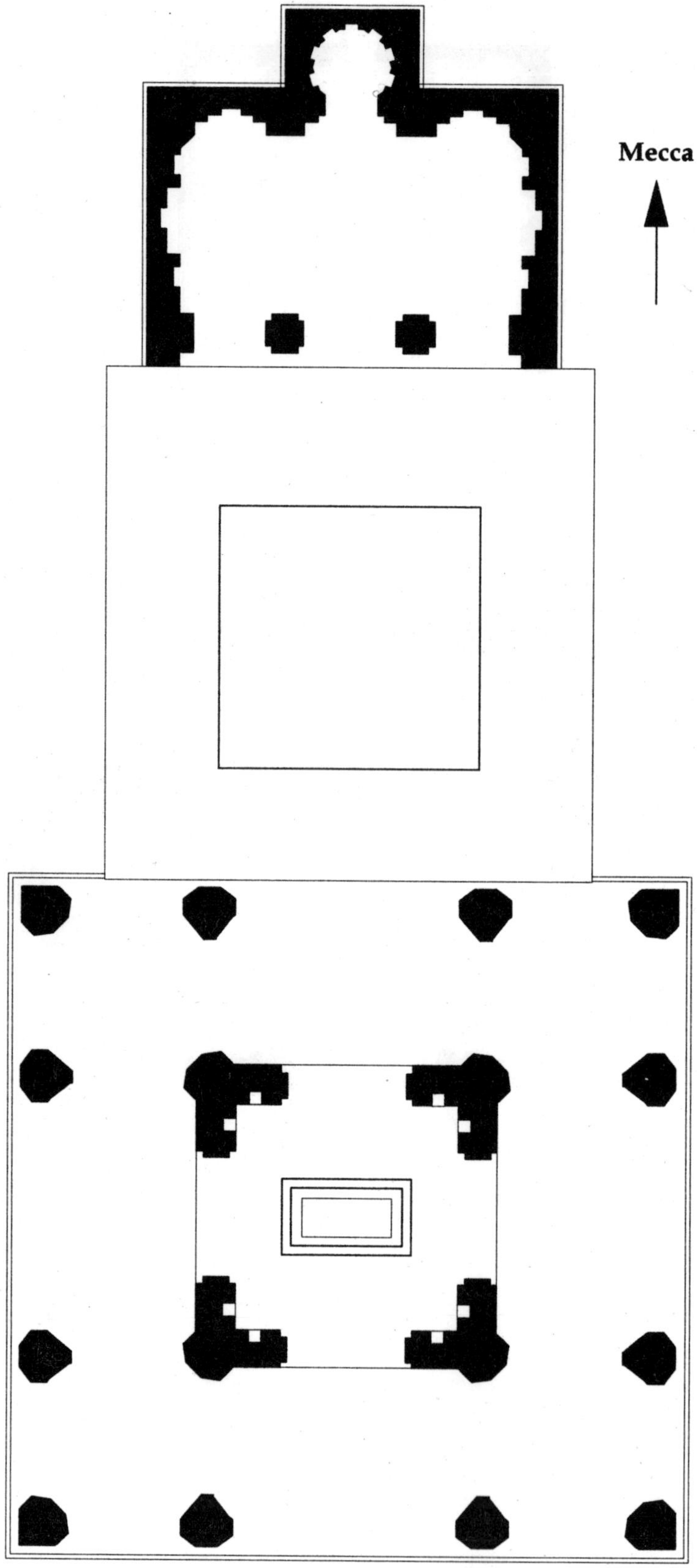

Plate 78 — Afzal Khan Rauza (Plan)

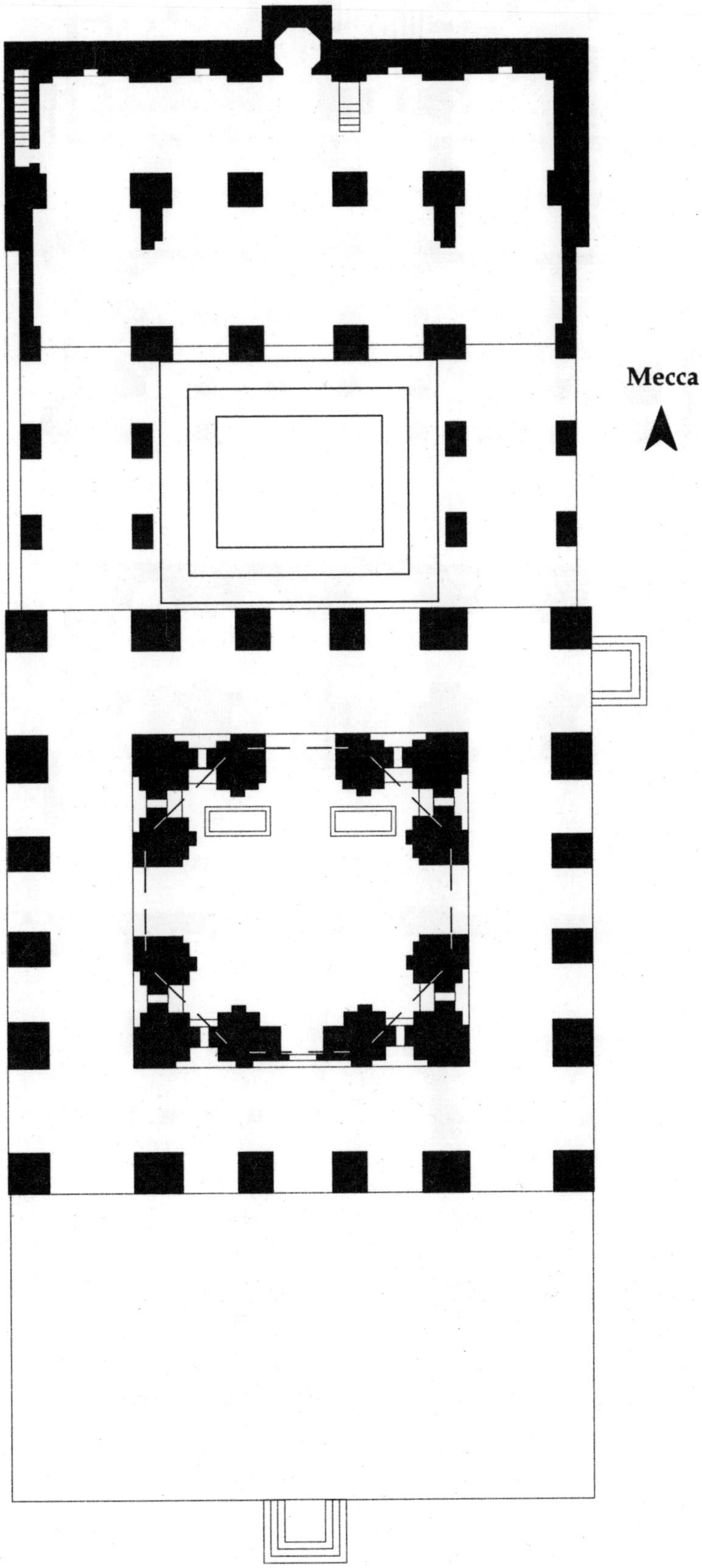

Plate 79 — Mughal *haram*-screens

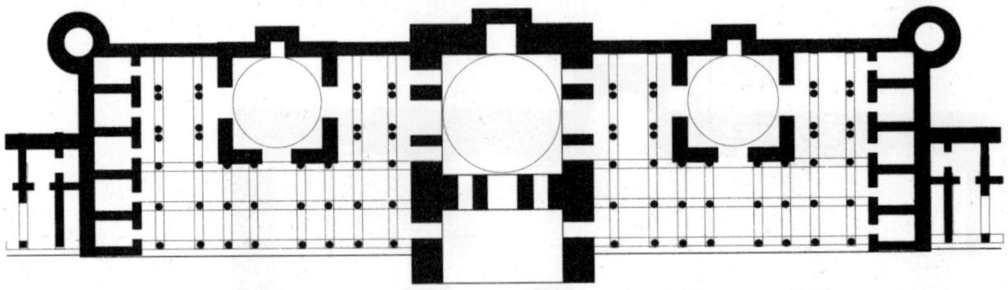

Masjid Badshahi, Fatehpur Sikri (CE 1568)

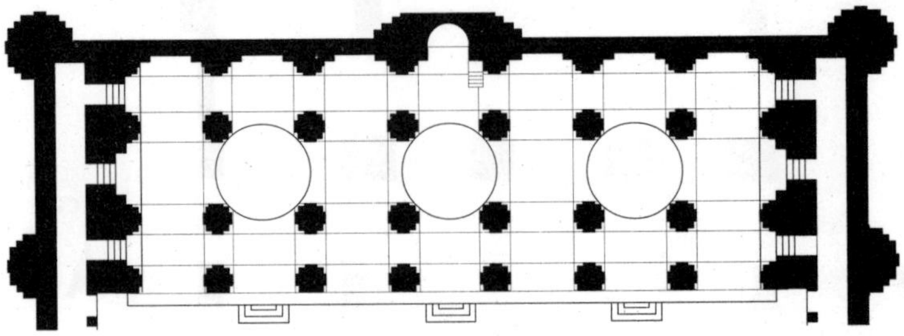

Mothi Masjid, Agra (CE 1628)

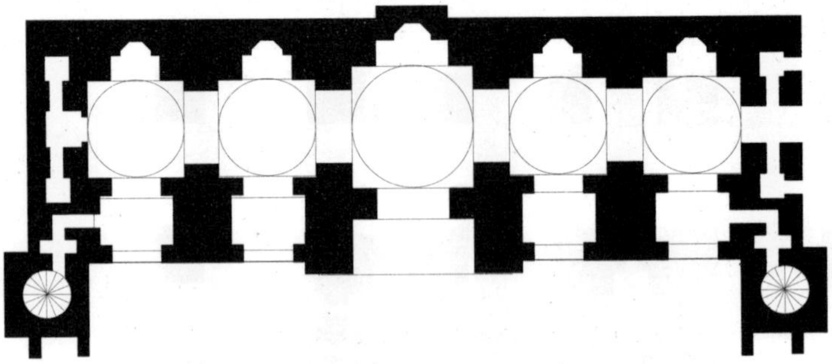

Masjid Wazir Khan, Lahore (CE 1634)

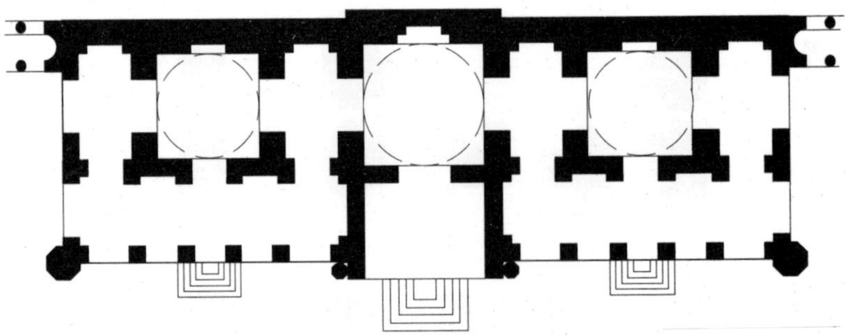

Masjid-i Jami, Delhi (CE 1644)

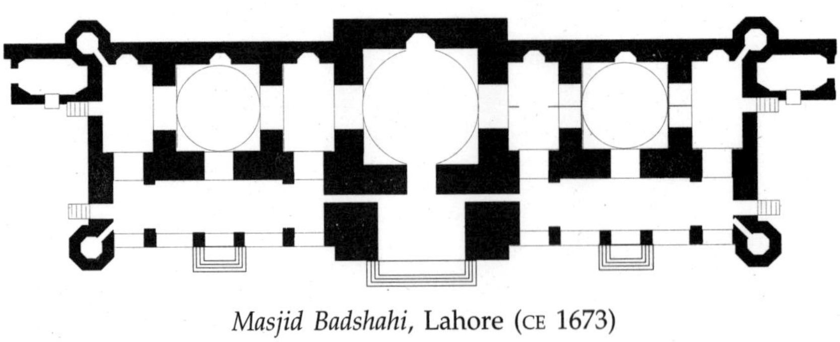

Masjid Badshahi, Lahore (CE 1673)

Plate 80 — Square Islamic tombs

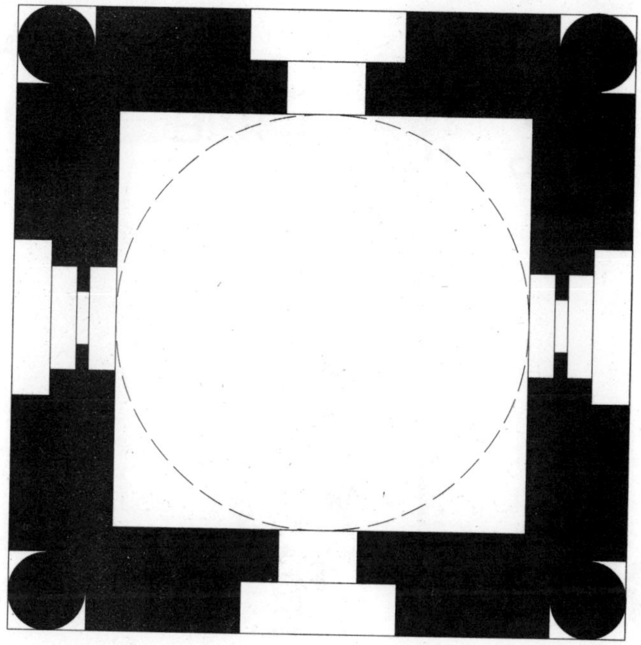

Tomb of the Samanids (plan), Bukhara, Uzbekistan (c.CE 920)

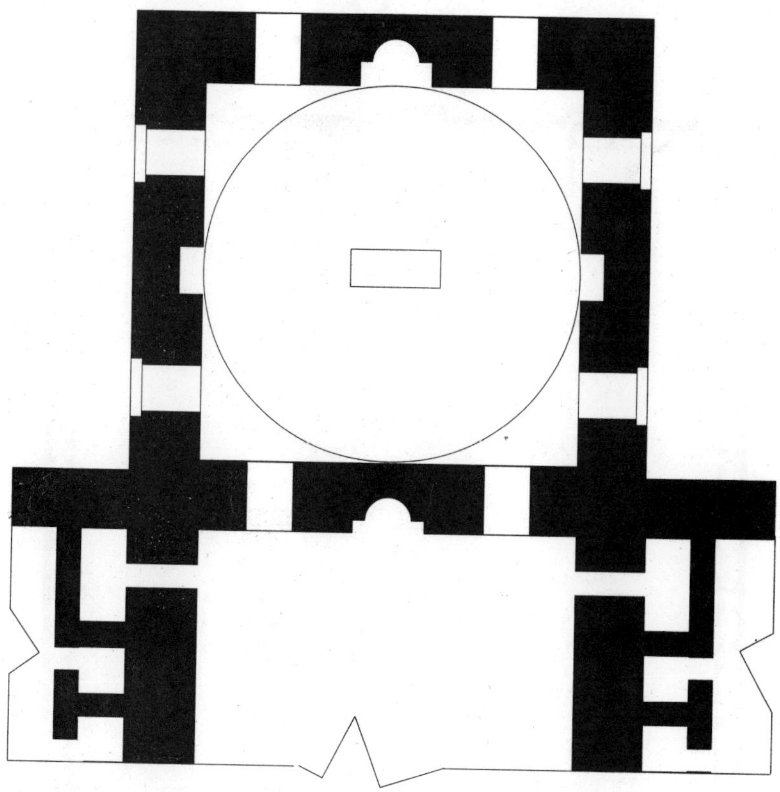

Tomb of Sultan Hasan (plan), Cairo, Egypt (CE 1356-1363)

Plate 81 — Relative size: Masjid-i Jami, Delhi (top left), Bahshahi Masjid, Fatehpur Sikri (top right) & Bahshahi Masjid, Lahore (bottom)

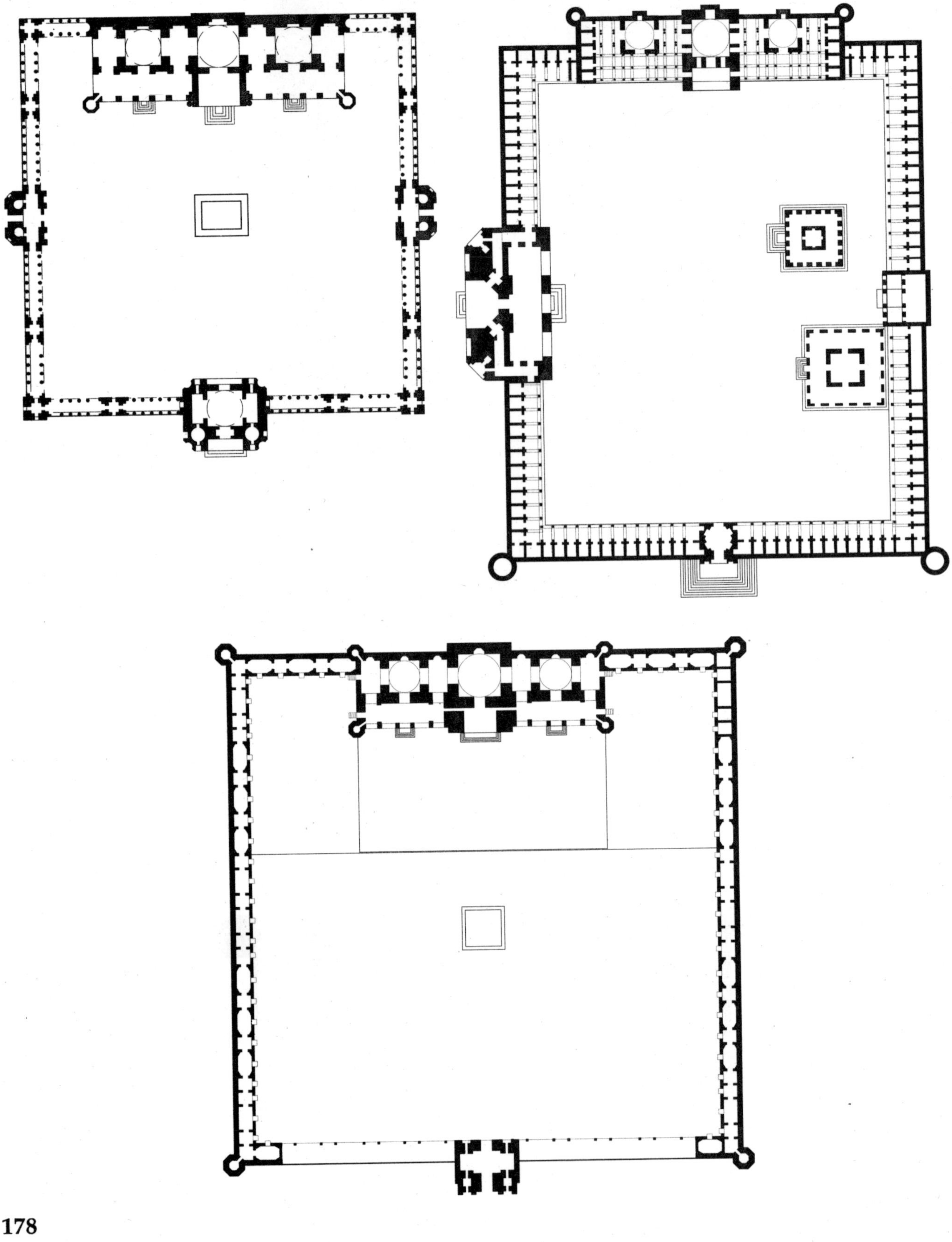

Plate 82 — arch construction techniques

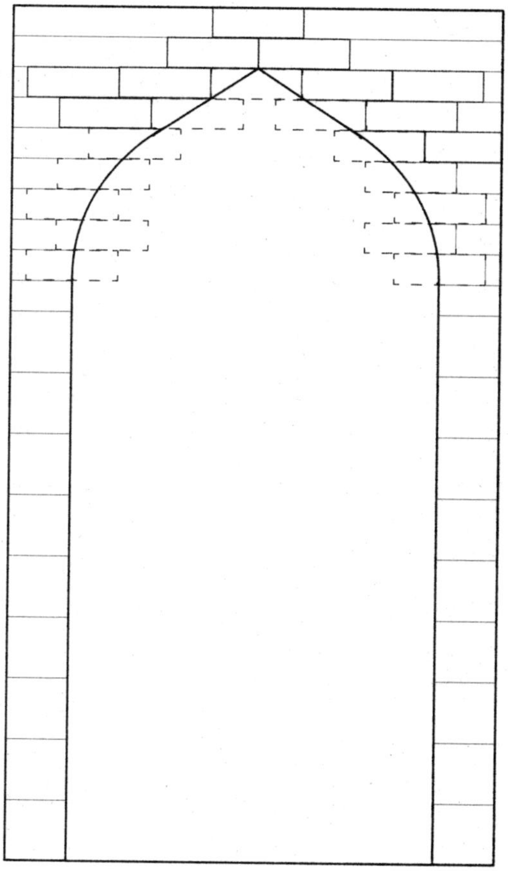

Hindu corbelled arch

Islamic ogive voussoir arch

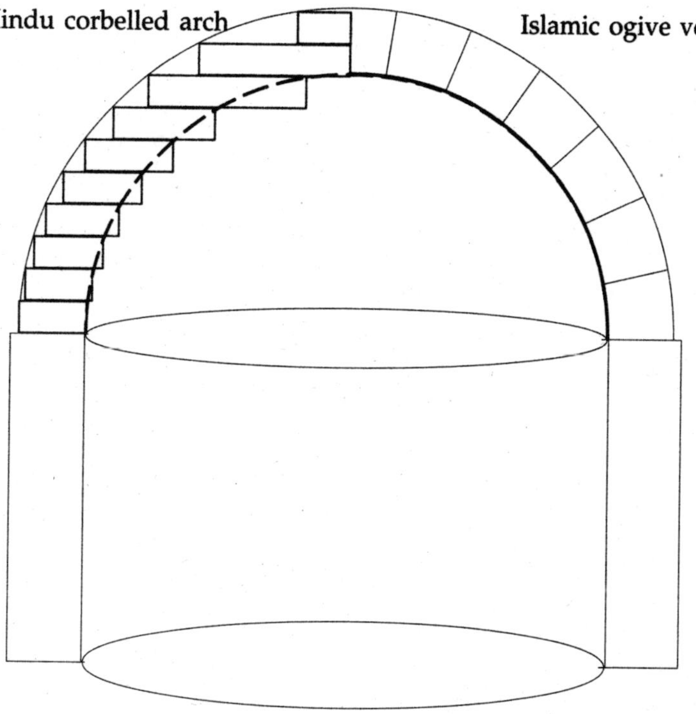

Hindu corbelled dome (left) and voussoir-style dome (right)

Plate 83 — Dome types

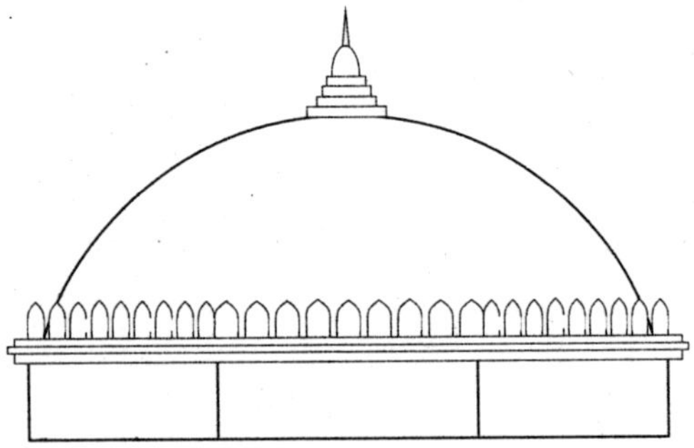

Delhi (*Tomb 36*)
1230

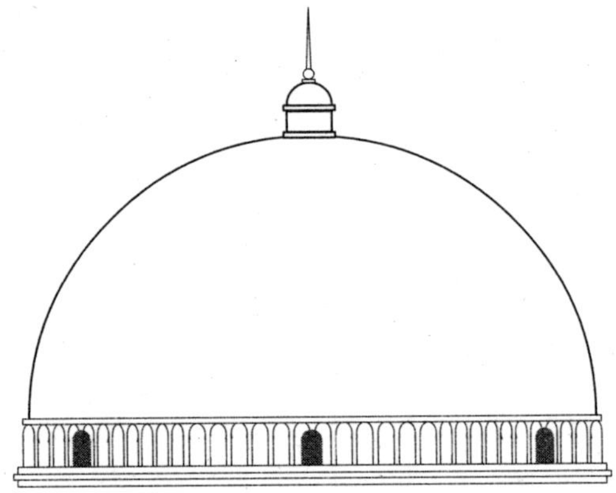

Multan (*Tomb of Sheikh Rukn-i 'Alam*)
1320

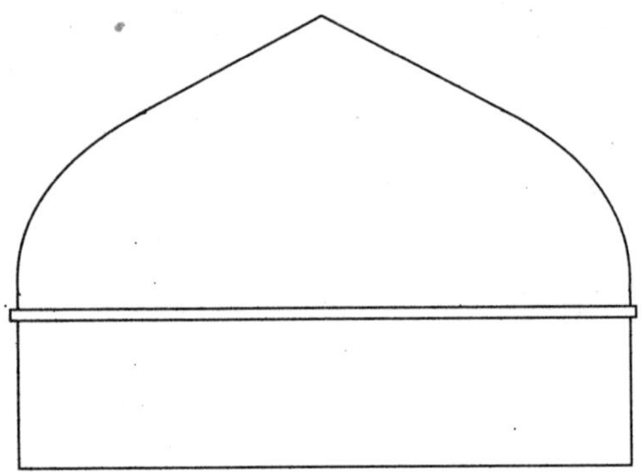

Mandu (*Jahaz Mahal*)
a. 1410

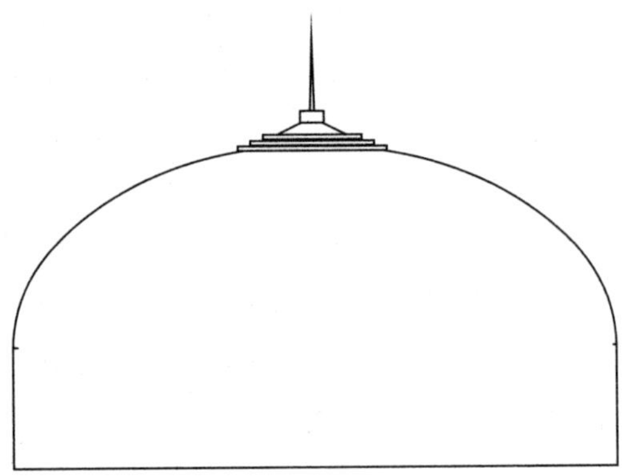

Bīdar/Gulbarga (*Solah Khamba Masjid*)
1424

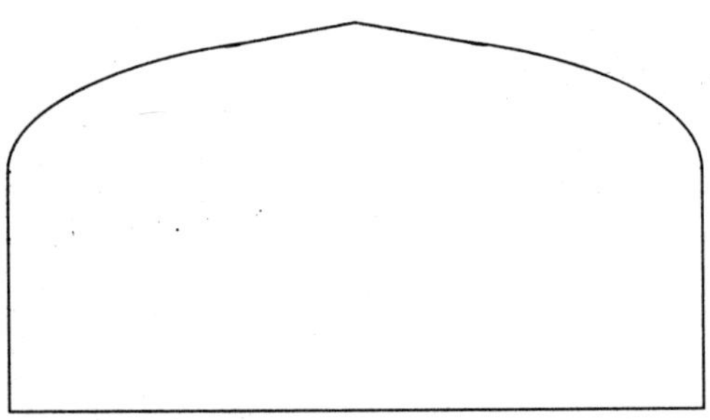

Mandu, secondary domes (*Masjid-i Jami*)
1440

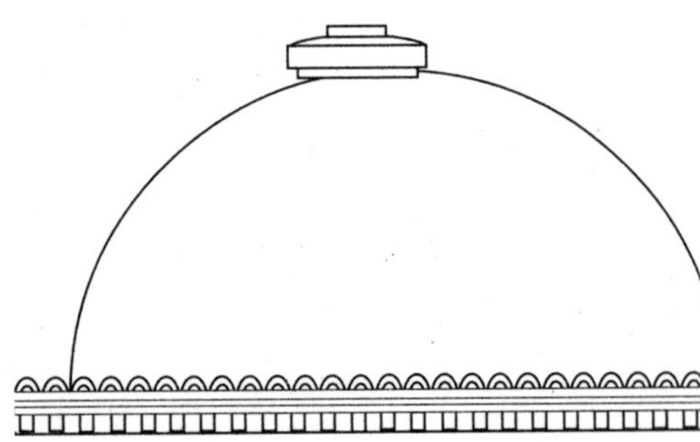

Usmanpur (*Sayyid Usman Rauza*)
1460

Plate 84 — Dome types (Continued)

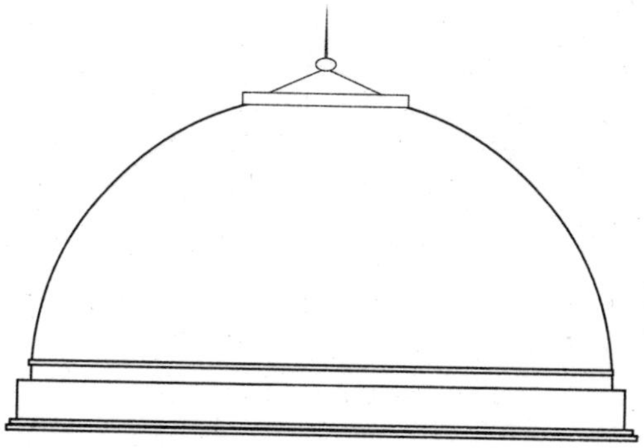

Delhi (*Tomb of Sikandar Lodi*)
1518

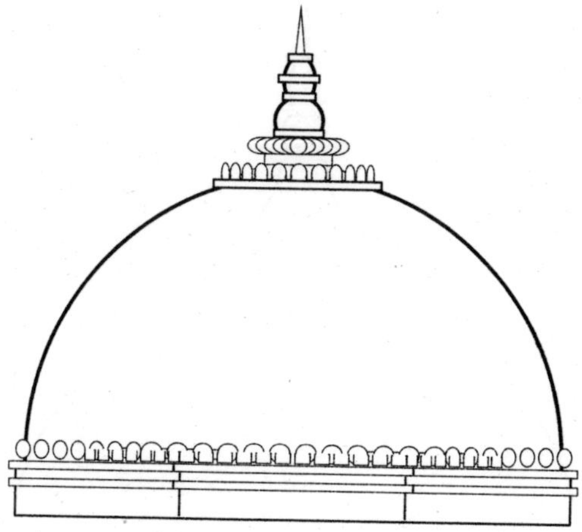

Saseram (*Tomb of Hasan Khan Sur*)
1535

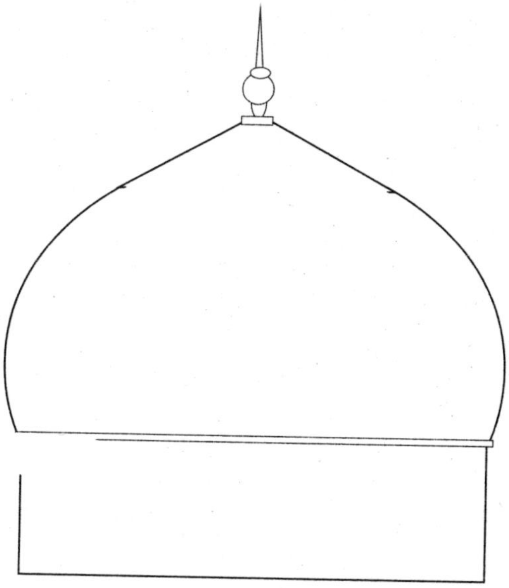

Delhi (*Tomb of Humayun*)
1565

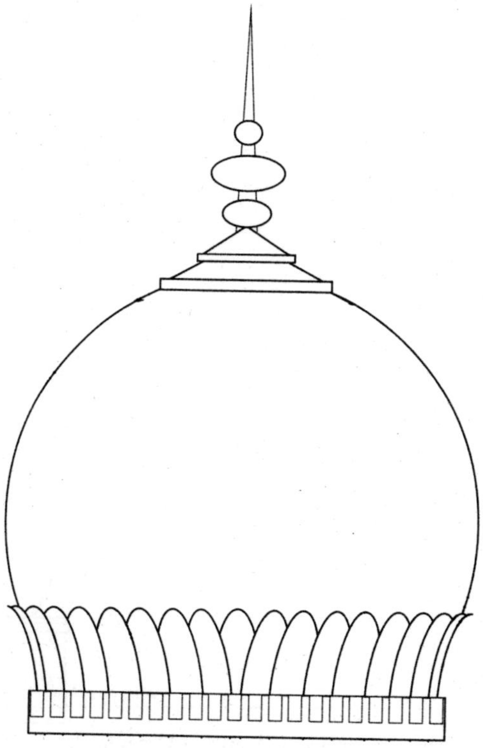

Bījāpur (*Ibrahim Rauza*)
1615

Plate 85 — Dome types (Concluded)

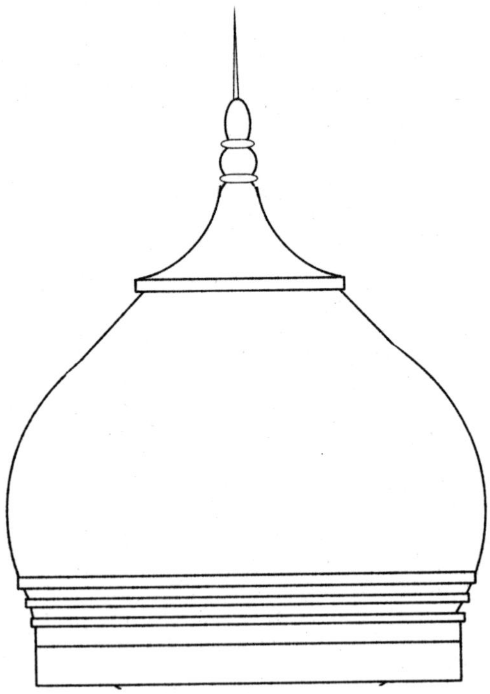

Agra (*Taj Mahal*)
a. 1632

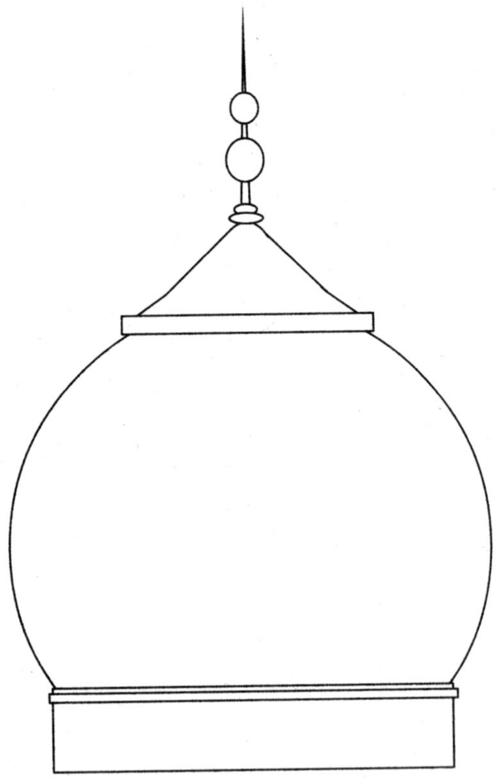

Agra (*Moti Masjid*)
1655

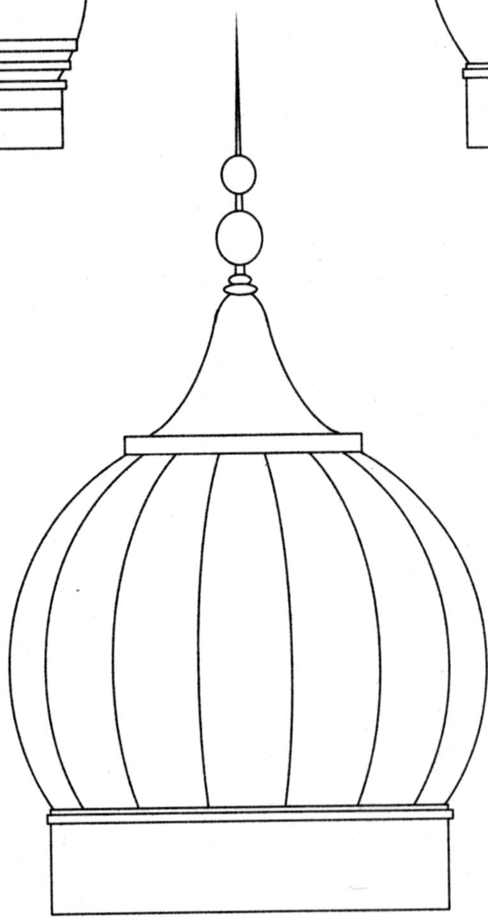

Delhi (*Moti Masjid*)
1659

Appendix C

Miscellaneous Proportional Elevations

Plate 86 — Solahkhambi Masjid, north elevation & half-plan (top) and Chhoti Masjid, north elevation & half-plan (bottom)

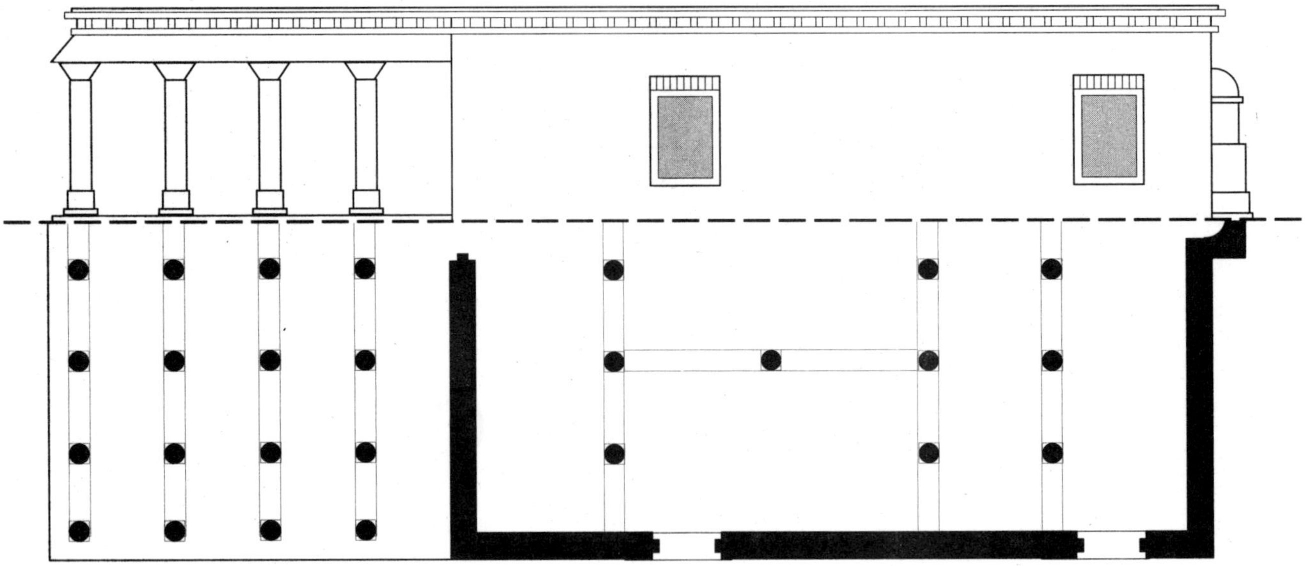

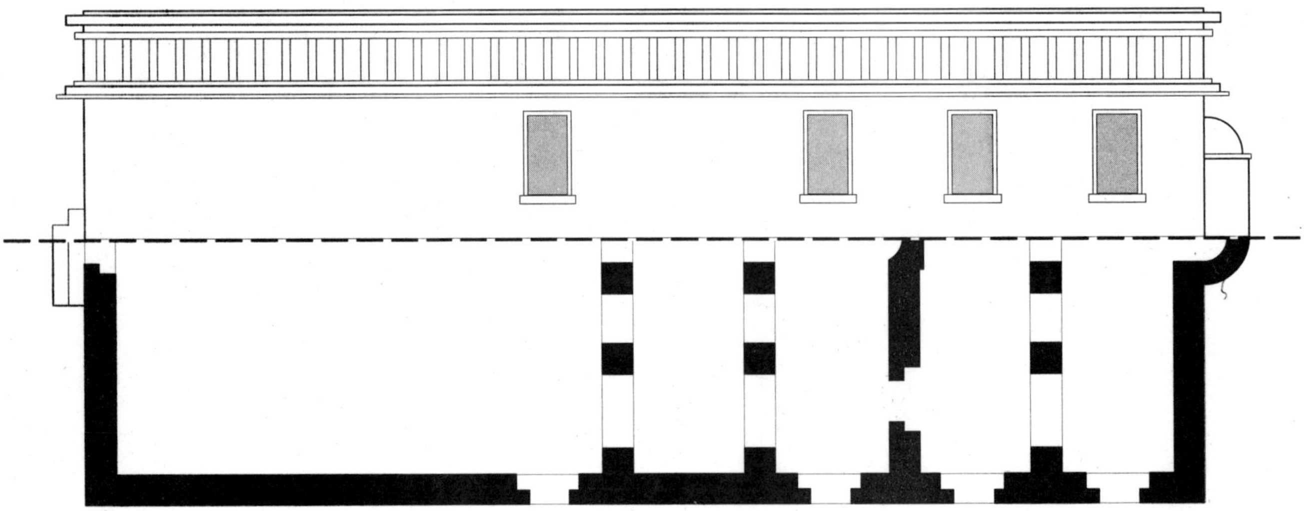

Plate 87 — Qadi Taj al-din, north elevation & half-plan (top) and Jami' al-Kabir, north elevation & half-plan (bottom)

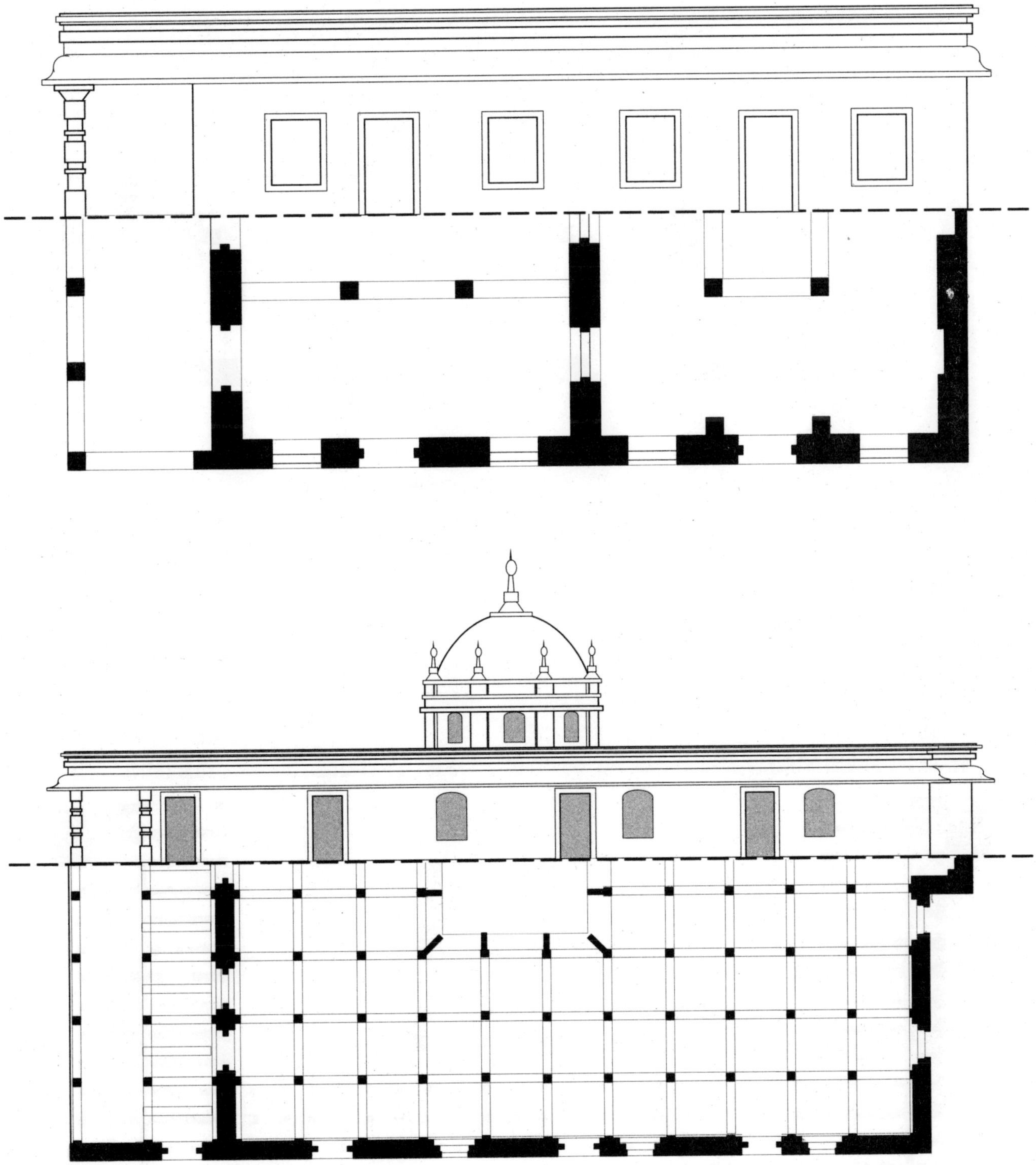

Plate 88 — Ahmad Nainar Masjid, north elevation & half-plan (top) and Atala Masjid, east elevation & east half-plan (bottom)

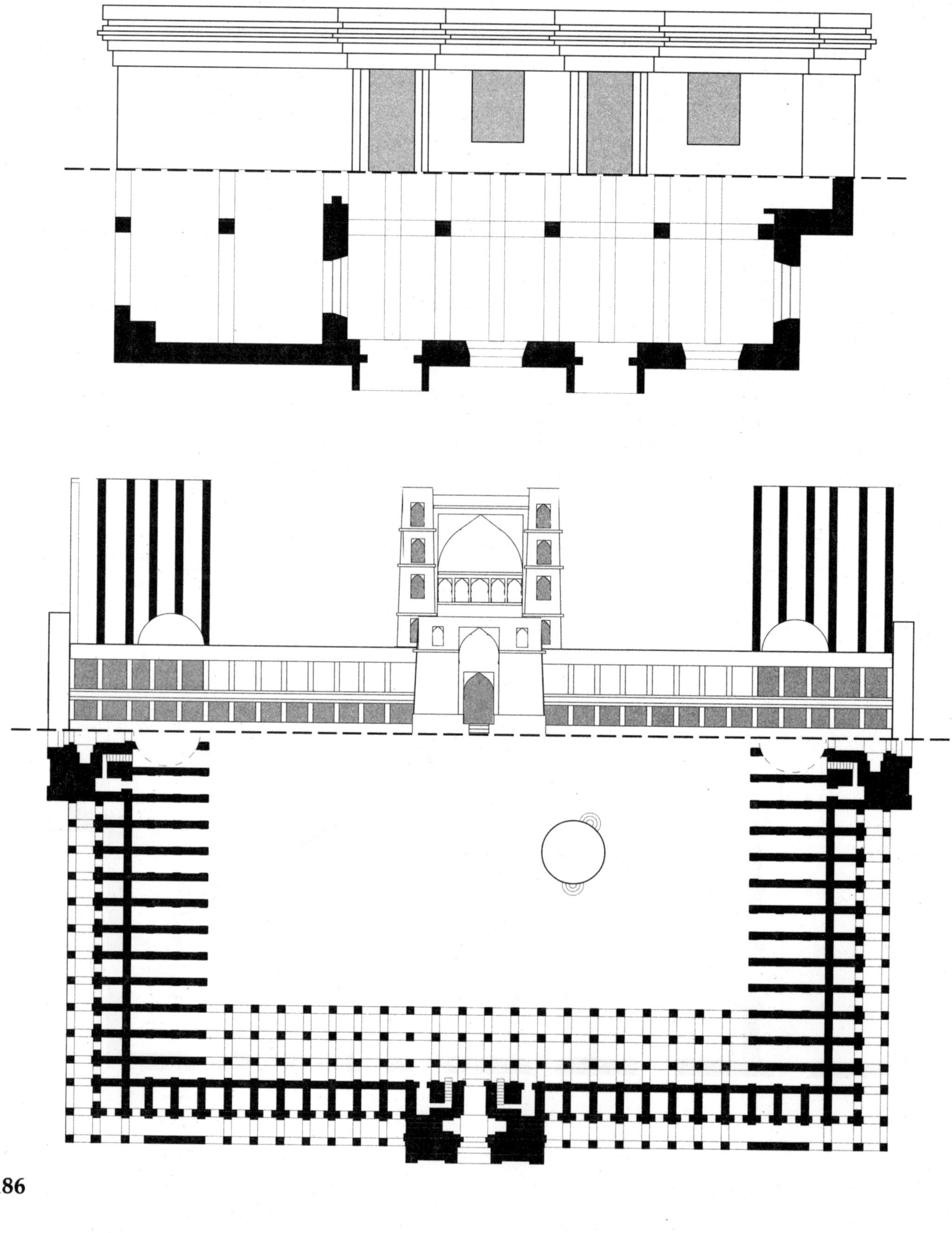

Plate 89 — Masjid-i Jami, Ahmedabad, side elevation (simplified) (top) and Masjid-i Jami, Jaunpur, maqsura elevation & partial plan (bottom)

Plate 90 — Qadiriya Masjid, north elevation & half-plan (top) and Choṭā Sonā Masjid, east elevation & east half-plan (bottom)

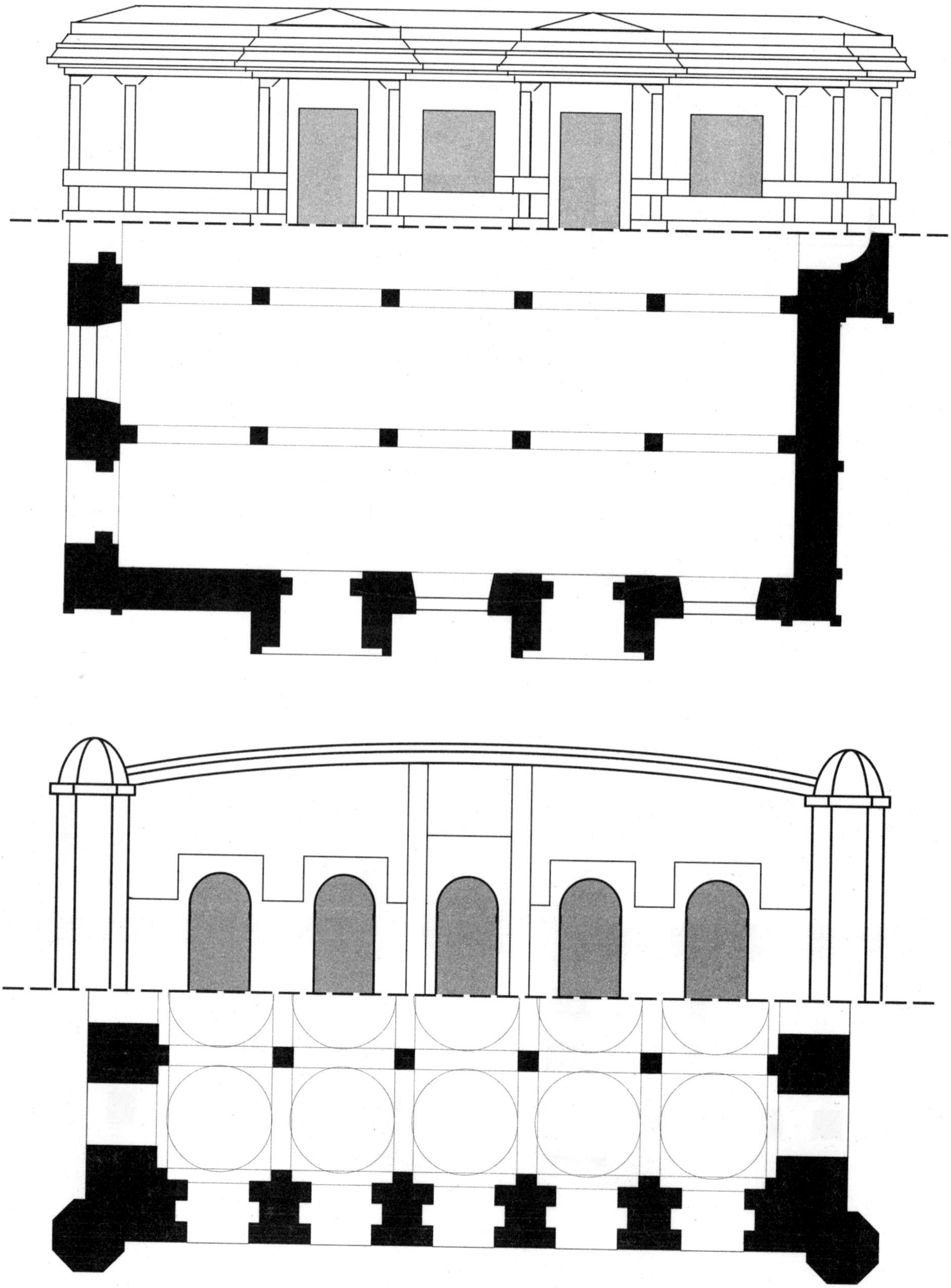

Plate 91 — Qadam Rasul Masjid, east elevation & east half-plan (top) and Rettaikulampalli, north elevation & half-plan (bottom)

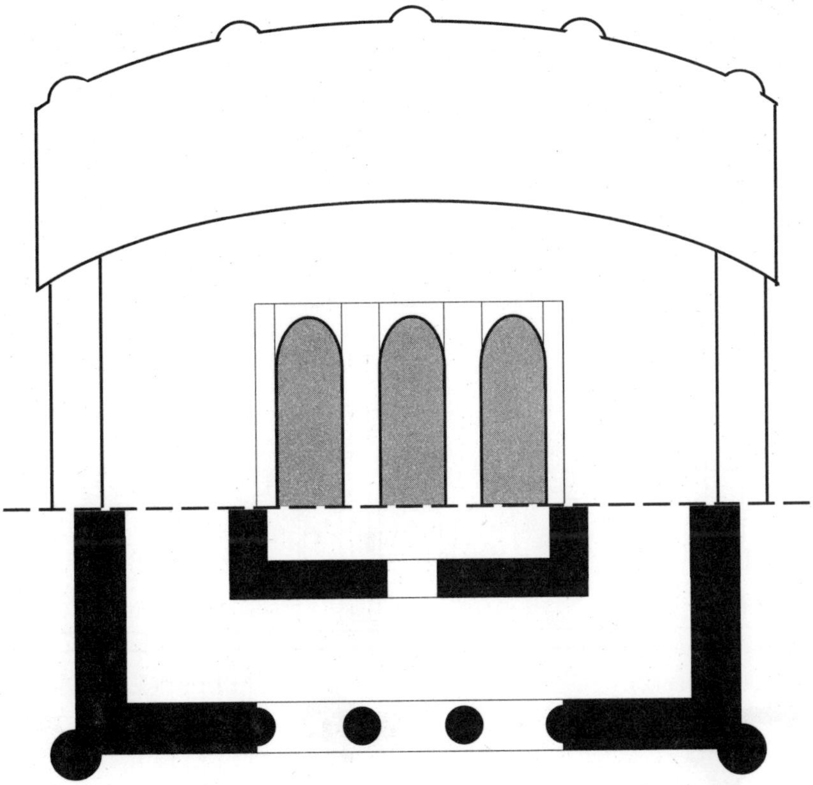

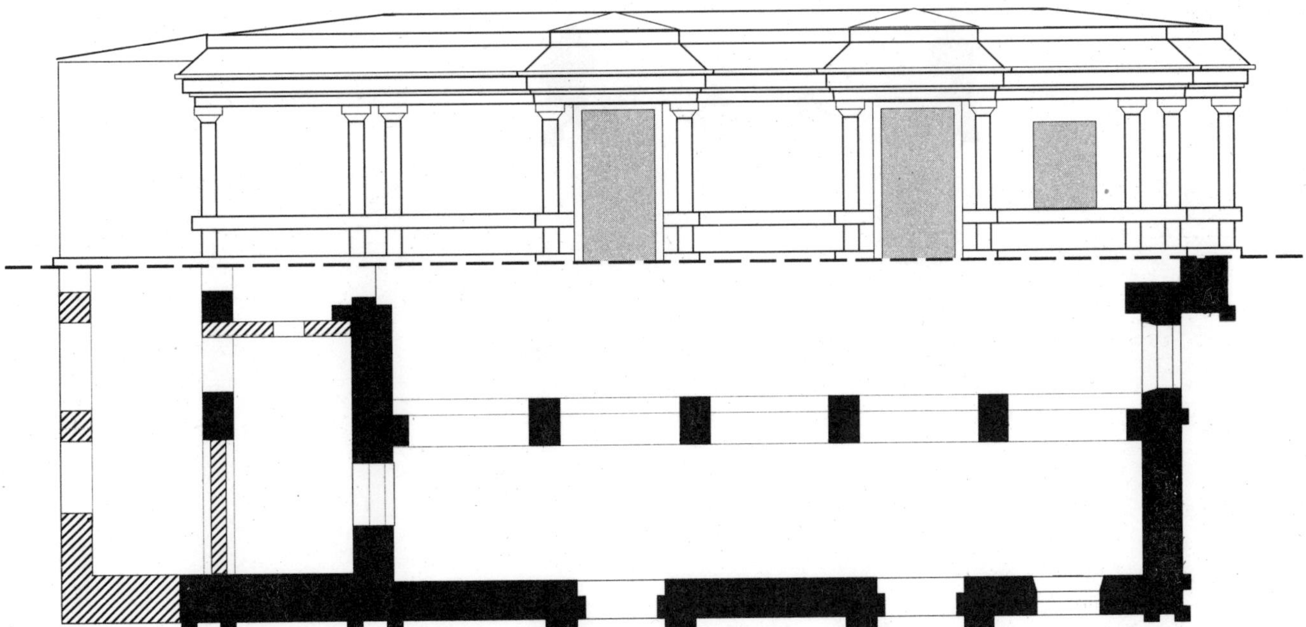

Plate 92 — Safa Masjid, north elevation & half-plan

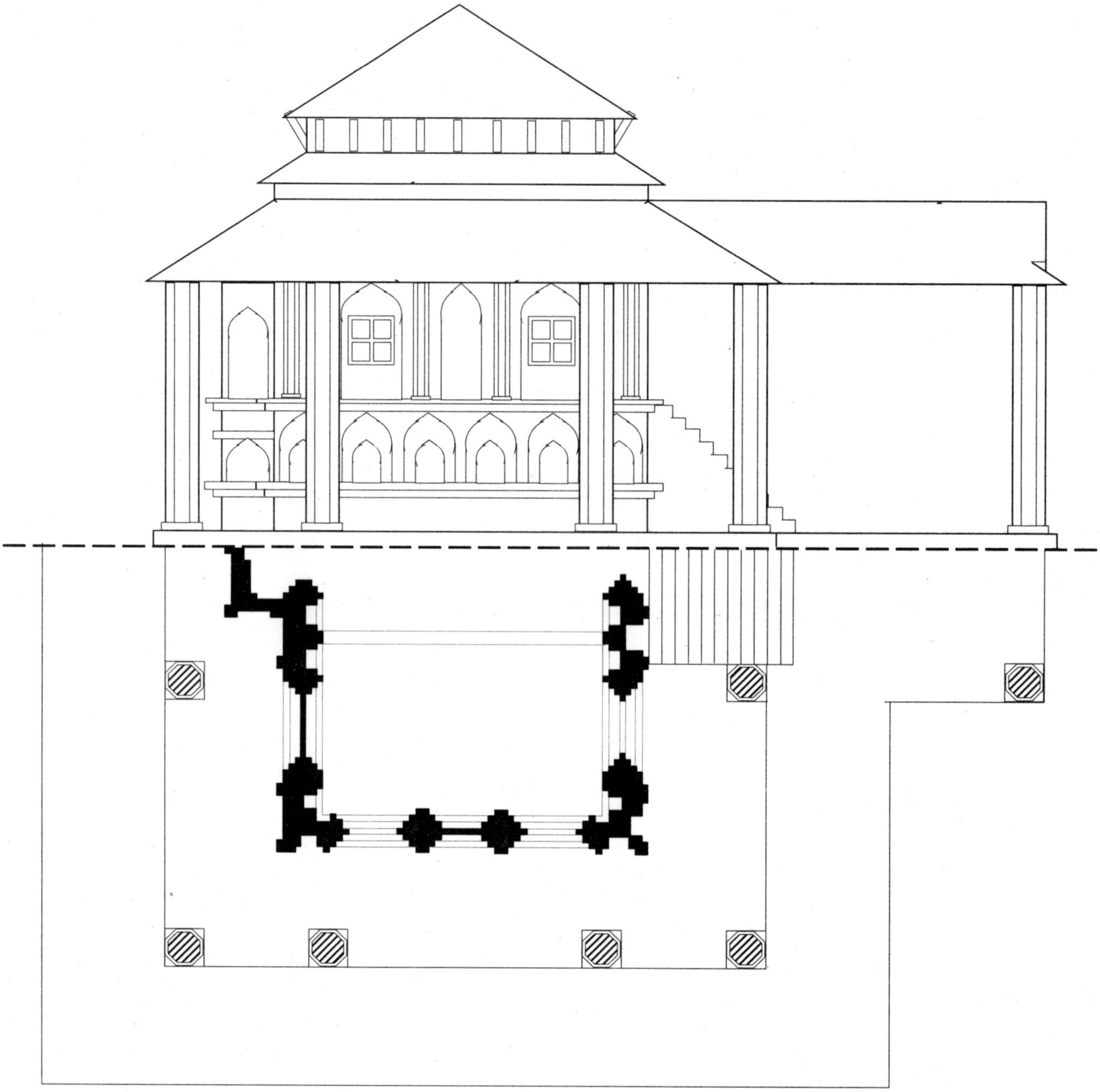

Plate 92 — Safa Masjid, north elevation & half-plan

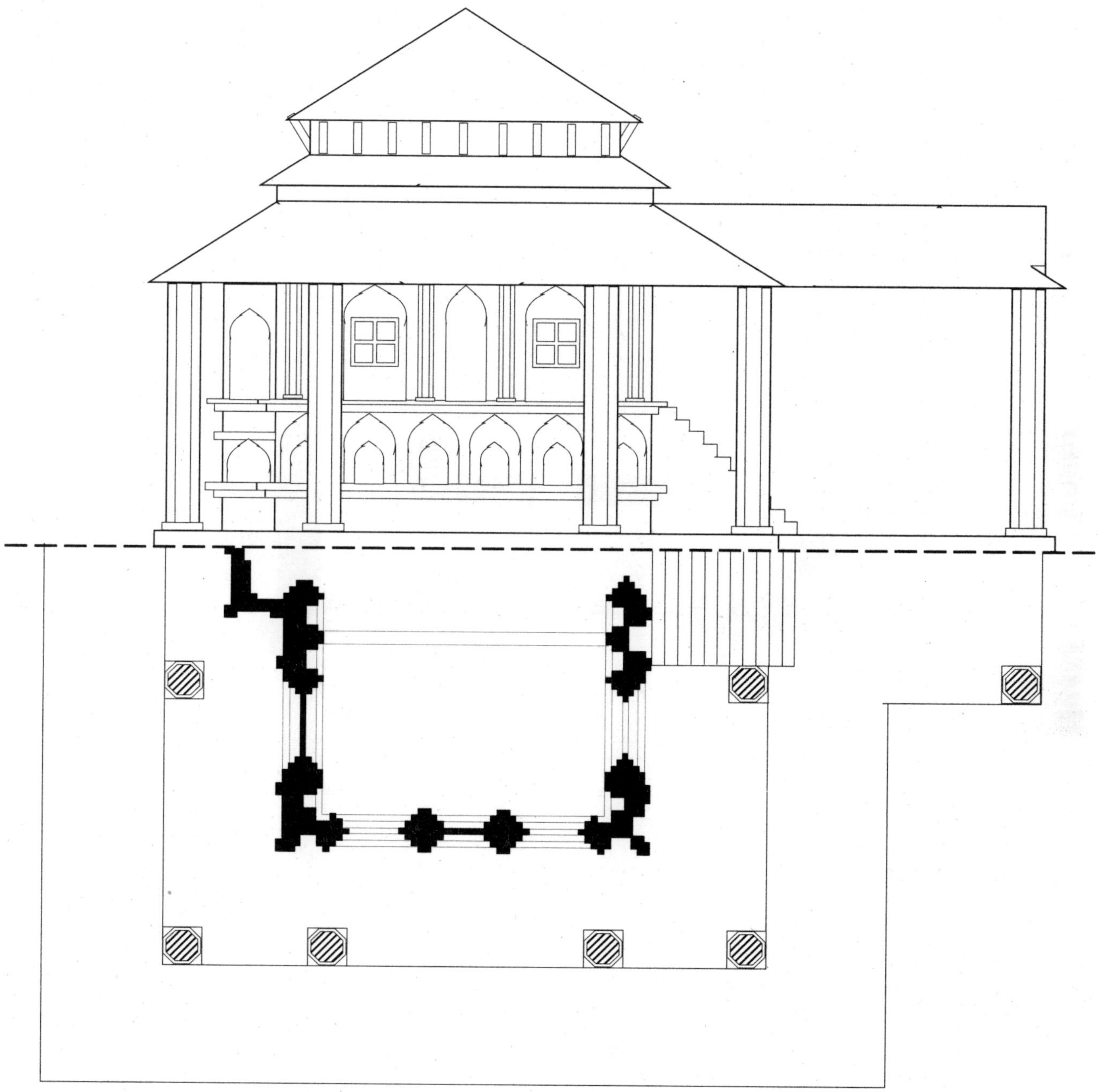

Plate 91 — Qadam Rasul Masjid, east elevation & east half-plan (top) and Rettaikulampalli, north elevation & half-plan (bottom)

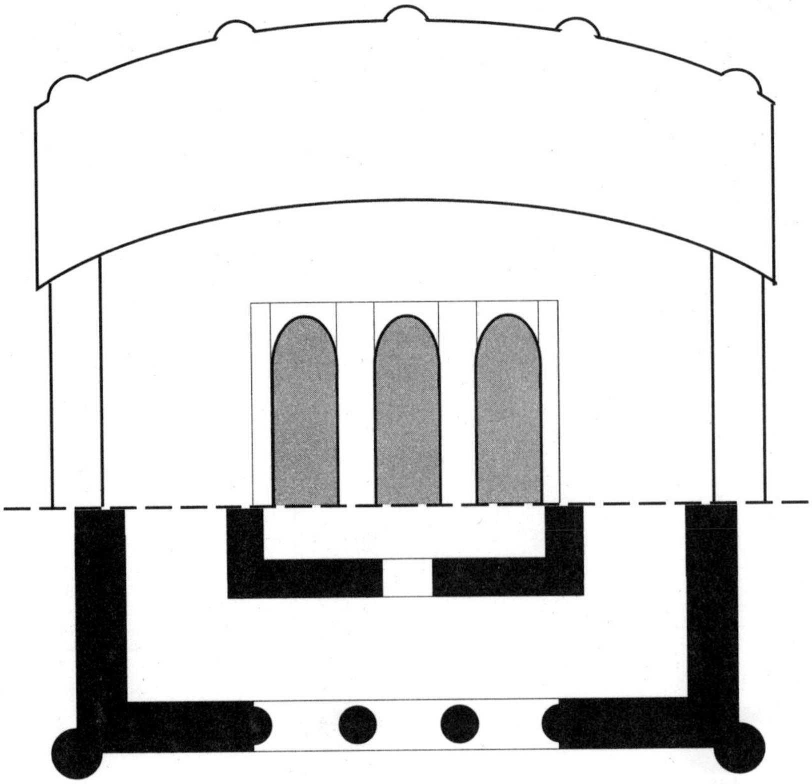

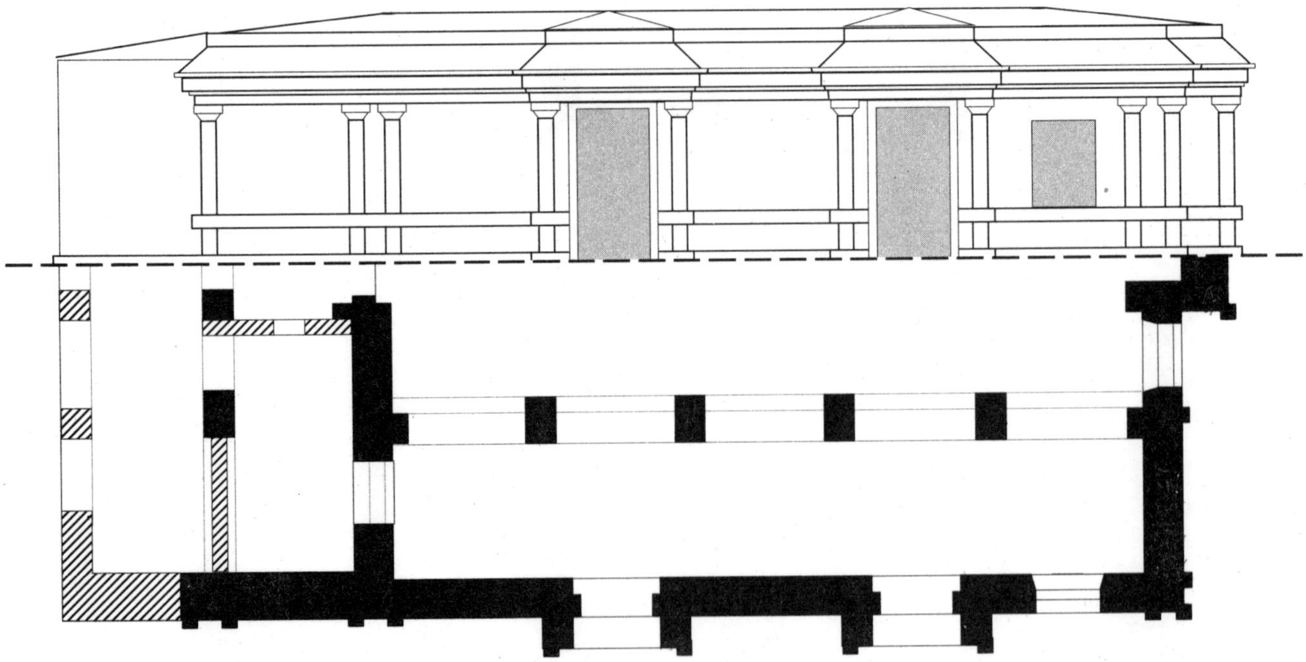

Plate 93 — Mithqalpalli Masjid, north elevation (original) & half-plan

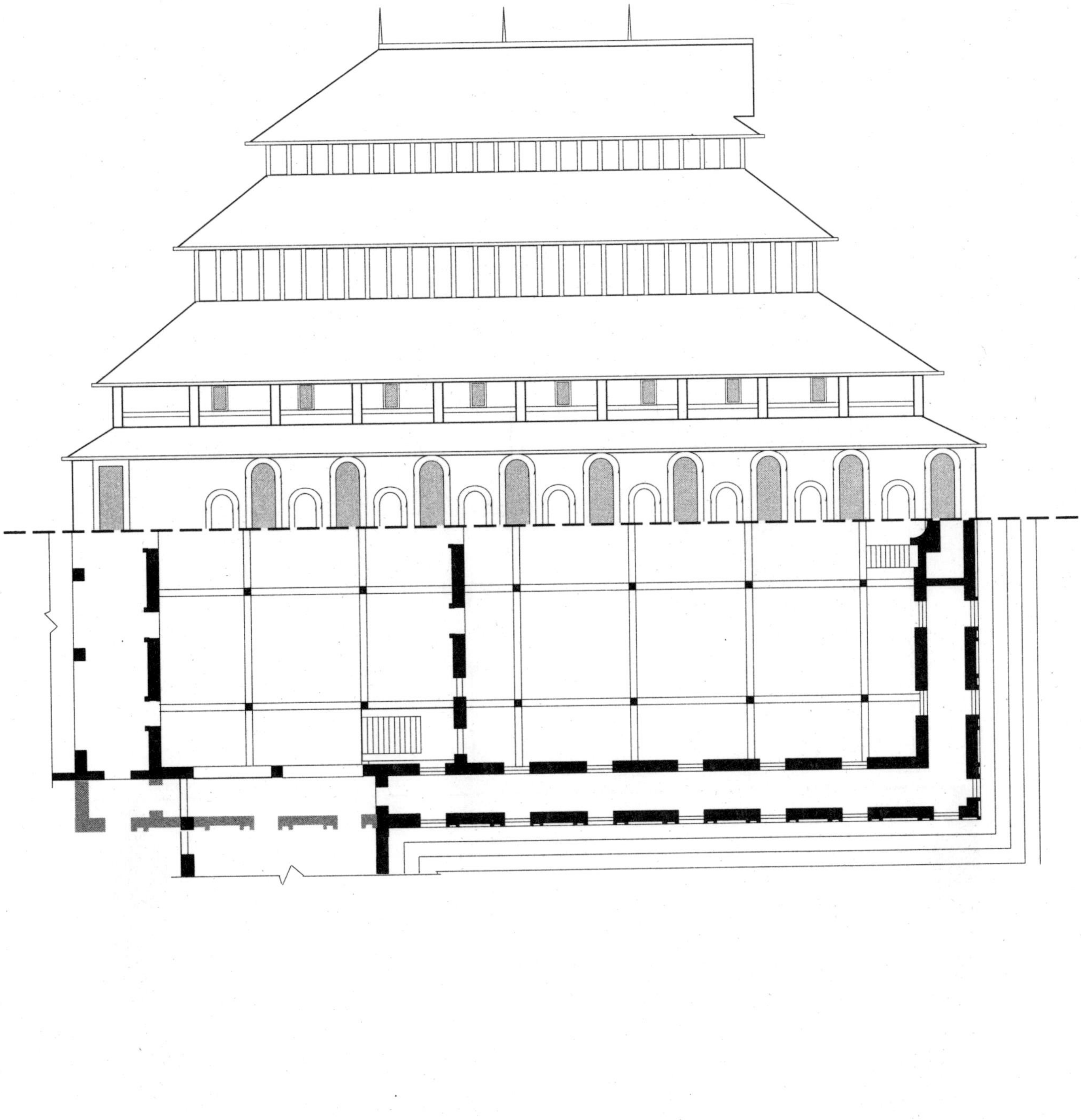

Plate 94 — Ali Shāhid Pir Masjid, east elevation & east half-plan

Plate 95 — Anda Masjid, east elevation

Plate 96 — Ibrahim Rauza Masjid, east elevation & east half-plan

Plate 97 — Gol Gumbaz Masjid, superimposed over Gol Gumbaz

Plate 98 — Mothi Masjid, Agra, east elevation & partial plan

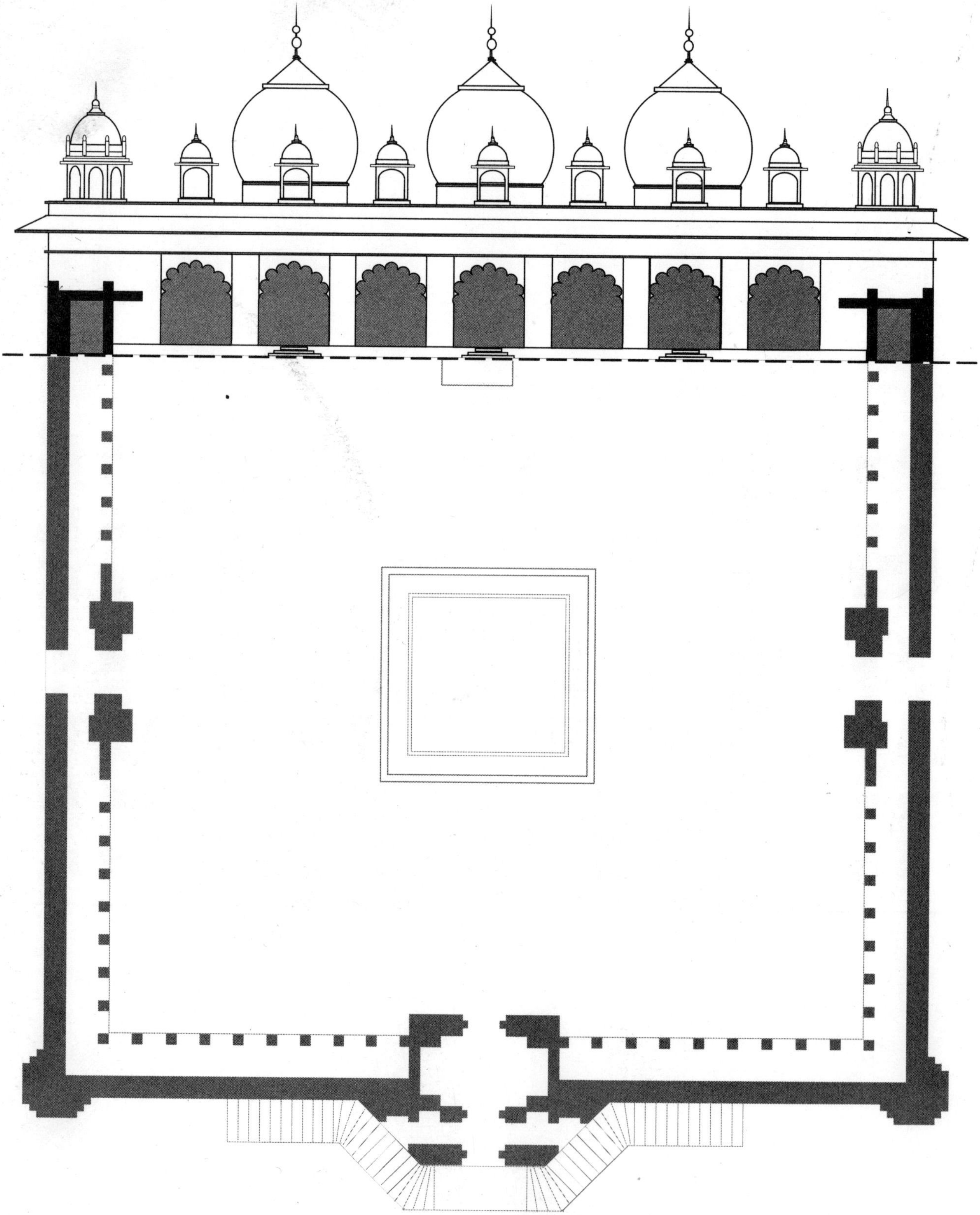

Plate 99 — Wazir Khan Masjid, Lahore, proportional elevation of the haram & partial plan

Plate 100 — Masjid-i Jami, Delhi, proportional elevation of the haram & partial plan

Plate 101 — Shāh Navaz Khan Rauza, north elevation of mausoleum

Plate 102 — Afzal Khan Rauza, north elevation & half-plan

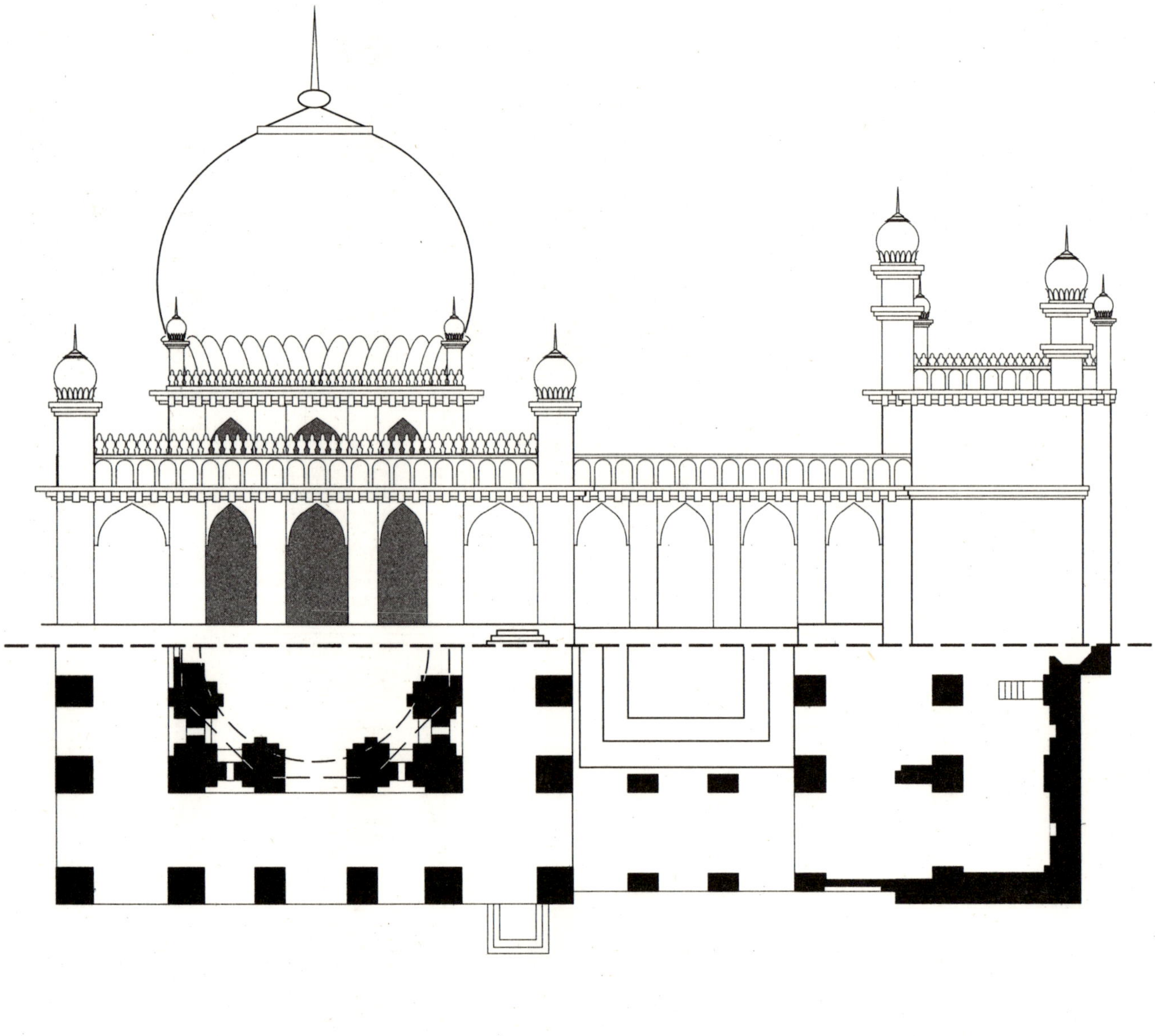

Appendix D

Major Muslim Rulers

Major Muslim Rulers

Ghaznavid Dynasty
(977–1186)

Samanid Slave Commanders

Aptigin	*c.* 962–963
Abu-Ishaq	963–966
Bilgetigin	966–975
Piri	975–977

Yaminid Dynasty
(977–1186)

Sabuktigin of Ghazni (Sultan)	977–997
Ismail	997–998
Yamin-ud-Dawlah Mahmud .	998–1030
Jalal-ud-Dawlah Mohammad	1030–1031
Shihab-ud-Dawlah Masud I	1031–1041
Shihab-ud-Dawlah Mawdud	1041–1050
Masud II	1050
Baha-ud-Dalwah Ali	1050
Izz-ud-Dawlah Abdul al-Rashid	1050–1053
Qiwam-ud-Dawlah Tughril	1053
Jamal-ud-Dawlah Farrukhzad	1053–1059
Zahir-ud-Dawlah Ibrahim	1059–1099
'Ala-ud-Dawlah Masud III	1099–1115
Kamal-ud-Dawlah Shirzad	1115
Sultan-ud-Dawlah Arslan Shāh	1115–1118
Yamin-ud-Dawlah Bahram Shāh	1118–1152
Muizz-ud-Dawlah Khusrta Shāh	1152–1160
Taj-ud-Dawlah Khusraw Malik	1160–1186

Ghurid Dynasty
(1163–1215)

Ghiyath-ud-Din Mohammed II of Ghur	1163–1203
Shihab-ud-Din Mohammed III	1173–1206
Ghiyath-ud-Din Mahmud	1206–1212
Baha-ud-Din Sam II	1212–1213
'Ala-ud-Din Atsiz	1213–1214
'Ala-ud-Din Mohammed IV	1214–1215

Delhi Sultanates
(1206–1526)

Slave or Mamluk Dynasty
(1206–1320)

Qutb-ud-din Aibak, 1st Sultan of Delhi	1206–1210
Aram Shāh	1210–1211
Shams-ud-din Iltutmish	1211–1236

Major Muslim Rulers (Continued)

Rukn-ud-din Firuz	1236
Raziyya (Radiyya Begum)	1236–1240
Mu'izz-ud-din Bahram	1240–1242
'Al-ud-din Mas'ud	1242–1246
Nasir-ud-din Mahmud	1246–1266

House of Balban

Ghiyas-ud-din Balban	1266–1287
Mu'izz-ud-din Kaiqubad	1287–1290
Kaiumarth	1290

The Khalji

Jalal-ud-din Firuz Khalji	1290–1296
Rukn-ud-din Ibrahim (II)	1296
'Ala-ud-din Muhammad Khalji	1296–1316
Shihab-ud-din 'Umar	1316
Qutb-ud-din Mubarak	1316–1326
Nasir-ud-din Khusrav	1320

Tughluq Dynasty
(1320–1414)

Ghiyas-ud-din Tughluq Shāh I (Ghazi Malik)	1320–1325
Muhammad Shāh Tughluq Shāh (II)	1325–1351
Mahmud Ibn Mohammed	1351
Firuz Shāh Tughluq	1351–1388
Ghiyas-ud-din Tughluq Shāh II	1388–1389
Abu Bakr Tughluq	1389–1390
Mohammed Tughluq Shāh (III)	1390–1393
Sikandar Tughluq Shāh I	1393
Mahmud Tughluq Shāh II	1394–1396
interregnum	
Mahmud Tughluq	1399–1413
Daulat Khan Lodi	1413–1414

Sayyid Dynasty
(1414–1450)

Khizir Khan Sayyid	1414–1421
Mu'izz-ud-din Mubarak Shāh II Sayyid	1421–1434
Muhammed Shāh Sayyid (IV)	1434–1444
'Ala-ud-din Alam Shāh Sayyid	1444–1451

Lodi Dynasty
(1451–1526)

Buhlul Lodi	1451–1489
Nizam Khan, Sikandar Lodi	1489–1517
Ibrahim Shāh Lodi (II)	1517–1526

Major Muslim Rulers (Continued)

Bengal Sultanate
(1282–1576)

Iliyas Shāhi Dynasty
(1282–1415)

Nasir-ud-din Bughra	1282–1291
Rukn-ud-din Kaukaus	1291–1301
Shams-ud-din Firuz Shāh	1301–1322
Shihab-ud-din Bughra Shāh	1322–1324
Ghiyas-ud-din Bahadur Shāh	1324–1336
Fakhr-ud-Din Mubarak Shāh	1336–1350
Ali Mubarak, 'Ala-ud-din Ali Shāh	1341–1342
Malik Iliyas Haji, Shams-ud-din Iliyas Shāh	1342–1358
Ikhtiyar-ud-din Gaji Shāh	1349–1352
Sikandar Shāh	1358–1390
Ghiyas-ud-din Azam Shāh	1390–1410 or 1396?
Sultan-ud-Salatin Saif-ud-din Hamza Shāh	1142 or 1396–1405?
Shihab-ud-din Bayazid Shāh	1412–1414 or 1405–1415?
Ala-ud-din Firoz Shāh	1414?–15

Gaṇeśa-Shāhī Dynasty
(1493–1538)

Rājā Gaṇeśa	1415–1418
Jalal-ud-din Muhammed Shāh	1419–1431 or 1432?
Shams-ud-Din Ahmad Shāh	1431 or 1433? – 1435? 1437?

Ilyas-Shāhi Dynasty
(1435–1487)

Nasir-ud-din Mahmud Shāh	1435 or 1437?–1459
Rukn-ud-din Barbak Shāh	1455–1476
Shams-ud-din Yusuf Shāh	1474–1481 or 1483?
Sultan Sikandar Shāh II	1482
Jalal-ud-Din Fateh Shāh	1482–1484 or 1487

Hussain-Shāhī Dynasty
(1493–1538)

Alauddin Hussain Shāh	1493–1519
Nasib Shāh, Nasir-ud-Din Nusrat Shāh	1519–1533
'Ala-ud-Din Firuz Shāh II	1533
Ghiyas-ud-din Mahmud Shāh	1533–1538

Shir Shāh Sūr Dynasty
(1538–1563)

Farid-ud-din Abul Muzaffar Shir Shāh Sūr	1538–1545
Islam Shāh	1545–1553
Firuz Shāh	1553
Muhammad Mubariz Khan, Muhammad Shāh Adil	1553–1555

Major Muslim Rulers (Continued)

Ghiyas-ud-din Bahadur Shāh	1555–1560
Jalal-ud-din, Ghiasuddin II Abul Muzaffar Jalal Shāh	1560–1563
Ghiasuddin III	1563

Taj Karrani Dynasty (1563–1576)

Taj Khan Karrani	1563–1565
Sulaiman (II) Khan Karrani	1565–1572
Bayazid Karrani	1572
Daud Khan	1572–1576

Ma'bar Sultanate (Damghan) (1333–1356)

al-Sharif Jalal al-din Ahsan Shāh	1333–1338
'Ala al-din Udauji	1338–1339
Qutb al-din Firuz Shāh	1339
Ghiyath al-din Muhammad Damghan Shāh	1339–1345
Nasir al-din Mahmud Damghan Shāh	1345–1356
Shams 'Adil Shāh	1356–1372
Fakhr al-din Mubarak Shāh	1372–1377
'Ala al-din Sikandar Shāh	1377–1378

Kashmir Sultanate (1346–1589)

Shāh Mirza, Shams-ud-Din I	1346–1349
Jamshid	1349–1350
'Ali Sher, 'Ala-ud-Din	1350–1359
Shirashamak Shihab-ud-din	1359–1378
Hindal Qutb-ud-Din	1378–1393
Sikandar Butshikan	1393–1413
'Ali Shāh	1413–1420
Zainal-'Abidin	1420–1470
Haidar Shāh	1470–1472
Hasan Shāh	1472–1484
Muhammad Shāh	1484–1487
Fath Shāh	1487–1499
Muhammad Shāh (2nd reign)	1499–1505
Fath Shāh (2nd reign)	1505–1514
Muhammad Shāh (3rd reign)	1514–1515
Fath Shāh (3rd reign)	1515–1517
Muhammad Shāh (4th reign)	1517–1528
Ibrahim Shāh I	1528–1529
Nazuk Shāh, Nadir	1529–1530
Muhammad Shāh (5th reign)	1530–1537
Shams-ud-Din II	1537–1538
Isma'il Shāh I	1538–1540
Ibrahim Shāh II	1540
Nazuk Shāh, Nadir (2nd reign)	1540-1546
Haidar Dughlat	1546–1550

Major Muslim Rulers (Continued)

Nazuk Shāh, Nadir (3rd reign)	1550–1551
Ibrahim Shāh II (2nd reign)	1552–1334
Isma'il Shāh II	1554
Habib Shāh, Mahmud	1555

Chakk Dynasty

Muhammad Ghazi Shāh	1555–1562
Nasir-ud-Din Husain Shāh	1562–1570
Muhammad 'Ali Shāh	1570–1579
Muhammad Yusuf Shāh	1579
Mubarak Shāh	1579
Lohar Shāh	1580
Muhammad Yusuf Shāh (2nd reign)	1580–1586
Muhammaad Ya'qub Shāh	1586–1589

Bahmanī Sultanate (1347–1527)

Ismail Mukh (Afghani)	1347
Hasan Bahman Shāh ('Ala-ud-din I)	1347–1358
Muhammad Shāh I	1358–1377
Mujahid Shāh	1377
Daub Khan	1377
Muhammad Shāh II	1377–1397
Yaj-ud-din Firoz Shāh	1397–1422
Ahmad Shāh	1422–1435
'Ala-ud-din II	1436–1458
Humayun	1458–1461
Nizam Shāh	1461–1463
Muhammad Shāh III Lashkari	1463–1482
Mahmud Shāh	1482–1518
Ahmad Shāh III	1518–1521
'Ala-ud-Din	1521–1522
Wali-Allah Shāh	1522–1525
Kalim-Allah Shāh	1525–1527

(*See*: 'Adil Shāh of Bījāpur, Qutab Shāhī of Golconda, 'Imad Shāhī of Berar, Niẓām Shāhī of Ahmednagar and Barid Shāhī of Bīdar)

Muzaffarid Shāhi of Gujarat Sultanate (1391–1583)

Muzaffar (Khan) Shāh I	1391–1411
Shams-ud-Din Muzaffar Ahmad Shāh I	1411–1442
Mohammed Karim Shāh	1442–1451
Nasir-ud-Din Ahmad Shāh I	1442–1451
Qutb-ud-Din Ahmad Shāh II	1451–1458
Da'ud Shāh	1458–1459
Nasir-ud-Din Mahmud Shāh I Beghara	1459–1511
Shams-ud-Din Muzaffar Shāh II	1511–1526
Nasir-ud-Din Sikandar Shāh	1526
Nasir-ud-Din Mahmud Shāh II	1526
Qutb-ud-Din Bahadur Shāh	1526–1535

Major Muslim Rulers (Continued)

Humayun occupies Gujarat	(1535–1536)
Qutb-ud-Din Bahadur Shāh	1536–1537
Miran Muhammad Shāh III	1537
Nasir-ud-Din Mahmud Shāh III	1537–1554
Ghiyath-ud-Din Ahmad Shāh III	1554–1561
Shams-ud-Din Muzaffar Shāh III	1561–1573
Akbar occupies Gujarat	(1573–1583)
Shams-ud-Din Muzaffar Shāh III	1573–1583

Malwar Sultanate of Māṇḍu (1392–1531)

Ghuri Dynasty 1392–1436

Dilvar Khan Ghuri	1392–1405
Husam-ud-Din Hushang Shāh	1405–1435
Ghazni Khan, Muhammad Shāh I	1435–1436
Masud Khan, Masud Shāh	1436

Khalji Dynasty (1436–1531)

Mahmud I, Khalji	1436–1469
Ghiyath Shāh	1469–1500
Nasir Shāh	1500–1510
Mahmud II	1510–1531

Sharqi of Jaunpur Sultanate (1394–1476)

Khwaja Jahan Malik Sarvar Sharqi	1394–1399
Malik Qaranful, Mubarak Shāh	1399–1402
Shams-ud-Din Ibrahim Shāh	1402–1440
Nasir-ud-Din Mahmud Shāh	1440–1457
Muhammad Shāh	1457–1458
Husen (Husain) Shāh	1458–1476

'Adil Shāh of Bījāpur Sultanate (1489–1686)

Yusuf 'Adil Shāh	1489–1512
Ismail 'Adil Shāh	1512–1534
Mallu 'Adil Shāh	1534–1535
Ibrahim 'Adil Shāh I	1536–1557
Ali 'Adil Shāh I	1557–1580
Ibrahim 'Adil Shāh II	1580–1626
Muhammad 'Adil Shāh	1626–1656
Ali 'Adil Shāh II	1656–1672
Sikandar 'Adil Shāh	1672–1686

Qutab Shāhī of Golconda Sultanate (1512–1687)

Quli Qutub Qutbul-mulk Shāh	1512–1543
Jamsheed Quli Qutub Shāh	1543–1550

Major Muslim Rulers (Continued)

Subhan Quli Qutub Shāh	1550
Ibrahim Quli Qutub Shāh	1550–1580
Muhammad Quli Qutub Shāh	1580–1612
Muhammad Qutub Shāh	1612–1626
'Abdullah Qutub Shāh	1626–1672
Abdul Hasan (Qutub) Tana Shāh	1672–1687

'Imad Shāhī of Berar Sultanate (1490–1574)

Fath-Allah 'Imad ul-Mulk Shāh	1490–1504
'Ala-ud-Din 'Imad Shāh	1504–1529
Darya 'Imad Shāh	1529–1562
Burhan 'Imad Shāh	1562–1568
Tufal Khan Dakhni	1568–1572

Nizam Shāhī of Ahmednagar Sultanate (1490–1680)

Nizam-ul-Mulk Bahri.	1490
Malik Ahmad, Ahmad Nizam Shāh I	1490–1509
Burhan Nizam Shāh I	1509–1553
Hussain Nizam Shāh I	1553–1565
Murtaza Nizam Shāh I	1565–1586
Hussain Nizam Shāh II	1586–1589
Isma'il Nizam Shāh	1589–1591
Burhan Nizam Shāh II	1591–1595
Ibrahim Nizam Shāh	1595–1596
Bahadur Nizam Shāh	1596–1603
Murtaza Nizam Shāh II	1603–1610
Burhan Shāh III	1610–1631
Hussain Nizam Shāh III	1631–1633

Barid Shāhī of Bīdar Sultanate (1492–1687)

Amir Qasim Barid Shāh I	1492–1504
Amir Barid Shāh I	1504–1542
'Ali Barid Shāh I	1542–1579
Ibrahim Barid Shāh	1579–1587
Qasim Barid Shāh II	1587–1591
'Ali Barid Shāh II	1591
Amir Barid Shāh II	1591–1600
Mirza 'Ali Barid Shāh	1600–1609
Amir Barid Shāh III ('Ali Shāh II)	1609–1618

Major Muslim Rulers (Continued)

Mughal India
(1526–1876)

Timurud Dynasty
(1526–1531)

Zahir-ud-din Muhammad Babur, King of Ferghana, "the Great Mughal"	1526–1530
Nasir-ud-din Humayun	1530–1540

Suri Period
(1540–1555)

Sher Khan (Sur Sher Shāh)	1540–1545
Islam Sur Shāh	1545–1553
Firuz	1553
Mohammed Adil	1553–1555
Sikandar	(opposition) 1554–1555

Timurud Dynasty
(1555–1876)

Nasir-ud-din Humayun	1555–1556
"Rājā" (General) Himu	1556
Jalal-ud-din Akbar the Great	1556–1605
Nur-ud-din Jahangir	1606–1627
Dawar Bakhsh	1627–1628
Shihab-ud-din Shāh Jahan	1628–1666
Murab Bakhsh	(1657)
Shāh Shuja'	(1657–1658)
Muhiy-ud-din Aurangzib	1658–1707
A'zam Shāh	1707
Kam Bakhsh	1707
Qutb-ud-din Shāh Alam Bahadur	1707–1712
'Azim-ush-Shan	1712
Mu'izz-ud-din Jahandar Shāh	1712–1713
Muhiy-ud-din Farrukh-siyar	1713–1719
Rafi'-ud-Darajat	1719
Rafi'-ud-Daula Shāh Jahan II	1719
Nasir-ud-din Muhammad Shāh	1719–1748
Mujahid-ud-din Ahmad Shāh Bahadur	1748–1754
'Aziz-ud-din 'Alamgir II	1754–1759
Shāh Jahan III	1759
Jalal-ud-din Shāh 'Alam II	1759–1788
Bīdar Bakht	1788–1806
Mu'in-ud-din Muhamad Akbar II	1806–1857
Siraz-ud-din Bahadur Shāh II	1857–1876

(1878-1947 — British rule)

Acknowledgements

I wish to particularly acknowledge the works of: Catherine B. Asher, Percy Brown, Henry Cousens, Martin J. Frishman and Hasan-Uddin Khan, Satish Grover, Mohammad Waliullah Khan, Rustam Mehta, George Michell, Anisha Shekhar Mukherji, R. Nath, K.V. Soundara Rajan, Shehbaz H. Safrani, Mehrdad Shokoohy, Henri Stierlin, Christopher Tadgell, and G.H.R. Tillotson, from which the various plans were found and redrawn.

I dedicate this work to my many Muslim friends in Malaysia.

Note: Throughout this work, I have employed the entwined "eight-point star" or "octagram" shown above. Eight is considered to be an auspicious number. It denotes perfection, good fortune, and on the divine plane: justice and balance between attraction and repulsion, positive and negative. It is an evenly even number and the first cube number — 2^3. Particularly in Islam it is indicative of the eight paradises (*hasht bihisht*) and the eight rivers of paradise. The octagon is a geometric form that is frequently found in Islamic architecture. In addition, the octagram seen above is so constructed as to imply eternity. It is never ending.